P9-BIB-363

The Sentimental Years

By E. DOUGLAS BRANCH

THE SENTIMENTAL YEARS

WESTWARD: THE ROMANCE OF
THE AMERICAN FRONTIER

THE HUNTING OF THE BUFFALO

THE COWBOY AND HIS INTERPRETERS

T-319-A

The
Sentimental Years

1836-1860

E. DOUGLAS BRANCH

American Century Series
HILL AND WANG · NEW YORK
A division of Farrar, Straus and Giroux

Manufactured in the United States of America
4567890

PREFACE

*T*HE little boy, the huckleberries, and Henry David Thoreau: they meet in a patch on the outskirts of Concord, in the summer of 1853. (That was the year when the American Secretary of State warned all his country's diplomats that they must on no account wear medals or knee-breeches; the year when a genius in up-state New York invented the cast-iron bathtub.) The little boy, his basket filled with fine fruit of his own picking, took a tumble and spilled it all. He cried, and was not consoled when his adult fellows offered to share their baskets with him. Then Thoreau put his arm about the woeful child, and explained that if the crop of huckleberries were to continue, it was necessary now and then that boys should spill their pickings and tread the berries into new earth.

And in the lush patches of other generations' experience, writers pluck and redistribute. With integrity and luck, they may plant truth and life in new places. Transplant, rather. The plucker who works in old books, old letters, newspapers, discovers that nothing is old. And if he is worth the grubby spots on his fingers, he discovers that very little is new. Not even literary treacle; philosophical mush; widespread poverty; or the groans of dying capitalism.

The patch of my picking-over lies within the twenty-five years between Andrew Jackson's descent from the Presidency and Abraham Lincoln's accession. My interest has been with the free-state Americans; I have wanted to bring together their hopes and accomplishments in literature, religion, the art of living together, education, mechanical and industrial technic, the fine arts, economic equality, political idealism—to bring these facets of a people's life into one view.

And the view is not merely a maze of diverse things. Common threads are discernible often, a continuity. In behalf of my labeling of that continuity a bit of definition may be in order. Romanticism I take to be three-pronged: the recognition of the reality; the passing of judgment upon it; and the clinging to the myth. Sentimentalism is the refusal to recognize the reality; or the inability to pass judgment upon it; and the clinging to the myth. It is the immature phase of the Romantic Movement. This immaturity is of two sorts: fresh, adolescent; and precious, evasive.

Now that my pickings from that twenty-five-year field are distributed, with such order as I can manage, the emergent book is a social discussion of the first generation of the American middle class. Their era is, I think, the first modern quarter-century of our national life.

This book is based upon the generation's own printed record, which Professor Schlesinger of Harvard called "the most abundant outpouring the nation had ever known." I have traveled pretty far in that rag-paper Concord; bibliography and footnotes becoming cumbersome, I have culled them from the book and stowed them away—in a file which shall be opened, in helpfulness or in defense as may be, when an interested reader raises a query.

E. Douglas Branch

CONTENTS

ILLUSTRATIONS

CHAPTER ONE

Progress and a Doubt

NEW YORK was a white blur. The walks were choked with snow. At night, with the temperature below zero, a northwesterly gale was knifing and rippling the drifts in the deserted streets. Pity the poor watchman making his solitary rounds — in the bitter darkness of December 16, 1835. He was employed by the insurance companies to patrol the district of the great warehouses in lower Manhattan. From an upper storey of Number 25 Merchant Street the telltale flare darted into his sight.

The jangle of the bell on the old jail back of City Hall gave the alarm; the volunteer firemen shivered, cursed the day of their enlistment, and rushed to the engines. But the machines had been used on the previous night; the pumps were envised with ice and had to be thawed out with hot water. Meanwhile the flames passed from loft to loft, through the great series of dry-goods fabrics and into the flooring. The wooden gutters along the eaves and the wooden shutters upon the windows were two common details of construction which the insurance underwriters had ignored. Merchant Street was narrow; the fire leapt the open space without half trying.

The fire-hose was stiff and intractable; most of the water outlets were frozen. Both sides of Pearl Street were soon ablaze; Water Street was next to be fireswept, and within two hours after the first alarm, vessels lying beside Coffee House Slip were burning. All the buildings in Merchant Street below the Merchants' Exchange were destroyed, and at midnight the Exchange, whose thick stone walls had been thought impregnable, was afire. Letters and government funds were hurriedly transported from the Post Office before that building was abandoned. At one o'clock the fire had claimed South Street and was roaring along the piers. A chain of engines stretching from the water-front relayed East River water from pump to pump, and from emergency sources absurd trickles were being piped through ice-choked logs.

The Exchange was in ruins at three o'clock on that implacable morning, and Ball Hughes' famous statue of Alexander Hamilton was torn from its pedestal and crushed under the avalanche of falling stone. The fire was raging along both sides of William Street; if it gained entrance into the residential district, with its rows of tinder-boxes, there would be no stopping the blaze south of Fourteenth. Gunpowder was needed to blast an open space. From the Navy Yard a barge was sent to the magazine at Red Hook, fighting against a head tide and the vicious gale; meanwhile the small supply on Governors Island was rushed to Manhattan. The editor of the *Morning Advertiser,* completing perhaps the first job of "flash" reporting in the history of American journalism, made a last note: "5 o'clock. We go to press while the fire is still raging. It is said to have extended below Old Slip on Pearl Street." Six daily newspapers did not appear that day, because their plants had been burned out.

The *Evening Post* took up the story six hours later. The flames had been arrested on the north side of Wall Street, thanks to Engine Number 13 and its company; blocked in its uptown sweep, the fire was raging between Old Slip and Coenties Slip. Several stores had been blown up ("We have seen nothing more characteristic than the sang froid with which the sailors of Captain Mix's party carried about, wrapped up in a blanket, or pea-jacket, as it might happen, kegs and barrels of gunpowder, amid a constant shower of fire, as they followed their officers to the various buildings indicated"), but the flames had leaped each gap. On the river great pools of burning turpentine, pouring from the chaos on Old Slip, swirled down the channel. Sparks whipped by the wind across the river ignited the naval storehouses in Brooklyn.

Exhausted firemen were relieved at the pumps by volunteer citizens. Some of the fighters, averred the *Evening Post,* "had their clothes frozen so stiff upon them, that they were obliged to cut them from their bodies." At noon the saving chasm was made at Coenties Slip: the large brick warehouse of Wyncoop and Company, grocers, was blown up, and the fire was checked. But in basements enclosed by fallen wreckage smoldering embers fed upon the stores of merchandise and burned until the first of January, 1836—fade-outs of the most colorful and destructive spectacle the city was to see until the night of May 13, 1863, when the incendiary and murderous carnival of the Draft Riots began.

The Great Fire was a costly show. Forty blocks were consumed; one newspaper's count was that 674 stores and residences had been leveled. The bill for the spectacle was between sixteen and twenty million dollars. Payment was evaded with a dexterity which bore tribute to the spirit of American enterprise. Much of the fabrics had come from Lyons, on consignment; the commission houses refused to acknowledge responsibility, and the French city was all but prostrated by the loss. The insurance companies promptly declared bankruptcy, while "widows and orphans; unmarried females; domestics who have prudently husbanded their earnings or legacies; aged men who invested for annuity" were left destitute and bewildered, as their traditional fate prescribed, at the strange dénouements of gilt-edged investments. On February 23 Philip Hone noted in his diary: "Twenty lots in the 'burned district' were sold at auction this day . . . at most enormous prices, greater than they would have brought before the fire in 1835, when covered with valuable buildings."

And on the first Sunday in 1836 the Reverend Orville Dewey took his text from the Great Fire. His clientele included many of New York's worthiest merchants, ripe for consolation. "We are, in a life of business, surrounded by fearful exposures, and especially in this very city, whose prosperity has been invaded by such a sudden and dreadful calamity." Then he spun the moral: consider the captive Indian, singing his tribal war-song, stoical under the most excruciating tortures; and the Christian martyr, supernaturally calm, lifting his gaze heavenward while the pyre crackles. The merchant must not be outdone in fortitude. "Wealth is valuable, doubtless, but its value is contingent—it depends on what has a far higher value, the intelligence, liberality, and purity of the mind." And Dr. Dewey indulged in a parable. He had encountered on the highways a callous, pelf-crammed merchant whom he recollected with distaste. "But again I went forth, and another man I saw, and he too was opulent." This second merchant was the poor man's friend, the young man's adviser, a liberal patron of science and education, and goodfellow of many charities. "And then it seemed to me that wealth was a good and beautiful thing—a blessed stewardship in the service of God, and a divine manifestation of mercy to man."

While Dr. Dewey's audience was being thus comforted and heartened, a number of other persons, in a different aftermath of the Fire, were listening to the visiting parson at the Tombs. On that night of December 16, the rabble had swarmed for whatever booty they could grab. The man-animals from their warrens in the dark streets of the Bowery and the human flotsam from the wharves had scurried among the crowd and past the fire-fighters, darted into stores or clawed among the debris, and scuttled away again with their pilferings. A hundred of the wretches were caught red-handed on the night of the fire; during the next few days the police searched through the tenement district for stolen goods and arrested hundreds more of the slum-dwellers.

Every place capable of serving as a detention-house was crammed, and for want of jail-room hundreds of the scavengers were discharged with no other punishment than a lecture on the laws of private property. The reporter for the *Evening Post* discerned a human waste of more consequence than the value of the stolen articles. "The squalid misery of the greater part of those taken with the goods in their possession," he wrote, "the lies and prevarications to which they resorted to induce the magistrates not to commit them to prison, their screechings and wailings when they found they must relinquish the splendid prizes they had made during the raging of the fire, and the numbers in which they were brought by the police and the military, exceeded any scene of a similar kind on record."

If there be one earnest, honest purpose beneath the strata of American society, declared Frederick Cozzens, a New Yorker, "it is the desire to ameliorate the condition of two classes, rich and poor." The rich, earnestly maintaining that they were common citizens at heart, and the poor, vigorously denying that they were a proletariat, would have agreed. Probably one's personal experience did not prove the equalitarian ideal, but that would not make the sentiment less praiseworthy. If equality was a legend, the middle class was real enough. From the merchant princes and the master shipwrights of the Atlantic seaboard, the peddlers in the New England back country, the ironmongers who worked their smelters in defiance of the Trade and Navigation Acts—from the mercantile interests of eighteenth-century America runs one ancestral strain of the middle class. And the rough democracy of the frontier, after the wilderness had been cleared and small towns had sprung up, also gave rise to a middle class. About 1835 this class became the dominant element, cultural and economic, in American life. New York, among the cities, was to profit most by this new dominance.

In the afterglow of the Great Fire appears a city of not quite 275,000 inhabitants, the largest aggregation of the fifteen million people in the United States. (Philadelphia is next, then Baltimore and Boston.) On Broadway, opposite City Hall Park, a huge box with a dignified Grecian pediment is being built— the Astor House, promising a new standard of magnificence in hostelries. A group of capitalists have applied for a charter to build a free bridge across the Harlem River ("Haarlem," adds a *vox populi*, "is destined to be a place of considerable importance. All that is wanted is free intercourse with the neighbor-

MAY-DAY IN NEW YORK

Harper's Weekly, 1859: drawing by A. Fredericks.

ing country to add wings to her prosperity."). Chang and Eng, the Siamese Twins, have returned from a triumphant tour of the Continent and are back at Peale's Museum, taking headline honors from the Great Living Anaconda Serpent of Bengal, fourteen feet in length, so docile he may be handled by the most timid with perfect safety. Edwin Forrest is leaving for England, to show the British playgoers how American muscle and energy have made a second Roscius; but a friend accosts him on the sidewalk and says, "Washington never went to Europe to gain an immortality. Jackson never went there to extend his fame. Stay here, and build yourself an enduring place in the mind of your country alone. That is enough for any man!" Last year the citizens of New York voted for Croton water; there will be an aqueduct and reservoir excelling the greatest engineering triumphs of the ancient Romans. New York can afford it; the city has a valuation of $218,723,703 in real and personal property.

When the weather has thawed, New York's diversity includes color—and noise. Its streets are cluttered with private equipages, trucks and charcoal-carts, lemonade barrels, fruit-wagons. Mingled with the noise of rush, tack, and jib in a roadway without traffic conventions are the chant of the "Hot corn" girl, the "Hot bread, who buys?" and the baker's bell, the chimney-sweep's song, the down-South voice of a "free nigger" selling hominy, the buzz of woodsaws, and the cries of auctioneers. When the confusion in the streets is cleared, it is to make way for parades: the volunteer fire companies, with their musical bands and with their engines glorified by flags, streamers, and flowers; the militia; the Washington Market Chowder Guard, the Moustache Fusileers, Tompkin's Butchers' Association Guard, or another of the target companies; the Cold Water Army of the Temperance societies; fraternal orders and labor unions.

May First is a day of less organized processions. Vans weighted with household goods make their groaning journeys. The walks are encumbered with people carrying goods too fragile to be entrusted to the draymen: dusty-bonneted girls carrying mirrors wrapped in counterpanes, small boys staggering under China vases or porcelain griffins, embarrassed older boys smuggling ghastly portraits of the family ancestors to the new house. Papa has eaten his lunch standing, nothing more than cold ham, crackers, and a bottle of London stout. It is moving day, a new urban confusion, an entailed heritage to succeeding generations. In 1836 we live in a rented cottage in Greenwich or in the rooms over our store on Broadway; in fifteen years or so, with diligence and luck, we shall have a villa in Westchester or an elegant home on Staten Island. Then or now, "No house is large enough for two families."

New York had always been a trading post and commercial port. There were no skeins of Puritan tradition, as in Boston, or of social conservatism, as in Philadelphia, that had to be woven into the Sentimental fabric. New York was ambitious to acquire commercial and financial ascendancy; the opportunity came, in the Eighteen Thirties, and was seized. The romance of commercial expansion was a tonic factor in the new psychology. And this commercial expansion is an analogue to the material growth of the United States. Between 1830 and 1860 the United States added 1,234,566 square miles of territory; the center of population shifted from middle West Virginia to the longitude of Chillicothe, Ohio; and the total population of the Republic increased to 30,986,851.

The Honorable Gulian Verplanck, in 1836, saluted the rising generation with a report on the present condition and future prospects of the American Republic. Praiseworthy items were marshaled: our immense extent of fertile territory, opening an inexhaustible field for successful enterprise; our magnificent system of federated sovereignties, carrying out principles of representative democracy never approached in the boldest theories of the Harringtons, Sidneys, and Lockes of former times; the reaction of our political system on our social and domestic concerns, bringing the influence of popular sentiment to bear upon all aspects of life; the unconstrained range of freedom of opinion, of speech, of the press; the absence of all serious inequality of fortune and rank; our divisions into numerous religious sects, with synchronous harmony of toleration and evangelical zeal; our intimate connection with the older world beyond the Atlantic, "communicating to us, through the press and emigration, much of good and much of evil not our own;" the fact that in America talent cannot slumber, and knowledge always may find some fit application; "the quick and keen sense of self-interest, that gives such energy and sagacity to the business operations of this country." And so on, while the young men of Union College fidgeted in their black gowns and wondered if their names were spelled right on the diplomas.

Moving, parading; progress, expansion; triumphs and self-congratulations, for almost a quarter of a century. Then, in 1859, seventeen days after John Brown had been hanged by the State of Virginia for the crime of inciting an insurrection, the President of the United States issued his report on the condition of the Republic. Nearly everything, James Buchanan remarked, was fine. "Prosperity smiles throughout the land. Indeed, notwithstanding our demerits, we have reason to believe, from the past events in our history, that we have enjoyed the special protection of Divine Providence ever since our origin as a nation." Cheerful, as Verplanck had been in 1836. But Verplanck's optimism was sturdy and confident; President Buchanan was making hopeful, desperate mumbo-jumbo.

The span of the Sentimental generation is from the blaze in lower Manhattan to the holocaust over the nation. Beginning and ending with a conflagration, the span itself is a rainbow—even if the sunshine is occasionally synthetic. The generation believed in the goodness of man—and allowed the left hand a little predatory liberty. Altruisms and evasions, the pebbles of fact and the cement of illusion: so was builded an American tradition of being socially comfortable, practically successful, spiritually progressive, and privately warmed with self-esteem. It was a grand idea; and if the smooth philosophy had been able to encyst a certain few irritant elements, it might have survived for another fifteen years. There is no second-guessing of history, and perhaps small profit in quarreling with it; but we have the privilege of resenting that Civil War, inevitable or avoidable as it may have been, whose forecast shadow blighted the major Romantic tendencies in American life and literature.

The United States in 1836 was well aware of the Industrial Revolution. That force was manifest by 1820, when steamboats were navigating the Ohio and the Mississippi, Eli Whitney's cotton-gin was being adopted throughout the South, and in Lowell, Massachusetts, the first city founded expressly to be a manufacturing center, the mills began to turn. The foundations of the revolution had been laid in eighteenth-century Britain. Machinery and artisans were imported into the United States, and the early triumphs and mistakes of the British industrialists reënacted. But in 1836 there were more significant evidences of the technical change than the transplanted ones. With its own creative vitality the nation was building its modern structure.

In less than a decade after the first locomotive had been put into service on the Baltimore and Ohio track between Baltimore and Ellicott's Mills, in 1829, railroads emerged from the experimental stage. In 1836 railroad shares were being listed by the New York brokerages, sharing that distinction with insurance stocks and government bonds. At first merely feeders to water transportation, by 1840 the railroads were driving the canal companies to default. Short lines were linking up with one another; the venules were becoming veins, carrying a flow of increasing richness. By 1845 the rails joined Boston with the Erie Canal at Albany and with the St. Lawrence at Ogdensburg. New York five years later, despite the interest of the State in protecting the Erie Canal from rail competition, was linked with Buffalo by a continuous line. In

1853 a trunk line between New York and Chicago was completed; Philadelphia was connected by rail with St. Louis in 1855, and with Chicago three years later. Nine thousand miles of railroad were built in the United States before 1850, and twenty thousand miles were built in the next decade.

Street-railways were laid in the Fifties. But horse-drawn trams were feeble innovations compared with the little instruments that represented the first capturing of electrical energy for the service of communication. Samuel F. B. Morse, an odd pedagogue who ate, slept, and pursued his experiments in his classroom at the University of the City of New York, completed the first practicable telegraph in January, 1836. After Congress in 1843 appropriated funds for a large-scale experiment, several intercity telegraph-lines were constructed; these were linked in 1856 to form the Western Union. The magnetic telegraph brought new conceptions of speed into business transactions; with the new printing-presses (Richard M. Hoe's patents of 1842 and 1846 increased the capacity of the machines to six thousand impressions hourly) it accelerated every department of the newspaper industry. The telegraph was a notable influence toward the standardizing of prices; and, as became dramatically evident with the completion of the line to San Francisco in 1861, it was an essential link in the tangible chain of nationalism.

The United States Mint on March 23, 1836, struck its first coinage to be made by steam-power, on the new press designed by Franklin Beale. The next twenty-five years multiplied the uses of steam in industry. When in 1844 the Land Reform Union surveyed the Industrial Revolution, machinery had taken almost complete possession of the manufacture of cloth; it was making rapid advances upon all branches of iron manufacture and other mineral industries. Newly invented machine-saws which worked in curves as well as in straight lines; a new machine for planing and grooving; the tenon-and-mortise machine—these and other revolutionary tools were taking command of the wood-working industries. The Union's survey concluded, "While some of our handicrafts are already extinct, there is not one of them but has foretasted the overwhelming competition of this occult power."

The wooden pitchback wheels that propelled the factory machines were supplanted, in the Fifties, by iron turbines. Away from the streams, in Western districts where coal was cheap, steam-driven mills were being built. The extension of railroad systems permitted industry to overcome the geographical restrictions imposed by the location of water-power sites and anthracite deposits. Technical progress of the primary furnace industries was accompanied by economies in labor, while similar progress was creating a proletariat in the textile mills. The foundry steadily displaced the forgeman. The use of malleable iron and improvements in casting accelerated the tendency toward standardization of parts, while type-founding machines and the application of molding machinery to glass manufacture further limited the occupations open to independent artisans.

And machinery came to agriculture. At county fairs new inventions and improvements were demonstrated; the most conservative of crafts gradually acknowledged and adopted the new tools. From such ingenious spectacles as the "Endless Chain Horse Power" machines patented in 1841 to the steam-driven threshers introduced in the Fifties, science and invention provided the instruments of a better technique—which made practicable the conquering of the prairies and freed the Eastern farmer and his wife from ancient burdens. In the North, at least, the importance of soil conservation was acknowledged; commercial fertilizers were introduced, and the use of cover crops became prevalent. Cyrus McCormick patented the first satisfactory automatic reaper in 1835; John Deere made his first steel plow in 1837; seed-drills were introduced in the Forties. In 1835 grain was still threshed with a flail; hay mown with a scythe, raked and pitched by hand; corn planted by hand and cultivated with a hoe. Thirty years later every one of these operations, in districts woven into the mesh of railroads and canals, was done by machinery driven by horsepower. The patient ox, after a hundred thousand years as drawer of farm carts and wagons, was pensioned off. About four decades in the future was the mechanical animal designed to supplant the horse.

In the ante-bellum United States agriculture provided livelihood for the greatest number; and after agriculture, transportation—the sea, the inland waters, and the rails. As farming methods were systematized, over a range ever widening to the westward, the strands of communication led to the cities. Ideas as well as goods were carried and exchanged. In this exchange many provincial characteristics of back-country districts were recut according to common fashion: just as, in the early years of the twentieth century, mail-order houses in Chicago set the styles for Sunday dress in many thousand communities. And, in the Sentimental generation, an "agrarian consciousness" does not emerge as a political force.

The slaveholding South was a region apart. Committed, in the early Thirties, to the ideals of an exploitative aristocracy, entrusting its political and cultural destinies to a minority group of planters and lawyers, the South provided militant opposition to the ideals of the middle class. Here and there in the North, too, were elements that resisted or escaped the impulses toward national, cultural unity. Some of these groups were encased by hard-shell religious creeds; others were insulated by genteel complacency. These latter groups were the trivial remnants of an endowed aristocracy. Charles Carroll of Carrollton, last surviving signer of the Declaration of Independence, died in 1832; and so passed the last symbol of the intellectual leadership which had wrought stability and law out of the Revolution. John Marshall, the Chief Justice who had given authority to Federalist ideas in government, died in 1835; Stephen Van Rensselaer, last of the semi-feudal aristocracy of New York patroons, in 1839. Paine Wingate had preceded him by a few months—the Honorable Paine Wingate, of Stratham, New Hampshire; ninety-nine years old; Harvard, class of 1759; barrister, judge, Washington's confidant; who wore, until the day of his death, a cocked hat, breeches and top-boots, and cambric ruffles. After his death there was no one who dressed in his fashion, and there were very few who thought in his fashion.

Beyond the area of middle-class dominance lay the frontier, a proud, crude society rampant in contradictions—democratic equalitarianism and individual license, laissez-faire and paternalism, malaria and insatiable vigor, quinine and corn whiskey. But the frontier was a phase of rapid transition, and a generalization said of New York in 1835 is apt to be true of Cincinnati in 1850 and of Chicago in 1860. The frontier's determining factors of abundant lands, rapidly increasing population, inflationist currency, and easy credit bred an unteachable, speculative optimism, which by 1836 had become part and parcel of middle-class ideals.

Andrew Jackson's election to the presidency in 1828 was the effect of the frontiersman and the "common man" of more stabilized communities working in coöperation. Qualifications, of property or religious faith, that had restricted the franchise were being discarded; the electorate was being broadened to include all males "free, white, and twenty-one." The election of 1828 was a triumph of new voters; its primary aim was to destroy the aristocratic principle in government. And the broom swept clean. "To the victors belong the spoils," said Jackson's lieutenant, William L. Marcy. Within the next few years Jackson's aides built the Democratic party into a mutual-profit society which could almost dispense with principles; the cohesive factor was the spoils system, with political appointment the reward for party service and enjoyment of these rewards contingent on unstinting service to the party in the future. Opposition, too, coalesced into a practicable unit, and the two-party basis became the characteristic expression of American politics. The Whig party contained the men who desired centralization of finance and such "protection of the rights of property" as a high tariff on manufactures, a higher price on the public lands, and federal promotion of internal improvements and maritime trade. But in working effect the real significance of the Whig party was that it was the alternative one—the ticket to select when the voter wanted to scratch the Democrats.

The second Bank of the United States, chartered in 1817, had become the nucleus of an aristocracy of finance. Headquarters were in Philadelphia; the guiding genius was Nicholas Biddle. The Bank's note-circulation, less than five million dollars in 1823, was increased to twenty million by 1832. Through its branches the Bank could stimulate or depress, within limits, the credit of state-chartered banks. Jackson's equalitarian followers raised the cry of monopoly. The President spoke of "this hydra of corruption," and to prevent government funds and credit from being turned into private profit—to level down the aristocracy he called "moneyed capitalists"—he adopted a drastic remedy. The Bank of the United States was denied renewal of its charter, and with it Philadelphia lost its financial supremacy. In New York, capitalists began the slow work of piecing together a new centralization of finance—a work which needed the Civil War for its completion.

Government, during this generation, did not represent the moneyed interests. Nor did it represent the opposition to those interests. Jackson had offended the frontier element by vetoing an active policy of federal support of road-building, canal-dredging, and other internal improvements. In 1836 the frontier vote was almost equally divided; the West was not again united with the "plain people" of the East until 1860. The machinery of government in this interval was intrusted to a convenient element, the professional politicians—who maintained themselves by being professional democrats. The political convention, a system extending from county caucuses to the meetings for nomination of a national ticket, was the form of representative action finally adopted by 1840. This system, with its ample opportunities for manipulation by professionals who knew the right maneuvers and the right platitudes, throve as the franchise was extended and prospered by the exploitation of newly naturalized voters. The Whig party quickly learned that business interests had little to fear from a democratic

THE NATURALIZATION OF VOTERS

A scene in Tammany Hall the day before election. *Frank Leslie's Illustrated Newspaper,* 1856.

electorate. Both parties found the great majority pleased and flattered to vote access to the public purse to one set of politicians and another. New York City provided an exemplary demonstration of this truth; only a comparative modesty of peculation distinguishes its municipal government of the Fifties from that of later years.

In 1836, when the population of the United States was about fifteen million, the national election polled 1,600,000 ballots. Four years later, with the population at seventeen million, about 2,400,000 votes were cast. Such a sudden increase nearly always means, "Turn the rascals out!" And so it meant in 1840. The business-cycle manufactures the rascals, and in four years it had made a pregnant rotation.

Prices were rising, credit expanding, in 1836. In the four years from 1834 through 1837, 194 new banks were chartered, and existing banks increased their currency issues by fifty per cent. A writer in the *Christian Review* explained, with little exaggeration, "A man had nothing to do but borrow of a bank, give it his note, buy up anything on which he could lay his hand, wait until the increase of the circulating medium had raised the price of his product, sell, borrow yet more on the credit which his first speculation had established, and repeat the process as often as the times would allow." The tariff was accumulating revenue faster than it could be spent, and Congress voted a generous hand-out to the states. It was labeled "a temporary deposit without interest," but, in intent and effect, the money was a gift. The wheat crop of 1835 in the Western states had been a failure, and the trade-balance with England was running heavily against the United States; but these things did not seem dangerous at the moment.

Coincidental with the creative and destructive forces of the economic cycle were the ardent, heedless desires of Imperialism. Each current reaches crest and trough in synchrony with the other; and in 1836 the national ego was embarked on a course of unlimited expansion and unqualified virtue—in a single phrase, Manifest Destiny. Canada was bound to come into the Union ultimately; there were other inevitable domains in the Caribbean. But at the moment the birth travails of Texas invited the aid of the great Republic. The democratic majority in the United States was in lively sympathy with the struggle of its Southwestern fellows for self-determination—a sympathy in some instances whetted by the promise of Texas agents that for a six months' enlistment in the revolutionary army 640 acres of land, besides pay of twenty dollars a month, would be granted. New Orleans was a rendezvous of recruits; battalions of volunteers were raised and outfitted in Louisville and Nashville. Harry R. W. Hill, the Nashville merchant, sent five thousand dollars from his own purse—as the story has it, the sum that purchased the ammunition used by the victors at the Battle of San Jacinto. Cincinnati donated cannon; New Englanders sent money. In New York one of the evidences of popular sympathy was the Giant Benefit for the "Texians" announced by the American Theatre in December, 1835, delayed by the Great Fire, but presented in January—the play *Hyder Ali; or, the Grateful Lion,* in which anticipation of George Bernard Shaw the canine star, Bruin, appeared in costume as the Lion. "After which, the comedy of *The Jew; or, the Benevolent Hebrew.* A Tyrolean Dance. A Farce." President Jackson gave aid and comfort, in the devious ways his high office permitted; and the Senate readily concurred in his hasty recognition of the infant Republic of Texas.

In 1836, too, Congress authorized an expedition to the South Seas, with Captain Charles Wilkes of the United States Navy as its commander. Sent forth primarily to investigate the seal-fishery possibilities of the southern ocean, the expedition bestowed upon the United States plausible title to a continent —Antarctica, discovered on January 19, 1840.

President Jackson, in 1836, had an eye to the expansion of his private fortunes, and he despatched an agent to the Southwest to buy lands suitable for cotton plantations. The agent reported that no good investments were left, the improved

lands being quoted at unreasonable prices and the unimproved
lands being held by speculators. Alarmed at the rapid disposal
of public lands to speculators who paid in state bank-notes of
doubtful integrity, the President directed his Secretary of the
Treasury to instruct government land-offices to accept only
specie. If the bank-notes were not good enough for the Federal
Government, they were not good enough for the British creditors of American merchants; and the paper castle began to
tumble. Martin Van Buren, Jackson's handpicked successor to
the Presidency, inherited the crash.

In May, 1837, eight hundred banks suspended, and $120,-
000,000 in bank deposits became inaccessible.

> Why speak of schemes, begot with every sun,
> Whose paths were many, but their purpose one?

put Champion Bissell in cadenced arraignment of

> The BANK, whose shares, on bright crisp paper wrote,
> Were based upon the PROMISSORY NOTE,
> Sublimest fiction of the age of brass,
> When borrowers organized to lend each other. . . .

The democracy was inclined to agree with Jackson and
Van Buren that the Bank was to blame for it all. After having
ventured the legislative gantlet three times without success, in
1840 Van Buren's plan for an Independent Treasury was
passed. It meant, simply, that government money should be
bullion while the common currency should be the inflated
issues of state banks. The Executive delayed his formal assent
for a few days, signing the bill on the Fourth of July so that
the ceremonial tollings and cannonades should signalize to
Democrats a dual independence—from the British in '76, from
the banks in '40. It was a hollow celebration, since the National
Government was in debt, business was sluggish, and the states
carried such staggering indebtedness that legislatures were
inclined to disown the burden. Repudiation did follow shortly,
and $200,000,000 in bonds and interest were defaulted. It was
a consolation that these issues had been floated in large part in

London, where small investors had given them preference over British government securities, which had a lower interest-rate.

On the political rebound from the Panic of 1837, General William Henry Harrison, who had been something of a hero in the War of 1812, became President. After his nomination a delegate at the Whig convention called for the routine adoption of an address to the people—that is, the party platform. There was no need for an address, he was answered; the voice of the West, rolling down from the mountains and along the valleys of the Atlantic, was more compulsive than all the addresses that had ever been written. And the General was presented to the people sans platform or program, with but his military past and his sterling character.

Harrison had been trounced in the previous election, and Democratic orators and newspapers, at the start of the campaign of 1840, mentioned him disrespectfully—as a dotard, a granny, one who should be content with a log cabin and a barrel of hard cider without aspiring to the Presidency. This last line of attack recoiled in Harrison's favor; it took the starch out of the gentleman's shirt-frills and brought him closer to the people. The issue of the campaign became honest sentiment versus snobbery, Harrison's mythical drinking-gourd against Van Buren's legendary silver goblets, hard cider against the imported champagne reputed to be Van Buren's tipple. Harrison discarded the silk topper he had usually worn and adopted a soft, broad-brimmed hat. "It is to him," said Whig spellbinders, "that we look for a restoration of all the privileges and blessings of freemen"—in particular, Two Dollars a Day and Roast Beef.

Verso, the Democratic candidate for reëlection to the presidency became a profligate spendthrift. A Whig Congressman, in one of the most amazing and mendacious speeches ever heard in the national legislature, offered a scent-by-scent description of Van Buren at his morning toiletries, described the full-length French mirrors in the President's bedroom and a scale of living as lavish as the Bourbon's—"Substitute in his stead, at the head of the Government, that plain, frugal, and well-tried citizen, William Henry Harrison." Van Buren was Jackson's pupil in Executive usurpation. "Through the official agencies, scattered throughout the land, and absolutely subject to his will, he executes according to his pleasure or caprice," declared Henry Clay, who knew he was talking nonsense; but he was playing according to the rules. The distinguishing mark of a President thereafter, until 1861, was to be his lack of distinction; and of a successful political campaign, a rapturous appeal to the golden mean of the middle class.

Slogans and community singing; canvasses taken in steamboats and stage-coaches, at church-raisings and baby-christenings; emblematic push-balls, rolled from town to town and state to state to signify Harrison's cumulative majority—the people were given their first opportunity to exalt one of their own kind. Even the small city of Utica could put on a Harrison parade nine miles long.

So much for the mass libido, ardently responsive to the Sentimental appeal. The kindly old General had not been allowed to pull in his latch-string for a little privacy since the campaign opened; he had been half-killed by his friends before he went to Washington for his inauguration. Harrison's first speech embodied the promise to shape his policies for "the greatest good to the greatest number." The next four weeks were given over to the patronage tumult; the party ax decapitated large and small office-holders alike. Every morning Harrison communed with his Bible and prayer-book and took a walk before breakfast. It rained, and he caught pneumonia. One month from the date of his inauguration he died. The popular enthusiasm for the Hero of Tippecanoe was to have been the cloak for a rechartering of the Bank of the United States and the enactment of other legislation favorable to moneyed interests. But the opportunity vanished. The Whig nomination for Vice-President had been bestowed upon John Tyler, as a Virginian with a "favorite-son" appeal and because Tyler was a friend of Henry Clay. The compliment became a party calamity when Tyler inherited the presidency and vetoed the Whigs' pet measures.

And the political and economic effects of the Panic of 1837 remained impressed upon American life until another outburst of Manifest Destiny had changed the geography and the fortunes of the country. Without an attractive figurehead the Whigs could not mass public sentiment for their financial program. Southern Democrats readily chose Northern men as their candidates for highest office; but, even so, the slavery interests could not dictate legislation. The middle class held the balance of power—a precarious and unwieldy power. Government followed a course of vacillation and mediocrity. A national bank system was not reëstablished. The public-land policy was not liberal enough to satisfy Westerners and laborers, nor on the restrictive basis desired by Eastern capitalists and Southern planters. The tariff remained a political makeshift; neither the manufacturing interests of the North nor the raw-material interests of the South obtained the economic legislation they wanted.

To this blockade of the political avenues of the "money-power" there was one exception, in which the middle class acquiesced because the move seemed of general benefit. In February, 1840, a petition reached the Senate from a New York merchant, Silas M. Stilwell, for a "single and direct" law that, on the surrender of his property, the debtor should be released from all his obligations—the first proposal for a new type of bankruptcy law, to release not only the person of the debtor but the debt itself. Senator Daniel Webster, spokesman of the Whig party, introduced such a bill two months later, and in the autumn of 1841 a bankruptcy statute was enacted. Middle-class aversion to such a grant of financial irresponsibility was expressed as soon as the statute had done its work—the cancellation of $400,000,000 in private obligations and $200,000,-000 of bank debts. Eleven months after its passage the law was repealed.

President Harrison had pledged himself not to seek a second term—a gesture of submission to the popular will and a pledge not to exalt his personal influence as Jackson had done. When Tyler attempted to win the Whig nomination in 1844, after having served practically the whole of Harrison's term, the Democratic party made political capital of this "defilement of Harrison's sepulchre"; and the candidates in successive elections professed a modesty which inhibited their considering the possibility of reëlection. The exception, Pierce, found that his four years of faithful service to the Democratic party did not avail to break the tradition.

It was a tradition for little men. Polk, elected President in 1844, was a Tennessee politician without record save in the safe grooves of party loyalty. James Buchanan, angling for the succession, was told by Polk that "no man would ever be President who was prominently before the public for that office for two or three years or a longer time before the nomination." In 1848 the Whig ticket of Taylor and Fillmore was irresistible. Taylor was a Southern Whig who had never shown interest in politics; he owned a sugar plantation worked by slave labor, but no one knew his views on the "peculiar institution." He promised to be "the President of the whole people," followed the example of his party's convention in announcing no platform, and was enthusiastically elected, for much the same reasons that had won Harrison the presidency: in the Mexican War Taylor had "overstept his duty, and blundered on to that victory at Buena Vista"; and, in the words of Horace Greeley, Taylor was " 'that noblest work of God, an honest man.' "

Another military hero, Winfield Scott, was the Whig nominee in 1852; the Democratic convention countered with yet another wearer of the braid, General Franklin Pierce. The generalship was a political favor: Pierce had been wounded in the Mexican War, but by a fall from his horse; called into action at Chapultepec, he had responded by fainting. His years in Congress had shown no more distinctive qualities than modesty and affability. When Major Jack Downing returned from the convention to Downingville, Maine, he related the nomination to Uncle Joshua. "And then he looked up again, and says he, 'Major, *who is General Pierce?* It ain't a *fictious* name, is it? Well, now, Major, are you sure there is such a person, or did someone play a hoax on the Baltimore convention?' 'Yes,' says I. 'To make sure of it all and no mistake, I come through New Hampshire, and went to Concord, where they said he lived, and inquired all about it. The neighbors there all know him perfectly well, and showed me the house he lives in.' " But Pierce was a likable man, as Marcy said; and he moved to Washington.

More compelling evidence of political mediocrity was the obsequious attention given by Executive and Congressmen alike to matters of patronage—the importance of the machine and the fear of being impolite to a constituent. Polk's diary describes an instance when the Executive patience wore thin: "Had many visitors today, mostly office seekers. Among them was a man named Emanuel Fisher, who had repeatedly called on me before to be appointed Keeper of a Light House on the Lakes and had been as repeatedly referred to the Secretary of the Treasury, who was charged by law with the appointment of such officers. On being informed again that I would not interfere in such appointments . . . he acted and spoke rudely and insolently; when I told him that I did not desire to be insulted in my own office, and he retired." Pierce, traveling to Washington to be inaugurated, found that to escape the pestering swarm he had to ride in the baggage-car and disguise himself in old clothes.

The bulky correspondence of Senator Thomas Ewing of Ohio is almost entirely a record of patronage and pork-barrel —a dismal picture of a Senator perpetually busied with what his constituents and friends conceived to be the primary duties of his office. One McElrain wishes his son admitted to West Point: "I herein enclose you a copy of a petition (*which I beg of you to read*) which I calculate to git [*sic*] our governor and all our State officers to sign, also the Whig state central committee, and, if need be, the Whig members of our legislature and other distinguished individuals of the Whig party"; if

Senator Ewing will promise to nominate the young man, "I will take my son out of a store where he is now engaged, and send him to some good school, in order the better to prepare him to enter said institution." One Winright, set upon being named Commissioner of Pensions, drools his appeal: "My friend Ewing permit me to ask you if something cannot be done through your influence, and let me be relieved from further suspense and anxiety, and become settled in the evening of my life. How long our lives may continue, is very uncertain; for death is now stalking through our land [the cholera, in 1849], in an alarming manner. Yet we are in duty bound to live, as though we were under mutual obligations to live for, and assist each other in the best possible manner that we can. For the good Book says that he who will not provide for his friends, (or which is the same thing) 'for his own household,' is 'worse than an infidel.' " So the plums were squabbled over and handed around, while Manifest Destiny was stating a problem which the middle class and their politicians had trained themselves not to solve. Their evasiveness must be imitated here, and a discussion of the problem postponed until our diorama of the Sentimental Years creaks into its final frame.

The problem was whether expansion of slavery should accompany territorial expansion. In 1845 Texas entered the Union, and the westward movement had leaped from the Mississippi Valley to the far reaches of Oregon, whither for five years the overland caravans had borne a steady stream of emigration. The ruts of ox-team freighters from the Missouri River towns to Santa Fé were twenty-four years old. Several colonies of Americans had established themselves in the nominally forbidden territory of California.

"It looks as if a great day was coming," declared Margaret Fuller, "and that time one of democracy. Our country will play a leading part. Her eagle will lead the van; but whether to soar upward to the sun or stoop for helpless prey, who dares promise?" Another lady, Anna Ella Carroll, gave the answer, strangely phrased: the Fathers of the Republic had indicated the way; "spreading their Protestant Bible and their American Constitution of Government on the wings of the American Eagle, they left us to burst its pinions, and soar toward the sun." The eagle seemed minded (like Stephen Leacock's knight) to soar in all directions.

A succession of treaties had left a region on the Pacific coast, between latitudes 42° and 54° 40′, open to the joint occupation of the United States and Great Britain. The American popular demand was for exclusive title to the whole; "Fifty-four forty or fight" was a campaign slogan in 1844, making votes for the party that shouted it. Two years later, by treaty with Great Britain, that part of Oregon most valuable for agriculture and fisheries became United States domain. Almost at the same time the United States became engaged in a war with Mexico.

This war had seemed inevitable after Texas became one of the United States; the prospect was welcomed by expansionists. If the continental domain of the United States could not be stretched to the utmost limits by purchase, another instrument would serve. President Polk instructed a confidential agent in California to promote dissatisfaction with the Mexican government among the natives—looking toward an independent California under American protection or an annexation of the region to the United States. And in 1846 a party of civilian Americans, possibly having an understanding with Captain John C. Frémont (then in California at the head of a United States Army expedition), took possession of a California town and hoisted a flag of their original designing.

With the National Administration in full accord with the Texan claim that the new state extended to the Rio Grande, as against the Mexican assertion that the Nueces was the western boundary, a military force was sent to patrol the farther stream. In the view of the Mexicans this movement was a wanton invasion of their own soil, and Mexican troops congregated on the west bank of the Rio Grande. On May 11, 1846, Congress was informed by the President that American blood had been shed on American soil by Mexican aggressors; and although Congress moved expeditiously, General Zachary Taylor had won two battles before war was formally declared. By October the task was simply to persuade the Mexicans to acknowledge the futility of resistance—a task requiring a military demonstration which lasted until mid-September, 1847, and parleys which ended on February 2, 1848. The new boundary between the United States and Mexico was, roughly, to follow the Gila River westward and thence the Colorado—to extend from the Rio Grande to the Pacific. The United States acquired a domain greater than the area of the original thirteen states. Two members of the Cabinet, James Buchanan and Robert J. Walker, felt that the President had let them down: they had urged the conquest and annexation of all of Mexico.

The beginning of the war found the Northern middle class casually acquiescent. The righteousness of the struggle was a matter of opinion; opposition was not treason. But excitement and enthusiasm grew while the war lasted. The zest for adventure found a national stage; the American regulars and volunteers behaved splendidly and so glorified the war. "Our beloved country," Polk announced after the new domain had been claimed, "presents a sublime moral spectacle to the world." In behalf of Manifest Destiny, buyers had been despatched to market again, this time for the Pearl of the Antilles. Within the next few years three filibustering expeditions were outfitted in Southern ports to expel the Spanish authority from Cuba; American agents, with promises of as much as one hundred million dollars for the island, beleaguered the Spanish court; and three American diplomatists of high rank collaborated in a public statement that if Spain persisted in its refusal to sell, the United States should consider whether every human and divine law did not justify the seizure of Cuba by force.

Lieutenant Lucien Loeser, courier of the American military commandant in California, reached Washington in December,

1848, bringing with him a tea-caddy filled with gold-dust and nuggets, and tendered the commandant's report that in the region about the Sacramento and San Joaquin rivers was probably more gold than would pay the cost of the Mexican War a hundredfold. In the new year Americans swarmed through the rills of the Sierras, and Eastern newspaper advertisements were abundant with bargains in mining boots, gold-sifters, and processed foodstuffs. The overland travelers to California passed what had been the isolated outpost of American settlement—the Mormon colony in Utah, now thriving and widely distributed, organized as the State of Deseret and petitioning for admission to the Union.

If Eastern labor received a better wage in the Fifties, it could thank California gold for that. In the quiescent years after the Panic, industry rescaled its operating costs, and with the upturn of business in 1841 it was in excellent position to make a profit. For the next decade wages and costs did not rise above the 1840 level, and they were actually lowered in the textile and other industries shifting from a handicraft to a factory basis. In this laissez-faire world the capitalistic machine became more complex and more extensive; Europe poured new labor into the machine, the South and West poured swelling quantities of farm produce, and the portentious differences between the economic interests of the North and the South were obscured by the general profit-taking. The value of American exports in 1836 was little more than a third of the $316,-000,000 which represented the exports of 1860. Imports fluctuated considerably, more because of European conditions than of domestic factors, but usually were in excess of the exports; the flow of European capital into American joint-stock corporations more than redressed the balance. The value of interstate commerce increased from two billion dollars in 1850 to three and a half billion in 1860. The national wealth, in the same decade, mounted from $7,136,000,000 to $16,160,000,000.

But within this last and most prosperous of the antebellum decades the evil genius of capitalism made its periodical appearance.

California's output of gold passed $40,000,000 in 1849, the first full year in which the startling discoveries were exploited; in 1853 the state's output reached its maximum of $65,000,000. Discoveries in Australia served further to increase the world's supply of the standard moneys; within the ten years ending in 1848 about $800,000,000 of gold and silver was added to the world's store. This abundance was reflected, magnified, in American speculation; and, as in the Thirties, the states encouraged rather than restricted the outcropping of mushroom banks. The 691 banking houses in 1843 had become 1,416 in 1857, and their liabilities were mounting much more rapidly than their resources. The westward movement of population and the general increase in the volume of agricultural crops made the construction and stock-jobbing of railroads a most tempting activity; and over one and a quarter billion dollars was invested in the rails. Bissell, the bard of depressions, lamented

> the madness that possessed
> One half the nation, and amazed the rest—
> That threw the ponderous chain of iron road
> O'er lonely plains where man had scarcely trod!
> As if the long-drawn lines of rusted bar,
> The jangling rattle of the empty car,
> Had magic potence to produce the birth
> Of full-grown cities from the lonely earth;
> As if the secret of the wealth of states,
> Long hid from mortal eyes by envious fates,
> Were now revealed, as if by sudden shock,
> To wondering eyes, in form of RAILROAD STOCK!

The Ohio Life Insurance Trust Company of Cincinnati, with too many of its eggs in one basket—five million dollars in railroad loans—dropped the basket in August, 1857. This incident began the crisis. All but one of the New York banks suspended payment in specie; in October the monetary system of the country declared an enforced holiday. The depression was lifted by 1860; meanwhile the Treasury had accumulated a deficit, which served merely to bind the financial groups in New York and Philadelphia closer to the Government. But the

Panic of 1857 had a unique consequence—a religious revival, non-sectarian, among the business folk. Its agency was the noonday prayer-meeting, sponsored by young men; the Young Men's Christian Association, arranging many of these gatherings, then came into its earliest prominence. More than a dozen prayer-meetings were held daily in the New York downtown district, five in Washington, three in Baltimore; the record touches all Northern and Western cities. In this sudden confession of bankruptcy about five hundred thousand people attained a "general awakening and sense of grace." The key desire of this almost spontaneous revival was expressed at a midday meeting in Burton's Theatre in New York. "I probably shall offer the united petition of every Christian here present, when I say, 'Come, Lord Jesus, come quickly.' " It was a cleanly note, in contrast with the message New York merchants had vicariously spoken not quite twenty-five years before: "Come, with money-bags."

CHAPTER TWO

This Fine Busy World

A FOUNT of learning in New Hampshire, the Holmes Plymouth Academy, broadened its field of instruction in 1836 by adding a course on "Anatomy and Natural History, as Illustrating the Divine Existence." In New York the Reverend Dr. Dewey was offering his worthy parishioners a series of sermons which might well have been entitled "The Divine Existence, as Illustrated and Exemplified by Our Commerce, Society, and Politics." Dewey put his sermons into a book (1838), where they formed a harmonious demonstration that "there is an object, in the accumulation of wealth, beyond success; there is a final cause of human traffic; and that is virtue." But in 1836 the Reverend Thomas P. Hunt had performed the theomorphic task so patly that Dewey, or anyone else, could do no more than add another halo. Spoke Mr. Hunt in *The Book of Wealth*: The desire to possess more property than is sufficient for our maintenance is almost universal, so common an emotion that it must be a law of human nature. Since it *is* a law of human nature, its purpose must be wise and benevolent. (Both boys and girls were made of sugar and spice.) "From this common desire, may it not be presumed that it is a duty to be rich? And one thing is certain: no man can be obedient to God's will. as revealed in the Bible, without becoming wealthy."

The merchant's guide to virtue was embodied in a printed copy of maxims, available in broadsheet or pocket size. Stephen Allen, successful merchant and benevolent gentleman, kept this card always about his person; and when his body was recovered from the Hudson after the explosion of the steamboat

Henry Clay, the water-logged list was in his pocket. "When you speak to a person, look him in the face. Good company and good conversation are the very sinews of virtue. Avoid temptation, for fear that you may not withstand it. When you retire to bed, think over what you have done during the day. Do not marry until you are able to support a wife." And so they ran, twenty-seven capsule admonitions in all, preaching a sedulous, unctuous type of virtue for gentlemen who elected to pursue wealth and salvation in one process.

What did constitute a merchant? Charles Edwards answered, in a lecture published in 1839: decision of character ("confidence without obstinacy, and constancy of purpose under all circumstances"); a cheerful disposition ("for it helps wonderfully in making a good bargain"); ambition ("to accomplish a name which will give to his bill of exchange the currency of the world, and to his merchandise the best price and the highest consideration"); truth ("a deposition at the custom-house is considered a solemn declaration"); scholarship—that is, a knowledge of geography and arithmetic; and honor ("an aid and consolation in adversity"). And, whenever the merchant could afford it, benevolence.

Elizabeth Oakes Smith, in her novel *The Newsboy,* depicts the Merchant with tender respectfulness. If none of us is embarrassed by being seen with a lady of feminist repute, we may follow the authoress into the scene. Quietly the Merchant sits in his counting-room, with its sofas and stuffed chairs and carpets, a room "reverently ornamented with a bust of Webster and Clay, while from the tall desk looks down Shakespeare and Milton." (Merger!) The Merchant is planning an expedition, and spiritual good shall be an unbilled part of the outbound cargo. "Thank God there is a wake of broad, generous, manly, and Christian principles following the pathway of an American ship." But let us venture to disturb him. His office is in the rear of the store; we must pass through a broad area filled with merchandise, where the stout Irishman shoves aside huge boxes and bags and coils of rope, for a consignment has just arrived; we noticed a dray, with Negro driver, outside. The head clerk stands, tablets in hand, "taking account" and directing the movements of the porters. Farther in the interior we enter a large room floored with manila matting. This is the room of the bookkeeper and clerks. Desks are ranged about, but not many high stools, "for the smart, handsome clerk prefers to stand, and his faultless tights have no 'stick out' at the knees." Beyond is the Merchant's sanctum. Can you find anything about him to criticize? Unrestrained adulation, remember, is not an American trait. "In our day the merchant is a little more reserved than is essential to his position; he does not treat his dependents with quite the fatherly care which his situation would justify; but time and culture will amend this."

Some old women and shabby children wander into the front room, the warehouse; they do not seem to belong in this pleasing scene, but the lady novelist thinks they are quaint adornments and keeps them in. They are the favored scavengers, whom the Merchant allows to come in and pick up the coffee-beans spilled from the bags and to claim the barrels and boxes for kindling-wood.

The commission merchant was, as late as the Mexican War, the typical moderate capitalist. The old, conservative house of Goodhue and Company affords a good example, for Jonathan Goodhue and his partners never speculated in any of the grandiose "internal-improvement" schemes of the Western states which devoured huge sums of Eastern and British capital. Goodhue and Company followed sound pursuits with a minimum of risk. Commercial houses from widely scattered ports sent them consignments; they were the New York agents of the largest line of Liverpool packets and correspondents of eminent European bankers—Baring Brothers of London and Steiglitz of St. Petersburg. They disposed of goods at auction or through brokers, taking usually a commission of five per cent on the proceeds. They guaranteed the consignees against loss. Goodhue and Company necessarily had to accept "paper," extending credit of from four to six months, even from the most reliable jobbers and merchants. The vicissitudes of collection were such that the house, conservative as it was, found its profits reduced to about two and one-half per cent; but the volume of business, and the fact that a very small working capital was needed in the usual run of transactions, accounted for a sizable emolument.

In firms of this type, and in the many mercantile houses that dealt broadly in both wholesale and retail trade, the good old story of *Pluck and Luck; or, from Messenger Boy to Merchant Prince,* was often rewritten. Bright young fellows of fourteen or fifteen, verdant from a New England district school, had the best chances; for urban merchants believed as strongly as anyone in rural virtue and knew besides that they could extract the maximum of work from a country boy. Besieged every year by hundreds of applications from well-to-do families in behalf of their young men, who professed themselves willing to start without salary, the magnates of trade preferred to pick applicants who had no acquaintances in the big city (with whom they might loiter when despatched on errands) and had no toplofty prejudices against such tasks as sweeping out litter and scraping their employers' boots.

The young American at the bottom rung of the ladder got fifty dollars, or at the most seventy-five, for his year's labor. His greatest reward, for the first three or four years, was that something called "learning the business." The young men toiled while they learned—sweeping, doing errands, taking letters to the post-office, keeping the store-book, entering packages at the Custom House, delivering goods, assisting the bookkeeper or the porter, and copying letters. This letter-copying was a wearisome art, for duplicates and triplicates had generally to be made and despatched against the uncertainties of marine shipping and inland post. And after the years in the counting-room, perhaps varied by a trip or two as supercargo, even a partnership was not improbable for a diligent young man who had been sufficiently obtrusive with his merits. (As the century advanced past its meridian, however, when moderate wealth was no longer conspicuous and the tradition of "diligence" began to appear rather Georgian, the enterprising clerk perhaps discovered a boulder in the path of opportunity—the new idea that the capitalist's son, educated outside the business, was qualified to step into a high position.)

A hair shirt of virtue went with the job. Most of the commission firms and many industrial corporations expected their clerks to observe an explicit morality. A lapse in compliance was accounted ample reason for summary discharge.

The posted rules for employees of Arthur Tappan and Company in 1836 represent the finest flower of the disposition to shepherd the morals of one's clerks. The brothers, Arthur and Lewis, were congenital reformers identified with many "causes," and, contrary to the sage practice of most merchants, they subordinated their mercantile interests to their crusading passion. Arthur Douglas, to be sure, refused to accept a cargo of wines and liquors, sacrificing thirty thousand dollars rather than blemish his record of no dealings with the rum demon. Many merchants imposed teetotal abstinence on their employees. But the Tappans' clerks were gaited to a virtuous lockstep: strict temperance; divine service twice on the Sabbath day; attendance at prayer-meetings twice a week; no acquaintance, front- or back-stage, with members of the theatrical profession. A clerk was required to belong to an Abolition society, and to gain favor with the Tappans he had to make converts. He was not permitted, of course, to visit houses of ill fame or indulge in fast habits; he must not be out of his boarding-house or residence after ten in the evening. (This last rule was favored by many commission houses; for young ladies are fond of silks, and it was no difficult matter, in the days before cash-girls and doorkeepers, to smuggle out a bolt or two.)

Arthur Tappan and Company expected its clerks to be at their posts before half-past seven on summer mornings and before eight in winter. Except during the slack months the store closed at eight. The hours were typical of mercantile practice. The ceremony of morning prayers, in which everyone from capitalist to apprentice joined, was still common in 1836, but it disappeared within the next fifteen years.

SHAKESPEARE FOR THE COUNTER-JUMPERS

"You should be women, and yet your beards forbid me to interpret that you are so.—MACBETH, Act I, Scene 3."

Vanity Fair, 1860.

Clever employees attended church whether their overlords expressly required it or no, and the wiser clerks attended Sunday School as well. Homer Ramsdell, counter-jumper in a small dry-goods store, got sixpenny dinners at Seely Brown's eating-house in Nassau Street and slept on a cot in a boarding-house at 60 Dey Street, where his two dollars per week paid also for breakfast and tea. He slept, however, with his trousers smoothly impressed beneath the mattress; he combed his hair beautifully; and he taught in the Sunday School of the Reverend Dr. George Potts, whose Presbyterian church was generally accounted to have the richest members with the prettiest daughters. And the enterprising young man, in consequence, met and captivated the daughter of Thomas Powell. They were happily married. And Powell, at his daughter's fond request, forced his son-in-law upon the directors of Erie as president of the railroad.

Joseph A. Scoville, a dependable chronicler of the commercial history of New York City, avers that a group of ten counter-jumpers so acutely interpreted the times that they all taught in Sunday Schools, curled each other's hair on Saturday nights, and otherwise fraternally coöperated; and each of the ten landed a daughter of fortune. Ramsdell was one of these; George R. Ives, who married the daughter of Ralph Olmstead, the wealthy dry-goods merchant, was another.

Amos Lawrence was the generation's favorite example of a merchant whose virtue paid dividends in currency. Gerrit Smith (not so popular because he was inflexibly Abolitionist) was another capitalist whose life pointed a romantic moral. Unlike Lawrence, he had been wicked in his youth—poetic, epicurean, with flowing locks and broad Byronic collar, the young man had played cards for stakes on Sunday and otherwise dabbled in youthful folly. But before his thirtieth year he had "abjured the castors" (by this phrase Mr. Smith meant that he had given up putting salt, pepper, and vinegar on his food); in 1832 he swore off tea and coffee, and, taking up moral hygiene in earnest, in 1835 he abandoned fish, flesh, and gravies. In the next year he forswore butter. He conscientiously observed the Sabbath, regularly held family prayer, and was identified with many worthy causes. His interests as landlord and capitalist prospered. (But unregenerates may derive some satisfaction from his diary, which records a train of colds, rheumatic pains, giddiness, and other interesting symptoms.)

Perhaps the sudden popular deification of Stephen Girard, little esteemed during his lifetime of rigorous trading and implacable acquisitiveness but discovered to have been a great and good man when his will was read and its munificent provisions for the education of orphans made known, had something to do with the planting of the crop of philanthropic capitalists. But, in the language of the times, emulation was not the exclusive motive. Philanthropy was the final, self-pleasurable fruit of complacent success. The princes of commerce really enjoyed it.

Amos Lawrence sent stuffs for poor students, to be distributed by college professors, to the seminaries; donated goods to poor ministers and widows; founded a children's infirmary in Boston; gave nearly forty thousand dollars to Williams College and smaller sums to Groton, Wabash, Kenyon, and the Theological School at Bangor. He filled his carriage with tracts published by the American Temperance Society and the Sunday School Union, to be showered upon acquaintances and strangers alike whenever the good merchant took the air. He had several thousand copies of *Uncle Toby's Thoughts on Tobacco,* a pamphlet of obvious message, printed for his carriage system of distribution. His brother William gave ten thousand dollars to Groton Academy in 1844, the most generous donation that the academy, founded in 1793, had received; the grateful trustees changed the name to Lawrence Academy at Groton. Abbott Lawrence, a younger brother, gave fifty thousand dollars to found the scientific school of Harvard College; thus, as the eulogist pronounced at his funeral in 1855, he "indulged a well-directed generosity."

These donations were not happenstance. Amos Lawrence left, at his death in 1852, entries for all of the $639,000 he had given away. Harry Hill, the Southern merchant, kept a volume labeled "Charity Register," as carefully posted as was any other entry-book in his establishment—was not the keeping of good books itself a primary virtue in a merchant?

John Bromfield's donations reflect a typical division of the objects of benevolence. Bromfield, who made his money at first in the Canton trade and later in "investments" (note-shaving and the like), gave away $110,000, to these enterprises: the Massachusetts General Hospital, the McLean Asylum, the Farm School at Thompson's Island, the Asylum for Indigent Boys and the Seamen's Aid Society, both of Boston, and the Town of Newburyport. The donation to his natal city was half to be used for keeping the sidewalks in good order and half "for the planting and preserving of trees in said streets, for the embellishing and ornamenting of said streets for the pleasure and comfort of the inhabitants."

Even John Jacob Astor, who was never really Americanized, came to appreciate the place of benevolence in the capitalist's life. During his lifetime he made large donations to the German Society and to the Association for the Relief of Respectable, Aged, and Indigent Females. His will directed further contributions to these societies, as well as to the poor of his native village; on the advice of friends, in 1836 he added a codicil for the founding of the Astor Library, with a legacy of $400,000. The Library, built on Lafayette Place near Astor Place, was opened in 1854, six years after Astor's death. With its fifty thousand volumes and more it was then the largest library in the United States.

Astor's estate at his death was valued at about $20,000,000, a sum unique and almost incredible in 1848. It would have been more had not Astor diverted several millions to his son. The press and public were respectfully awed at the magnitude of the estate, the bulk of which descended to William B. Astor.

Only James Gordon Bennett—who was, of course, a demagogue, the publisher of a dreadful one-penny paper which carried the advertisements of obstetricians and ladies of convenience—ventured the opinion that the late Mr. Astor might have given ten of those twenty millions back to the people of New York.

In 1830 Astor was the only man in New York City with an accumulation of more than a million dollars. Robert Lenox, Nathaniel Prime, Stephen Whitney, and John G. Coster completed the city's roster of the very wealthy—a larger list, by two or three names, than Philadelphia or Boston could exhibit. The era when ship-owners were the dominant capitalists, stretching from the beginning of the century, culminated in Stephen Girard's hoard of eight millions. Very respectable fortunes were still to be made in shipping as late as the mid-Fifties. But wise ship-owners invested their surplus profits in real estate, banks, turnpikes, insurance companies, railroads, lotteries, and particularly in factories. The shift of investments from maritime commerce to manufacturing plants, a process begun in the Eighteen-Twenties and well-nigh completed in the late Fifties, when the Cunard Line put American shipping to shame, was practically a common chapter in the history of the wealthy families of New England.

John Jacob Astor's fortune, with its diverse tales of embarrassed families, governmental favors, mortgages, office-holders in need of ready cash, and the recurrent phrase, "seven per cent," owed its greater bulk to Astor's interest in city lands. The fur trade had made the butcher's son a millionaire; but he retired from Western ventures in 1834, to multiply his wealth by a surer means. The Panic of 1837 gave the capitalist with unencumbered cash chance after chance to purchase mortgages at much less than their face value; and Astor, in due time, took full title to many lots and buildings. Leasing real property but not selling it, he acted sagaciously for himself and his descendants. The increase of capital as the nation expanded in commerce and agriculture and the rise in rental values as the large towns of 1830 became the great cities of 1860 produced wealth without sweat.

Astor had the largest amount of funds ready for investment at the trough of the economic wave and so gained the most on the upward swell. Except in its volume the rise of his fortune was typical of the other great accumulations of the period. The growth of the urban middle class and the increasing density of the slums manufactured, for the holders of real estate, wealth to an amount hitherto incredible—not for one land magnate, but for twenty. When Pierre Lorillard, landholder, banker, and tobacconist, died in 1843, his fortune of one million dollars was so notable that the newspapers coined a word to describe the new breed of capitalist—*millionaire*. Within less than five years the novelty had worn off, and the word was being printed without italics. The Goelet, Dodge, Schermerhorn, Rhinelander, Longworth, Lispenard, and Lenox fortunes all owed their momentum to the rise of city land-values. In the smaller cities in the growing West the process was being repeated on a commensurate scale.

Meanwhile the ramifications of the complex commercial set-up were producing a goodly quantity of moderate fortunes. Moses Yale Beach, proprietor of the New York *Sun* and a hail fellow with the townsfolk, compiled in 1844 the first practical guide-book to credit and marriage, *The Wealth and Biography of the Wealthy Citizens of the City of New York*. The booklet had reached its tenth, revised, edition in 1846, and it was revised twice during the next decade. The edition of 1846 disposes of 212 gentlemen in the first fifteen of its fifty-nine columns; the volume lists, then, about 850 names in all. The city then numbered about 400,000 people. Of the first 212 names (the A, B, and C of the directory), eighty-seven were credited with fortunes ranging from $100,000 to $250,000; eighty-nine had accumulated from a quarter-million to a half-million dollars; twenty-eight had fortunes between $500,000 and $750,000; three citizens of New York were amassing the final quarter of the million-dollar goal; and five were bona-fide millionaires. Of these, the Astors, John Jacob and his son William Backhouse, led everybody else, with a little nest-egg of thirty million dollars between them. The other great fortunes in this sector of the alphabet belonged to William B. Crosby, who had gained his by the comparatively effortless process of inheriting it; to the estate of Isaac Bronson, the banker, who had died in 1838; and to Henry Brevoort, Jr., whose wealth had been amassed by the triplicate means of buying city lands, playing the market, and marrying a rich Southern lady.

The *Wealth and Biography* amply reveals the diversity of opportunities for heaping up dollars in urban mid-century America. The first forty-two fortunes listed are attributed to twenty-four different activities. Lawyers, newspaper publishers, retail merchants, dry-goods wholesalers, auctioneers, and iron merchants each claimed three of the fortunes; two belonged to hack-writing professors who turned out texts and encyclopædias cribbed, in great part, from English books; and one, gained by more imaginative labor, was accredited to Phineas Taylor Barnum.

The wealthy citizens were listed alphabetically. Opposite the name of the possessor was set the amount of the fortune; a biographical sketch followed, varying in length from a line to a page. These sketches make an inspiring tale, of a land of opportunity delivering the goods. From Andariese Barnet, who owed his fortune to being "an excellent Tailor and very amiable man," to Benjamin Brandreth, the celebrated manufacturer and vendor of Brandreth's Pills (bread-crumbs coated with sugar they were, testifying in their success to the partnership of Advertising and Progress), of whom Mr. Beach noted, without irony, "He resides mostly at Sing-Sing, where he has a splendid seat," the reader comes in time to N. T. Hubbard, "of an excellent and honored New England family. Is largely interested in the pork business."

Among others of the estimable and wealthy, Thomas W. Thorne merits notice: "Formerly engaged in the lottery business, but at present President of the Jefferson Insurance Company." Of Henry E. Pierpont, possessing $250,000, Mr. Beach wrote the one needful line, and no more: "Married a daughter of John Jay." Beach handled John I. Morgan discreetly, describing him as "rich and of no calling as far as we know, but has been a political man." And in one conjunction of father and son, John W. and William B. Moffat, emerges, simply and beautifully, the picture of an aristocrat in the making. The elder Moffat's paragraph states, in part: "The founder of the celebrated 'Life Pills and Phœnix Bitters,' by the manufacture and sale of which he has amassed his present fortune. He has now retired from active business and is succeeded by his son William B. Moffat." The latter gentleman is thus described: "An only son and the successor in business of his father as stated above. Possessed of that greatest mine of wealth —a thorough and complete education—his recent travels in Europe have so polished the jewel that its owner must shine in future years as a distinguished man."

Jesse Chickering in 1847 prepared tables of "The Progress of Wealth in Massachusetts," from the tax valuations—surely a conservative index. The data are scant but significant. In 1820 the assessed valuation was $153,545,171; in 1830 the sum had risen to $208,856,423. And in 1840, increasing at a rate which it may be assumed did not diminish until the middle Fifties, the assessed valuation was $299,880,338. The greater part of the increase was in the urban counties, notably the district about Boston; some of the agricultural counties show an actual loss in the 1840 computation. And when the striking increase of wealth in Boston is reckoned against the increase of population, the average citizen of that metropolis appears much poorer than he was in 1790. Of course, the average citizen is a myth; the smaller individual share of capital in 1840 is accounted for by the swarm of immigration and the receding of the handicraft trades.

The middle class was heartily attached to the rights of property, but not so heartily devoted to the rights of aggrandizement. The concentrated "money-power" which President Jackson dreaded so fiercely was balked in its legislative program, by inadequate support in the North as well as by the checkmate of sectional interests, and did not become a fact until after the

THE BOARD OF BROKERS IN SESSION IN THE NEW YORK STOCK EXCHANGE

Illustrated News, 1853.

Civil War. The investment market shows a corresponding decentralization. Wall Street was Wall Street, but it was not an octopus.

The New York Stock Exchange had rooms in the Merchants' Exchange until the Great Fire forced it to seek less Corinthian lodgings. The years 1835 and 1836 were lively ones for the brokers, but there was no such business on the Exchange again until the middle Fifties. The Stock Exchange moved into its own building a few years after the Fire; Philip Hone called the handsome structure a "mausoleum," probably in memory of the burial of his own investments. The aggregate value of the listed stocks, estimated a writer in the *Democratic Review* for September, 1850, was under a fiftieth of the value of the British stocks negotiable in London. The admission fee to Exchange membership was then four hundred dollars; members were admitted by ballot, in which three blackballs meant exclusion. The usual session was but an hour and a half, from ten-thirty until noon. The president (whose salary was two thousand dollars annually) called off the list of stocks, pausing after each name for the babel of offers to buy and sell; din and apparent confusion were already a tradition of the Exchange. In 1835 Jacob Little staged a bear raid on the market; in this unfamiliar situation some of the brokers were badly singed, and the upshot was a by-law of the Exchange prohibiting the borrowing of stock for "short"-covering.

But the jobbing of stocks to the public—shares to be held as permanent investments, not to be juggled in and out of the market—was the established mode of financing. Charles Francis Adams wrote in 1840, "An accurate survey of our joint-stock banks would, if I am not much mistaken, establish the fact, that the shares are in general held in very small sums, and by persons of moderate means"; as much could be said of other types of business, although shares were certainly not distributed so equally as it was pleasant to suppose.

The incorporated company steadily gained ascendency, superseding proprietorships and partnerships as the typical form of organization. In New York the constitution of 1841 recognized the corporation as one of the interests that the organic law should regulate and sought to curb "odious monopolies" by requiring a two-thirds vote in each branch of the legislature for the chartering of any new corporation. Prevailing sentiment regarded such drastic scrutiny as unreasonable restraint upon the spirit of enterprise, and an affirmative vote on a special incorporating act became the common thing, a simple pork-barrel courtesy to the legislators financially or affectionally concerned in the granting of the charter. A banking charter, because of the great rewards to be had in high finance in the middle Thirties, was especially valuable, and especially expensive to obtain. It was against "the granting of charters to Banking Companies, with the privilege of issuing notes as a circulating medium, or as money," that the Anti-Monopoly Party tilted in 1835–36; and this agitation for "Equal Rights" was victorious in 1838, when a statute was enacted whereby banks could be instituted by voluntary associations, under certain general regulations. Two years earlier the State of Connecticut enacted the first important general incorporation law.

Louisiana provided for general incorporation in its constitution of 1845; and in the New York constitution of 1846, when the Anti-Monopoly tenets had been absorbed by the Democratic party, "the corrupting influence of private solicitation for the consummation of personal advantages" was apparently put at naught by provision for a general law. But a proviso that "where, in the judgment of the legislature, the objects of the corporation cannot be obtained under the general laws," specific businesses might be reserved for incorporation by special laws, preserved a number of profitable enterprises from unrestricted competition. The democracy removed the insurance business from this protected class in 1849, and railroads in 1850; but savings-banks and other excepted businesses managed to resist the forceful and undiscriminating idea that every citizen should enjoy "legal facilities in enterprise" equally. Two other states, California (1849) and Michigan (1850), made general incorporation the rule.

The advantages and disadvantages of the corporate form were still being debated in 1850. Popular concepts of equality and opportunity were difficult to reshape, but the clinching arguments turned these very concepts against the doubting individualist: corporations "aggregate the resources of many persons, and thereby yield the advantages of great capitals without the supposed disadvantages of private fortunes"; and, by means of the capital-gathering processes of a corporation, "the greatest enterprises are within the capacity of any man who can inspire his fellow-men with confidence in his project." The manager of one of the Lowell, Massachusetts, textile companies, in pointing out to Sir Charles Lyell how equality and industry were entwined in the United States, remarked that stock in the Lowell corporations (the smallest share was five hundred dollars!) was often held by operatives: "By this system the work-people are prevented from looking on the master manufacturers as belonging to a distinct class."

The corporate system developed even to that precious stage where the company directors became adept in the tricks of diverting profits from the shareholders to the directors. That very factor which proved the republicanism of industrial corporations, the wide distribution of stock among the public, persuaded the treasurers and directors of the Lowell mills that the shortest road to wealth was to unload, at a good price, all but a minimum of their holdings of the company's stock and then to bleed the company as long as there was a surplus left. Stockholders in these mills, during the late Fifties and the Sixties, received shrinking dividends while the textile business paradoxically increased. A certain insurance company of Boston made loans to industrial corporations for quite unnecessary purposes—loans which could not be met at maturity. The insurance company took possession of the factories or used its power to depress the stock for its own benefit. The directorates of the distressed corporations curiously interlocked with the group financially interested in the insurance company.

As the threads of the economic rete multiplied, interstitial businesses arose to serve new wants. Life insurance was one of these new enterprises. The Insurance Company of North America, founded in 1796, the first effort in this country to transact a general business in life insurance, ran afoul an ethical prejudice—a wager on one's life was a gamble with Divinity. The Massachusetts Hospital Life Insurance Company, chartered in 1818, flourished as a house of commercial insurance; its eponymic business received scant attention. No other life-insurance company was founded until 1832, when three entered the field, in Baltimore, Philadelphia, and New York. Then in 1836 seven new companies appeared, most of them in New York. "Nothing is now wanting," wrote E. W. Stoughton in 1840, "but a correct appreciation of its nature, to induce an indefinite multiplication of its policies." He added the warning that a person should not be permitted to take insurance on the life of one for whom he "entertains no affectionate regard calculated to prevent him from endeavoring to hasten that contingency upon which depends his pecuniary reward." But in an urban society legitimate reasons for life insurance became evident; and with the founding of the Mutual Life Assurance Company in New York in 1842, the business entered a period of rapid expansion.

When his dry-goods business failed in 1837, Arthur Tappan was left with one asset—an extensive knowledge of out-of-town buyers, accumulated through the years when he sat at the proprietor's desk, met every visitor, and inquired narrowly about his credit. He enlisted his brother Lewis Tappan, and later George Douglas, in furnishing the first private information service to merchants. Subscribers received manuals listing the principal capitalists and tradesmen in the United States and the Canadas, which were supplemented by prompt advice of deaths, changes of partnership, defalcations, and other matters of interest to creditors. The Tappans retired in their old age with a ripe fortune; the firm was for a while Benjamin Douglas and Company, and then became Dun, Boyd and Company. The mercantile agency did much to stabilize a flimsy credit system. Two hundred clerks or more (as the force numbered in the Fifties) were a capable body of inquisitors. And concerning the value of currency issued by outlying banks, Eastern financiers and merchants pooled their information to set uniform rates of discounting.

Newspapers underwent a notable revolution in the quarter-century following the appearance of the New York *Sun,* the first successful penny paper, in 1833. Changes in technical production, methods of news-gathering, and financial set-up marked the evolution from political essay and informational bulletin to complex business enterprise. But of all the adaptions that expanded the rôle of the newspaper in a merchant-dominated society, most significant was the efflorescence of advertising.

In 1835 the advertising rate of the six morning papers and three evening papers in New York City was uniform—forty dollars a year, including the newspaper delivered daily to the advertiser by carrier. There was no set limit upon space; merchants were upon honor not to overdo their displays, in a tradition like that which today limits an attorney's advertisement to a "card." The *Herald,* founded in 1835, overrode custom; the *Sun* and the two papers established within the next few years, the *Tribune* and the *Times,* also sold the use of their columns at space rates. The new system produced competitive superlatives in copy, bizarre uses of type-fonts, and other forms of "stunt" advertising. The most conservative of the established jobbers and commission merchants, not to be stampeded into modernity, for a time refused to advertise in these papers. But that prejudice disappeared by quick attrition, and editorial criticism of business enterprises also became hard to find. Even the bridle-shy Greeley, proprietor of the *Tribune,* offered dissatisfied workingmen advice no more radical than "Don't strike; don't drink; save your money and start in business for yourself."

The pill-venders were first to appreciate the possibilities of new-style advertising. In 1838 a viewer-with-alarm counted in a single issue of the *New York Herald* 130 inches of advertisements, of which 54 inches were puffs of doctors and their proprietary remedies; in a *Boston Transcript* of the same date 134 of its 224 inches of advertising were devoted to the cure-alls. Within the next decade various businesses had cut into that ratio, as newspapers increased the size of the page and advertisers preëmpted the extra space.

The penny newspapers inaugurated a contagious practice of dramatizing the news, discovering a romantic interest in crime-stories and publicized immoralities. Horace Greeley, launching the *Tribune* in 1841, promised that "the unmoral and degrading Police Reports, Advertisements, and other matters which have been allowed to disgrace the columns of our leading Penny Papers will be carefully excluded from this one, and no exertion spared to render it worthy of the hearty approval of the virtuous and refined, and a welcome visitant to the family fireside." But the metropolitan sheet that captured the hearty approval of the virtuous was the *New York Times,* founded by Henry Jarvis Raymond in 1851. Its capitalization was one hundred thousand dollars—a hundred times the fund on which the *Tribune* had been begun. The *Times'* European news, of unprecedented fullness and merit, was indicative of a higher operating cost; capital investment and overhead were such that the product had to be generally acceptable. And the *Times,* like most good commercial articles of that period, was a blended package of the useful, the virtuous, and the expedient.

To their editorials and the variety of topical and commercial reports, newspapers were adding the miscellany of a general magazine. Only metropolitan newspapers could afford a staff of specialized talents, and the burden of multiple labors on the average paper substituted facile versatility for the phlegmatic dignity which old-school editors had aped. J. L. M'Crackan lamented the change in the profession: what an unenviable life, he declared, "to have no one of your talents exercised enough to improve it, but all tantalized and teased; to have your faculties beaten up into a chowder of universal gossip; to review books unread, puff new inventions unseen, battle for party politics undigested, to give reports on Wall Street, . . . a chapter on abolition, or usury, or whatever the topic may be, and then to ply the scissors."

Aut scissors aut nullus, indeed, for most newspapers outside the larger cities. A complaint that "the newspaper now is a lame thing, and quite uniform from New York to Maine, Arkansas and Mississippi," may be found in the *American Monthly Review* for January, 1838—six years before that great agent of uniformity, the telegraph wire, was first strung up! New York newspapers received European news earliest, and people especially interested in foreign intelligence subscribed for a New York newspaper no matter where in the hinterland they lived. Local journalism, as yet little interested in home-town news, buttressed its editorials and political stories with essays clipped from the magazines, miscellaneous news-items clipped from the New York papers, and miscellaneous tidbits from anywhere. The notable editors in the smaller cities were those who could express a political message most effectively; these men, the Kendalls, Daniels, and Hammonds, got their rewards in political influence.

The telegraph, conveying news from the seaboard to the Mississippi by 1850; the spurt in railroad-building following the Mexican War; the steam press and successive inventions to speed up publishing—these mechanical factors accelerated the broadening of the news field, multiplied the capital invest-ment of a publisher, and settled finally that the newspaper should become a commercial institution, identified in every essential respect with the business community about it.

And advertising agencies were duly introduced. Mr. V. B. Palmer's American Newspaper Advertising Agency was the first such concern of truly modern dimensions; he had offices in New York, Boston, and Philadelphia. His object, reads his card in the 1850 issues of *Hunt's Merchant's Magazine,* was "to afford every facility for the transaction of business with the most widely circulated journals of all the cities and principal towns in the United States, British Provinces, &c." Horace Greeley's article on "The Philosophy of Advertising," which won the prize essay-contest in Palmer's *Business Men's Almanac* for 1851, declared that henceforth large profits were to be made only in very exceptional instances. "The general diffusion of intelligence and the improvement of the facilities for direct exchanges between producer and consumer render extensive and regular trade on the basis of small sales and large profits impossible." That was in a measure true; and in the shift to a basis of large sales and possibly small profits the art of advertising was an indispensable factor. A certain article ($3 per bottle, or $24 the dozen), when presented to readers of newspapers as

> Lucina Cordial!—barren wives
> It turns to mothers fair;
> And the fond name of father gives
> To husbands in despair,

fetched the business.

While ingenious Americans were multiplying such dubious boons as the Lucina Cordial, their mechanically-minded fellows were with more laudable zest playing an important part in broadening the scope of commercial enterprise. The rôle of newly invented processes and tools in the growth of fundamental industries is by no means the whole story; patent bootjacks and "Artificial Teeth without Clasps, Springs, etc., on the principle of atmospheric pressure," testify as surely as Mr. Morse's telegraph to the quickened inventiveness which went into the making of the new world.

Congress authorized a timely reconstruction of the patent system in July, 1836. The Patent Office was elevated to the dignity of a separate bureaucracy and ordered to publish annual reports. For the first time the examiners were required to entertain considerations of the "novelty, utility, and priority" of inventions; their work was no longer to mean a mere registry which left wide avenues for litigation. "Models and specimens" were to be placed on public exhibition. The tenure of a patent was extended from fourteen to twenty-one years. And then, by way of giving the new generation a clean start, in December the Patent Office was destroyed by fire, and with it the old records.

To improvements in heating and lighting, "the art of calorifics," Yankee ingenuity gave much attention. Within the short span from 1834 to 1837 over one hundred patents were granted for new stoves or stove appliances. The American Caloric Company offered to the public in 1836 a "Compound Heater, an apparatus newly invented," with which "almost any degree of heat may be produced, merely by burning the steam of Alcohol, Rum, Whisky, or other Ardent Spirits. The intensity of the heat may be graduated in such a way as to raise the Mercury in a thermometer to any required degree, and to retain the same temperature or change it at pleasure. It has proved very useful in Counting Parlors, Bed Rooms, etc." Even this device was not to be compared with that instrument which was then being exhibited at Peale's Museum (where it shared honors with a Grand Cosmorama; the living Anaconda Serpent from Bengal, the largest ever brought into the United States; and Mr. Hart, the celebrated English Fire King, or Salamander, who ate oakum, alcohol, sulphur, and firebrands while in full flame)—Mr. Wenn's newly patented Solar Stove, which cooked food and boiled water "without either fire, flame, steam, gas, oil, or friction," commencing every evening at half-past seven.

As many improvements were designed for lamps burning lard-oil, camphene, or proprietary mixtures. Lewis Rice opened the American House at Boston in 1835, the first hotel to have gas-light in the guest-rooms and the upstairs halls. The Astor House ("designed entirely for strangers during the traveling season . . . city boarders will be received for the rest of the year only"), which opened in New York on May 31, 1836, provided an innovation by having steam-heat—though

A SLEEPING-CAR OF THE FIFTIES

Frank Leslie's Illustrated Newspaper, 1859.

only in the laundry-rooms of the basement. The Eastern Exchange Hotel of Boston, opened in 1846, was the first public building in America to be heated by steam. The evolution was all but completed when, in 1855, a genius living in Clifton, Connecticut, received the first patent on a steam radiator.

The first "modern" hotel in the United States was the Tremont House in Boston, which had swung open its palatial doors on October 16, 1829. The Tremont House had eight water-closets, probably the first in any public building in the country. The swank hotels of the next three decades, whose architects almost uniformly relied on the Tremont for their inspiration, extended and improved this amenity; and in 1852 the Tremont itself was forced to remodel, extending its plumbing to all parts of the house. Water-closets, for many years considered an affectation of the wealthy, had become a not uncommon luxury of the middle classes by that date. Hotel proprietors, having learned the commercial advantages of glitter and ostentation, sponsored other new luxuries: the New York Hotel introduced the private bath in 1844; the Irving House, which supplanted the Astor House as New York's leading hostelry in 1844, had the first bridal chambers; and in 1859 the first elevators were installed, in the Fifth Avenue Hotel of the same fortunate city. It was permissible in the name of democracy to call the hotels "monstrous palaces of gorgeous sloth and immoral ease," but the instruments of ostentatious luxury in one generation became middle-class comforts in the next.

The Cumberland Valley Railroad, running between Harrisburg and Chambersburg, Pennsylvania, introduced the first sleeping-car service in 1836. The berths included no bedding except mattresses, and modesty forbade undressing, in the absence of curtains. But the tradition of comfort had been implanted, and in 1858 George M. Pullman built Number Nine, the first "palace" sleeping-car, for the Chicago and Alton. Another notable contribution to physical comfort was forecast in Alexander Twining's invention of an inexpensive process of making artificial ice. His first patent was granted in 1850, in which year he built his first machine. Rebuilding and improving, in 1857 Twining published tested plans for the construction of freezing-plants which could manufacture ice at a cost of less than one dollar and a half a ton. Benjamin Silliman, professor emeritus of chemistry and natural history at Yale, was pleased to endorse the product, but he displayed a strange myopia of imagination in saying no more than, "Your invention is, I conceive, of great importance to the South and to all hot countries, and even to temperate regions where ice is not easily accessible."

Akin to the fecund ambition to promote comfort was the interest of inventors in compressing things—in devising a great number of portable objects to prepare the carrier against all emergencies from sudden appetite to shipwreck. Of folding lifeboats and collapsible bathtubs sang the Muse of Invention. There is record in 1851 of "a new kind of bed—one of the neatest and most convenient inventions of our day, a downy and comfortable couch which can be shut up like an umbrella." Gail Borden in 1850 invented a "meat biscuit" of concentrated extract of beef mixed with flour and thoroughly desiccated. Having opened the way to the manufacture of concentrated foods, he proceeded to invent condensed milk. This product and concentrated coffee (you took cream and sugar whether you liked or not; it was all in the cube) were on the market in the late Fifties.

Among the chemical processes that underwent great improvement in the generation were commercial treatments of gutta-percha and caoutchouc. Charles Goodyear was rewarded for his years of slavery to the intractable gum when, in 1839, he discovered the means of vulcanizing the whole thickness of rubber. As Daniel Webster declared, "It introduces quite a new material into the manufacture of the arts, that material being nothing less than ELASTIC METAL." Many commercial uses of rubber were developed before 1860.

Charles Thurber constructed a "mechanical chirographer" in 1843 which actually worked, and within the next few years Alfred Ely Beach built several practicable typewriters. Samuel

Ward Francis patented his machine in 1857, incorporating the first satisfactory method of inking the types; but the typewriter was to remain in the commercial status of an "ingenious novelty" until after the Civil War. Meanwhile, however, Stephen Pearl Andrews opened schools of "phonography" in Boston (1845) and New York (1847), teaching a shorthand modeled upon the system Isaac Pitman had introduced in England. Andrews was editor of two magazines printed in phonographic type and was co-publisher of two stenographic manuals, each of which had reached its sixteenth edition in 1855.

The polite arts were relatively neglected by the mechanical geniuses, but Jonas Chickering, in 1840, patented those improvements which bridge the difference between the pianoforte and the upright piano. Jeremiah Carhart with other inventors contributed to the introduction of the calliope into the world of music.

In somewhat allied zeal for the progress of the arts George V. Callendine of New York undertook the studies that culminated in the publication of *The Geometrical Regulator, or Circular Transfer; being a Scientific Guide for Draughting, Balancing, and Cutting Pantaloons.* The inventor-author charged ten dollars for the use of a copy of his book, but it was worth the sum for a tailor to align himself with the spirit of the times. "The art of cutting pantaloons has been so much neglected," lamented Mr. Callendine in 1847, "that many of the trade have regarded it as a trifling subject, until within the last few years. I am sorry that truth compels me to add that my extensive intercourse with the trade has convinced me that not more than one tailor out of twenty even knows how to fold a pair of pantaloons correctly after they are made." Some fifteen hundred tailors paid the inventor his fee for instruction in the improvement of their laggard art. The key to the art seems to have been that the thigh measure should not be taken from the thigh, but, with the aid of a mathematical formula, from the hip measure. "You may be curious to know why. Well, if you adopt the thigh measure, you will, in nine cases out of ten, have the fork too long, and the hips too

SALES HEADQUARTERS FOR SINGER SEWING-MACHINES IN NEW YORK

Frank Leslie's Illustrated Newspaper, 1857.

large, which will not only make the Pants too full about the crotch and seat, but will destroy the proportionate appearance the leg should have to the body; which is, to say the least, a superfluous display of bad taste."

Samuel Colt, after some years of trouping about the country as a "Professor of Chemistry," attracting the yokels' small coins with a scientific peep-show, began to take his talents seriously and in 1836 took out his first American patent on a rapid-firing gun. Colt's revolvers sold extensively in Texas, and they had significance in the winning of the Southwest frontier which historians have only lately recognized. At the beginning of the Mexican War, General Zachary Taylor demanded that the War Department adopt Colt's automatics as standard equipment. Then Colt became an important figure in the progress of industry; his immense armory at Hartford was a pioneering exemplification of the standardization of parts. In the improvement of machine-shop methods he shared distinction with Thomas Blanchard, inventor of many invaluable tools, including the first lathes that could copy any pattern precisely.

Moses Gerrish Farmer, too, was a professor of public entertainment for a while. Inventor and manufacturer of the first paper window-shades, he became tired of the business after the first forty thousand were printed and sold, and constructed a miniature electric train offered in 1847 to the juvenile public at a penny a ride. Farmer was co-inventor, with Dr. William P. Channing, of the first electric fire-alarm system, installed by the city of Boston in 1851. Isaac Merritt Singer, the sewing-machine inventor and impresario, had been a theatrical manager before he began tinkering with needles and cogs. His sewing-machine was displayed in ornate show-rooms, starred in Barnumesque advertisements, and outsold its competitors in an overcrowded field.

The Genius of Invention has an irritating custom of flitting about at large, inoculating more than one receptive mind with the same brand-new idea. In the matter of the sewing-machine the Genius abused her prerogative. There were so many authors of this invention that in 1856 the manufacturers created a precedent by pooling their patents. Beginning from scratch in 1849, the production of sewing-machines rose amazingly; in 1860 the industry was distributed over twelve states and had an annual output of over 111,000 machines. As yet, the instrument was a luxury in the home; but it had revolutionized the manufacture of clothing, caps, boots, shoes, and harness—in each instance displacing a handicraft and substituting factory production.

When the New York *Sun* announced, on April 13, 1844, "ASTOUNDING NEWS! By Express via Norfolk! The Atlantic Crossed in Three Days! Signal Triumph of Mr. Monck Mason's FLYING MACHINE! ! !" it was a scoop for the paper, and also a hoax. The multitude read, and believed, until the Southern mails arrived in New York. The transatlantic flight of the "Steering Balloon 'Victoria' " was more credible in 1844 than was the few minutes' flight at Kitty Hawk in 1903. As Edgar Allan Poe, author of the hoax, stated, "In fact, if the 'Victoria' did not absolutely accomplish the voyage recorded, it will be difficult to assign a reason why she *should not* have accomplished it." Itinerant professors of aërial navigation were making balloon ascensions at fairs; in the Fifties there were balloon-races, which newspapers and public followed avidly.

Mr. Abner Lane of Killingworth, Connecticut, originated the gyroscope and induced a school-apparatus company to manufacture it. "The Gyroscope, or Mechanical Paradox," said the first advertisements (1856), "is attracting much attention from the scientific world. Whoever shall account for them satisfactorily to himself, or shall discover new phenomena, will confer a great favor" by notifying the proprietors. And promptly numerous essays appeared in the learned journals, accounting for the phenomena by means of mathematical equations almost as remarkable as the instrument—the gyroscope which aviation was to appropriate three generations later. Of one potential Wright the *American Magazine* of August, 1841, reported: "The model of a flying-machine has been deposited in the Patent Office by Jacob F. Hestor of Philadelphia County, Pa. The aeronaut is to be put into a kind of garment or bag, and suspended to a balloon, then wings are to be used, by means of which he is to mount upward."

From the six hundred patents granted in 1836, the registration increased nearly every year, at a rate sharply accelerated after 1850, until by 1860 nearly five thousand patents were being issued annually. Invention does not flourish unless there is demand. Labor was cheap, but labor-saving devices were cheaper.

The Government's first attempt to gage the productive industries of the country was made in the census of 1850. Excluding any establishment that did not produce five hundred dollars in goods annually, the total value of the yearly production was placed at about $1,020,000,000. The computation listed 186 industries: 968 distilleries, 74 daguerrotypists, 64 mineral-water and soda-pop concerns, five suspender factories, three pyrotechnists. . . . In 1860 the annual production of American industries, again leaving out the very small plants, was estimated at $1,900,000,000. The census of 1850 gave the number of wage-earners in these industries as about 960,000. The census of a decade later reported 1,300,000—an increase, but not commensurate with the increase in the value of the manufactured products.

The nation's dynamic growth, geographically and commercially, as an influence upon social thought much overweighed the repressive by-products of the new industrialism. Edward Everett recurringly brought to the young men of the Mercantile Library Associations, and other auditors, this plausible message: The poor man who nourished feelings of unkindness and bitterness toward wealth made war upon the prospects of his children and the order of things in which he lived. In the United States the roads toward wealth—industry and frugality—were open to all, the golden opportunity might come in anyone's life, for "the wheel of fortune is in constant revolution." And so, my less fortunate friends, *honi soit qui mal capitalisme pense.*

CHAPTER THREE

The Honest Mechanic

ROM the beginning in '76 the American people had entered into a compact to play the part of good fellow to one another, not elbowing roughly or extinguishing the neighbors' rushlights with one's own glitter. "Therefore," continued Donald Grant Mitchell, "it is reasonable, and natural, that in view of the splendid trappings of our growing houses, and our metropolitan hotels, that the gasfitters, and cordwains, and ladies' shoemakers, and saloon-servants, should hold out their hands for their share of the excess." But when they held out their hands, their palms got smacked.

In the early Thirties workingmen were fast developing trades-unions which brought all craftsmen, from cigar-makers to saddlers, into one civic organization. One of these bodies, the Trades Union of the City and County of Philadelphia, in 1835 undertook the first successful general strike, gaining a ten-hour day for the municipal employees. This reduction in the working-day was the immediate goal of the other city unions, and it was claimed in the interests of good citizen ship—to provide leisure for mental cultivation, permitting laborers to share with employers the ethical responsibilities of republican citizenship. Education and enlightenment! Æsop had once been a slave, Adam Ferguson a shepherd's boy, Franklin a friendless apprentice, Christian Heyne the son of a poor weaver. . . . Robert Francis Astrop gave "The Honest Mechanic" his ballad of sturdy pride:

> I envy no king, lord, or great emperor;
> No general, nor doctor, nor man of the law.

No coxcomb his pleasure, nor miser his wealth
(I live not by cunning or yet lower stealth).
I envy no mortal that ever was made
While I'm a mechanic who lives by my trade.

The right to work, the principle of free competition, was an inalienable privilege in the Republic. The national union of carpenters resented the canard that the association limited the number of apprentices, and in its public denial (March, 1836) stated that every boy had the right to select his trade or calling for himself. It was in such a spirit of sturdy democracy that the National Trades Union, in its convention of 1836, passed beyond the mere matter of hours and wages to discuss equal rights for women and the abolition of monopolies and to resolve at length in favor of equal, universal, and republican education.

But prices were rising in 1836, and labor's necessary concern was to obtain commensurately higher wages. This demand produced the more convenient unit, the union of the craftsmen of a single trade. The first national trade-union, the cordwainers', founded early in 1836, was followed by several others within a few weeks. And the strikes began—seventy-two of them in that one year, representing forty-three crafts in all. Then came the Panic, and in the following year there were only nine strikes, most of these in sections of the West that the distress was slow in reaching. Of the eighty-one strikes in 1836 and 1837, sixty-three were for higher wages and thirteen in protest against reduction in pay. Not even the right to strike was gained by the flurry; twenty striking tailors in New York City were sentenced on indictments for conspiracy. Unionism for direct economic purposes was practically destroyed; and for the next fifteen years labor leadership rested with social revisionists, Land Reformers, coöperationists, and gentlemen who put complete faith in universal common-school education.

The generation's lone episode of mass sabotage, which occurred early in 1837, led to nothing except prison terms for some four hundred of the rioters. The Great Fire in New York had made thousands of people jobless while the cost of living was climbing. Coal was at ten dollars a ton in the winter of 1836–37; flour, thanks to the enterprise of Eli Hart and Company and S. B. Herrick and Company, was selling at eleven dollars a barrel in early February—a profit in excess of six dollars a barrel to the two commission houses that had cornered the market. On Friday, February 10, handbills were posted: "BREAD, MEAT, RENT, FUEL! *The voice of the people shall be heard and will prevail.* The people will meet in the [City Hall] Park, *rain or shine,* at four o'clock on Monday afternoon . . . to devise a suitable remedy." On Monday, despite the intense cold, six thousand people gathered in the Park, listened until night to a succession of rabid speeches, then mobbed the flour warehouses. On Tuesday, the 14th, flour was selling at twelve dollars a barrel.

The *Knickerbocker* inquired in 1835, "When was so general an anxiety manifested to extend the privileges of the people, to ameliorate their condition, to give them facilities for instruction and fit them for the free, honest, and intelligent exercise of their rights?" But this amiable, self-gratulatory desire was blind to the less attractive aspects of the economic shift. The market had outgrown the limitations of the master mechanic working with one or two journeymen. Canals and railroads permitted the "mammoth establishments" to send their stuffs to remote parts of the country, crowding out the local producers. The merchant-capitalist gained control not only of the market, but, to a large extent, of the productive processes also; he encouraged ruinous competition between the master craftsmen and even resorted to prison labor. The competitive pressure was passed on to the journeyman, whose professional skill lost its value as new industrial techniques permitted unskilled labor to produce satisfactory articles at a lower rate.

In New York State in 1825 household textile manufactures accounted for 16,469,422 yards of goods, a production of almost nine yards for each person in the state; in 1835 the year's production was 8,773,813 yards. Within that decade the family factory had practically disappeared from the urban districts, and the New England mills had taken over the bulk of the textile market in the state. In the rural districts the household system was tenacious. Hand-loom weaving was generally done at home; sometimes the manufacturer had ten or twelve looms in a building attached to his dwelling, and then he employed journeymen. The competition of the power looms was painful and impoverishing to the hand-loom workers; after a steady decline beginning in 1837, by 1845 earnings had been reduced fifty per cent.

The history of the cordwainers was typical. The journey-men of a shoe-shop were guildsmen, almost in the Chestertonian sense. The labor was quiet and social; the mind was free while the skilled hand worked, and the journeymen usually hired a boy to read to the group. The product was carefully finished. Then in 1837 the companies of Lynn, the center of the industry in New England, discontinued payment of wages in cash (pleading the exigencies of the depression) and substituted scrip redeemable only in goods at the company stores. The degradation of the craft began. The merchandise in these favored establishments was marked up to exorbitant prices. The "order system" of awarding work made earnings uncertain; the average in the Forties was about $250 a year.

When in 1844 the Lynn shoemen founded a Cordwainers' Society and began an organized protest, it was of business practices "anti-republican in character, which assimilate very nearly to those that exist between the aristocracy and the laboring classes of Europe" that they complained. Where once they had recognized a community of interest between employer and workers, they now denounced the "money-power." Even so they acknowledged the fact of class distinction reluctantly, claiming no disposition to profit at the expense of the employers: "We hold it our duty to maintain the value of labor that it may be respectable . . . and respected." And they added a wistfully antiquated note, strangely out of key in the new industrialism: if they were given a fair proportion of the profits, they would do their work more conscientiously and better the reputation of Lynn shoes.

They did not get their demands; they talked of going on strike, but did not. Several groups of twenty-five or thirty journeymen formed "Associated Labor" societies and made the first attempts in the United States at coöperative production. But the coöperatives encountered cutthroat competition from the regular factories, and the ventures failed.

In the immigration of the mid-Forties came German and French cordwainers, entering into bitter competition for work. In New York the American artisan, to survive, was forced into the tenement cellar, where workshop and family residence were comprised in one room. At the close of the decade machinery was transforming the occupation into a factory industry. In 1852 the women, whose part in the craft had been the binding of the upper part of the shoe to the lower, were drafted into the factories to tend the newly invented machines, and received wages cut by more than half from the handicraft scale. Ten years later the journeymen cordwainers had to abandon the home benches and go into the factories. There duly appeared that good American, the skilled machinist. He had his own merits, but he was not the skilled craftsman.

Where the new industrialism was most completely expressed, in the textile mills of Massachusetts, there was also a moral blossom which warrants rather extended inspection. In the mills of Rhode Island and the Middle States the general tendency was a continuance of the British policy: the companies hired and fired as they chose, making no discrimination on account of age or sex except in the wage-scale and taking no concern in the living conditions and moral folkways of their employees. Children were kept out of mischief and rescued from idleness by their interminable hours at the work-bench. Adults were protected from the follies of extravagance by being paid a wage hardly adequate for sheer maintenance. But in Lowell and Waltham, and in other mill towns of the Commonwealth, the shoguns elaborated a benevolent despotism which left no hours of the employee's day untouched.

Lowell was the prize exhibit. The town was founded, with aforethought, to be a metropolis of the cotton textile industry. The foundation of the system was the exploitation of female labor; in 1845, when there were eight thousand workers in the mills, seven thousand were women. The average age of these women was twenty-three; their average service in the mills, under three years. These figures were fairly constant throughout the generation.

The Massachusetts textile industry confronted, in its early years, the want of a labor force and a popular distrust of factory discipline. The "bone and sinew" of Massachusetts were literate folk, well acquainted with the results of the factory system in England; they had no wish to see their children macerated in the industrial maw. The frontier took away many of the young men, leaving an excess of feminine population in the older states; the mill-owners discovered a vast potential source of labor in the women and children of New England, if they could attract them. So they painted roses over the factory gates. All the girls at Lowell were required to reside in boarding-houses supervised by their employing companies, to be in bed at the respectable hour of ten, and at all times to observe specific rules of Christian decorum. Agents hustled among the farm people, described the superior attractions, the pecuniary opportunities, and the moral safeguards of Lowell, and packed their buggies with young ladies agog to be self-supporting workers. As was reported in *Hunt's Merchant's Magazine,* the factory operatives were "recruited, in a circulating current, from the healthy and virtuous population of the country." In other words, they came (mostly) from the farm and stayed at Lowell as long as they could stand it.

The hours of labor varied somewhat with the season. The morning bell rang at five in midwinter; the girls dressed and breakfasted hurriedly, beginning their work by lamplight.

Most of the tasks required that the operatives continually stand beside their machines. At noon came a half-hour recess for dinner. The hurried walk to and from the factory to the boarding-house usually accounted for two-thirds of that half hour. The girls returned, to work until seven—ending the working-day, as it had been begun, under lighted lamps.

Because of the requirements of manufacturing processes the rooms were maintained at uniformly high temperatures throughout the year. The windows were not opened at the close of work; whatever fresh air entered the rooms was a vagrant wisp with the occasional opening of a door. The cards, spindles, and looms gave off numberless motes of cotton to befoul the air, and the lamps vied with the young ladies in the burning of oxygen. Perhaps the working conditions were not quite ideal, and the hours may have been exhausting; but popular opinion credited the captains of industry with excellent intentions and natural benevolence, factors which would in time eradicate the discomforts. A commentator ventured, in 1847, "We should much prefer a shorter term, if the period during the intervals of labor could be filled up with profitable employment, although that, of course, would depend upon various local circumstances which are best known to those who are immediately concerned in the manufacturing establishments themselves." On Saturday evenings, whatever the season of the year, the girls were never retained after dusk.

Only the actual experience of labor tended to contradict the Sentimental sanctions with which the Lowell system was enveloped. Even after several months in the mills a girl could discover compensations. The pecuniary drive was powerful; although a girl could save but little from her wages at the textile factory, she received no money at all for her work on the farm. Many circumstances might persuade a young lady that she contribute to the family funds, or at least be self-supporting for a while.

In the *Lowell Offering* is a sketch by a factory girl, "Elmira," which sets forth the rarefied course of argument whereby life in the mills appeared quite tolerable. Elmira herself figures as the conservative; "Ellen Collins," a room-mate, is the malcontent. The tolling of the waking-up bell provoked Ellen's petulance: "I will not stay in Lowell any longer; I am determined to give notice this very day." (She had already worked in the mill for longer than twelve months, else she would not have had the privilege of giving notice.) She told Elmira, "I am going home, where I shall not be obliged to rise so early in the morning, nor be dragged about by the ringing of a bell, nor be confined in a close noisy room from morning until night." That evening Ellen was still gloomy, and Elmira undertook to reason her out of her dissatisfaction.

"We must not forget that there are advantages," said Elmira. "We have the evening to ourselves, with no one to dictate to or control us. I have frequently heard you say, that you would not be confined to household duties, and that you disliked the millinery business altogether, because you could not have your evenings for leisure. You know that in Lowell we have schools, lectures, and meetings of every description, for moral and intellectual improvement."

But, Ellen pointed out, these things required a fee; if one attended them all and then got sick in Lowell, what then? No work, no money, no friends! Elmira answered, very prettily but not exactly to the point: "A person has only to be honest, industrious, and moral, to secure the respect of the virtuous and good, though he may not be worth a dollar; while on the other hand, an immoral person, though he should possess wealth, is not respected."

The *Lowell Offering,* in which Elmira and Ellen had their say, was the outgrowth of two "improvement circles" sponsored by the Universalist churches of the town. Some of the original compositions read at the meetings were published by the Reverend Abel C. Thomas in 1840, and they were received so favorably that the benevolent pastor founded the *Offering* as a monthly magazine in the following year. Its very existence was a tribute to the conditions of Lowell employment. Its contents, written by girls who licked their pencils and were terribly serious about self-improvement, obviously had propagandistic value. It happened, therefore, that when the Reverend Mr. Thomas discovered the *Offering* to be too much of a financial burden, the proprietor of a local newspaper, the *Courier*, purchased the operatives' journal. (The *Courier*, bank-rolled by one of the great corporations of Lowell, was edited by, in the elegant language of the opposition newspaper, "one of those miserable, pettifogging young lawyers who cringe and crawl beneath the nod of wealth and power.")

"A repository of Original Articles, written exclusively by Females actively employed in the Mills," runs the subhead on the first issue of the *Lowell Offering* (October, 1840). In the five years of its existence sixty or seventy girls wrote for the journal: Tabitha, Ella, Jemima, Susanna, Lisetta, Ethelinda, Theresa, Annette, and others who, not christened so happily, signed only their initials. The *"Daily Worker"* of the time, a sheet called the *Voice of Industry,* growled that the operatives' magazine proved nothing except that, out of six or eight thousand girls employed in the Lowell factories, a sufficient number had been found qualified by previous education to edit a monthly magazine. The mill executives subscribed to more copies of the *Offering* than did the working-force; and once, very helpfully, the corporations purchased the back numbers of the *Offering* at their own price of one thousand dollars. But to most people the *Lowell Offering* was wholly acceptable proof of "mind amongst the spindles." Dickens boasted of having read four hundred pages of it, calling it good, solid reading—as one might boast, justifiably, of having read so many pages of *Sir Charles Grandison.*

Whatever literature the young hopefuls produced was written in the two hours between supper and curfew. Within those two hours had to be crowded the shopping, mending, the little personal tasks, recreation, and the intellectual improvement every Lowell girl was officially supposed to acquire. On Sundays church-attendance was compulsory.

When Harriet Martineau visited Lowell, in the mid-Thirties, she found the boarding-houses not unattractive. Pretty frame houses, as she described them, with broad piazzas and green Venetian blinds. Within, the large, airy eating-room, with a few prints on the walls, the piano at one end, and the amalgamated libraries of the girls; rocking-chairs in the parlor, and an iron stove, ornamented in summer with flowers. "The chambers," however, "do not answer to our English ideas of comfort. There is a strange absence of the wish for privacy; and more girls are accommodated in one room than we should see any reason for." Six or eight commonly slept in a room. The price for board and lodging, fixed by the corporations, was $1.37½ a week from 1836 until 1841, and in the following years a half-shilling less. This sum was deducted from wages and paid directly to the housekeeper. It allowed her little surplus, or none without skimping; and skimp she did, in quality of food and in matters of sanitation.

It is somewhat comforting to find occasional hints of improper goings-on involving Lowell girls with the young men of the vicinity. Immoral conduct was cause for dismissal, as was bad language, disrespect, "improper attitude," or slackness. Tenure of one year was required before a worker was entitled to "honorable discharge," and in any event two weeks' notice had to be given of intention to leave. The company assumed no responsibility as to length of employment and changed wages, hours, and conditions of work as it found expedient. The factories were in close agreement on these matters and made wide and effective use of the black-list—an instrument which right-thinking people applauded as an effective means of maintaining the moral character of the operatives.

This was the system, with its adept intertwining of morality and industriousness, that radical malcontents attacked more savagely than they did the laissez-faire methods of other factories; that distinguished British visitors were shown for their admiration; of which several books were written in defense and praise, presenting imposing statistics about church-attendance and savings-bank accounts, and applauding every curlycue in the elaborate façade of moral censorship. This was the system over which Edward Everett sprinkled pearls of literary appreciation: Twenty years ago, he remarked, two or three miserable farms occupied the entire space. Behold, in 1838, the same spot: Lowell's palaces of industry, side by side with her churches and school-houses; the long lines of her shops and warehouses, her streets filled with the comfortable abodes of an enterprising and intelligent population. "To denounce the capital which has been the agent of this wonderful and beneficent creation," he warned his audience of young clerks and aspiring mechanics, was to emulate the malignant sorcerer in the Oriental tale, "who, potent only for mischief, utters the baleful spell which breaks the chain, and heaves the mighty pillars of the palace from their foundation."

The eleven textile mills of Lowell in 1844 paid 7,430 female employees an average weekly wage of two dollars. In 1845 their 7,000 female employees received an average wage of one dollar and seventy-five cents a week. But the weekly production of cloth was increased from 1,435,450 yards in 1844 to 1,500,000 yards in the following year. In the *Merchant's Magazine* for 1847 a writer estimated the wages of the Lowell operatives at from fifty cents to one dollar and a half weekly in excess of the deduction for board. The average was higher in 1836; it was lower in 1860.

It became common knowledge in 1841 that the working-week in the British textile mills was more than four hours shorter than the hours of the Massachusetts textile workers, and apologists had to shine up the whole panoply of moral improvement in Lowell to prove that the American operatives were happier. The operatives themselves were not convinced, and from 1842 onward they memorialized the state legislature for relief. They began with no very clear idea of what they wanted, deploring the influx of foreigners "whose cheap habits of living enable them to work at very low wages," protesting the employment of children in flagrant violation of the state law, and asking that ten hours be made a legal day's work. (President Van Buren, by executive order in 1840, had established that limit for the working-day of laborers and mechanics in the federal employ.) Whether the ten-hour requirement should be imposed on corporations only, or on unincorporated companies and individuals as well; whether it should be inflexible, or capable of modification by "special agreement"—there was no unanimity, and consequently little strength.

But the sheer volume of the petitions in 1845 demanded some recognition from the legislature, and a committee was appointed, with William Schouler as chairman. This gentleman was the proprietor of the Lowell *Courier,* who had obligingly taken over the *Lowell Offering* when that exemplary child was in failing health. The committee went to Lowell, donned pious blinders, and walked about; "grass plots have been laid out," they reported, "trees have been planted and fine varieties of flowers in their season are cultivated within the factory grounds. . . . Your committee returned fully satisfied that the order, decorum, and general appearance of things in and about the mills could not be improved by any suggestion of theirs or by any act of the legislature." Statistics exhibiting the health and morality of the operatives were marshaled from the old written-to-order descriptions of Lowell. The committee acknowledged that the hours seemed long and the ventilation inadequate, and that possibly other abuses existed. But the remedy, they concluded, was not within the province of the legislature. "We look for it in the progressive development in art and science, in a higher appreciation of man's destiny, in a less love for money, and a more ardent love for social happiness and intellectual superiority."

The lady malcontents, organized into the Lowell Female Reform Association, resolved to exercise their utmost influence to detain Mr. Schouler in Lowell when he presented himself for reëlection to the legislature. But of course they could not vote. With the unlimited quantity of European labor pouring into the United States, they did not dare to strike. They did enter into correspondence with the similarly restive girls in the Pittsburgh factories, and they jointly agreed to declare, upon the Fourth of July, 1846, their independence of "the oppressive manufacturing power now being engrafted upon the business institutions of our country." But they didn't.

Whatever amelioration the later years brought to the Lowell operatives was a respite of minutes. In 1847 the corporations extended the lunch period by twenty minutes; six years later the working-day was reduced to eleven hours. Snipping into these reductions, however, was the venerable custom of "fixing" the factory clock.

A ten-hour law was approved in New Hampshire in 1847; one was enacted by Pennsylvania in 1848. Both these statutes contained a considerate proviso, "in the absence of special contract." The common result was that employers distributed among the mill workers and machinists little slips for the workers to sign, agreeing to labor for as many hours as the employers thought proper. The law even had its meritorious aspects from the capitalists' point of view: it provided an easy method of detecting the trouble-makers among the working-forces. Operatives who refused to sign the special contracts binding them to work "as long as the mills run" daily were discharged and black-listed. Freedom of contract and moral censorship—could not one call such a reconciling of contradictions a pleasing evidence of American ingenuity? The *Dover Enquirer* implied as much, and remarked, "The largest portion of those who are employed in our mills—working as they do by the job and piece—are desirous of working as many hours as they can. Those who take a different view of the matter can seek other employers or different occupations. It is a free country."

A free country, but. . . . Agents of the Land Reform Association, who would have advised the workers to vote for the free distribution of the public domain, were refused the use of a hall in Manchester, New Hampshire, at the instance of the mill-owners—because the proposal was "regardless of the regulations of society and the commandments of heaven." When the ten-hour agitation got into Massachusetts politics, in 1851, the corporations exercised their paternal right to threaten, and administer, chastisement. Applicants for work had to submit their political opinions for approval; Whig clubs were pro-

ARRIVAL OF EMIGRANTS AT BOSTON

Ballou's Pictorial Drawing-Room Companion, 1857.

moted in the mills, to present educational and more persuasive arguments in behalf of the proper ticket; and the directors of the Hamilton Company, with shocking disregard for appearances, had a notice posted on the factory gate: "Whoever, employed by this corporation, votes the Ben Butler, Ten-Hour ticket on Monday will be discharged."

Wages generally declined by a third or a half between 1838 and 1843, and the business pick-up of the early Forties was not reflected in the wage-scales. George Henry Evans estimated in 1844 that in New York City 51,600 persons, one in every seven of the city's population, were paupers. Greeley's *Tribune* in 1845 stated the regular pay of laborers as one dollar a day, with an average of four days' work a week—an earning which would hardly represent a dollar a week for each worker and dependent. Out of that, "three hundred thousand persons within sight of Trinity Steeple must pay rents, buy their clothing, and obtain such medical attendance, religious consolation, mental culture, and means of enjoyment as they have." The "three hundred thousand" was a Greeleyesque exaggeration, but there was no doubt that the Industrial Revolution and the unchecked swarm of immigration were together bearing down heavily upon the dignity of labor. It was at this time that George Henry Evans launched his "Vote Yourself a Farm" campaign for the worker's salvation.

Evans was a belated edition of eighteenth-century liberalism. His father had indoctrinated him with Thomas Spence's agrarian philosophy; he discovered Thomas Paine for himself. *The Man,* published by Evans at Ithaca early in the Twenties, was the first labor paper in the United States; he launched, at intervals, five other working-men's papers, knelling an impressive sequence of journalistic mortality. In 1844 he gathered a half dozen likely acolytes in a New York printing-office and expounded his principles of social regeneration. The group, converted, went out into the highways and on street corners and in parks harangued the passing throng. Within a few days working-men's interest justified a "Giant Meeting," and the National Reform Association was organized.

Evans began with the theory that man possessed certain inalienable rights. The basis of life, liberty, pursuit of happiness, and the rest of them was the right to own land. Each person had, equally, natural wants—light, warmth, air, water, food, clothing, shelter. These needs demanded that each person have, equally, a share of earth that he could call home. It wasn't necessary, in the United States, to stage an insurrection to obtain for every man his homestead birthright, because the land already existed, unoccupied and ready. The Government was holding it, calling it the "public domain," and feloniously selling it at a dollar and a quarter an acre. This estate had been "redeemed from the British Crown by the priceless blood that flowed in our Revolution" and "from the aboriginal tribes by moneys paid into the Treasury by the productive classes of the whole United States"; therefore it belonged to the people and not to the National Government. Evans wrote a pamphlet, *Vote Yourself a Farm*, explaining just how Congress was to be bent to the sovereign will.

Land Reform harked back to a medieval localism. For each person Evans proposed a homestead of one hundred and sixty acres of farm land or two acres in the center of a township. The "Rural Republic Township" was to be six miles square, a completely self-sustaining unit with its own village. The system of trade was to be simple: land could be exchanged only for land (and then only to provide "the proper freedom of emigration") and products only for products; artisans were to exchange their artifacts directly with the farmers or through local traders in the village square. No one was to be permitted to acquire more land than the single homestead. Ultimately, with the increase in progeny, it would be necessary to subdivide the homestead unit, but a ten-acre subdivision was to be the minimum. "When the earth can feed no more," announced the far-seeing Evans, "the laws of physiology will have to keep the race at a standstill."

An appeal to Congress seemed most unpromising because there was nothing in the Land Reform scheme to endear it to the slaveholding element. Abolitionists pointed out that their own reform was a prerequisite, and William Lloyd Garrison, through the *Liberator*, inquired, "What hope, nay, what possibility is there, that in a nation where it is reputable to steal men [an allusion to the Fugitive Slave Law], the right of every man to a just portion of the soil will be conceded and enjoyed?" But Evans was an arch-doctrinaire; absolutely nothing took precedence over Land Reform. He addressed an open letter to Gerrit Smith which must have sorely wounded the sensibilities of that devout man: he was informed that Mr. Smith was one of the largest landholders in the state, a very good and benevolent gentleman, who carried his opposition to Negro slavery so far as to hold outdoor meetings on Sundays at which to promulgate his views. "I am constrained to tell you, that you are one of the largest slaveholders in the United States"—because Mr. Smith had prospered through the economic crime of buying and selling land, of acquiring much more than was necessary for his existence and taxing other individuals for their use of their rightful heritage.

Evans was as rigidly dogmatic in his preachments to labor. The immediate remedy for unemployment was the placing of the surplus mechanics on their own land in Rural Republican Townships "with their large Public Square and Public Hall in the center of each." His followers explained to workmen that land-monopoly was at the root of all their difficulties, and for every workers' meeting or factory strike called in the mid-Forties there was a Land Reformer with his message. Every expedient course for the improvement of wages and hours Evans rejected, with the pronouncement that the ballot-box was the only hope of the worker. If they did little but clutter the way to immediate betterment, the Land Reformers did that neatly. For the workers listened respectfully and cheered at the finish.

An Industrial Congress was held at Boston in June, 1846. Adding a rider or two to his stock in argument, Evans captured the organization. The conferees were pledged to "a reasonable limitation of the quantity of land that any individual may acquire possession of hereafter; exemption of the homestead from mortgage or debt hereafter; the freedom of the public lands to actual settlers; the limitation of the hours of daily labor for wages in all public works and in all establishments authorized by law, to ten." And a committee was appointed to discover the best methods of electing a President and Vice-President pledged to this program.

Industrial Congresses were held annually, each of them attended by a fervent group of talented gentlemen and a progressively insignificant number of working-men. The strongest labor-union in the late Forties and early Fifties was the New England Working-men's Association, tinged with coöperationism and numbering among its leaders and mentors George Ripley, Wendell Phillips, Charles A. Dana, Albert Brisbane, and others of Perfectionist hopes.

Antedating Land Reform and still influential in the Fifties was the Fourier-Brisbane scheme of social reconstruction which would have struck the chains from the working-men and from everyone else.

Albert Brisbane, as a youth in Batavia, New York, had meditated on the social destiny of man and discerned the changes wrought by the Industrial Revolution even upon a small town such as his Batavia; but neither there nor in Europe, where from 1827 until 1835 he shifted between several universities and as many social theories, did he acquire any direct industrial experience which might have leavened his idealism. The definitive impression upon his thought was made by Fourier's *Traité de l'association agricole domestique,* which Brisbane discovered in 1831, ten years after its publication. François Marie Charles Fourier was a solitary philosopher with a chess-player's mind. In his cramped room he disposed his pieces, Labor, Capital, and Talent, into a symmetrical pattern, reconstructing society grandly and in its tiniest details. He wrote six volumes describing his gambit; and every morning he waited in his room until noon to receive the moneyed philanthropist who was to propel the first moves, and who never came.

Brisbane suffered five years of ill health after his return to the United States, then began the crusade. In 1840 he published *The Social Destiny of Man,* followed that with a *Concise Exposition* of the social plan, and in 1842, by courtesy of Horace Greeley, discussed the great desideratum weekly or oftener in the *New York Tribune.*

"L'homme est né libre," and his terrestrial destiny, as Fourier and Brisbane agreed, was to be the benevolent guardian of the earth and its fruits. Natural man had been entrusted with the cultivation and improvement of the earth's surface, the development of its resources, the perfecting of the kingdoms of Nature, and the overlordship of the vast scale of creation from inert matter to the gorilla. What had happened, alas, was the growth of social duplicity and discord, fostered by false customs and artificial industries. And, with man neglectful of his trust, the earth was in a sorry condition. Not a tenth of it was under cultivation. The uncurried state of the Arctic soils caused an excess of cold beyond the natural order of things, deranging the system of winds and producing violent irregularities of climate. About the equator the rays of tropical sun, beating down incessantly upon a vast uncultivated waste of sand, produced pestilential winds which bore their baleful influences far beyond the desert borders, parching vegetable life and enervating man and beast. The aromal system ("those invisible, imponderable fluids, a few only of which are known to science under the name of electricity, magnetism, galvanism") was deranged, and the condition of the human race was in keeping. The arts and sciences were unknown to the overwhelming majority, and the exercise of industry coerced either by fear of the whip or by fear of starvation. The passions had become distorted; society was characterized by hypocrisy, vice, and crime. Capacities and talents were smothered, genius mute, morality perverted.

Philosophers of inferior courage might reasonably conclude, as certain ones did later, that the only remedy for this warped state of things was to select twenty or forty of the best people, undress them and give them a sunny island to play in, and eliminate the rest of the population. But the Fourier-Brisbane combine had its panacea all bottled and ready for dispensing. It was labeled "Joint-Stock Association," or, for popular purposes, "Phalanx," but the label hardly indicated the complexity of the recipe. At the base was the conception of the paramount dignity of manual labor. (This exaltation of physical work was an importation from the Continent and has never been quite at home in the United States.) The custom of living in isolated household units was to be scrapped. Labor, talent, and capital were to coöperate—though certainly not on equal shares of the profits—in the management of self-sufficing social organisms. Idlers and non-producers (merchants, middlemen, bankers, lawyers) were to be eradicated. Children were to receive, in common, a practical industrial education. Each laborer was to pursue the task he preferred, reward being meted out in proportion to the disagreeableness of the operation. The system was, in short, a Perfectionist variety of industrial communism.

Of course such a social reconstruction was possible! The plan was based on "positive and mathematical truths," the laws of *exact* social science. The benevolent scheme of the universe admitted no exceptions: the human passions, like chemical affinities, the notes of music, and the planetary order, were governed by fixed laws. Certainly the Divinity, in creating the "passions, attractions, and instincts," precalculated their effects and adapted them to some order of society where they would produce harmony and virtue. The laws that regulated the passions had fortunately been discovered, and Fourier's joint-stock association was designed in accord with them.

The cause flourished; most of the minor intelligentsia were drawn toward the light. In the list of contributors to *The Phalanx, or, Journal of Modern Science,* and its successor, *The Harbinger,* which together ran from the autumn of 1843 to the spring of 1849, were enrolled Christopher P. Cranch, Francis G. Shaw, Osborne Macdaniel, Henry James, Parke Godwin, William H. Channing, Charles A. Dana, Horace Greeley, Timothy Dwight, George William Curtis, and many another eminent dabbler in uplift. Fourier clubs were organized; Fourier books, conventions, "conversations," and even a Fourierist "Church of Humanity" were shining indications of a happier time ahead.

And the agitation produced results. About forty idealistic communities, inspired altogether or in part by the Fourier-Brisbane message, were founded in the United States between 1840 and 1850. All the Sentimental aspirations were dumped into the new cart. John White declared, "We behold in the science of associated industry, a new social edifice, of matchless and indescribable beauty, and true architectural symmetry! Surely it must be no other than that 'house made without hands, eternal in the heavens,' for its foundation is justice, and the superstructure, praise; in every department of which dwell peace and smiling plenty, and whose walls are everywhere inscribed with manifold representations of the highest Divine attribute—love."

Only one element was lacking—the progressive capitalists ready to invest their wealth in a social adventure to make labor attractive. Brisbane in 1840 put the minimum population of a self-sufficing "phalanx" at two thousand people, declaring that number necessary for a stimulating social life and the joint development of all branches of art, industry, and science. In 1842 he scaled the figure down to five hundred and published a detailed scheme for such an association. The Alphadelphia Phalanx, founded in 1844, with a domain of almost three thousand acres in Kalamazoo County, Michigan, had almost five hundred members; but internal bickerings dissolved it within less than three years. The Wisconsin Phalanx, established in 1844 by thirty-two families who purchased about two thousand acres of public lands in Wisconsin, near Green Lake, prospered under the expert management of Warren Chase. Speculative interest in Wisconsin lands pushed the value of its domain sharply upward, and in 1850 the Wisconsin Phalanx yielded to temptation. The lands were sold, and the stockholders received the whole of their investment plus eight per cent. No other phalanx wound up with a profit.

The North American Phalanx had the longest existence of any. It was organized in a convention at Albany, where a constitution (following Brisbane's model closely) was drafted and a covenant signed by twelve men to invest in the capital stock. The ultimate subscription was eight thousand dollars. A tract of six hundred acres in Monmouth County, New Jersey, was purchased, and in the autumn of 1843 a few families took up residence as the pioneer inhabitants of this industrialized Eden. By December of the following year the colony included about eighty people (at its most populous the Phalanx contained about one hundred and twenty-five members), crops had been planted and gathered, a large building had been constructed to supplement the two farm-houses on the property, and workshops and mills were under way. The reading-rooms displayed the *Tribune,* other progressive papers, and agricultural journals; there were a few books in the "library." Not the least of the cultural innovations was a community bathing-house.

Enlightened gentlemen from New York commuted frequently to observe the gradual unfolding of the social virtues and to enjoy an equalitarian holiday of manual work. A visitor on Independence Day, 1845, transcribed the idyl: As soon as the morning dew had risen, a group went to the meadows to spread the hay, "with good-will and quickness illustrating the attractiveness of combined industry"; others, meanwhile, gathered vegetables for the pots in the communal kitchen. Guests, arriving at desultory intervals during the morning, were shown "Brisbane Hill" (the eminence on which a bigger and better phalanstery was to be erected) and the other points of present and future attractiveness. In time a bell summoned the husbandmen, and the population dispersed itself over a semicircle of seats in the cool shade of the walnut grove. There William Henry Channing and Horace Greeley made speeches. After those ninety minutes were gone, the company had dinner, with cold water as the drink. Then the guests had opportunity to play at being workers. Every rake and hay-fork was put in use, and the meadow was "dexterously cleared"—too early in the afternoon, for there was expressed "a demand that the right to labor should be honored by fresh work, which the chief of the group lamented that he could not at the moment gratify." The young people danced cotillions that night while the philosophers had their conversation.

THE PHALANSTERY NURSERY

Yankee Doodle, 1847, taking as its text the following quotation from Godwin's *Popular View of the Doctrines of Fourier*: "A series is charged with the care of the younger children, which are raised in saloons perfectly appropriate to their destination. During the night, the different groups of this series will alternate in the discharge of the duties of that season, so that the work will not fall frequently or heavily upon any class of persons. . . . This series is in close relation with the series of physicians, who watch over the sickness of the younger children, and especially charge themselves with the arrangement of those parts of their clothing and rooms which have an influence upon health."

A visitor in 1851 found the men "unshaven and unshorn" and complained of the lack of a few niceties—of, for instance, chairs or pegs to hang his clothes upon when he retired. He was shown into "a spacious garret with four cots in it"; the residents at eve simply pitched their garments upon the floor. The experience of the North American Phalanx, and of all

Fourierist communities, was that the basic industry of agriculture crowded out the other industries; that the necessary devotions to the soil left infinitesimal time and energy for cultivation of the arts and sciences; and that persons who practised social reconstruction by the primary mediums of plough and grub-hoe neglected the little personal amenities they had practised in their cravat days and ultimately got pretty tired of it all. The women gained little from "joint-stock association" except an increased likelihood of collapsing from overwork; and several did wilt under the grind at the North American Phalanx. The children gained more idle play, less education, and were swinged much less frequently than would have been their meed in more conventional society.

A correspondent of the *Tribune* reported in September, 1853, that "the younger females wear bloomers; are beautiful and apparently refined; but both sexes grow up in ignorance, and seem to have little desire for mental progression." The reading-room, then, had dwindled to two (complimentary) copies of the *New York Tribune*, a *Nauvoo Tribune*—retailing the progress of the Icarian (French) Community in Illinois—and two Monmouth County papers. The gentlemen, "in the absence of any rational mode of applying their small amount of leisure," had fallen into the vacant-minded exercises of chewing and smoking.

The unsettled question of religion harried every community founded for social-economic motives. Fourierism contained, when the intellectuals were done with expounding it, enough of the generation's "love-force" to satisfy the religious wants of its leading reformers, but not enough to satisfy the working-men and their wives. People could be liberal enough, devotees of the religion of manual labor and social progress, six days a week, but on the Sabbath old nostalgias mustered themselves. From the beginning of the North American Phalanx religious services, vaguely non-sectarian and of course optional, were offered on Sundays; but an intensified demand for a qualified minister, to be maintained by the Association funds, provoked an open controversy.

Schismatics founded a new Fourierist community at Perth Amboy in 1853 without removing the difficulties of the old one. The mills and shops about "Brisbane Hill" burned down in the autumn of 1854, and the stockholders were not eager to provide funds for replacement. The members, somewhat to their surprise as a group, found the idea of dissolution not without its charms. The physical assets were disposed of by general sale; thanks to the increase in land values since 1843, the stockholders did not lose much. Its leading advocates insisted that the community had been a success, demonstrating, as conclusively as its small capital permitted, the harmony of labor, capital, and talent in coöperative endeavor for the glory of labor. This was a Barmecide solace.

The few persistent communes were those representing a religious creed and dominated by one racial stock. Robert Owen's New Harmony, the first communal enterprise in the United States not connected with a sect, ended its three years' existence in 1827, and the several Owenite communities it had fathered were also dissolved by the close of that year. Owen spent most of his later life in his native England but twice returned to America, once to attempt a grand negotiation with Mexico for several thousand acres on which to develop a new social system. He was darting about the United States in 1845, buoyantly hoping to interest capitalists or Congress in providing a million dollars for the building of a model community.

Joseph Warren, meanwhile, was scouting all forms of social organization as unscientific. His book *The True Civilization* set forth the doctrines of Individual Sovereignty and Equitable Commerce. Warren operated a "Time Store" in Cincinnati for two years, and later opened such an establishment at New Harmony, Indiana. This storekeeper would not accept cash; his medium of exchange was "labor notes," devised on the principle that the proper reward of labor was a like amount of labor. A visitor in 1842 described Warren "with a large bundle of these notes, representing various kinds and quantities of labor, from mechanics and others in New Harmony and its vicinity. Each individual who gave a note, affixed his or her price per hour of labor. . . . I heard him complain of the difficulties he had to contend with, and especially of the want of common honesty." In 1851 Warren founded the village Modern Times, on Long Island, which maintained itself for several years on the principles of Individual Sovereignty—with some radical compromises, which Warren explained were forced by the depraved state of present society. But in essentials, he declared, the community was demonstrating the social worth of *"Individuality.* Any difference between us confirms our position. Differences, therefore, like the admissible discords in music, are a valuable part of our harmony."

The clerisy interested in social betterment skirted the realistic crux of labor's problem with frictionless ease. To have approached it directly would have been alien to the generation's ways of thought. Instead, they preached "education," or betterment by escape. Some urged a return to romantic primitiveness; others sought to arrange a leap into an intricate millennial society. Institutions were plastic, human nature tended toward perfection; the present discomfort needed only the lever of faith, with the grease of a little capital, to be overturned. But, reversing an ancient tableau, Cyrus paid no attention to Archimedes.

The idea that, even in a society characterized by acquisitiveness, it was quite possible to stimulate wages and to improve conditions of labor without remodeling the economic structure gained no headway at all until the Fifties. Then, partly because of the hectic exploitation of the California gold-deposits, speculation and business had taken on new zest, prices were rising, and money was being spent with a new freedom. At this time appeared trade-unions which limited their activities to trade problems, utilized the strike and the boycott, and worked directly toward inducing employers to enter into agreements concerning wages, hours, and conditions of work. And it was not until then that free labor recognized Southern slavery as an implacable foe. Northern working-men had a tangible stake in the fate of the public lands in the West. The new Republican party promised to free the soil to actual settlers; and labor, in 1860, voted for Lincoln.

CHAPTER FOUR

Literature: The Scene

*O*N the western side of the Atlantic bloomed a nation self-consciously very superior. Occasionally, from the east, came the congealing air of British condescension, and the bloom was nipped. Beginning soon after the War of 1812, a goodly succession of British travelers toured the States, detailed trivial vulgarities out of all due importance, and were wilfully blind to the merits of American institutions. " 'My dear son Jonathan,' says the good lady mother, 'I wish to keep up the relations of blood and friendship with you, though it must be confessed that you have been an undutiful young rascal. Come, receive my blessing, you gouging, spitting, lynching, ignorant, boasting, self-sufficient, roaring, roystering, cheating, impious caitiff. You ought to have been gibbeted long ago.' " And the *Democratic Review* concluded, "Never did one nation woo the friendship of another by such an unaccountable and original mode of courtship." Worse than the travelers were the beef-eaters who, never having got as far west as Land's End, wrote sneers at things American for a steady market in the British reviews. American sensibilities were wounded, and pride answered with a counter bumptiousness. It was not an entirely successful answer.

This uneasiness was reflected politically in a thoroughgoing distrust of British intentions. British foreign policy, ran the common suspicion, was forever conniving at new aggrandizements, and British diplomats were skilled in tricks which honest American representatives could meet only with unceasing vigilance. The esteemed *North American Review,* in its summer number of 1844, sketched the past and present of England:

the population was made up of masters and serfs, otherwise called the aristocracy and the people. The former were the illegitimate descendants of the marauding tribes who had conquered the country, and the latter were the present representatives of the barbarous, ignorant races whom the marauders had subjugated. No other explanation could account for "the insufferable arrogance and haughtiness" of the higher class or the "cringing servility" of the lower. The colonization experiments in Australia were evidence that "England produces criminals enough, not only to fill her own borders, but to people other islands and continents with them."

During the rebellion of 1837 in Canada many American citizens near the international boundary gave aid and comfort to the insurrectionists; President Van Buren was only partially successful in enforcing neutrality. Three other occasions for twisting the Lion's tail followed in the next few years: a dispute over timber lands on the northeastern boundary; the question of jurisdiction in the trial of a Canadian sheriff for murder of an American citizen; the refusal of the British Government to return a number of slaves who had found refuge in Nassau. British creditors made acerbate comments on a national government so negligent of its honor that it did not assume the bond issues which state legislatures had repudiated; and American maritime interests were riled by British selfishness in the matter of certain fisheries and by the British exercise of the "right of search" on the high seas to enforce the suppression of the West Indian slave trade. The Webster-Ashburton Treaty of 1842, establishing the boundary between Maine and Canada, was a compromise, not a complete recognition of American claims, and therefore was very nearly guillotined by Congress and the press. The Clayton-Bulwer Treaty of 1850, pledging the United States and Great Britain to complete equality in the project of a trans-Isthmian canal, was quite an amicable agreement; but it was soon discovered that the negotiations owed their amiability to a misunderstanding, for the American belief that Great Britain was obligated to abandon her protectorate over a part of the Caribbean shore

DANIEL IN THE LION'S DEN

The Lantern, 1852, quoting from the *Democratic Review:* "The fish question
will be settled, as the Bulwer Treaty was, with the British Minister over a bottle
of brandy." This cartoon relates to the negotiations of Secretary of State Webster
in the perennial dispute with Great Britain over the rights of American fisher-
men in British waters, which reached an acute stage at the period of bitterest
disillusion over the interpretation of the Clayton-Bulwer Treaty.

(the "Mosquito Coast") proved to be not the British idea. When Secretary of State William L. Marcy, in 1856, rejected an invitation that the United States join a concert of Powers in establishing rules of maritime warfare, his reason was that the proposed abolition of privateering would deprive the United States of a needed weapon in the event of a war with Great Britain.

With political relationships unstable, social variances overstressed, and religious systems practically unrelated, the United States was none the less bound closely to Great Britain, by commerce and by literature. English literature was part of the American tradition. It exercised a dominant influence upon American writers, and then it competed with them in the American market.

It was good literature. The English language was (save for a group of Yankee dialecticians and a few "backwoods" authors) the American literary language. And current British books could be reprinted in the States to sell for less than the original editions, for the American publisher did not have to reckon with payments to the authors. The tariff practically excluded British imprints, and there was no international copyright. The American Government represented the ideals of an active, prosperous merchant. The protection of the rights of commercial property was one of its chief concerns; but literary and artistic productions were creations of the spirit and, in a class with Congressional orations or musical performances, were the gift of the best minds to the common weal. That there was an American registry was in recognition of the property rights of publishers, not of authors.

In the Eighteen Thirties Theodore Foster and Leonard Scott, of New York, were reprinting British magazines without change in title or contents. A year's subscription to Foster's reprints of all four *Reviews,* the *London, Edinburgh, Foreign,* and *Westminster,* cost but eight dollars; the reprints sold in Canada for two pounds and sixteen shillings, only eight shillings more than half the sum that the British reader paid for the original magazines. *Harper's Monthly,* founded as late as 1850, was entirely "eclectic" in its contents. Its prospectus was unblushing: "The magazine will transfer to its pages as rapidly as they appear all the continuous tales of Dickens, Bulwer, Croly, Lever, Warren, and other distinguished contributors to British periodicals." "As rapidly" indeed, for fear that some other American publisher would get the jump on Harper and Brothers. Steam navigation of the Atlantic, which began in 1838, permitted American-made copies of a British book to reach the stalls within as little as three weeks after the release of the book in England; if the American publisher's agent could obtain a set of the proofs, the pirated book might be actually the first edition. American publishers made some payment to the British authors whose output they particularly desired when the writer agreed to send over his work in manuscript or in first proof.

The British authors who were popular in the United States had significant place, then, in the American scene; by their sales and by their influence upon American writers they became integrants of a national literature of which they knew little and perhaps cared less.

"The author of 'Waverley,' " like the lesser figure whom reviewers had dubbed "the American Scott," was still widely read and esteemed in the United States of 1836, but the gradual decline of his reputation had already set in. Scott lost none of his importance in the South, however, where his *Ivanhoe* in particular coddled the illusion of a second age of chivalry. Cooper's least productive period happened to coincide with the most prolific and brilliant period of Bulwer-Lytton. *Pelham* appeared in 1828; this intimate, worldly romance established Bulwer's reputation almost as quickly in the United States as in England. There followed *The Disowned, Rienzi, The Last Days of Pompeii, Eugene Aram, Alice,* and the rest—all of them reprinted in American magazines as fast as British copies became available, and clapped between boards with the same rapidity.

The "spice of elegant deviltry under the most irreproachable moral" was a fetching combination; the glimpses into the *déshabillé* life of the aristocracy, Bulwer's vivid fancy and elaborate imagery were delightful to American readers. And the educational value of *The Last Days of Pompeii*—for the author had visited the ruins—did not pass unremarked. But, the *Southern Literary Messenger* objected, Bulwer's pictures were gaudy, too highly wrought, and therefore "too much above nature." The same spice of elegant deviltry that spurred his popularity made him no favorite with critics, who had the national virtue to protect. The *American Monthly Magazine* in 1838 called the first lord of Lytton "an essential and pernicious humbug" and queried, "Does he not put forth the most familiar commonplaces with such an air and strut of novelty as if he deemed them absolute revelations?" Sumner Lincoln Fairfield, editor of the *North American Magazine*, had a particular reason for his vitriol. He believed that his epic poem, "The Last Night of Pompeii," had been foully plundered by Bulwer; and he described Bulwer as "a sophist in ethics and a libertine in love," ranking him in those respects with Fielding and Smollett.

Popular opinion, however, linked Bulwer with Charles Dickens as twin brilliants of English fiction. The second volume of *Sketches by Boz* appeared in 1836, and the incomparable *Posthumous Papers of the Pickwick Club* was finished in 1837. The immediate acclaim, the tremendous outpouring of public affection for the author were evidences of a success with few parallels in England or in America. "How lovingly he enters into the slender joys and brief amusements of the poor," "With his sensitive reader smiles and tears chase each other," rolled up the chorus of praise. The *North American Review* put Dickens' appeal into eight words: "His fellow-feeling with the race is his genius."

American critics remarked on the oddity that popularity should be bestowed so evenly upon the Baron and the commoner. But the complacent Baron did not invite affection; it was to Dickens that the American audience gave its heart. And how he macerated it!

Dickens came to the United States in 1842, "the Guest of the Nation." The editors of the *Arcturus* extended a welcome to "Boz, the painter of the poor," characteristic of a hundred editorial greetings: "Go where he will, the quick eye, the right heart, the generous hand of the British writer cannot avoid a humanity he loves to delineate, and is proud, by the persuasive influence of his kindly page, to soothe. As authors, and as men, we would claim for our country a character above or beneath humanity, did it furnish no element suggestive of beauty, love, charity, to a mind like his. One thing he cannot fail to see, that men here have a higher, more pervading idea of fraternity and fellowship; that many, many social evils are trodden down and suppressed, by the great, paramount conviction, that all men are born free and equal. Here is a truth that strikes at much wrong at which he has aimed his trenchant and vigorous pen."

Dickens' previous journeyings had probably not extended farther than the immortal travels of the Pickwickians; and Dickens, in America, made note of the discomforts and exasperations of travel by steamboat and stage-coach. Since he had publicly bespoken international copyright, a few American presses suggested that Dickens' expenses were being defrayed by British publishers; and he made note of the craven chicanery of American newspapers. At banquets and fêtes America dolled up in her prettiest for the distinguished guest; and he made note of the pigs on Broadway. When *American Notes for General Circulation* was published in 1842, a nation hopeful for praise was disappointed and indignant. *Martin Chuzzlewit* doubled the insult. No one but Dickens could have so bruised the feelings of his American audience and then have regained its affections; but the restoration did not follow quickly.

The dreadful revenge of the citizenry of Lewistown, New York, upon Captain Frederick Marryat for a lesser offense is worthy of parenthetical mention. The Captain, at Toronto in the spring of 1838, gave a toast complimentary to the officers and crew who had destroyed the American steamboat *Caroline*; and it was also alleged, albeit falsely, that Marryat had "insulted and contradicted and refused to drink with Henry Clay." The folk of Lewistown assembled in town meeting and resolved to burn all the copies of Captain Marryat's works they could find. "A bonfire was kindled on the shore directly opposite Queenstown," recorded Philip Hone, "and all the 'Peter Simples,' 'Jacob Faithfuls,' 'Japhets,' etc., which could be found, were cast into the flames; the officiating high priest at the altar of absurdity pronouncing aloud the title of each as it was immolated."

Thackeray came to the United States for a lecture tour in the winter of 1852, and again three years later; in the interval his popularity in America became second only to Dickens'. For his first engagement he read his papers on the English Humorists; the series on the Four Georges served him for the later tour. "The publishers tell us," wrote the occupant of *Harper's* "Easy Chair" in January, 1853, "that the subject of Mr. Thackeray's talk has given start to a Swift, and Congreve, and Addison furor"; and the next issue of *Harper's* discusses "the Henry Esmond and Thackeray fever of the winter." *Vanity Fair,* published in 1848, had been widely read in the United States, but it was not a comfortable book. Young men and ladies resolved, in earnest conclaves, that *Vanity Fair* was a libel upon human nature; and George William Curtis wrote, "The reader closes it with grief beyond tears. It leaves a vague apprehension in the mind, as if we should suspect the air to be poisoned. It suggests the terrible thought of the enfeebling of moral power, and the deterioration of character, as a necessary consequence of contact with 'society.' "

Byron, Young, and Mrs. Hemans were the particular stars of English poesy who were brightest in the American sky. The three favorites of the Eighteen Tens, Scott, Thomas Campbell, and Samuel Rogers, were by 1835 in the status of minor classics —esteemed, but hardly a living influence. Henry Kirke White

was not yet forgotten. A Vermont poetess in 1830 acknowledged, for many of her sisters,

> But O! one lyre above the rest
> Awak'd emotions in my breast;
> 'T was thine,—lamented youthful White,
> I listened to it with delight.
> Misfortune standing by his side,
> And as his hand to harp he plied,
> Slow moved a string—his bosom glowed
> And struck to "Disappointment's Ode."

At that date the Byronic collar was yet in mode in the United
States; ambitious disciples were writing new stanzas for *Don
Juan,* and even poets of established reputation were writing in
Byronic stanzas. Within the next few years the Byronic fever
cooled, and by 1845 Tennyson had overtaken his dazzling
predecessor in favor.

The dolorous expanse of Edward Young's *Night Thoughts*
was frequently visited by American admirers. New editions of
Young's poetry, for school, dressing-table, or Christmas gift,
appeared in surprising number as late as the Fifties. The first
two or three of the *Night Thoughts* were the ones that mattered, and neophytes dipped for inspiration into that emotional
sea of bobbing generalities and derelict abstractions. The first
Night probably invoked more imitative poetry in this country
than any other one item of English literature—with the exception of "The Graves of a Household" by Mrs. Felicia Dorothea
Hemans.

There was a woman who had suffered, whose every unshed
tear had become a pearl of poetic sentiment. No other poet
was so cherished by American readers, no other spoken of with
such unanimous respect. The critic of the *American Monthly
Magazine* who, in an essay otherwise genuflexive, complained
that the lady's poems breathed an undue admiration of the
pomp of war narrowly approached heresy.

Mrs. Hemans went to heaven in 1835, but most American
patrons of literature in the next generation could recite the
story of her life—the story of a high-minded, affectionate per-

son whose years were seared with grief, whose tenderness and sorrows had found a sublimated expression in verse. The child of sensitive fancy, living in a vivid dream of moral and natural beauty, she had seen her first volume of poetry published in her fourteenth year. The naïve, romantic maiden—she married a uniform, alas, a captain of militia. The matron of sorrows— five children and belated, reluctant separation from her scamp of a husband. Then the professional poetess, inadequately paid and necessarily writing much that she knew posterity would reject. Late in life Mrs. Hemans declared, "It has ever been one of my regrets, that the constant necessity of providing sums of money to meet the exigencies of the boys' education, has compelled me to waste my mind in what I consider mere desultory effusions."

She was a singer of wide range. Her verses dealt with mountains, sea, and forest; with nature's tinier felicities, the silken rustle of the bending grass, the fragile beauty of wild flowers, the joyous life of the uncaged birds; with childhood, its angelic innocence and mystic flashes of truth, its overflowing fulness of affection; with history (as a critic said, "Many are the beautiful garlands which she suspended in the temple of Clio"); and with noble and affecting delineations of humanity, favoring lofty Stoic virtues in her men and gentle ardors in her women.

"The volume of life, to her, ever opened at the moral." Her metrical variations were not many; the rhymes were exact, the melody was usually a mournful and melting cadence. This sameness of key tended to enforce the sameness of message—the beauty of pathos. A man dying the patriot's death on the battlefield; the boy upon the burning deck, whence all but he had fled; woman enhallowing the modest scenes of home, or brooding over a little grave, or "watching the stars out by the bed of pain"—these were the tableaux of virtue she depicted in her most characteristic poems. She subscribed to the dearest confusion of romanticists, in making "external beauty" emblematic of the human affections; and her many nature-poems, exhibiting "the moulding power of scenery over the susceptible spirit of childhood," were also moral gems. Mrs. Hemans was a middle-class product, aware and proud of her cultivated refinement, humorless, ardently moral, expansively sympathetic. She sang in tender verses of the humble poor; there was not one syllable of social criticism in her: to her, every condition of life was sacred, because . . . because it was the lot of humanity. By every standard of supply and demand she was eminently deserving of her high place in the hearts of Americans.

In 1830, $3,500,000 worth of books were manufactured and sold in the United States; about a third of the amount was represented by school-books, and another third by classical, theological, legal, and medical books. (These are the estimates of Samuel Griswold Goodrich, and they must serve in the absence of any more authoritative.) School-books accounted for $2,000,000 of the aggregate $5,500,000 in 1840. Ten years later the annual value of the book-publishers' product was no less than $12,000,000 (school-books, $5,000,000; classical, $1,000,000; theological, legal, and medical, $1,600,000; "all others," $4,400,000). In 1830, forty per cent of the publishers' output was credited to American writers; in 1840, fifty-five per cent; and in 1850, seventy per cent. But the product of American genius was actually smaller, for textbooks and scientific manuals nominally of domestic authorship were often practically literal "adaptations" from British or Continental books. When the Grub Street puppies of New York and Philadelphia were yapping at Poe, they accused him of plagiarism in the making of *The Conchologist's First Book,* published under his name in 1839. Poe's reply that *"All* school books are made in the same way" was not a great exaggeration. Charles Anthon, LL.D., Jay Professor of the Greek and Latin Languages in Columbia College, by general repute the most learned classicist in the United States, in 1841 published a *Classical Dictionary* in which an English reviewer counted one hundred and forty articles lifted bodily, with their citations, from the popular

Penny Cyclopædia of England. This circumstance in no way affected the preëminence of Anthon's book in the American field.

In 1836 Boston and Philadelphia were the publishing centers, by inheritance rather than by enterprise. Most of their publishers had learned to think of literature solely as a commodity; school-books (of which Philadelphia published the bulk) and medical and legal books were the backbone of their trade. In Boston the publishing business remained on a "six per cent and safety" basis until in 1843 two young men willing to gamble, Charles Sampson and Moses D. Phillips, set up a partnership. As the leaven of public-school education raised a new buying appetite and eagerness for self-progress grew up beside a demand to be amused, it was possible for energetic New York publishers to prosper by representing the "newness" without having to fight with the Boston and Philadelphia houses for the technical-book trade. And with the hustle that distinguished the commercial life of the growing metropolis, the New York publishers took the ranking position. The fact that the most and the fastest of the steam vessels that plied to the States came into the port of New York was a great advantage; and New York's eleven daily newspapers, a much greater number than any other city could boast of, lent distinctive freshness and vigor to the literary competition.

Goodrich made a careful estimate of the geographical distribution of the business in 1856, when he placed the value of books manufactured and sold in the United States at $16,000,-000. New York had become unquestionably the literary capital, with $6,000,000 worth of books. Philadelphia had subsided to a poor second, with $3,400,000. The Boston publishers accounted for $2,500,000; and in the West had arisen a literary capital, Cincinnati, with a book production of $1,300,000 for the year. Not more than one hundred and fifty magazines had been current in 1836; twenty years later at least six hundred were being published. Five or six literary magazines published in Philadelphia which claimed the bulk of the "family trade" accounted for the fact that the aggregate circulation of the

Philadelphia magazines was larger than that of the New York journals although a greater number of magazines were published in the metropolis.

꙳

Writing was emerging from its amateur status, and the moths flocked to the candle. But there was not much for them to feed on. The editors of the *Arcturus* lamented, in December, 1840, "As yet literature has been dependent upon chance or caprice; it has been the gratification of idleness, a relaxation from other duties, but very rarely the true and constant aim of an entire life. A young collegian publishes a poetical address, a gentleman of taste and fashion gets out a dull octavo, a senator writes sonnets; we hear periodically of a new Epic growing portentious in the backwoods; those who can write and do write well have not sufficient impulse of genius to carry them through any great work, and drop off quietly into other pursuits." A truer rendition would have been, they have not likely prospects of getting a fair payment.

Emerson received no money from any of his books until 1850, when Phillips and Sampson issued *English Traits*. Washington Irving enjoyed a unique esteem. The *Hesperian* saluted him in 1838: "If we should ask, in what does Mr. Irving excel, as a writer? the reply would be almost instantaneous, from almost every intelligent reader, In every thing!"—but Irving, in the Forties, got only a thousand dollars a year from his publisher. Emerson had a private income and his lecture fees. Hawthorne was barely sustained by a government appointment; Poe and Melville sought vainly for a like answer to the economic problem; Thoreau succeeded in managing his life so that his lack of money didn't matter. When publishers invited authors to table, the juicier portions fell to writers whom belletristic critics ignore.

Louis Antoine Godey, proprietor of the *Lady's Book,* boasted in 1836 that he had engaged the services of several American writers of the highest literary reputation, to whom were to be paid "the highest rate of remuneration offered by any periodical in this country." That meant that favored contributors received something over two dollars a page. Most of *Godey's* contributors were rewarded simply by the honor of publication, and in submitting material they ran the risk that Mrs. Sarah Josepha Hale, the editor, would publish her reason for rejecting it—thus, in her personal department in the back pages of the magazine: " 'A Father's Lament on Parting with his Daughter' is lamentable."

In 1842 George Rex Graham, editor of a ladies' magazine, suddenly offered dazzling rewards—as much as twelve dollars a page for prose, fifty dollars for a long poem, and even higher rates to the most famous *litterateurs*. It was a competitive weapon; Godey and other rival proprietors followed suit and found that liberality was profitable to magazines of their sort—addressed to the newly literate middle classes and particularly to the ladies, echoing their pretensions and exploiting their leisure. Fortunate writers threw away their commonplace nibs and bought Rapp's Gold Pens ("goose quill size, $2; condor quill size, $5; holders extra, in onyx, silver, pearl, ivory, or gold"). From the rates set by *Graham's* and *Godey's* in 1842 may be dated the beginning of that literary dispensation whereby successful writers have trimmed their jibs to meet, first and foremost, the demands of family-circulation periodicals.

Charles J. Peterson, himself the publisher of a family magazine, paid tribute to *Graham's*: "No sooner were Longfellow, Bryant, and Cooper discovered to be permanent contributors than thousands who had hitherto looked with contempt on American monthlies hastened to subscribe. The benefit thus done to popular literature cannot be calculated." In other respects Graham enlivened the profession. He took space in the *New York Tribune* to jibe at the wretched woodcuts in *Harper's,* and it was probably no coincidence that the cuts were improved. His publicity was in a brisk, most unusual style—thus: "GREAT TIME FOR 1852—GRAHAM AND GODEY. This fast team has started around the track of 1852, at the rate of 2:36, topping time, and no mistake. We intend to keep Godey up to his work until we come in at the winning post in December. He is in good condition, a little overfed, and therefore touched in the wind; but he is doing all a pony in such condition can be expected to do, and strikes out as if he had bottom, and intends to keep step or die. The Harper horse is the only other nag on the track who has a show; the rest are NOWHERE! The fact is, the owners of Harper's have no right to win the stakes; they are rich enough already." But the Harper nag, as a matter of record, won that race.

In the early issues of *Harper's* borrowings were credited to their sources, but shortly even this acknowledgment was omitted. The "Easy Chair" during the first few years was mainly a compilation of Parisian gossip, and the literary notices for the most part clipped comments on foreign books. But the magazine's double-columned pages, in six-point, admitted an attractive quantity of matter; it was wholly "safe" morally and gave no inkling that there were political controversies in the United States. Its circulation in 1850, after the sixth issue had appeared, was given at 50,000, and after three years 130,000 subscribers were claimed. American writers might call it "The Buccaneer's Bag," "The Monthly Corn-Plaster," or some less gentle sobriquet; but editors of rival, more "American" magazines had seriously to reckon with it.

Competition among the general literary magazines, which had promoted fair payment to writers, in time had the opposite effect, and in the early Fifties only opulent and haughty writers who positively scorned pin-money were being well paid for the hire of their reputations. *Putnam's Monthly,* founded in 1853, for the four years of its existence used only American pieces and paid a good rate; but that largess probably hastened the magazine's failure. The *Atlantic Monthly* was identified with the New England literati from its inception. It is worth remembering, however, that the first issue (November, 1857), which contained the first papers of the "Autocrat," Emerson's "Days" and "Brahma," and other memorable pieces, also contained a story, "The Mourning Veil," about a heroine who underwent very tearful woes and sought the traditional escape of *Lady's Book* unfortunates: "Olivia became known in the abodes of sorrow, and a deep power seemed given her to console the oppressed." The publishers of the *Atlantic* were well aware of the quality of that story.

Another literary outlet which sometimes paid handsomely was the special item for the Christmas and birthday trade. As yet unused to spending its money without thought of a lean tomorrow, the middle class had to coddle itself into buying expensive pleasantries. The commonest self-excuse for a depleted pocket-book was the special occasion when the most important thing was sentiment—Christmas, the darling's birthday, holidays and anniversaries. The Christmas trade became a phenomenon beloved of shopkeepers and booksellers. The holiday of gladsome buying owed a great deal to Charles Dickens. *A Christmas Carol* appeared in 1843, followed within two years by *The Chimes* and *The Cricket on the Hearth*; and by 1845 the Christmas cult was firmly a part of the national manners in England and America.

Literary miscellanies and gift-books designed for the open-hearted season were more elaborately made than the general run of publishers' items. They varied in many respects, but they were alike in that, as format and literary content indicated, the purchaser was expected to give them away. Some were huge and beautiful, designed to please heiresses; others were diminutive and pretty, intended, say, for teacher's present to the pupil who came to school every day with his face washed. The bindings of the best gift-books were in tooled leather, with gilded traceries, or inlaid with mother-of-pearl, or in some other manner glorified. Pictorial art entered the American home by way of these gift-books; since in them extravagance was a virtue, they were all "embellished" with illustrations. Steel engravings were features of the annuals before the ladies' magazines took up art; as Goodrich, editor of *The Token,* said, the gift-books "scattered the very gems of art far and wide, exalting the general standard of taste." Some of the presentation volumes were elaborately decorated with hand-colored plates.

Steel engraving or water-color, the plates were at harmony in their rampant sweetness—florid landscapes; female figures, generous-breasted and olive-eyed; tableaux in the pastoral, or delicately amorous, or pathetic veins. Often, and especially if mendacious publishers were using the plates for a second time, the stories and poems were written to fit the pictures. Hawthorne's early tales were printed in *The Token,* to his pecuniary gain. Bryant, Poe, Longfellow, Whittier, Miss Catherine Maria Sedgwick, and Mr. Nathaniel Parker Willis found it profitable to write for the gift-books. Well they might pay: the demand for the embellished volumes did not fade until the middle Fifties. The success of many of these books warranted their serial appearance. *The Rose of Sharon, a Religious Souvenir,* first appeared in 1840; the last of its annual editions invited Christmas money in 1858. *The Amaranth, The Floral Offering, The Garland, The Remember Me, The Pearl of the West, The Magnolia, The Keepsake of Friendship, The Opal: a Pure Gift for the Holy Days,* had their followings who were ready for another volume every season. From 1846 to 1852, the crest of the wave, an average of sixty gift-books appeared each year. Not belying their seductive titles, the gift-books became, as one of their editors was proud to write, "messengers of love, tokens of friendship, signs and symbols of affection, and luxury and refinement, and thus they stole alike into the palace and the cottage, the library, the parlor, and the boudoir."

The annuals, the magazines, the newspapers, the "abridgments and epitomes" which publishers issued in quantity for an education-eager generation, offered some justification for leading the life in the West End, and the young egoists came to the big city. Bayard Taylor, in 1847 part owner of a country newspaper, wrote to Horace Greeley, as, doubtless, did scores of others, asking about chances in New York. Greeley was always ready to aid an honest country lad if he could, but he wrote, "I know nothing at present wherewith to tempt you toward this city. . . . All the aspiring talent and conceit of our own country and of Europe confront and crowd on our pavements, and every newspaper or other periodical establish-

AN EVENING PARTY IN BOSTON

Ballou's Pictorial Drawing-Room Companion, 1855.

ment is crowded with assistants and weighed down with promises." Of course, despite the letter, Taylor went to New York. P. S. He got the job.

The literary professionals and hopefuls in New York soon had their favorite bars and boarding-houses; and by 1845 several coteries were holding weekly *réunions* during the winter season. Anna C. Lynch, authoress of "Bones in the Desert" and other poems, queened it in Waverly Place; over in Brooklyn, Sarah Anna Lewis played hostess to the starlets; Mrs. Seba Smith was at home every other Sunday evening in her Greenwich Street house; Mrs. Fannie Osgood, Marcus Spring, James Lawson, and Orville Dewey had their salons. Let us peek into a Valentine party in 1848, "to which all the male and female authors have contributed for the purpose of saying on paper charming things about each other." A young man on the *Tribune* will be our guide. "Here is a sunny-faced, smiling gentleman, who cannot stand still, but capers and prances about with an exuberance of animal spirits . . . his merry and infectious laughter lights the room . . . LEWIS GAYLORD CLARKE." And there is "the stately MRS. SEBA SMITH, talking in a bright, cold, steady stream, like an antique fountain by moonlight; and yonder, nestled under a light shawl of heraldic red and blue, like a bird escaped from its cage and longing to get back again, is the spiritual and dainty FANNIE OSGOOD, clapping her hands and crowing like a baby." By the fireplace sits "the dark-eyed and poetic-faced GRACE GREENWOOD, talking earnestly and casting bright glances of lambent defiance about her." And near-by rests "the heart and soul of tenderness and poetry, in the plump and temporal person of LYDIA MARIA CHILD." Amid such a party as this, we may well imagine conversation flows and sparkles incessantly, and eleven o'clock—breaking-up time—comes quite unbidden.

The brilliant gatherings of the Boston and Cambridge literati have been described often; and if this narrative were

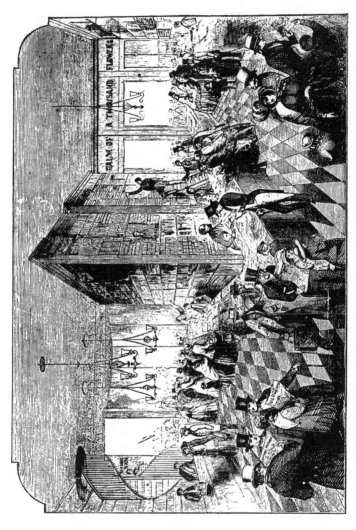

FETRIDGE'S PERIODICAL ARCADE AND READING-ROOM, BOSTON

Gleason's Pictorial Drawing-Room Companion, 1851.

concerned with æsthetic judgments, it might not wander much farther from Boston than the eighteen miles to Concord. One of Alexander Mackay's notes on Boston society relates that the traveler who meets "a gentlemanly-looking person with a decent coat and a clean shirt" in the Washington Street neighborhood "may safely put him down as either a lecturer, a Unitarian minister, or a poet; possibly the man may be all three at once." The Brahmin world had its own provincial boundaries and was proud of them. It partook very sparingly of the popular literature and had no representative literary magazine of its own until 1857. The books it bought were not the new books. The paradoxical fact was that the most literate region of the United States preferred to receive its potions of current thought from the lecture platform.

The American Institute of Instruction, with local associations throughout New England, and the American Lyceum Association, which by 1836 represented almost a thousand local societies throughout the North generally, were the distributive channels of an eager curiosity about literature, the arts, the sciences, moral ideas, and the new social and educational movements. In 1839 the Lowell Institute was opened in Boston, with an ample endowment, and began a service of the highest worth, providing a stimulating intellectual diet at very low cost to the listener but with a respectable fee for the speaker.

The most numerous reading public the world had yet known, the Sentimental generation in the United States, had no free libraries with shelves of popular literature; but it had that other economical device, the circulating library. These libraries trebled in number between 1825 and 1850. There were, besides, literary reading-rooms, stocked with periodicals, which charged an annual fee—ten dollars, usually. The reading-room at Number One Ann Street, New York, advertised in 1839 that it contained the current numbers of the leading British and American journals and new books and pamphlets —and boasted a bargain admission of five dollars a year. The mercantile associations, too, had reading-rooms whose stock included the current journals.

The literary salon was a far cry from the theatrical green-room. The commercial dramatist was usually one of the house staff, with other duties besides his auctorial carpentry. He could revamp French and English successes, and he could whack a play out of a novel.

Dickens was tremendously useful. His name drew the crowds, and his novels were a joy to adapt. Dramatic scenes could be transported almost bodily from his written text to the stage. His characters had that touch of caricature which simplified the actor's task—eccentricities of dress and speech: Tiny Tim his crutch, Mrs. Gamp her umbrella and pattens, Micawber his tasseled cane. . . . Dickens liked to have his characters at table; and did any play ever fail in which the actors ate real food on the stage? His pathos was irresistible; the sympathetic handling of children, the terror and suspense which were truly dramatic on the printed page, were the stuff of successful plays. From *Pickwick* to the posthumous *Edwin Drood* Dickens' novels were the theater's grist. *Oliver Twist, Dombey and Son, The Cricket on the Hearth,* and *David Copperfield* were the most successful on the stage; two of these appeared in as many as eight versions. The *Christmas Carol,* of course, made a delicious afterpiece.

Bulwer-Lytton was that rare creature, an expert novelist and an expert playwright; his *Richelieu* and *The Lady of Lyons* became stock items in the better repertories. But for those novels which the author did not care to adapt, the theater hack obligingly did the job. *Jane Eyre* and *Camille* were most successful adaptations; versions of Scott's and Cooper's novels, adapted in earlier years, still held the boards. *Evangeline* and *Hiawatha* were translated into acts and scenes; and Poe unwittingly became a dramatic property, when "The Gold Bug" appeared under the more sprightly title, *The Pirate's Treasure.*

The novelist received no fee for his borrowed material; even the original dramatist had no legal protection until 1856.

In this world of easy piracy it behooved the dramatist to keep his plays out of print; managers paid royalty only when there was no other means of obtaining the script. There was not much that managers wished to obtain by this radical means; the original play that was not hashed together backstage was likely to be overliterary, a morsel for the library but indigestible in the theater. Longfellow and Willis, who each made one attempt to uplift the American drama, George Henry Boker, Epes Sargent, and Nathaniel Bannister, who made several, wrote not for their own times but for the theater of Sheridan Knowles; in other words, they wrote Elizabethan drama at third hand. But the American stage, with indiscriminate appetite, accommodated some of these blank-verse anomalies very nicely. Sargent's *Velasco,* Charlotte Barnes' *Octavia Bragaldi,* Robert Conrad's *Jack Cade,* and Willis' *Tortesa the Usurer* were the most successful.

The more characteristic fare exhibited the situations immortally dear to the Sentimental mind. The heroine a delicate, beautiful creature, blessed by the hero's devotion so long as she is not suspected of being unchaste. The heroine a pawn in the game of life; shall she obey her Papa and marry the viper, or follow the dictates of her own heart and incur Papa's displeasure? The hero under a cloud of suspicion, the lady aweep, until the Convenient Friend settles everything. The moneyed hero disguised as a mechanic, to win love by virtue alone. The poor girl–rich villain–honest lover combination. The seduced heroine; and the thoughtless gentleman suddenly become remorseful, ready to atone at the altar. Fifth act: the sun shining on the good, the wicked pelted with hailstones. It was all sturdy, familiar; customers came early, mayhap bringing peanuts and hard-boiled eggs to nibble between the acts. American history—in particular, Revolutionary battles and Indian wars —made excellent melodramatic fodder; and the list of historical protagonists whose speeches thundered in this generation included Tecumseh, Aaron Burr, Pontiac, Mary Tudor, Marion the Swamp Fox, Kit Carson, General Israel Putnam, Montezuma, Mohammed, Ethan Allen, and Charlotte Corday.

Historical or domestic, the melodrama owed its customers variety and action. The *comédie larmoyante* in its earliest and most monotonous form was outdated. Such a one—*Second Love,* an importation from London—turned up in 1856 and was trounced. "Very much diluted," reported the *Tribune,* "by copious floods of tears, which are shed in copious profusion by the 'entire strength of the company.' The first act is showery, and there is quite a little deluge in the second; it clears off in the last, and the curtain comes down just as the audience begins to look for better weather. The heroine cries occasionally, and the hero is quite a perambulating hydrant." The ideal combination was represented by *Uncle Tom's Cabin.* In any of its several versions the play was execrable drama; but it was superb theater, through its melodramatic tableaux and comic interludes to the poignant hushes of the final two scenes—one, the death of Uncle Tom, and the ultimate tableau, as in George Aiken's version: "Gorgeous clouds, tinted with sunlight. Eva, robed in white, is discovered on the back of a milk-white dove, with expanded wings, as if just soaring upward. Her hands are extended in benediction over St. Clare and Uncle Tom, who are kneeling and gazing up at her. Impressive music. Slow curtain."

The *Democratic Review* in 1857 summed up the generation's progress in dramaturgy fairly enough: "It is generally conceded that the American Drama, as a national institution, is as yet unborn." Until Dion Boucicault, the playwright-manager who came to New York in the early Fifties, emphasized the value of the *play,* the acting personalities were the most important part of the theater. Stars from Europe—Junius Brutus Booth, Fanny Kemble, Rachel—were avidly welcomed and prospered unless they stayed too long. Usually making their début in New York, these imported headliners contributed toward making the metropolis "the spot to which the whole country looks for precedence and example in matters of refinement and artistic culture." And the star system kept the plays of Shakespeare, with their magnificent acting opportunities, almost constantly on the boards; a few semiclassic tragedies completed their repertory. The American-born actor of unparalleled popularity, Edwin Forrest, added to a stormy Lear and a cyclonic Othello several tempestuous characters created by American authors. Three of his vehicles were written by Robert Montgomery Bird between 1830 and 1834—who then quit playwrighting in disgust at the small returns. To the great actor belonged the spoils, and the plaudits. As a culmination of this popular devotion to the acting personality occurred the Astor Place riots in New York in 1849, when one hundred and thirty-four rioters were killed—the intended victim being William C. Macready, a British tragedian whom Forrest did not like.

If the native drama was to show that "highest purity in every department" which philosophers hoped for everything American, the triumph remained for later generations. In the Sentimental years playwriting was not part of the literary profession (except in the likeness of native plays to the serials in the fourpenny weeklies—*The Yankee Privateer, Uncle Samuel,* Street and Smith's *New York Weekly, Ned Buntline's,* and the rest); and in this separate world of the theater the regular drama was deformed by vaudeville incrustations. Lady stars had a penchant for transvestite parts; Charlotte Cushman, for instance, was very popular as Hamlet. Negro minstrelsy (after 1841), equestrian dramas, and "tableaux vivants" sometimes crowded the drama off the bill, and the evening's performance usually included some freak attractions. Among these interspersed novelties were "somerset men," the Learned Canary Birds, the Automaton Speaking Figure (with the ventriloquist concealed in a cabinet); "M. Casimir, first Drum Major of France, beating TWELVE DRUMS AT THE SAME TIME"; the only live Egyptian giraffe, or camelopard, in captivity; and "the Giant Boy of Vermont, 3½ years old, weighs about 100 pounds, and has a splendid pair of whiskers." The dress that Queen Victoria wore at her marriage played a three weeks' engagement on Broadway.

CHAPTER FIVE

Literature: The Stuff

"*W*HEN a new work is to be purchased," advised a lady writer in *The Lily*, "let the inquiry be, will it promote virtuous and useful knowledge, will it afford innocent pleasure, will it cheer the hour of sorrow, or console the heart in its moments of affliction." The general reader in 1836 had reached the emancipated belief that even fictitious narratives might do these things. Novels were still denounced as naturally pernicious by a cleric here and there; but the amen corner was almost vacant for such sermons. William Patton lamented that the obscene fiction of Bulwer-Lytton and Eugene Sue was being circulated among young men and women; and the Reverend Stephen Phillips assailed "book match-makers, in the form of love-sick tales and poetry, containing Eugene Aram adventures, and scrapes of languishing girls with titled swains running off, calculated to heat the youthful imagination, and giving to marriage the air of a romantic adventure, leading the young off into a world of dreams." But that was precisely where "the young," and matrons for that matter, wanted to be led. Women preferred to read fiction (why shouldn't they— the novel had been twice invented for them); authors and readers preferred the easiest way, and narrative prose attained its permanent commercial supremacy among literary forms.

From Scott's *Waverley* in 1814 to Dickens' *Mystery of Edwin Drood* in 1870, nearly every year produced at least one British novel of international popularity. American novelists, in bitter competition with this British stream, were handicapped by the low prices of the republished novels; but they owed to Scott, Dickens, and Mrs. Susannah Rowson the fact that there was an extensive novel-reading public in the United States. And the American writers had the competitive advantage of a national brand of morality. When Donald Grant Mitchell was graduated from Yale College in 1841, the pith of his valedictorian address on "The Dignity of Learning" was that the real superiority of American literature should be "its grasp and subordination to morality." And from the *Saturday Evening Post* (which advertised itself as "a strictly moral paper, one that a parent may allow freely to go before his innocent sons and daughters") to the wild novels that George Lippard wrote in 'Monk's Hall" runs a common, loudly iterated concern for the national morals.

Godey's in 1849 called Lippard "unquestionably the most popular writer of the day," and, although the best people of Philadelphia pretended not to know him, his novels and plays found large, enthusiastic—and sometimes furious—audiences. He slept in an abandoned house where ghostly bodies clanked on the stairs and the moonlight filtered through memories of *Vathek* and *The Castle of Otranto*. The novel for which Lippard may be best remembered, *Blanche of Brandywine,* is a comparatively sober historical romance. The weird *Monk of Wissahikon* and his several novels about the modern Sodom, Philadelphia, represent the full unbuckling of his talents. In such discourse as this, from *New York* (a joy of 1853), Lippard shines: " 'You have a fine bust, my girl,' he continued, as though he were repeating the 'points' of a horse; 'a magnificent arm, a foot that beats the Medicean Venus all hollow, and limbs'—he paused and sipped his wine, protruding his nether lip which was now scarlet red—'such limbs! I like the expression of your eyes—there's fire in them, and your clear brown complexion, and your moist red lips, and'—he sipped his wine again,—'altogether an elegantly built female.' And he rose and approached me."

Of how the scoundrel was vanquished by Female Virtue and the strong right arm of coincidence, thousands of customers were enraptured in the reading. Lippard's *The Quaker City,* first published in 1844, ran through twenty-seven editions in its first five years. The vices and abuses of a great city, hidden trap-doors and murderous hirelings, voluptuousness and chastity, seduction and revenge—this was the meat of his success. Poe was a better reporter of the terrible things in a death-haunted world—too good. It was one thing to read a story written by the light of a candle set in a skull, and quite another to take pleasure in a story written, so to speak, from within the dark crannies of that skull. The generation acclaimed Poe for "The Gold Bug" and "The Raven" and offered him several opportunities to make a living as an editor. If he forfeited them all and did not accept the Petersons and the Griswolds as his brothers in art, it was not the generation's fault. The surprising thing is that, in a world of people desperately determined to be complacent, editors who catered to that audience welcomed Poe's strange, disquieting tales. Poe could boast a dozen psychoneuroses before even the Œdipus complex had been catalogued; he had the stuff to make the Starving Poet of any generation, and the "neglect" his contemporaries accorded him might have been in another time absolute indifference.[1]

Lippard was no truckling hack; he delighted in the weird for its own sake, and he was imbued with creative zealotry in behalf of Virtue, which it was his pleasure to manifest in graphic, libidinous descriptions of Vice. Lippard's heroes heaped maledictions upon the rich for their immoralities and their cruelties to the poor, and denounced churchmen (preferably Catholic churchmen) for hypocrisy and arrogance. The shaggy-haired author had no patience with literature "too dignified or too good to picture the wrongs of the great mass of humanity"; he was contributing his excitable best toward a national literature. And Lippard took comfort that the evils he flayed were not native, but transplanted, evils: "the whole list of British absurdities from absurdity A No. 1 of supporting a female Pope called a queen, to Z No. 99, of pouring all the

---

[1] Poe and Hawthorne present a situation—the introspective genius who weaves an escape-world out of the fine stuff of his mind—too nearly unique to find place in this survey of general tendencies; and which must be discussed elsewhere.

life and blood of a people into that great funnel of degradation called the 'Factory system.' "

A brother Philadelphian of great popularity, whose audience was not at all identical with Lippard's, was Timothy Shay Arthur. Arthur pushed the game of making the public pay for the same Barmecide dish of morality, served again and again with only the faintest change in the sauce, to its utmost possibilities. Godey puffed him: "No editor that we know of has been more deserving the approbation of his fellow-citizens, and of the esteem and confidence of the entire reading public of America, than Mr. Arthur. He has been leading the minds of thousands, almost imperceptibly, into the paths of virtue." As editor of the *Ladies' Magazine of Literature, Fashion, and the Fine Arts,* and later of *Arthur's Home Gazette,* he devoted many advertising campaigns to establishing T. S. Arthur as "the conservator of morals and well-being." Meanwhile he published an incredible number of books—novels and collections of his short stories. *The Withered Heart, The Tried and the Tempted, Lizzy Glenn; or, Trials of a Seamstress, True Riches, The Martyr Wife,* and the others were liked well enough; but the crowning triumph of the prolific Mr. Arthur was *Ten Nights in a Bar-Room,* an immediate success as a novel and of durable esteem as a play.

The stately meters of Thomas R. Whitney, the Know-Nothing, advised the ladies,

> Clothe all the attributes of *mind* in robes
> Of intellectual light and purity;
> Whence thou may'st draw, as from a well of wealth,
> True elements of loveliness, and thus
> Make toilet of the graces of the soul.
> Thy jewels shall be *words,* more worth, more bright,
> Than diamonds. . . .

and some of the ladies did very well indeed in the novel-writing business. Mrs. "Eden" Southworth, author of *The Dis-*

carded Daughter, Virginia and Magdalene, and other well-spiced novels; Mary Jane Holmes, whose *Lena Rivers* has become a lachrymal classic; Caroline Chesbro', author of *The Children of Light*; Maria Cummings, perhaps still known for *The Lamplighter*—these novelists were popular and prolific. Augusta Jane Evans' *Beulah* was an enviable success in the Fifties—an autobiographical fantasy wherein Beulah, the heroine, is an orphan endowed with such extraordinary intellect and such resolute spirit that she rises from a menial and destitute childhood to the highest rank in literary and social life. Mrs. Maria J. McIntosh, author of *The Lofty and the Lowly; or, Good in All, and None All-Good,* was immensely successful with her *Violet; or, the Cross and the Crown,* in which distinguished criticasters declared they found the united genius of Irving and Cooper. The novel begins with a shipwreck off the New Jersey coast; all on shipboard are lost except a sweet babe, found and adopted by rude beach-combers. The further adventures of Violet enthralled readers, whose susceptibilities made the novel the "best seller" of 1856; and there is still a teardrop or two to be coaxed from the book which reviewers pronounced "a work which alone would confer upon any writer high and enduring fame."

The greatest achievement of any of the lady novelists, by the twin tests of copies sold and tears coaxed, was *The Wide, Wide World,* by Mrs. Susan Warner ("Elizabeth Wetherell"). Her novels were tales of rural life, rich in pathos. "The favorite characters of Miss Wetherell," a *Tribune* reviewer commented, "are distinguished for the union of purity, sweetness, and admirable sense—the quaint archness of their conversation has an irresistible charm . . . and although often placed in incredible situations they display a naturalness and beauty of conduct which never fails to touch the moral sensibilities." A critic has reckoned that the heroine of *The Wide, Wide World* bursts into tears, silent or paroxysmal, at a numerical average of every other page through the two volumes.

Mrs. Harriet Beecher Stowe tried, with *The Minister's Wooing,* to become a lady novelist, but she could not reach that

particular eminence. She was compensated, probably, by knowing that her regional sketches had a gentle, more than effable
merit, and by the immeasurable influence of *Uncle Tom's
Cabin; or, Life Among the Lowly*—which incidentally outsold
any other novel of the generation and made fortunes for several
theatrical managers. And Mrs. Anna Cora Mowatt tried and
failed, with *Evelyn, a Domestic Tale*—the story, she said, "of
one whom I had dearly loved—over whose tomb there are few
to weep, but whose sin we may dare to hope was forgiven, for
she loved much." Mrs. Mowatt had the consolation that her
instructive manuals—*Housekeeping Made Easy, Book of the
Toilette, Cookery for the Sick, Etiquette of Matrimony,* and
several others—were contributing to the refinement and happiness of thousands of homes; and she had the pleasure of having
written that sprightly, very likable play, *Fashion.*

There is no evidence in the fragmentary memoirs of the
lady novelists, and certainly none in the novels themselves, that
the birth of a book involved redaction and pain. It was an
age of effervescent, unlabored expression. Legislative halls,
courts of justice, pulpits, saloons, and street-corners abounded
with eager and fluent speakers. Poets blossomed as lushly as
the wild flowers they celebrated. "We have very few great
poets," explained George Bethune, "but we have many whose
artless fingers draw sweet and glowing strains from the lute
and lyre."

Editors who commented on the abundance of the poet crop
were inclined to credit the varied grandeur of American
scenery and the high aspirations that republican freedom
awakened. Another influence was local pride, which welcomed
and encouraged all home-grown refinements (as the *Western
Monthly Magazine* commented in 1837, "Notwithstanding the
devotion of Ohio to pork, railroads, and banks, and of Kentucky to tobacco, we are doing a pretty fair business out here
in the literary line"). Another was the helpful circumstance

that technical niceties were not of common interest. Poe was
the sole critic who had anything intelligent to say to his contemporaries about mechanical execution—the only critic except
possibly Lowell capable of dissecting a poem and pointing out
the flaws in the mechanism. It was to "that natural standard
of criticism which is implanted in the human heart" that poets
directed their appeal. Except that the professed humility is
laid on too thickly, the preface to Zelotes Adams' *Musings*
(1835) expresses this general aim: "Though the elegance of
diction—the harmony of thought—the perspicacity of imagination indigenous to a natural writer, do not flow through the
subsequent pages, yet if they are destined to awaken one sweet
recollection within the bosom of a friend, or add to the serenity
of one moment's enjoyment, or guide the sedulous aspirings
of some heart . . . ample will the author think the remuneration bestowed upon his first efforts."

James Russell Lowell set up, as the test of good American
poetry, the correspondence between the sense of the verse and
the sentiments that good Americans felt in common: "the proof
of poetry is, in my mind, that it reduce to the essence of a
single line the vague philosophy which is floating in all men's
minds, and so render it portable and ready to the hand." That
philosophy, in the ante-bellum generation, was an intermixing
of humanitarianism and self-indulgence, was naïve, uncritical,
affirmative, conceptualist, sometimes mawkish and sometimes
almost beautiful. Lowell caught one aspect of it in "The Vision
of Sir Launfal," Whittier fastened upon another in the reminiscent idyl of "Snow-Bound," and Percival Chivers presented
another facet in his line,

And Lena was divinely fair but he swapped her for despair.

Bryant stalked daily in the streets of New York, proving
that greatness in poetry still lived. He was called "our Magnus
Apollo" by his friends, and (in his absence) "the Grand Pan-
jandrum." Bryant's vein of creative poetry had been exhausted
before he was thirty. He produced very little verse during his
long career as proprietor and editor of the *Evening Post;* yet

his renown had little to do with his cleanly, dignified journalism, but was a remembrance of "Thanatopsis" and its sister odes. In 1852 *Harper's* remarked upon the felicity that Cooper's funeral discourse should be pronounced by, "should we say the greatest living poet who speaks in the tongue of Milton and Shakespeare, who would dare to place another name in competition for the honor with that of Bryant?"

Longfellow reproduced the motifs of European sentimental verse in careful, genteel fashion, ranging from the Ossian-motif (as in his celebration of the Vikings) to the Noble Savage, melancholia, rural beatitude, and virtue in distress. From his own time he borrowed a later motif and became, for future school-teachers, the Children's Poet. His contemporary audience was respectful and pleased. "Evangeline" crowned his fame; persons who ordinarily were unresponsive to poetry found themselves stirred by that melancholy, gentle epic. The one poem of the period greeted more enthusiastically was Poe's "The Raven"; "the busy editorial scissors," as Poe's biographer relates, "reduplicated it in endless publications, everybody was demanding who the author was, and mouthing over the stanzas." Other favorite prey of our anthology-makers—Holmes, Lowell, Whittier,[2] Emerson—had national or regional audiences; certainly they did not suffer from lack of friendly magazines. These gentlemen might regret that George P. Morris, for one, enjoyed a greater popular reputation; but a general preference for poetry of familiar, everyday sentiment was by no means a characteristic peculiar to that generation. Of the author of "Woodman, Spare That Tree" Nathaniel P. Willis wrote truly, "Morris's heart is at the level of most other people's and his poetry flows out by that door. He stands breast-high in the common stream of sympathy"—a profitable and not unseemly place to stand.

Harbingers of the new feminine world, the lady poets abounded; their verses were in the rural newspapers, the family

[2] But Whittier, because of his prominence as an Abolitionist, was excluded from the family journals. And Emerson interested his generation not as a writer but as lecturer.

magazines, in jealously locked escritoires and in editors' hair. "The proportion of female writers in America," boasted their cicerone, Griswold, "far exceeds that which the present or any other age in England exhibits." Talent was indeed spread widely, if thinly. The first gleaning was Mrs. Sarah Josepha Hale's *The Ladies' Wreath,* in 1837. A collection of *Gems from American Female Poets* followed, in 1844; then, in 1848, the anthologies came faster and thicker—Thomas B. Read's *Female Poets of America* and Caroline May's *The American Female Poets.* Dr. Rufus W. Griswold's bulky anthology was published in the next year.

The lady poets were careful to avoid the reproach of immodesty. It was feminine, not feminist, to be an humble dilettante; and it also saved the poetess from the labor of revising her verses. In the coy disavowal wherewith Miss Charlotte Allen introduced her book of poems:

> Parnassus' top I never gained
>> To win a metric race;
> But am content to be allowed
>> To flutter round its base.
>
> I never yet have dipped my pen,
>> In deep poetic lore;
> But merely as a pastime sought,
>> Its surface to explore.

But a number of ladies made versifying a paying avocation; and there was one professional lady poet on whom a popular balloting undoubtedly would have bestowed the national laureateship. Mrs. Lydia Huntley Sigourney was an institution. She and George Washington were beyond criticism. Even that dreadful little drunkard, Edgar Poe, buttoned his rapier before he durst criticize her works; and having, tentatively and hedgingly, found a fault in her poetry, he apologized therefor in his private correspondence with the lady.

During her girlhood Lydia had been the constant ministrant and abiding solace of a senescent widow in Norwich, Connecticut. The widow's frequent amusements were to have her will read to her by Lydia and to have the girl read aloud from Young's *Night Thoughts*. Imbibing precepts of morality and poesy from the standard founts, Young and Hemans, Mrs. Sigourney added an evangelical fervor of her own, and a womanly daintiness quite too precious to expose to the dark and troubled heavings of the world. Nor did she expose it so; "woman is ever at home in the most peaceful circle, and among the less glaring topics," was the approving thought of the reviewer on the *Christian Spectator* after reading Mrs. Sigourney's poems. And Griswold, taking notice of the lack of vigor and "grandeur" in her poetry, suggested, "It is only because the flower has not been crushed that we have not had a sweeter perfume." In her letters the womanly daintiness seems somewhat extreme; she writes that she has come to the seaside for her "necessary annual inhalation of saline air," and apologizes over a blotted page because at the hotel "the instruments of chirography are not prone to be of the best quality, or fully available for any legible purpose."

Adoring critics dubbed her "the American Hemans," and not unjustly. The author of "Casabianca" died when her American disciple was forty-six years old; and Mrs. Sigourney, amid her tears, wrote a monody which was acclaimed her most exalted and sublime composition.

Mrs. Sigourney was a middle-aged woman when she published her first book (*Letters to Young Ladies,* inspirational prose, which appeared anonymously in 1833); she was twenty-three when the War of 1812 began. She had to subdue her own prejudices before she could invite the brazen publicity of the printed page, and only economic duress drove her to make an appearance outside (as it seemed to her at the time) the natural sphere of woman. But she was immediately successful; and when, in the middle Thirties, lady poetastry became definitely fashionable, Mrs. Sigourney was not only a fixed star in the literary firmament, but was making good money by her coruscatings. Even a very prominent star, however, had to glitter a great deal, until Graham and Godey boosted the value of literature. For three years (1840–42) Godey paid Mrs. Sigourney five hundred dollars annually for the use of her name, as associate editor, on the title-page of the *Lady's Book*. She had no part in the editorship of the magazine; she was simply selling "name value" to the first periodical to pay cash for that commodity.

She wrote much, yet not enough to satisfy the solicitations of editors. To produce such a quantity was physically impossible, but she did her best. In 1836 she took over the editorship of a gift-book, *The Religious Souvenir,* and saw it through three Christmases. To her professional labors her kindliness imposed the burden of replying to a swarm of letter-writers, advising girlish neophytes in the poetic art, and even writing elegaic verses upon request. One of these poems was to console "the owner of a canary-bird, which had been accidentally starved to death," and another was written for the father of a child "drowned in a barrel of swine's food." The latter elegy was rich in consolatory sentiment but left the manner of the child's death to be explained in a prosaic subtitle. For there were conventions of speech, then. In Mrs. Sigourney's autobiography occurs a reference to "a quadruped member of our establishment which has not been mentioned, and is, I suppose, scarcely mentionable to ears polite. Yet I never could understand why it should be an offense to delicacy to mention the name of"—and she trails off into a circumlocution, for not even in her private diary would she write the word "hog."

"Her poetry," wrote a panegyrist in 1836, "is the poetry of home life; the affections clustering around the manifold objects of the domestic circle, and exhibiting in the varied scenes of man's changeful trial, the necessity and beneficial influence of virtuous feelings." Not surprisingly, she was especially fond of the pathos of death—the death of infants, foreign missionaries, sailors, cripples, poets. . . . Mrs. Sigourney was a good woman and honored versifier in her time, and she never offended anyone—except, possibly, visually. (Jane Welsh Carlyle, neither beautiful nor amiable, described Mrs. Sigourney, in 1840, as "this figure of an over-the-water Poetess—beplastered with rouge and pomatum—bare-necked in an age which had left *certainty* far behind—with long ringlets that never grew where they were hung—smelling marvellously of camphor or hart-shorn and oil—all glistening in black satin . . . and staring her eyes out, to give them animation.")

Quite as fugitive as the multitude of verses, and written with the same artful spontaneity, were the little sketches and narrative-essays swarming thickly in the magazines and some-times clustered into the undeserved permanence of book form. The family journals, the ladies' magazines, the *Southern Liter-ary Messenger,* and even the *Knickerbocker* were weighted with them. The stream of casual thought, running from a trifle toward a generalization, meandering into a kindly or satirical digression or two—that was the method. Ephemeral little sketches, they conjured a mood, fondled it, and let it trickle away, leaving a few jelly-like paragraphs about love, the land-scape, sympathy, virtue, or death stranded on the flabby nar-rative. Donald Grant Mitchell's *Reveries* and the *Prue* essays of George William Curtis were both elaborations of this popular device.

Reveries of a Bachelor, "by Ik Marvel," appeared in 1850. The volume contained four "Reveries"—"over a wood fire," "by a city grate," "over the cigar," and one, an all-day dream, of "morning, noon, and evening"—in the Bachelor's analogy, past, present, and future.

The third Reverie, "A Cigar Three Times Lighted," intro-duced Aunt Tabithy, who could not abide cigars; the Bachelor, in return for permission to smoke, offered "to make up such a series of reflections out of my cigar, as would do your heart good to listen to. . . . About love, which is easy enough lighted, but wants constancy to keep it in a glow; or about matrimony, which has a great deal of fire in the beginning, but it is a fire that consumes all that feeds the blaze; or about life, which at the first is fresh and odorous, but ends shortly in a withered cinder, that is fit only for the ground." And Aunt Tabithy listens as the Bachelor evokes wisps of sentiment and puffs ring upon ring of quaint conceits.

The first taste of the fragrant leaf is like one's first love, "fresh, genial, and rapturous"; the Bachelor reviews his young devotion, the jealousy and the sorrows—and the ash cools. "There are those who throw away a cigar, when once gone out; they must needs have plenty more. But nobody that I ever heard of, kept a cedar box of hearts, labelled at Havanna. Alas, there is but one to light!" And so into a recalling of "the love of youth which succeeds the crackling blaze of boyhood." The beloved Nelly becomes another's; you meet her years afterward, "a comely, matronly dame in gingham, with her curls all gathered under a high-topped comb; and she presents to you two little boys in smart crimson jackets, dressed up with braid." And, after the cigar has been relit, with the remark that "brimstone matches were never made in heaven," the Bachelor has blazed his trail into a discussion of match-making and marriage. He imagines himself "married well," in the worldly phrase, and very unhappy about it. "But you have a little boy, thank God"; and you love to catch him in his respites from the nursery "and to spread upon him a little of that depth of feeling, which through so many years has scarce been stirred." This time it is you, the Bachelor, who becomes sick and dies; and after your boy has received his blessing, your wife bends over you, "and you feel a bound at your heart—the same bound that you felt on your bridal morning—the same bound which you used to feel in the springtime of your life." (In another Reverie it will be the little boy who dies; and in another, your wife.) The cigar is consumed; the Reverie is over.

Reveries of a Bachelor was the most cherished piece of belles-lettres that the Fifties produced. Over a million copies have been sold in authorized printings, and there were more than fifty pirated editions. Only the propaganda novel *Uncle Tom's Cabin* may have outsold it. Ladies showered the author with valentines and proposals of wedlock; the love-lorn wrote to him for advice and sympathy. Mitchell was still in his twenties; "young sentiment was then so jubilant in me that it seemed to me I could have reeled it off by scores; nor did spontaneity prove lacking." To evoke the delicate mood again, he took lodgings in an old farm-house; and, finding "a world of encouragement in the play of sun and shadow over the tranquil valley landscape," he there wrote *Dream Life,* a second volume of Bachelor musings. *Dream Life* was still being reprinted well into the present century; an expensive, newly illustrated edition of the *Reveries* was among the de luxe publications of 1931.

It is a cloud-cuckoo-land of the heart that these books describe, a world of sentiment purely for sentiment's sake. Rousseau, hanging his head over the cliff's edge to experience, together, the thrill of falling and the comfort of safety, is the spiritual antecedent of the Bachelor beside his hearth—rollicking with his imaginary children, killing off his mythical wife, sorrowing at his own death-bed, while he has an excellent smoke. "I dashed a tear or two from my eyes;—how they came there I know not. I half ejaculated a prayer of thanks, that such desolation had not yet come nigh to me; and a prayer of hope—that it might never come. In a half hour more, I was sleeping soundly."

Mitchell never emerged from the charm of the Bachelor he had created. He made his money, of course, as author and editor; but he affected to disavow his status as a professional writer and insisted that his really important accomplishments were his æsthetic adventures in landscape-gardening and in being a gentleman farmer. It was Mitchell who was offered a nomination for the governorship of Connecticut in 1876, but it was the Bachelor of the *Reveries* who declined the nomination: "Suppose I should be elected and compelled to take up my abode in brick-and-mortar-environed Hartford, while all the coppices of Edgewood are bright with summer bloom. I would rather be farmer than governor; I would rather sit in my library of an afternoon and watch the growing corn undulating in the western wind, than sit in the chair of state signing bills for public acts; and the bright flag floating above the capitol would not be so pleasing in my eyes as the smoky banner of the far-off steamer athwart the dancing waters silvered in the June sunshine." Over one million copies. . . .

Prue and I, the aimless, tranquil narrative of the thoughts of a bookkeeper who has wealth greater than riches—in a perfect wife and a talent for being interested in people and landscapes—accounted for itself nicely with an estimated sale of five hundred thousand copies between its appearance in 1856 and the turn of the century. This business of putting into print "a phrase or two of passion, of endurance, of love, of sorrow" which Mitchell and Curtis did tenderly, Sara Payson Willis (whose pen-name was Fanny Fern) performed in a nervous dash. Hers was a new style of essay, and it produced a brood of short-lived imitators. *Fern Leaves,* the lady's first book, sold fifty thousand copies within the first six months of publication. It was made up of essays no longer than a page or two—sharp and rapid little sketches without beginning and without end, striking one clear, emphatic note and breaking off before the pitch subsided. Of the Model Wife, beginning without prelude: "She don't know a word of French, Italian, or German, never reads anything but 'Hints to Married Women' and 'The Cookery Book'—don't play on the piano, don't keep but one girl, does half the washing and ironing, makes all the cakes and pies, cuts her husband's vests, her own dresses, mends all the stockings, turns her husband's pants inside out and hindside before when they get shabby—presents Mr. Snooks with an heir once a year—nurses the baby while papa is shaving, for fear its crying will make him cut his face with the razor"—a page more of that, an exclamation point, and bang! it's done.

Sara's brother, Nathaniel Parker Willis, had genuine talent for handling a subject lightly, without pretense of significance. In a generation busily playing find-the-moral, Willis distinguished himself by finding the ornamental. He prattled about his japonica and his pastilles, quoted the intimate gossip and described the personal failings of his European hosts, itemized the felicities of his everyday existence, and expressed the last word in fashions and etiquette, in essays "transparent like a lump of sugar in champagne—soft-tempered like the sea-breeze at night." *Pencillings by the Way, Fun-Jottings, The Rag-Bag, Life Here and There,* and the many other titles indicate by their own fluffiness their light, purposively unimportant materials. The depth of his social thought is suggested by his complaint on the too general prosperity of Westchester—"It wants a dash of wretchedness to relieve the eye"; and the nature of his private fantasies may be gleaned from his semi-fictional writings about all-conquering young literary men who luxuriate in the boudoirs of adoring heiresses. Poe wrote of him, "At a very early age Mr. Willis seems to have arrived at an understanding that, in a republic like ours, the *mere* man of letters must ever be a cipher, and endeavoured, accordingly, to unite the *éclat* of the *littérateur* with that of the man of fashion or of society." Willis was successful, as author and as exquisite.

In literature and life Virtue received its garlands and Vice its scorn. "What shall be said," inquired Willis Gaylord Clark, "of those fiends in human form, who poison the fountains of virtue in the innocent bosom; whose lips breathe the black lie and the broken vow?" In print, a great deal. "Is there a punishment too great to be inflicted upon the villain who approaches the fair fabric of virtue only to leave it in ruin and desolation? Is *hell* too much? NO!" A Miss Clay of Seneca Falls, New York, was seduced, and mortally shot the scoundrel. The grand jury found no bill against her, and the newspapers congratulated the lady on her deed. So vigilant was this public sense of virtue that Emma Willard's husband was suspect when he escorted Sarah Josepha Hale, a widow, to a commencement exercise at Harvard College when his wife was out of town; his offended helpmeet had no difficulty in getting a divorce.

"Be good, be womanly, be gentle," was Whittier's excellent advice, "generous in your sympathies, heedful of the well-being of those around you, and my word for it, you will not lack kind words or admiration." Never mind the homely image in the mirror; quite another picture was registered on the retina of human sympathy. "Every mother's daughter of you can be beautiful. You can envelope yourselves in an atmosphere of moral and intellectual beauty, through which your otherwise plain faces will look forth like those of angels." External beauty, to reach the springs of æsthetic appreciation, must filter through the social conscience. Extreme beauty (like the peacock's) was the least substantial and the farthest removed from love, the center of beauty. And essayists deplored the idle lives of those ladies who spent their souls in admiration of external beauty—vying with one another in dress and in mere brilliancy of eyes and complexion, courting flatteries and delighted with adulation, for social effect simulating a specious counterpart of love, purity, devotion, sincerity, honor, until in time these pretensions displaced the capacity for genuine sentiments. A lady poet put all this into verse, "Lines Addressed to a Volatile Young Lady." The poetess saw a rose-bud opening fair, and dewdrops glittered on its stem;

> I saw admirers round it move,
>   All flattering its loveliness,
> While each declared unchanging love
>   For the fair flower, with fond caress.

Again she saw that floweret when the lovely bloom was all decayed and its admirers had forgotten it:

> And thus that maid, who seeks to shine
>   And in false colors blazen forth,
> Shall see her influence decline,
>   And tribute paid to modest worth.

In Anna Alcott's diary is a charming entry for a day in her thirteenth year: "I take so much pleasure in reading beautiful stories and poetry. I like to hear beautiful words and thoughts. Beautiful is my favorite word. If I like anything I always say it is beautiful. It is a beautiful word. I can't tell the color of it. Louisa and I took a walk. It was pleasant if it had only been a little warmer. When we returned we sat in our chamber. I wrote down all the beautiful names we could think of, and in the evening wrote the colors of them." When Anna became a little older, she was to learn that the Beautiful was not idle

and self-sufficient, like a butterfly, but that it had a mission—
benevolence. God had ordained the usefulness of the beautiful,
declared Henry Ward Beecher; and many literary persons
remarked that a man lacking a love of music or an eye for
natural scenery was, so experience confirmed, dishonest and
secretly vicious.

The Reverend John Abbott in a Fourth of July oration
dwelt upon the relation between beauty and the profitable life.
Who would not, he inquired, give a few dollars more for a
farm-house because it was planted about with trees, in whose
shade the children could play and the cattle slumber in the
noontime heat? The poor man, toiling hard for frugal fare,
would be more than repaid for the extra labor of keeping the
plat before his door clean and green; "and you will love your
home the better for the rose bush which blooms in the yard,
looking up into your eye, as it were with gratitude, through its
green leaves and blushing flowers."

Mr. Abbott's theme was a felicitous choice for a Fourth of
July speech. Nationalism was too pervasive a thing not to affect
one's ideas of virtue and beauty. A sprig of whiteweed raised
in American soil was sweeter than the marjoram of Italian
bowers. Leonard Withington averred, with what seems exaggeration, that the softest warblings of a European nightingale
were poorer melody in his ears than the screaking of the night-
hawk's wings as the bird swooped in the New England sky. As
Mrs. R. J. Avery declared, in a book of verse entitled *Wood
Notes Wild:*

> From France we ne'er can copy airs,
>   Nor ape her courtly etiquette;
> Our sons—like bold and hardy Tars,—
>   Our daughters—*Violets.*
>
> Nor yet from Italy's soft sky,
>   From citron groves, or spicy bowers,
> Do we twine wreathes of roseate die,
>   Or cull sweet flowers.

> Our bouquets simple though they be,
> In our own native woods they bloom,
> Uncultured—in our Tennessee
> They yield perfume.

"I affect the country," declared Lewis Gaylord Clark, by which he meant that he doted on natural scenery. He had company. Everyone of some degree of "soul" was attuned to the natural world. The trim woods and "templed hills" of Samuel Francis Smith's neoclassic out-of-doors no longer existed. Nature, too, had gone romantic.

On a summer afternoon Henry Tuckerman walked through a wood, with a poet for companion. The poet uttered exclamations of delight when he saw a grass-blade glint in the sunshine; not a fir cone slept amid the herbage, not a moss-clump gleaned from a rotting root, not a pale wild flower shot its slender stem through the moldering leaves, but elicited his articulate delight. Mr. Tuckerman was transported with appreciation; at last he had corralled a prime specimen of the effervescent nature-sampler.

The sparrow twittering outside one's window called up memories that reached back half a lifetime, and hope that reached farther than the flight of terns. The rose-tree clambering beside the kitchen door offered, with each bud and blossom, a token of promises covering life and reaching beyond death. The quiet sunshine of a warm afternoon quickened into activity a thousand vagrant thoughts—of the meadow, the blue hills beyond, the mountains of years over which Youth climbs to the slope of Age. Extravagant imagery? Donald Grant Mitchell tossed off sentiments like these by the candyboxful; his reward was in hundreds of letters in appreciation of his talent for expressing the common sympathies, and in the currency of the realm.

> Rocks, and woods, and water,
> I am now with ye!
> What a grateful daughter
> Ought I not to be!
> Alone with Nature—oh, what bliss,
> What a privilege is this!

> Give me now a blessing,
>   Help my tongue to speak
> The feelings that are pressing
>   Till my heart grows weak—
> Faint with the strange influence
> Of this wild magnificence.

Caroline May, the entranced authoress, was a city-dweller. There were good reasons for this prevalent emotion of nostalgia among the chimney-pots, reasons that have to do with the expansion of the ego toward a pleasurable, infinite haziness and with what Mr. Irving Babbitt sternly labels "the boundless sycophancy of human nature." Nature-sampling was, in simple, a protective adaptation. It is the common self-indulgence of the first generation of an urban middle class. It eases the transition, by glorifying the farm as it recedes adown the path of experience.

Traces of "nature" in the city intensified the nostalgia. Homes in the metropolis had their green lawns and their patches of garden in the back yard. One did not have to walk to the Battery to discover a tree. The smell of the sea was not also the smell of oily waste. The breezes bore the scent of growing plants, and (alas) their pollen, unweighted by coal-smut—although travelers were already complaining of the grimy belching of the smoke-stacks in Pittsburgh.

And the nature-addict sits by the casement, "with the gale melting all over my forehead, like an invisible touch of benediction from some spirit-land," and marks the rosy clouds moving along the West, as the hum of the city subsides and the aerial currents of evening take their course from Buttermilk Channel over the vast inland. "I feel at such moments," said Willis Gaylord Clark, "that I have an indestructible soul." A cloud was an opiate to the younger Clark. Clouds reminded him of flowers, in their fading and passing away. "We lose them with regret. Thoughts of our last hour come upon us, as we watch them die, and we almost wish to die with them." And from his immersion in melancholia he floated into a sea of analogies; but finally he decided that, whatever might be said for a cloud, "the richest thing in nature" was a wave in its dissolution.

In the popularity contest of the seasons autumn won by a margin of twelve essays, sixteen odes, and a triolet. Autumn, when the south wind seeks in vain for the summer flowers ("over which it had ranged in vain like a chartered libertine"), when the clouds lie in long red bars across the West and the falling leaves plap gently on the rill . . . the season most endeared, for the pleasant melancholy of its reveries. The soul perked up in winter, when "What loveliness, surpassing even the springtime, rests on the landscape! The hills, rising pale and blue afar; the vales and plains, dotted with farmyards, where the herds are huddled 'in their cots secure' and the yellow straw on the green marks the place of their pleased imprisonment. From the barn, you hear the hollow-sounding flail of the thresher; from the street, far and near, the cheerful jingling of bells. Woman looks sweeter now than ever. The demoiselle in her boa, with her muff and overshoes. . . . How the cutters, pungs, and fours-in-hand, sweep over the pave!" The mood is—debatably—a spontaneous response to the landscape; certainly the landscape is touched up to accommodate the mood.

The less trim the scene, the greater the adulation. Nature, like the soul, was at its loveliest when the fuzziness of the outline bespoke its artlessness. At the antipole of the Hellenic dislike of rugged country was the writer in the *Arcturus* (1842) who asserted, "A sunset at sea is not like a setting behind wooded mountains. It has not enough of the art in it; it is too simple, with not enough of scenery." This same anonymous exquisite, by the way, complained that "sun and moon lose all romantic interest when you see them bear to be peered at through such an inquisitive, steam engine, manual labor looking thing as what sailors call a sextant."

In the early Fifties flowers became marketable in New York; they appeared upon the stalls, flanking the lamb and the

butter, marking a noteworthy step in the evolution of urban-
ity. A twopenny bunch of roses on a merchant's desk harkened
him back to the days when flowers were profuse and unpriced,
when his urchin fingers depetaled buttercup and daisy. Of all
the beads on Nature's rosary, poets told off the Flower most
often. "There is not a spray which yields its tribute to the
wind, that hath not a lesson in its shiver, and a moral in its
sound"; not a species whose lure was not rediffused in essay
and verse. From edelweiss to *Houstonia cerulea,* the little star-
eyed "flower of innocence" abundant over the fields and hills
of New England and bespoken by Elizabeth Oakes Smith as
"like the homely virtues, strong and beautiful, and unthought
of because of their abundance," no bloom was safe from
nature-samplers who limned the petals and sketched a moral
significance.

Ladies pressed flowers between the pages of books, to brown
into sachet. Gentlemen did likewise, to preserve fragrant the
memory of an afternoon and a lady. "Forget-me-nots! the soft
tints slumber on your silken leaves yet. But the blue of her
eyes! We think sometimes it was stolen to be wrought into the
violets that summer winds sprinkle on her grave. And the red
on her cheeks! It was like the crimson on the breast of that
sweet bird that sings of morning on her little tombstone." A
book (if it was a lady's gift-book, quite likely its title was of
floral inspiration) with its stuffing of garnered blossoms in
olent decay was a thing to be reopened for an emotional spree.
Here the folded spike of a lady's-slipper; next a buttercup that
had been paley-gold, and a sprig of clover that once was scarlet; then a pale red rose, almost turned Lancastrian upon the
fair beauty of the spotless page . . . a delectable reverie, soulful
and olfactory.

Always intermingled with the fragrances of nature was the
effluvium of the moral. Yield yourself to nature, surely; float,
like a mote in sunbeams, careless of direction, in a plenitude
of lovely sights and thoughts. But if you are an American, you
will not take your sensationalism undiluted as did your wilder
brethren of the *belle âme* or the *Weltschmerz.* Grasp, for

instance, the fading beauty of an autumn evening; observe the orange rays from the King of Day fall upon the dying habiliments of nature. Have you not something more than a pleasant, idle languor? You'd better have. Mr. Roswell Rice, author of *Orations and Poetry on Moral and Religious Subjects* (1849), announced, "It is no mere bubble that I grasp, when I commune with Autumn's final groans." No indeed, but a dripping analogy of the evening when the clod of mortality called Roswell Rice should relinquish its ray of life. "It is humbling to one elated with high expectations and fond hopes, that the very leaf he treads beneath his feet, is emblematical of his mortality."

John S. Adams cast his plumb into the universe and struck another sounding. "Deep below us, high above us, far as the eye of the mind can see around us, are the works of our Creator, marshalled in countless hosts. All breathed upon by his life, inspired by his divinity, fostered by his love, supported by his power. And in all things there is beauty—sunbeams and rainbows; fragrant flowers whose color no art can equal. In every leaf, every branch, every fibre, every stone, there is a perfect symmetry."

Seeing symmetry in a dornick and good in every natural thing, the nature-sampler believed enthusiastically in Rural Virtue. Henry Ward Beecher, in his bucolic retreat at Woodstock, felt his own nature—his longings, his hopes and loves, faith and trust—come out from its interior recesses, and in the cool twilight, "where all is primeval, solitary, and rudely beautiful," expand rapturously. His true goodness he felt bobbing up to the surface of the world-soul, not hindered or driven back by all the burdens of his "multitudinous life" in Brooklyn. And why, he sighed, could he not carry back to Brooklyn that freshness of sensation, that simplicity, that repugnance to all that is sham? History deposes that Mr. Beecher did not carry it back to Brooklyn.

The involuntary reaches of the spirit tend toward the true and the natural—so, optimistically, declared the author of *Dream Life*. The boys who grew up in the country were better

THE APPLE BEE

An autumn joy of rustic life. *Harper's Weekly*, 1859: drawing by Winslow Homer.

boys. In the cities "children are not permitted to be children, but with fearful precocity are made up rapidly into men and women." One L. W. Mansfield—who lived in Albany, and was co-author of *Country Margins*—jabbed his lethal pen. "That is the way you have in town. But the cities, let us be thankful, do not contain everybody. There is a connection between God and Heaven still kept up, through the country and country life. Herein is the safety of the world, and of government, and of the perpetuity of good institutions—that you cannot wall up the country, you cannot pave the lakes, and the prairies, and the rivers; you cannot shut out the blue sky and the stars, you cannot fence in the mountains, you cannot bowl out the salt sea and make streets and picture palaces there. God reserves to himself all these." Reserves, in short, the pasturage of Virtue.

It behooved the village, then, to avoid imitating the city. Country roads, the nature-sampler insisted, *ought* to wind, and farm lots should not be rectangular. It was a pleasing thought from *Harper's* "Easy Chair" that zigzagging, lozenge-shaped lots tempted the pretty ingenuity of the agriculturist, that odd corners and nooks of a house lot enticed the architect to invent new gimcracks. And the matter of place-names: there was "many a natural beauty, destined to be the theme of our national poetry, which is desecrated with any vile name given to it by vulgar chance." New, euphonious, and poetical names should be chosen, by local committees "half composed of the more refined and imaginative sex," urged Willis. "The name once decided upon, its adoption might be the occasion of one general pic-nic, or of any number of private parties with excursions to the spot, or a poem might be delivered, or (why not?) a sermon." Frederick S. Cozzens, the grandest lily-gilder of them all, urged in public communications that the Palisades be painted white, for the æsthetic delight and moral improvement of the residents of Yonkers and adjacent villages.

Erato fared rather roughly in the back-to-nature movement, not from neglect but from being ravished overly often. Inexpert hands begrimed her chiton into the semblance of a printer's towel. Spontaneity, naturalness, was the thing; if the heart be attuned with nature, the rhymes must ring harmoniously. Perhaps. Mr. A. T. S. Barnitz, whose poems were assembled in a volume called *The Mystic Delvings,* had no poetic equipment except a good heart; and he was able to produce such morsels as,

> O, I love the little rainlets!
> Love the joyous little rainlets,
> When they laughing come together
> Telling all about the weather!
> And I'm sure a kindred feeling
> Over every breast is stealing,
> As the rainlets come together,
> Telling all about the weather.

Regrettably, Mr. Barnitz was very nearly right about the kindred feeling—to trap the rainlets into verses.

Margaret Fuller strolled along rural by-paths conscientiously, as did nearly all the New England literati. The asters she liked especially; their corollas looked like eyes, and she had a delicious sensation of being watched. As the stroll lengthened, nature's opiate took effect; "the disgust at unworthy care, the aching sense of how far deeds are transcended by our lowest aspirations, pass away, and for a while I lean on the bosom of nature, and inhale new life with her breath." Often in his college days Lewis Gaylord Clark, lolling in the dormitory, closed his Virgil and extended his telescope to peer "among the far-off hills in the lap of which the edifice was navelled," focusing upon the verdure and the milkmaids. "If I learned my Latin badly," was his serene comment, "I got many a leaf from the book of nature most deeply *by heart.*"

When the landscape and the soul are dallying together in an idyl, cerebration isn't at all necessary for the discovery of truth. Reverie is a preferable, pleasanter mode. Theodore Parker wrote to a Miss Cabot of Boston in 1837, "You know how I lamented the missing of Mr. Emerson's lectures, but a single walk along the banks of the Connecticut, or among the hills, or a moment's listening to the soft pine music, have taught me more than Mr. Emerson and all the Boston association of ministers."

It was the happy privilege of the Hutchinson family, a remarkable tribe of musicians and singers, to be grandly simple in their communing with nature. The Hutchinsons wore no gloves in the concert-room. Some friends were troubled by this breach of etiquette and presented them with the requisites. The Hutchinsons donned the gloves, one bright day, and went into the woods to see if the wearing of them corresponded with nature. Gloved, they felt miserably alien among the simple, unclothed fauna and herbage; when a woodsman came along the path, they hid their gloves in shame; and thereafter, in concert-hall or not, their hands were always unsheathed.

Common as the nature-cult, pervasive through literature and life as the smell of lavender pervades a hope-chest, was the gentle delight of melancholia. Not mourning or sorrow, but a vicarious titillation—Hannah Gould called it "melting," and the word serves admirably. What better place to "melt" in than an attic? The deep nooks housing ancient, worn-out furnishings; the unused spinning-wheel white with dust; the old faded bonnets hanging on the wall; and, with luck, the raindrops chanting upon the roof and the swallow twittering under the eave. Mary Andrews Dennison liked to remember such a place; "it gave me a dreamy sort of melancholy to sit in that room." Beecher indulged a floral lassitude: ah, roses! he remembered how mother loved roses; how she plucked a bud to give her little boy, and smiled such a look of love, that ever thereafter roses and mother and love were intertwined in his memory. Elizabeth Allen pined enjoyably for the sympathy of "a kinswoman whom I had never seen":

> I would *my* eye could rest on thine,
>   And read the movings of thy soul;
> I would *thy* heart could fathom mine,
>   And see what floods of anguish roll.

And Lowell sighed because other people did not know his attractive innate self. "I pass through the world and meet with scarcely a response to the affectionateness of my nature. I believe Maria only knows how loving I am truly," he wrote his friend Briggs in 1845. "I go out sometimes with my heart so full of yearning towards my fellows that the indifferent look with which even entire strangers pass me brings tears into my eyes."

The greatest enticement into romantic melancholy was probably the graveyard. The beguiling sadness of it evoked innumerable literary tributes, like Edward Darby's,

> Life is but a golden dewdrop
>   That will glitter for awhile,
> And bedazzle with its beauty
>   While the morning sunbeams smile.

The soul had been liberated, but social decorum still limited its opportunities for satisfying expression; therein, perhaps, lies the explanation of much of this inverted self-love, this pleasure in weeping at one's own bier—or the pleasure in prolonging a legitimate sorrow as long as one more tear, or one more poem, could be squeezed from it.

Miss Mary Todd sang her little plaint:

> Heart of mine, why are thou dreaming?
>   Dreaming through the weary day,
> While life's precious hours are wasting?
>   Fast and unimproved away?
>
> With a world of beauty round me,
>   Lone and sad I dwell apart;
> Changing scenes can bring no pleasure
>   To this wrecked and worn-out heart.
>
> In the grass-grown, silent churchyard
>   With a listless step I rove——

not because her lover was buried there; he wasn't dead; perhaps there wasn't any lover; certainly there was a volume of Tennyson near Miss Mary's ink-pot.

When Frederick von Raumer told his American hosts that he intended to visit Niagara, he was advised to stay at least a week, to capture its full message. "You will feel," said a gentleman, "quite depressed and annihilated." And a lady added: "The oppressed heart must be relieved by tears." It required nothing so real as Niagara or a lost love, however, to burst the flood-gates. The great success of *Reveries of a Bachelor* was demonstration of that; and Mitchell boasted, "If I have made the feeling real, I am content that the facts should be false. Feeling, indeed, has a higher truth in it than circumstance. It is approved or condemned by a better judge." Ah yes, the heart.

CHAPTER SIX

The Fine Arts

*P*ERHAPS "the United States have been hitherto too much engaged in the cultivation of the *utile,* to have been able to reach an extraordinary eminence in the *dulce,*" as Thomas Hofland winsomely apologized. But literature was in lush burgeon, and other stalks on the *dulce* bush—music, painting, and the plastic arts—were budding encouragingly, in these Sentimental years. Domestic architecture, however, remained parasitical or froward.

The ante-bellum generation inherited the Greek mode of building from the Eighteen Twenties, but—since, for imitative purposes, one historical period was about as good as another—the Gothic style was coming in. For his Grecian knowledge the local architect used Minard Lafever's *Modern Builders' Guide* or some other textbook, and characteristic temple-shaped houses, like the ones in the diagrams, dotted the country. The columns, pediments, and moldings of the approved Greek profile appeared, but with the variations suggested by the builder's ingenious taste. When the classic influence became suddenly *passé,* in about 1850, architects found in the English Gothic gladsome opportunity for decorative flourishes—in painted gables, steep roofs, diamond panes, broken silhouettes, the scalloped edges of the barge-boards; even, alas, the cast-iron piazza. "Imitation Italian" villas, too, appealed to the newly rich. And there appeared a jirbled mixture, the Hudson River Bracketed, which *Harper's* greeted in 1853 as "the improved taste which is consecrating the shores of the Hudson, of the East River, and of Staten Island." Orson Squire Fowler, repudiating the general tendency to borrow the preferences of

English architects, conceived an octagonal hive; and in *A Home for All* he proved the superiority of the octagonal style in hygiene, convenience, and elegance. On the grounds about the new suburban residences Andrew Jackson Downing was grooming the landscape into "an expressive, harmonious, and refined imitation of the agreeable forms of nature," and, with an expert knowledge of English precedent, doing a good job.

Like the professional development of literature, remunerative artistry in music and the fine arts was upborne by general creative interest—by dilettantism *en famille*. Paper lace, waxworks, embroidery, water-colors, lyrics, ballads—family art in the family parlor. The amative miss wrote her own threnody:

> I love him, but I can't say why;
> And though for me he would not die,
> I feel that I should *love* to lie
> In the cold grave, all silently,
> If he would strew upon my bier
> Sweet flowrets, wet with one sweet tear——

while mother was water-coloring an ideal landscape to brighten the space beside the hall-tree. A dialogue in a children's reader finds *Steady* drawing a bust of Epaminondas, when *Volatile* inquires why the draftsman does not spend his play hours at marbles and whipping-tops with the other boys. *Steady* answers, "As you have thought proper to doubt the utility of the favorite occupation of my play hours, just consider how important it is to the botanist, the chemist, the machinist, the foreign traveler . . . every kind of artizan has occasion for drawings of the work which he intends to execute"—cheaper to do one's own drawings, what? But *Volatile* is an heir, and these uses do not concern him. *Steady* advises, "In that case you should learn drawing as an elegant accomplishment, and rational amusement."

So, in one manner and another, artistic craft and art appreciation was of universal concern. The specialty-shop appeared, such a one as the "Repository of the Arts" which Messrs. Davis and Horn opened at 411 Broadway in 1838—"An extensive depot of the rarest English and French plain and colored engravings, imported from the most eminent houses in Europe, as soon as published, together with every variety of fine stationery and artists' materials"; classical music from German, French, and English presses; and an assortment of "superior pianofortes, flutes, guitars, violins, etc."

The American Academy of the Fine Arts was paying its way by popular exhibitions. Early in 1836 Colonel John Trumbull's paintings of Revolutionary subjects were on display; in April Benjamin West's "Death on the Pale Horse" was given the central spot and "splendidly lighted in the evening with gas." A generous love of the fine arts beguiled customers into such exhibits as Harrington's Diorama, which in the season of 1836 occupied an hour with this sequence:

1. The Deluge.
2. Brilliant display of Artificial Fireworks, introducing Washington in the center of the American Stars of Freedom, Napoleon Buonaparte, etc.
3. The Cave of Terror, with its awfully terrific scenery, which suddenly changes to
4. The enchanted grotto or Temple of Happiness, which for brilliancy and splendor of effects is unsurpassed.
5. Moonlight Sea View—Storm and Shipwreck.
6. Scene in Italy—displaying a variety of scenes—funeral by torch fire, etc.
7. Conflagration of Moscow.

No less encouraging was the popular interest in panoramas —Champney's "The Rhine," for instance, or Banvard's "Mississippi," the latter a magnificent unwinding depicting the Father of Waters, with the scenery along the banks, from New Orleans to St. Louis, "with all the accompanying incidents of trade and navigation." As a critic remarked of the panoramas, "A good picture is seldom to be measured by the mile; still, this is a fair field for talent, and in proportion as such works possess real merit, they open to the multitude a source of innocent gratification, and often of positive improvement."

Congratulations upon the refinement of popular taste and

the growing love of art among Americans took on a certain justification. The market in previous decades had been for little else than family portraits; but now self-made merchants were ready to gratify their wives' requests for showy adornment for house and person. In 1838 the American Art Union was founded in New York; within a year it had 914 subscribers, and in 1850 it claimed over 16,000, contributing $80,000 in annual dues. The Union's art gallery was open to the public without fee. Each year several paintings were distributed among the subscribers, by lottery; engravings and replicas of medallic art were awarded in the same manner. By 1850 the Union's wheel had guided the distribution of over 2,000 works of art painted by 231 different artists, besides about 150,000 copies of etchings and engravings; and the Union had expended $200,000 in special appropriations "for the advancement of art." Philadelphia, Boston, and Cincinnati by that date possessed their own Art Unions, operated on the same plan. A rising number of art institutes, galleries, and schools of design were doing their part to make truth and beauty visible. William H. Aspinwall, as became a benevolent capitalist, opened his private gallery to the public once a week. But it remained for the Civil War plutocracy to take art-collecting to that grandiose stage of which J. J. Jarvis remarked, "Private galleries in New York are becoming almost as common as private stables."

Henry Inman was still "important" in 1836; but he lost his money in the Panic next year, fretted himself into ill health, and was capable of only spasmodic work in his remaining years. The near-great of New York got little in the way of art from Inman for their three hundred dollars (half-length or portrait; full length, two hundred dollars more); they received dully pretentious canvases, executed truculently by an artist who wanted to paint landscapes but lacked the independence to follow his own bent. "Rydal Water," the view that Wordsworth pointed out to the artist, was by far his best picture, brilliantly contrasting warm colors with half-tints; but the bulk of Inman's work was in portraiture. "I made them pay for their own phizzes just as much as I should have asked them for a phiz of nature," was his glum boast.

At Inman's sickness Samuel Waldo succeeded him in fashion and prospered so handily that he accepted more commissions than he could execute, shunting the excess to a pupil, William Jewett. Thomas Sully, another who painted in the thin "intellectual" manner then popular in Britain, throve as portrait-painter to the elect of Philadelphia. In Boston a Massachusetts farm boy, Chester Harding, shared the pickings with George P. A. Healy. Sully and Healy were particularly adept at painting ladies—Healy, with his French training, giving full color and sweep to their draperies, and Sully emphasizing the femininity of his subjects. Henry Tuckerman called Sully's a "fairylike, unsubstantial manner," just the touch for the portraiture of American women, whose beauty was "winsome partly from the sense of fragility it conveys."

To the land of *Hermann und Dorothea,* where the heart of the folk was the fountainhead of art, went American neophytes to learn how to delineate pretty stories in emphatic colors. The gallery at Düsseldorf provided just the schooling in dramatic sentimentalism that they wished. "Genre" painting had great popular appeal in the United States. William Sidney Mount was endeared for his comic story-pictures—"Ringing the Pigs," "Dance of the Haymakers," "Boys Gambling in a Barn," "Bargaining for a Horse," among rural felicities, and his picturizations of rollicking Negroes. Two of Inman's best-liked canvases were in the anecdotal vein of sentiment—the often reproduced "Mumble the Peg," a recollection of schoolboy amusements, and his last picture, "An October Afternoon." This representation was of a district school-house at the edge of a wood; the children, just released, have loitered to frolic. "A blithe and buoyant rout of youngsters they are," ran a contemporary appreciation, "and some of them beautiful withal, as ever set philoprogentiveness a-yearning for the honors of paternity."

Caton Woodville, expatriating himself in devotion to his art, fetched up story-scenes from his American memories and translated them into strong, vivid color. George Inness in his middle period painted some beguiling instances of the genre, notably the great spread of "Peace and Plenty"—with an old soldier in the foreground, happy children clustered about him; a harvest field, stretching away to a village in the far background; a winding stream; a wagon with grain, on its way to the mill in the distance—all on one lavish canvas, and the veriest crack on the most distant water-wheel given its due stroke. Tompkins Matteson, whose "Spirit of '76" made him famous and prosperous, was given to things entitled "The Rustic Courtship," "Redeeming Forfeits," and "The Morning Meal" (wherein the farmer's daughter is feeding the chickens). Under contract with an art dealer, Matteson also made a number of historical pictures, including the well-known "Signing of the Compact on Board the *Mayflower*."

The historical variant of the story-telling idea nearly always implied a patriotic subject. Healy's most ambitious paintings were "Webster's Reply to Hayne" and the tableau of Franklin urging the claims of the colonists before Louis XVI. Peter Rothermel had notable ability for this branch of the art—an aptitude for grouping and for emphasizing costume, for facile brushwork, and the very rapid production of very large pictures. "Patrick Henry before the House of Burgesses," "De Soto Discovering the Mississippi," and "Columbus before Isabella" are from his workshop.

What customers liked in landscapes were striking, salient effects. François Regis Gignoux, probably the most popular artist in New York in the mid-Forties, gave them the broadly seasonal changes so satisfactorily that for two years or so he was allowed to paint only winter scenes; then he bolstered his trade with a cycle of autumn pictures. His "Niagara in Winter," "Niagara by Moonlight," and "Virginia in Indian Summer" were greatly admired; Gignoux duplicated or imitated them frequently.

The favored sketching-grounds of most landscape painters were the Hudson River region, the White Mountains, and the Catskills. By 1850 prejudice against spending money for pictures other than portraits had disappeared, and Nature was as greatly cherished in pictorial art as in the cheaper medium of literature. There were many landscape painters, with much in common besides their locale. In scenes as John Kensett painted them—"Hudson River from Fort Putnam," "Seacoast near Newport," "Sunset on the Adirondacks," and the like—the well-traveled Easterner could recognize the locations at a glance, to the glory of art. Sanford R. Gifford, faithful limner of the Catskills, reproduced local effects in a flood of yellow, misty sunlight. Frederick Edwin Church tackled icebergs, Niagara, the tropics, and the Andes with equal zest and was adept at picturesque arrangement and imitative naturalism; by 1860 Church was obtaining higher fees than any of his contemporaries. Asher B. Durand graduated from an anecdotal period (in which he produced his best-known canvas, the "Wrath of Peter Stuyvesant") to mature development as a painter of Catskill landscapes. Thomas Cole, "the father of landscape art in America" in point of time, also preferred the Catskills. Cole attempted to infuse into each landscape a moralizing message which was his substitute for beauty. His successors had no allegorical intent and were diffident as to the proper use of color. They worked either with brown sauce, strictly, producing crowded and unconvincing monochromes; or they attempted violent extremes of light and sky, as in their sunsets of most disquieting bloodiness.

"Go first to nature to learn to paint landscape," said Durand, "and when you have learned to imitate her, you may study the pictures of great artists with merit." In their conscientious endeavor to create an American art independent of foreign influences the Hudson River academicians (most of them educated in Paris) served to confirm the general expectation that the American genius, undisciplined and rampantly versatile, would become quite as successful in art as it had been in politics, mechanics, and banking. A critic remarked as early as 1839 that "We have seen works by young, uneducated American artists, which exhibit an originality and freshness of genius perfectly delightful. Knowing nothing of the technicalities and manners of schools, they derive their inspiration from the pure teachings of nature; an inspiration as true, as it is generous and unconfined." But happily the new amateurism had not advanced beyond the water-color stage by 1860. The outpouring of oil-paint daubs which martyred the sitting-rooms of a later generation probably was spared to the Fifties and Sixties because of the wide distribution of cheap engravings and the shrewdness of Messrs. Currier and Ives, lithographers, in meeting popular tastes in art.

George Inness, whose work is currently reckoned as the beginning of "the golden era of American landscape-painting," was to all evidences a failure in 1860, after he had been painting for twenty years. Inness opened a studio in New York in 1843, but his work was too far removed from the "Hudson River" manner with its meticulous brush-work; after four years Inness shut up his studio, to open another in New York in 1854. Again he failed to make a living. His work, meanwhile, was progressively subjective, and therefore increasingly unintelligible to the generation. Inness did not reach adequate recognition until long after the Civil War.

The much esteemed Washington Allston was at work in 1836 on his "Belshazzar's Feast"—so intently that he declined an invitation to paint a historical subject to occupy a panel in the Capitol rotunda. Seven years later, when Allston was buried by torch-light at Cambridge, "Belshazzar's Feast" was still unfinished. The one painter of religious subjects in the grand manner who was left, Daniel Huntington, shortly abandoned that branch of the art; and an epoch was closed. Upon Huntington descended the presidency of the National Academy of Design and the other highest honors of the profession. He showed the justness of the kudos by painting academic genre pictures, landscapes of approved literalness, and anecdotal figures of conventional archness. His areal masterpiece was the eighty square feet of canvas entitled "The Republican Court," depicting a reception given by Martha Custis Washington; sixty eminent guests were painted in, all presumably recognizable.

꧁꧂

The invention of the daguerrotype, with the several improvements in use by the early Fifties—the talbotype, the albumen process, the collodion method—released painting from any necessity to be graphic. American artists of the generation showed no awareness of that release; but the mechanical wonder excited public curiosity, and its reception was a delighted awe. François Gouraud, friend and pupil of the inventor, brought a collection of Daguerre's views to this country in the late autumn of 1839 and exhibited them privately. The editor of the *Knickerbocker* attempted to convey an understanding of the pictures ("their exquisite perfection almost transcends the bounds of sober belief"): "Let the reader suppose himself standing in the middle of Broadway, with a looking-glass held perpendicularly in his hand, in which is reflected the street, and all that therein is, for two or three miles, taking in the haziest distance. Then let him take the glass into the house, and find the impression of the entire view, in the softest light and shade, vividly retained upon its surface. This is the DAGUERROTYPE." Philip Hone's response was the exclamation, "How greatly ashamed of their ignorance the bygone generations of mankind ought to be!"

Within two years the daguerrotypists' shops were an established feature of urban business streets. Miniature painting disappeared under this competition. Monsieur Edouart, at 285 Broadway, New York, master artist in the cutting of silhouettes ("The first feeling is that of regret," wrote Lydia Maria Child, "that such an eye for form, such a decided love of art, should not have been employed in the more beautiful and enduring material of marble"), offered customers a choice between having their silhouettes made or their daguerrotypes taken—stabling the horse and the automobile together. An exceptionally talented artist, by name Peabody, opened a shop in Philadelphia in 1849, where he cut likenesses in cameo—a new and exquisite feature in the progress of the fine arts, said *Godey's,* which expected that ladies would make a fashion of wearing cameo-portrait pins and brooches "as memorials of love or friendship, parental or filial affection." But none of the crafts of dainty portraiture could survive; the camera won an easy victory.

Sculpture in the United States was sustained largely by the ardent patriotism of people and legislators, which demanded statuary memorials of its heroes; and an early outpouring of the æsthetic spirit placed hopefully beautiful works in cemeteries, paying joint tribute to the immediate dead and the enchanting melancholy of it all. Civic pride gave livelihood to a number of tradesmen sculptors, whose manufactures were planted in public squares and parks. Neither the National Government nor municipal bodies awarded contracts for art memorials on the basis of open competition, and patronage did its share in fostering visual annoyances. Persons of cultivated taste viewed the monstrosities leniently, on the optimistic principle that even bad statues familiarized the public with the idea of art and gradually created a desire for something better. The Italian cast-mongers, too, were missionaries of Art, as early as 1836 hawking their Napoleons, Graces, Walter Scotts, and Dianas in the city streets. "The lithographs may be rude and gaudy, cinerary urns be turned into flower vases, goddesses made to hold candles, and cross-legged Cupids to read little books," said a cheer-spreader in 1840; "but you will rarely find, in a humble family, a taste for these ornaments unaccompanied by neatness, temperance, and thrift. They are like the cherished plants in the window, the green creepers in the yard, or the caged singing-bird on the wall, signs of a fondness for home, and a desire to cultivate those virtues which make home peaceful and happy."

Clark Mills' figure of Jackson was the first equestrian statue executed for the National Government. Appropriately, the sculptor had never seen either an equestrian statue or General Jackson. After nine months' labor he completed a model exhibiting a new principle, the hind legs of the horse being exactly

THE DAGUERREOTYPIST

Godey's Lady's Book, 1849.

under the center of the General's torso and producing a perfect balance. This mechanical felicity won Mills the contract, awarded by the Jackson Monument Committee—the Honorable Cave Johnson, Postmaster-General, chairman. Mills worked two years, overcoming such difficulties as the breaking of cranes and the bursting of furnaces; the statue was dedicated in 1853, and a pleased Congress voted the sculptor twenty thousand dollars. The bright bronze wonder was a popular triumph; no other equestrian statue in the world balanced itself upon two legs, without help from the tail! Mr. J. H. Hammond of South Carolina won the competition to purchase the horse that Mills had used as a model, and added it to his stud-farm. The city of New Orleans paid Mills thirty-five thousand dollars to make a replica, and Congress awarded him fifty thousand to make another equestrian statue, this one of Washington. It was dedicated on February 22, 1860, and was conceded to beat even the Washington Statue in Union Square, New York.

The latter statue, the first bronze figure made entirely in this country, was the work of Henry Kirke Brown. Popular subscriptions, chiefly from the merchants, financed the production; the reward was a Washington fourteen feet high. Brown was commissioned by the State of North Carolina to execute a thirteen-figure group for the new capitol at Columbia. The design included Hope, Justice, and Liberty, flanked by black workers in the rice- and cotton-fields; the irony of it was too much, and the work was destroyed by an "act of God."

The pioneer of æsthetic sculptors in America was Horatio Greenough, a Bostonian, who spent most of his apprentice years in Florence. He was an idealist whose best works were story-telling groups of lofty sentiment, among them "Angel and Child," suggesting that the angel was guiding his little friend into the glories of heaven; and "The Rescue," exhibiting an athletic Caucasian rescuing a lady and infant from under the upraised tomahawk of a savage. Greenough's statue of Washington, now in the Smithsonian Institution, which professed to symbolize the ascendancy of the civil and the humane over the military virtues (Washington held a Roman sword point downward), was not a popular success; the ideal content seemed incongruous with the historical doings of the subject, and—worse—the General's bosom was naked. But connoisseurs admired the statue; and Alexander H. Everett spoke up, "I can say for myself, that after seeing the most celebrated specimens of ancient and modern sculpture to be found in Europe, including the Laocoön and the Apollo Belvedere, I consider the 'Washington' of Greenough as superior to any of them, and as the masterpiece of the art."

Hiram Powers and Thomas Crawford shared the peak of esteem. Powers was eminently characteristic of his times: he had technical aptitude and was particularly interested in the mechanical improvement of his craft; he produced statuary of invariably sentimental prettiness. It was proper, too, that he should have been one of a large family, born of "honest and harmonious" parents (the phrase is his own); that they should have moved from Vermont to western New York, thence to Ohio; and that the young man's first business experiences should have been in mechanic trades. His first work of art was a mechanical, moving representation of Hell—exhibited for a price, with lecture accompanying. The exhibit was purchased by a resident of Cincinnati, who improved it by adding thunder and lightning and passing electric shocks among the customers; he became a rich man.

Portrait sculptors were such rare creatures that Powers had molded the features of Jackson, Webster, Marshall, Calhoun, and other statesmen of highest rank before he produced any of the ambitious figures which won him his great fame. He took the plaster models of the statesmen sitters to Florence, where he set up a studio in 1837, and finished the busts in marble at his leisure. He invented an apparatus for hanging statues in gimbals for safer transportation and, among other technical novelties, devised a finish which made his statues gleam like polished ivory, imparting a flesh-like texture which spectators found exquisite. In the sculpture itself Powers was not so inventive. Aside from his conventional busts of the American great, his talent was in the literal reproduction of a pretty form; he was lauded, accordingly, for the "wonderful accuracy of his observation" and "the delicate truth of his manipulation."

His crowning triumph was "The Greek Slave," a September Morn which needed no press-agent to become a national sensation. The figure is that of a nude young lady of not excessive charms, her body languid, her head pensively inclined. But she made no light impression upon the generation for whom the statue was made. "The Greek Slave" told a story—of a beautiful woman in a position of humiliation and sorrow, but elevated above her condition by conscious virtue. Powers explained that she had been taken by the Turks and, standing exposed to the gaze of infidel strangers, was awaiting her sale in intense anxiety, tempered by her reliance on the goodness of God. Everybody saw the statue (Powers made six replicas of it, at excellent prices) and had an opinion to express. Sentiment was a very diaphanous veil for its carnal charm; but the veil was sentiment, and it served. The Reverend Orville Dewey stated the lady's defense: "The Greek Slave is clothed all over with sentiment, sheltered, protected by it from every profane eye. Brocade, cloth of gold, could not be a more complete protection. [This exemplifies] the highest point in all art. To make the spiritual reign over the corporeal; to sink form in ideality."

Powers selected his models from among "what are called the working classes," as he said, because "the best models are found in those walks of life where nature predominates over art." He modeled a pretty woman, leaving her prettiness as he found it; attached an allegory; and produced a success—sometimes called "Eve Tempted"; or "Eve Repentant"; or "California"; or "America." Two of his figures of another sort have been much reproduced in miniature—the "Fisher Boy," holding a shell to his ear, and "Proserpine," her head and bosom emerging from a nest of flowers.

Crawford, more versatile, also exceeded Powers in the loftiness of his ideality. Crawford's group-figures included "A Mother," attempting to save herself and child from the Deluge; "A Family," of five anguished figures "suffering under the reign of fiery serpents"; and "Adam and Eve," at the moment of their expulsion from the Garden, with Eve, overcome by shame and sorrow, clinging to an Adam majestic in his grief. Perhaps because he avoided the sex-perfumed figures that attracted Powers, Crawford was given preference on the award-ing of the commission to design the pediment of the new Capitol at Washington. The last statue to be shipped from his studio in Rome was of the First President, in colossal bronze, for the state of Virginia.

The arch prettiness of Crawford's lighter works may be read in a letter of the sculptor's concerning a statue of "Youth" then in progress—"a boy of seven or eight years, dancing in great glee, and tinkling a pair of cymbals, the music of which seems to amuse him exceedingly. The sentiment is joyousness throughout. It is evident that no thought of the future troubles his young mind; and he may consider himself very fortunate in being made of marble; for thus his youth remains without change."

Two gentlemen who abandoned merchantry for sculpture were commercial successes in the latter craft—Joseph Mozier, whose "Wept of Wish-ton-Wish" was popular enough to war-rant his reproducing it indefinitely; and Randolph Rogers, who was commissioned to design the doors for the National Capitol. He supplied an historical composition of the life of Columbus, stodgily executed and not original in idea. Rogers' most liked statue was of Nydia, the blind girl of Bulwer's _Last Days of Pompeii_; "in a listening, fugitive posture, she seems to hear the rushing of the lava about to overwhelm the city."

Late in the Fifties appeared the sculptresses. "Doubtless an amiable exaggeration has marked the public commendation of their efforts," Henry Tuckerman observed, "partly arising from the national deference to and sympathy with their sex." The most important was Harriet Hosmer—who would not wear a bonnet, incidentally, and wore her hair close-cropped. For a New England girl Miss Hosmer had enjoyed a markedly unusual education; she had been encouraged in athletic exer-cises, had attended lectures on anatomy, and traveled in the West unattended. After the almost uniform practice of Amer-ican sculptors, she studied in Rome. "Beatrice Cenci Asleep in her Cell" was her best.

The preëminent function of art, held the common definition, was to exert an elevating and humanizing influence—to
touch the finer sensibilities and bring the mind into sympathy
with the good and pure. It followed that, in an age of multiple
petticoats, the unclothed body was suspect. Could modern
painters of the naked woman lift her out of the mire of the
sensual? A difficult business, when critics were wont to discern
"sportive wantonness and conscious seductiveness" in very
nearly any representation of "the whole woman." Lewis Gaylord Clark accordingly objected to "omissions" in Edward A.
Brackett's marble group of "The Shipwrecked Mother and
Child": the expression of the mother's face was exceedingly
fine; the arms were admirably disposed; but the figure was
"almost painfully, certainly unnecessarily, nude. How easily
might a little drapery have been introduced, and with what
effect!" Even the classic stylization of the male anatomy was
realistic enough to be unbeautiful; and a verse in the *Knickerbocker,* inspired by "a naked statue of Apollo crowning Merit,"
admonished,

> Merit, if thou art blest with riches,
> For God's sake buy a pair of breeches!
> And give them to thy naked brother,
> For one good turn deserves another.

Hiram Powers discovered the sentimental channel to glide
around these objections, and after him artists were less bashful
—working in Paris or Rome, to be sure, for models for the
nude were not to be found in the United States save in bawdy
houses. A few sculptors prospered by the flurry of protest they
had anticipated, but "the whole woman" was not a paying
subject for painters. Artist's colors, like lip-rouge, simply
heightened the conscious seductiveness.

When Dr. W. B. Richmond, in about 1850, was examining
the curiosities of an asylum in Vermont, he saw the paintings
of a lady inmate, notably a canvas of the Garden of Eden. The
grounds of that classic estate were laid out skilfully (in the
Doctor's judgment), "and the whole animated with moss and
shrubbery in a tasteful manner." Adam was present, clad in

rather dandified garments, with a beaver hat on his head and an umbrella under his arm. Eve was a jolly thing in a wasp-waisted dress and flossy bonnet, regaling herself among the flowers. It was an insanely simple extension backward, into the time of the First Couple, of the taste of the artist's own decades.

Bowers of ambrosial brightness . . . flowery islands far away . . . a kindred spirit whose love envelops one as with an over-size mantua . . . rose shadows and silvery rivers . . . peace and harmony descending like white doves from the world supernal. These visions, it was presumed, came to the spirit eye of the lady attuned and submissive to music. The same family magazines that brought pleasing fiction and new dress- and doily-patterns into the home provided with each issue a new song to beguile voice or fingers. Such a one as Metcalf's (in *The Family Keepsake* for 1856):

> You are very lovely, lady,
>> Soft and fair your skin;
> Beauty's pencil has been there,
>> Blending colors fresh and rare;
>> Is all fair within?
> Yes! that blush, that modest glow,
>> Sweetly tells what I would know!

and two more verses, with the music. That was to be clipped, mounted on stiff paper, and played until the sheet was gummy with thumb-marks.

Was not the pride of the household the "instrument"—melodeon, pianoforte, or some other melophonic delight? Was there any soprano sweeter than daughter's? Daughter had studied under an accomplished *artiste,* one whom Lowell Mason had especially invited to the first annual convention of the Boston Academy of Music, in 1836, and who had addressed the first National Music Convention, in 1840, on the art of voice-culture. (If daughter's parents had real swank, it may be that

Call Me Pet Names.

WORDS

BY MRS. OSGOOD.

PUBLISHED BY PERMISSION OF E. FERRETT AND CO., PHILADELPHIA.

"CALL ME PET NAMES"

An example of the myriad sentimental songs purveyed by the popular magazines. *Sartain's Union Magazine of Literature and Art,* 1850.

CALL ME PET NAMES.

SECOND VERSE.

Call me fond names, dearest! call me a star,
Whose smiles beaming welcome thou feel'st from afar;
Whose light is the clearest, the truest to thee,
When the "night time of sorrow" steals over life's sea,
Oh! trust thy rich bark, where its warm rays are—
Call me pet names, darling! call me thy star!

THIRD VERSE.

Call me sweet names, darling! call me a flower
That lives in the light of thy smile each hour,
That droops when its heaven, thy love, grows cold,
That shrinks from the wicked, the false, and bold,
That blooms for thee only, through sunlight and shower—
Call me pet names, darling! call me thy flower!

she had sojourned briefly in Europe under a Master.) Solo performance in singing and playing was, in the Sentimental generation, the prime short cut to social charm.

And, in New York, patronage of the opera was another evidence of social and æsthetic merit. But the *New York Times* of January 6, 1836, contained notice of a sale at auction: the trustees of the Italian Opera Association wished to dispose of everything—scenery, fixtures, theater; an elegant house, erected only two years before. Since the first troupe of musical Columbuses had come to America, in 1825, the history of opera had been like that: gratifying, delusory crowds at first, then rapid diminution in patronage as the novelty of the entertainment and the prestige of attendance wore away. Perhaps one had to be foreign-born to love Rossini after the third hearing.

Ann and Arthur Seguin, English singers, arrived in New York in 1838 and organized an English Opera Company. With a slender overhead and with no pretense of an adequate orchestra, the company survived to tour annually until 1847. French opera was firmly established in New Orleans, but there was a specially attuned racial clientele. New York had its flurry of an opera season every year, sometimes with as many as three companies. Conversation was annually set off with Italian expletives, and self-conscious ladies showed proof of their enthusiasm with bouquets and *bravo's* for the star performers. The season began in late November and lasted until January or March as luck might have it. The companies usually were Italian, built about one or two flashing stars—Caradori-Allan, Teresa Parodi, Guilletta Perrini, Teresa Truffi, Marietta Alboni, Louisa Pyne—to the comparative neglect of ensemble and orchestra. New York had no German opera until 1855. Boston withstood even the Italians until 1847.

The bright young men unaffected by "fashion" were skeptical of the whole business. The spectacle of oratorio-goers and opera-patrons listening, with some evidence of admiration, to foreign music-masters—bundles of shakes, trills, and whiskers, difficult passages and gaudy jewelry, conceitedness and quavers —didn't carry entire credibility. George William Curtis protested the incompleteness of the illusion, with a personal reference to Alboni: "Art and the dressmaker can do much, but they are not omnipotent. They can not undo the work of a quarter of a century, nor cheat the eye into a belief that a heroine of twelve stone is a sylph." In the *Knickerbocker* Clark insisted that the public taste needed only a proper direction to place it "above and beyond the influence of the elaborate Italian school."

The "proper direction" was toward a national music. Truly American were, for instance, the two families who gave musical concerts throughout the Northern states—the Baker family and the Hutchinson ménage. Both families were rooted in New Hampshire. The Baker group, four men and two ladies, offered popular programs of songs and glees, specializing in the lachrymal—"Mary's Last Words," "The Inebriate's Lament," "The Parting Requiem," "The Sailor's Grave." The astonishing Hutchinsons, sixteen sons and daughters of Jesse and Mary, plain farming people, were entertainers, and much besides—teetotalers, Abolitionists, and devout fundamentalists, which credos they celebrated in songs of their own writing. By some strange caper of their primal cells the children expressed themselves naturally in music, and not otherwise; they were not bright in worldly affairs, and they were diffident in conversation. In late November, 1839, one of the boys tacked up two placards in their native village of Milford: "The eleven sons and daughters of the tribe of Jesse will sing at the Baptist Meeting-House on Thanksgiving evening at seven o'clock." That concert launched an institution. The personnel changed from time to time, as marriage or trade beckoned some of the flock and younger children grew up to take their places before the lamps; but the Hutchinson family held the boards until rheumatism claimed the last quartette.

The program invariably began with the "Family Song," written by Jesse Junior. The fourth of the ten verses of the original song tells them off:

> David, Noah, Andrew, Zephy,
> Caleb, Joshua, Jess and Benny,
> Judson, Rhoda, John and Asa,
> and Abby are our names . . .

The favorites of their repertory included "The Cot Where We
Were Born," "The Grave of Bonaparte," "The Irish Emi-
grant's Lament," "The Angel's Invitation to the Pilgrim,"
"The Maniac"; a Temperance ballad entitled "Cold Water";
musical settings of Longfellow's "Excelsior" and Morris' "My
Mother's Bible"; the battle-song of Abolitionism, "Get off the
Track"; and the camp-meeting echo which ran,

> The fatherhood of God, and the brotherhood of man,
> The cause of true religion is spreading through the land.
> Oh, the fatherhood of God and the brotherhood of man,
> We'll talk and sing while on the wing, and ring it through
>   the land.

William Lloyd Garrison announced, of the Hutchinsons, that
never before had the singing of ballads been made directly
subservient to the freedom and moral elevation of the people:
"Let the example become contagious!"

Several resounding elegies written between 1816 and 1836
—Woodworth's "The Old Oaken Bucket," Morris' "Woodman,
Spare That Tree," Sargent's "A Life on the Ocean Wave,"
Mrs. Willard's "Rocked in the Cradle of the Deep"—were set
to music in the late Thirties and became the classic ballads of
the generation. Henry Russell and Joseph Philip Knight, two
English soloists whose series of concerts in the States were
markedly successful, were inspired by this generous Republic
to write ballads which remained the property of the American
people long after the soloists had departed. Knight's setting of
Thomas H. Bayly's "She Wore a Wreath of Roses" and his
own "Oh, Fly to the Prairie," Russell's setting of Eliza Cook's
"The Old Arm-Chair" and his own "Wind of the Winter's
Night," became staples of the higher song-mongery. The common theater of the ballad was the family parlor, but male
soloists on the concert-platform fared somewhat better than

other visiting artists. The most renowned of these soloists was John Braham, the English tenor, who sang in the United States in 1840. The naval songs of old England and similarly hearty pieces were the stock of his repertory. The secret of Braham's powers, explained the critic of the *Arcturus,* "is not only the amazing extent or clearness, or melody of his verse, nor the brilliant expression merely, but (as in all men of true genius) it lies in the harmonious sympathy between the spirit of the man and the talent of the singer. He sung admirably the noble heroic songs from Scott and Burns, not only because he sung with power but also with love."

With the songs of Stephen Foster, American balladry reached probably its high mark for all time. A new style of theatrical show, Negro minstrelsy, did much to make Foster's songs nationally known and cherished. "Old Folks at Home," published in 1850, was the most popular piece of sheet music of the decade. The cork-and-satin troupes also introduced the Negro spiritual to the stage—the "native" melodies which D. H. Barlow interpreted to the ladies who read *Godey's:* "Sweet as they are, there breathes a plaintive, softly wailing tone. The ever-ready laugh is half smothered in a sigh."

But, aside from vocal music, the art remained annoyingly exotic. It seemed that if the composer essayed an opus above the artistic level of the Hutchinsons, his music employed recognizably European technique—as, if it had any merit, of course it did. William Henry Fry wrote a symphony, "Santa Claus," played in New York in 1853. The composer attempted such tone-pictures as the change from starlight to sunlight, delineated "by poetical analogies and mathematical facts," and the play of children on Christmas morning—for which effect members of the orchestra rattled and blared various toys. The critics did not like the toys, nor did they care for the device of the finale in introducing a concert of drums to represent the rolling of the spheres. Richard Storr Willis called the symphony "a kind of extravaganza which moves the audience to laughter, entertaining them seasonably with imitated snowstorms, trotting horses, sleigh-bells, cracking whips, etc." From

Boston came the weighted comment of John Sullivan Dwight that it wouldn't do to invite the public to "experimental feasts of possibilities."

Fry was the author of *Leonora,* the first grand opera by an American; it was written in his native language. *Leonora* was Bulwer's *Lady of Lyons* in new dress. Produced in Philadelphia in 1845, with a lavishness made possible by the author's own funds, it passed for an auspicious novelty. But when it was presented in New York, in 1858, *Leonora* had been translated into Italian, for the excellent reason that opera-singers acquainted with the English language were rare birds. The second native grand opera to reach the boards, George Frederick Bristow's *Rip Van Winkle,* which, operating at low expense, ran for four weeks at Niblo's, New York, in 1855, was thoroughly American in subject-matter. But the critic of the *Musical World* swung that familiar petard: "Is the music of Mr. Bristow quite American? Though agreeable and fluent it is somewhat devoid of character."

Antoine Philip Heinrich, who settled in the States in 1805, became excitedly devoted to his adopted country and wrote "national" music in quantities. "The Columbiad, Grand American national chivalrous symphony"; a "grand national song of triumph" entitled "Jubilee," scored for full orchestra and a vocal chorus; "The New England Feast of Shells," a "Divertimo Pastorale Oceanico," which included an Andantino describing "the fanciful curvetings of Mermaids in the ocean surf" off Cape Cod; and "The Wild Wood Spirits' Chant, or Scintillations of Yankee Doodle," were among Heinrich's compositions. But the first native American to produce a true percussion in the musical world was Louis Moreau Gottschalk. He was a Bohemian, a world-wanderer, and certain critics insist that Gottschalk was an exotic in the land of his birth. When he made his New York début in 1853, he aroused such hosannas that P. T. Barnum attempted (without success) to entice the pianist-composer under his management. Yet Gottschalk, too much the artist to welcome dealings with the proprietor of the American Museum, certainly favored the bravura in his laying; and, for all his private admiration of the classical onatas, he gave the customers "The Banjo," "Dance Ossian-que," "The Last Hope," "The Dying Poet," and similar com-ositions of his own. William Mason began his musical career s a piano virtuoso and toured as far west as Chicago in the niddle Fifties; but because he disliked the enforced repetition f the public's favorite pieces, he never made a second tour.

The pioneer of American critics of music, John Sullivan)wight, founded his *Journal of Music* in 1852. One of four ltruists who had organized, in 1837, the Harvard Musical ssociation for the purpose of elevating musical taste at the lma mater, Dwight had consorted with the Transcendentalists nd at Brook Farm had taught music and Latin. "He was all nusic," as an acquaintance said, constantly improvising on the iano and overflowing with interesting talk to demonstrate that nusic was the golden key to unlock all the analogies of the niverse. As became an æsthete, he was keenly sensitive to the harmonies" of rooms and of people and was bashful before trangers. Dwight was enamored of pure music, a worthy propa-andist of Beethoven, Mozart, and Bach in a ballad-loving nd. He exhorted technical musicians to forswear concessions) their audiences' taste and encouraged young scholars to udy abroad and to remain faithful to the Masters. To his :llow Transcendentalists he conveyed the word that man, in is social progress, had arrived at the dissonant Seventh—which lamored irresistibly for the coming octave. Classical music has :ldom been dissected into such precious metaphors and swoon-ig felicities of description as was Dwight's romantic wont.

Lesser critics, to whom any sequence of consonant notes was nusic, did their stint for the papers by writing in rapturous raise of the thing played, reserving their carps for the mere layer. Lydia Maria Child, who "covered" recitals for the *roadway Journal,* called music "the soprano, the feminine rinciple, the heart of the universe. Because it is the voice of >ve, because it is the highest type and aggregate expression f personal attraction, therefore it is infinite, therefore it per-ades all space and transcends all being like a divine influx."

Christopher P. Cranch essayed a further scramble: "Music i
an attempt to paint on the black canvas of the present, with
color-like melodies and tint-like harmonies, the soul's idea
reminiscences of the scenery of its native clime."

From the early Forties onward New York, Philadelphia, anc
Boston possessed chamber-music quintettes and philharmonic
orchestras, but most of the personnel were recruited among
German and Austrian immigrants. The greatest of these
ensembles, in point of excellence, was the Germania Society
(1848–54). As far as the advertisements and the public were
concerned, the greatest orchestra was Monsieur Louis Antoine
Jullien's—including "many of the most distinguished Profes
sors, selected from the Royal Opera Houses of London, Paris
Vienna, Berlin, St. Petersburg, Brussels, etc." Jullien's superla
tive orchestra opened at Castle Garden in 1853, and from tha
aquarian playhouse it went to Boston for a repetition of it
triumph. Even Dwight was melted. The repertoire included
an "American Quadrille" arranged by Jullien himself, con
taining all the national airs and embracing twenty solos anc
variations.

Ole Bull, the brilliant Norwegian violinist, so hefty a man
that he could play all four strings of his violin at once, made
his triumphant début in America in 1843. The unconventiona
genius, the comet rampaging through the world of virtuosity
he was a welcome excitant to American music-lovers; his tou
extended into a second year, and his receipts for the first excur
sion were about $400,000. Few classical numbers were in his
repertory; they required a precise compliance which irked him
Spiccatos and bizarre variations, while the orchestra carried the
melody, were his specialties. The composition most closely
identified with Ole Bull was the militant, noisy "Polaca
Guerriera," an inevitable encore. "There lies in this Scandi
navian a heartiness of impulse, and an exuberance of soul
which makes the better part of what men call genius," declared
Donald Grant Mitchell, paying tribute to "the spirit of the

man, creeping over him to the very finger-tips, and making music and melody of very necessity."

If the American people liked Ole Bull, the artist returned the compliment. He chose American subjects for his original compositions, which included the much applauded pair "Niagara" and "The Solitude of the Prairie." In the latter tone-poem, as Lydia Maria Child interpreted it, "the infinite stretches itself out, in darkness and storm. Through the fierce tempestuous struggle, it passes alone, alone, as the soul must ever go in all its sternest conflicts. Then comes humility and peace." "Niagara" too, it seems, dealt with a hegira of the soul "going forth peacefully into the calm bright atmosphere. It passes along, listening to the half-audible, many-voiced murmurings of the summer woods. Gradually, tremulous variations fill the air, as of a huge cauldron seething in the distance. The echoing sounds rise and swell, and finally roar and thunder. In the midst of this, stands the soul, striving to utter its feelings." Bull came back to the golden land in 1852 and stayed five years. It was during this visit that he planned the founding, on an extensive tract in Pennsylvania, of a New Norway consecrated to freedom. But his colony was never established, because he had bought the land from sleek liars who did not own it.

Edouard Remenyi, a greater violinist, made his first American tour in 1848. Henri Herz, who came to America in 1845, was dazzlingly nimble at the piano; his fantasias and florid variations kept him in the United States for six seasons and did much to miseducate American taste. Sigismund Thalberg, who came in 1856, was a master of arpeggios, shakes, and coruscations; his pyrotechnic fantasies were a craze until they were imitated to death. With Gottschalk and Thalberg playing simultaneously, in a dual concert, a special arrangement of *Il Trovatore,* there was produced possibly the greatest volume of music ever pounded from two pianos.

The evening of September 11, 1850, was the high mark of æsthetic rhapsody in the annals of the generation. On the stage of Castle Garden, underneath the entwined flags of Sweden and the United States, embanked by flowers, and looking out from a white and gold proscenium toward the floral legend on the balcony pillars, "Welcome Sweet Warbler," Jenny Lind made her American début. The entrepreneur of that occasion, P. T. Barnum, had offered the songstress a thousand dollars a night for one hundred concerts, plus an equal share of the surplus when any evening's receipts should exceed $6,500. The agreement was princely, unprecedented in any country. Jenny was the first great vocalist to come to the United States in the precise fullness of her powers, before time had corroded one small spot on the mortal perfection of her voice.

Barnum had not heard the lady sing until that September evening. He knew only of the admiration she had excited in Europe, and he knew his own abilities at ballyhoo. She became not only the greatest box-office attraction of the musical or spoken theater; Jenny Lind was a national love-affair. She lost a glove; the unselfish person who found it exhibited the glove to avid crowds, charging one shilling to kiss its outside and two shillings to kiss its inside. On a balcony she munched a peach and thoughtlessly dropped the pit to the walk below; the crowd engaged in a mêlée for the lucky endocarp which had been caressed by Jenny's lips. The Reverend Lebbeus Armstrong, son of a soldier of the American Revolution, Congregational minister of the gospel, and the oldest member of the Congregational Association of New York and Brooklyn, then in his seventy-seventh year of age and forty-fourth year after he had taken the total-abstinence pledge, addressed Jenny Lind in verse too pathetically amorous to bear quotation, added a prose salutation which began, "May divine grace prepare you to sing hallelujahs in heaven," and followed up with an "Ode on Scientific Harmony" using the acrostic, "TRIPLER'S AND BARNUM'S AMERICAN MD'LLE JENNY LIND MUSICAL METROPOLITAN HALL OF SCIENTIFIC HARMONY."

As part of his shrewd publicity, Barnum offered a prize of two hundred dollars for the best original song, written by an American, for the Nightingale to trill. Embryo song-writers all

over the land burst their shells, and the Jenny Lind Prize Song
Committee was showered with compositions. A hoaxing volume
entitled *Barnum's Parnassus* reported that about five thousand
songs in all were submitted and gave the distribution of "one
day's receipts":

Little Rock, Wisconsin, and entire West, including New Territories and Indian Reservations	10
Pontotoc, Miss., and entire South, including two from Cuba	3
Boston, East Boston, Cambridge, and suburbs, and New England in general	241
New York City, Brooklyn and Hoboken, and all other quarters	337
	591

But Bayard Taylor, winner of the contest, gave the number
of disappointed entrants as 752; and he probably knew, for his
publisher and his editorial associate on the *Tribune* were two
of the three members of the Committee. Inadequate consideration seems to have been given a suggested duet, written by
William Allen Butler, to be sung by Jenny Lind and Mr.
Barnum—one verse of which, addressed by Jenny to her col-
league, runs,

> Thy form is welcome as the sight
> Of diamonds sparkling in the night,
> Thy summons welcome as the cry
> That rent the California sky,
>   When first the adventurers bold
> Beheld the stream by Sutter's mill
> Begin the empty ditch to fill
> With sands of virgin gold!

Jenny's placid oval face was just plain enough for the spectator to endow with such ideal beauty as his imagination created.
Her large, steadfast eyes bespoke serenity, lambent radiance of
soul, fearless earnestness—all this, if you chose. Her ideals
endeared her. She had the simple piety of a child. She was
benevolent to a fault; newspapers reported such astounding

charities as the gift of twenty thousand dollars, when she was in New Orleans, to the poor of that city. And then she came out of the clouds and picked a clod for a husband—an Otto Goldschmidt, whose piano-playing interludes in her concerts were a bore to her audiences. The libido retreated; this Mrs. Goldschmidt was not such an incomparable singer. What a pity, as a critic sighed, "that her angel habit of song and charity should not have lifted her forever into a sphere above the weakness of human attachments."

A new Lucia made her operatic début at the Academy of Music, New York City, on November 24, 1859. She was Adelina Patti. But that is another love-story.

CHAPTER SEVEN

Garlands and Chains

$\mathcal{T}$HE human heart a garden is—Mrs. Harriot Arnold announced, in a pretty quatrain—and flowers there we raise; the blossoms and the fruit they bear, our skill reprove or praise. What an exuberant garden it was appears in the bridal bouquet of the American Moral Reform Society with its many blossoms of social improvement. "To practice and sustain the principles of Moral Reform in the United States, especially Education, Temperance, Economy, and Universal Liberty"—that was the pledge when the delegates assembled for their first convention, at Philadelphia in 1837. They authorized the Board of Managers to promote the founding of a manual-labor school, listened to lecturers on total abstinence and universal peace, then warmed to the serious business—the resolutions. These were adopted ("cordially," said the minutes):

Praise for George Thompson, the English Abolitionist; for Benjamin Lundy, the Quaker pioneer of the antislavery movement; and for the brave women who had put aside the traditional modesty of their sex to take public part against slavery. *Resolved,* in graceful acknowledgment of the martyr-complex, "That we will never separate ourselves voluntarily from the slave population in this country; they are our brethren by ties of consanguinity, of suffering, and of wrong." Resolutions against the custom of wearing mourning for the dead, and against parade and pomp on funeral occasions (because this tyranny of fashion imposed undue expense upon the poor). A resolution expressing great hopes for the rising generation; and one recommending agricultural pursuits to the colored people of the United States. Two memorials to be forwarded to Congress, one opposing the annexation of Texas, the other requesting that the Administration set a monthly concert of prayer for the promotion of human rights. A Declaration of Sentiment, to be given to the newspapers; and an Address to the American People, on a variety of topics.

Another such symposium might be gleaned from the minutes of the Brotherhood of the Union, which held its first convocation, with George Lippard as president, at Philadelphia in 1850. The purpose of the Brotherhood was, in its own simple statement, the amelioration of the wrongs of mankind. The convention adopted a manifesto stating that intention in greater detail—in part, "It seeks to destroy those social evils which produce poverty and crime," and "It seeks to inculcate correct views of the relations of capital and labor, so that the capitalist may no longer be the tyrant nor the laborer the victim, but both sharers of the produce of work on the platform of right and justice."

With such illimitable gestures and such expansive confidence the dynamic spirit of the age expressed its aspirations and proceeded to animate them. As a resolution adopted by the American Union of Associationists in 1848 phrased it, the ark of Social Science was floating serene upon the flood. Thomas Wentworth Higginson confided to a friend, "The more clearly I see, the more clearly I surrender myself to the new impulse that is come upon the world, the new dawning age of Faith." And John Sullivan Dwight composed a toast for Fourier's birthday: "To Joy! to Liberty! to Childhood's Mirth! to Youth's Enthusiasm! to the warm life-thrill of Attraction felt through every fibre of existence! The times are coming—the Harmonic Times of Unity and Love."

Moral Reform was a common enterprise. "There are not two or three stars which kindle up the Milky Way, but an innumerable host," said Saurin Lane, adding with generous imagery that the smallest pebble "may be of use as well as the corner stone of our political fabric." It behooved every citizen, by good example and kind deeds, to exercise a refining influence in his own sphere; and the greater the genius, the greater the obligation toward Moral Reform. True sentiment had a centrifugal force, and a scalpelist in the *Spirit of the Age* dissected the soul to prove it. That organ, analyzed as "a series of motive powers," possessed, besides five sensuous attractions and three distributive impulses, four affective attractions "tending to social groups, namely, friendship, ambition, love and famillism." These attractions sought their fulfilment in harmonized action, general well-being, and "coöperation with God in the movements of creation."

It was not belief or disbelief in this coöperative impulse in "the movements of creation" that separated conservative from radical, but a question of the manner in which harmonized action should best promote the common weal. As nearly as one idea may be the common idea of a people, the generation believed in perfectibility—or believed that, as William A. Alcott expressed it, "We are destined, if we are wise, to approach perfection forever." The distinction between the Horace Greeleys and the Orville Deweys, or between the Transcendentalists and the benevolent merchants, is analogous to the difference between two schools of thought concerning biological evolution—over the creation of new species by catastrophic change, or by gradual, tiny, but steady developments.

The common sympathetic interest in "the amelioration of the condition of the poor" expressed, besides its romantic components, the unspoken fear, it might be me. In a society without hereditary or institutional caste, chance played such part in the fortunes of an individual that no one could regard his inferior fellows indifferently. "The Great Searcher of Hearts alone knows," said Lydia Maria Child, "whether I should not have been as they are, with the same neglected childhood, the same vicious examples, the same overpowering temptation of misery and want." There was a provisional clause to this sympathy, however: "if they will but pay to virtue the outward homage of decorum."

A GENTEEL LODGING-HOUSE IN BAXTER STREET, NEW YORK

New-York Illustrated News, 1860.

In the decade 1825–35 the emigration of the human materials discarded by the Industrial Revolution in Great Britain created a "pauper problem" in the United States which the surviving eighteenth-century methods of poor-relief could not meet. The tendency of state government confronted with this avalanche of pauperism was to disown responsibility unless the destitute ones came into the almshouses. Benevolent citizens organized and sustained private philanthropies; the problem as they saw it was fundamentally a moral one, and the characteristic form of relief was linked with Protestant missionary work or the Temperance crusade. Readers of the *Moral Reformer* in 1835 were told that, as Christians, they had to be giving to the poor. Not money, necessarily; for money could be squandered or misapplied. But something more—time, assistance, instruction. "The poor and the ignorant mistake, most surprisingly, the importance of wealth on our immediate happiness. They seem to take it for granted, that men are happy in proportion to their possessions." The poor never thought of "the care, and anxiety, and perplexity, which property brings with it. Hence it is that they fall into a state of improper feeling towards the rich"—and the poor had to be educated out of these unseemly prejudices. Then benevolence would receive its due gratitude, and the world would be comfortable for both the have-nots and the haves.

Joseph Tuckerman, pioneer in the movement toward organized charity, was responsible for the Association of Delegates from the Benevolent Societies of Boston, which issued its first report in 1835, and for the Society for the Prevention of Pauperism, established in Boston that same year. Tuckerman's own idea was that inadequate wages and seasonal unemployment, with other economic evils, had to be disposed of before social evils could be prevented—a realistic approach quite unrelated to his cultural environment and as startling in that respect as the advice that the *Bunkum Flagstaff and Independent Echo*, in August, 1849, tendered to a precocious correspondent named Tommy: "We have only to say, patting him on the head with the hand of our mind, make the tail according to your kite, my boy, or if you have only so much rags, then your kite according to your tail."

The winter of the Bread Riots in New York called into existence a number of relief agencies, hastily devised for the emergency and working without concert. The citizens who then paused in life's pleasures and supped sorrow with the poor found that they had taken hand in a permanent problem. By 1840 there were over thirty relief-giving societies in New York. An investigative committee in 1842–43 condemned the lot of them for lack of coöperation, failure to discriminate among the means of relief, and failure to learn the "wants, capacities, and susceptibilities" of the poor by visiting their homes. The attempt at a remedy was the Association for Improving the Condition of the Poor of New York City, founded in 1843. Brooklyn, Baltimore, Boston, and (after the Panic of 1857) Chicago followed the New York model of comprehensive agency.

Under the guidance of Robert Hartley the New York Association attempted a city-wide plan of social service in the home. Each of the Association's volunteer workers lived in the district he investigated; he was pledged to withhold relief from persons unknown, visit the homes whose families appeared to require benevolent services, and, combining material aid with exhortations toward thrift, diligence, and Temperance, help the needy to "discover those hidden springs of virtue within themselves from which alone their prosperity might flow." The Association required every beneficiary to abstain from intoxicating liquors and to provide for the education of his children—the younger ones to be sent to school and the older ones to be apprenticed to some trade.

By 1850 one million natives of Ireland had been checked through the American ports of entry; another six hundred thousand came in the next decade. They were the largest national ingredient in the crowd that poured through the unguarded gates—almost six hundred thousand immigrants in the Thirties, seventeen hundred thousand in the Forties, twenty-six hundred thousand in the Fifties. The frontier claimed great numbers of these immigrants, and the factories took many. But the volume of immigration meant a labor-supply increasing at a rate greater than jobs were being created by the pushing-upward of American workers into middle-class occupations and the shift of population toward the West. And, worse, a large part of the influx was of families whose resources had been exhausted when the passage-money was paid, people unfitted for jobs—a condition particularly true of the Irish immigration, which owed its numbers not to any romantic impulse, but to the practical impossibility of keeping alive on John Bull's footstool.

Theodore Parker in 1850 drafted a memorandum on the charities of Boston, checking off "Anglo-Saxon," German, and Negro pauperism as trivial problems, noting that Jewish alms-giving cared for what little Jewish pauperism there was, then launching a violent tirade against the Irish. Parker was naturally a benevolent soul, and a Unitarian clergyman's extreme aversion to Irish immigrants cannot be charged off to economic determinism. The picture of the baffled philanthropist warrants a closer focus.

The unified agencies in New York and Boston were in theory nonsectarian, but they were endowed by Protestant benefactions and manned by Protestant workers. The prevalent attitude toward the Irish poor was expressed by Amos Lawrence: "I see no relief but to educate the children, and circulate the Bible and good books among them, which shall encourage them to do the best they can for themselves"—and with such an attitude the volunteers were scantily equipped to do preventive service against poverty in Catholic families. George Winfred Hervey in his *Principles of Courtesy* gave directions for the well-bred social worker: "No formal introduction will be found necessary; the poor are willing to dispense with the rules of refined life, if only they may be permitted to welcome to their needy hearths some generous almoner of the Divine bounty. And access to them will be the more easy when they ascertain that he belongs to the same household of faith with themselves." So the problem recurs to the generation's complacent exaction, "if they will but pay to virtue the outward homage of decorum." And it may be noticed that the philanthropists most liberal in supporting the cities' organized-charity agencies included those who maintained three societies (merged into one, the American and Foreign Christian Union, in 1849) whose object was the spreading of Protestant doctrines and practices in the benighted countries that persisted in the errors of Roman Catholicism.

A survival of the Atlantic cities' once-dominant interest in maritime trade was the large number of societies for seamen's aid. New York State controlled the Marine Hospital and the Sailors' Retreat, on Staten Island near Quarantine; a little to the northwest was Captain Robert Richard Randall's prosperous endowment, Sailors Snug Harbor; and near-by was a Home for Sailors' Children. The American Seamen's Society was the most ambitious of the New York agencies of its kind; for the sailors in port it provided boarding-houses, reading-rooms, savings-banks, and religious services; it published a monthly journal, the *Sailors' Magazine*; furnished ships with libraries of technical and religious books; and maintained chaplains in foreign ports. The Marine Society of the City of New York was devoted to the needs of the wives and orphans of sailors; and the Mariners' Family Industrial Society, also of Manhattan, supplied work to the female relatives of seamen and gave money in cases of urgent need.

Woman (in whom, as Willis Gaylord Clark said, "all that is sacred and lovely seem to meet, as in its natural center") was presumed to have a natural bent for sympathetic works, and the sex did not belie the compliment. Two of the societies just named were supported mainly by ladies, as was the Seamen's Aid Society of Boston. Samuel Woodworth, on reading the latter Society's annual report in 1836, put his appreciation in verse:

> The Sailor's best friend?—It is woman—dear woman—
>   She pities his errors she cannot approve,
> But prizes his daring, which seems super-human,
>   His coolness in peril—his ardor in love;

His patience in bearing fatigue and privation,
  When dangers, or famine, or agonies press him,
Elicits from woman the warm aspiration—
  "Oh! pity the sailor! God, bless him! God, bless him!"

This Society, with a higher virtue than consistency, established a trade-school for girls in 1836; most of the attendants were taught to be seamstresses. Later the Seamen's Aid ladies were pioneers in offering a new benevolence, a day-nursery in which employed mothers could leave their children during working-hours.

By 1850 New York City had an Asylum for the Relief of Respectable, Aged, and Indigent Females; a Society for the Relief of Poor Widows with Small Children; several orphans' homes; a Protestant Half-Orphan Asylum, which collected a fee of fifty cents a week from the surviving parent; a People's Bathing and Washing Asylum; and an American Female Guardian Society. This last Society maintained a "House of Industry and Home for the Friendless," opened in 1847; published and distributed several tracts, notably one entitled *Friendly Advice to Domestics*; and pursued in various ways its original object of "throwing good influences around poor young women." But in the early Fifties the American Female Guardian Society placed increasing emphasis on the relief of abandoned and neglected children. The new importance of this humanitarian interest was marked by the founding of the Asylum for Friendless Boys in 1851 and its reorganization into a semicivic institution in 1853 as the Juvenile Asylum, to which the courts were authorized to commit not only vagrants, but—the first legislative invasion of the patriarchal supremacy over the child—children neglected or grossly abused by their parents. In 1854 the Children's Aid Society opened a lodging-house for boys, combining with it an Industrial School and "Boys' Meetings" for religious education.

A list of benevolent associations in New York in 1853 names ninety charities besides twenty-two asylums, eight hospitals, and seven dispensaries. A liberal interpretation of "benevolence" might add to the list most of the seventy-five fraternal societies (their number is eloquent testimony that the average American was a joiner), with their three hundred and fifty chapters in the city.

Mrs. Cornelius Dubois, who had converted part of her Gramercy Park home into a nursery for a particular class of neglected children—the younglings of the wet-nurses who nurtured the babies of the rich,—and Mrs. Thomas Addis Emmet, sponsor of the Marion Street Lying-In Asylum, united in 1854 in a splendid demonstration of Earnestness overcoming the handicap of Sex; within a month the two ladies had raised a subscription of ten thousand dollars, the endowment for the Nursery for the Children of Poor Women. The plan was enlarged, and a second charter, in 1857, rechristened the institution as the Nursery and Child's Hospital. Funds to supplement voluntary donations were annually raised by entertainments, arranged by a committee of women and presented before a "society" audience at the Academy of Music. It was in 1857, too, that the ingenious combination of benevolence and vanity, the Charity Ball, was invented.

Ladies' charities assumed the burden of caring for their errant sisters when repentance or distress brought them within reach. In New York the Female Benevolent Society, a venerable organization among its class, since the early Thirties had maintained a home where a Christian matron taught the penitent residents trades that might procure an honest living. The New York Prison Association, a gentlemen's organization founded in 1844 "to take into consideration the destitute condition of discharged convicts," issued a call for a "female department"; the result was the opening of "The Home"—delicately named—in 1845. Its purpose was the shelter of female convicts after their release; a sewing department, a school, and a laundry were to provide a useful education. The one condition of admission was "a sorrow for what has been, and a desire to do better hereafter." By 1854 the connection with the New York Prison Asso-

ciation was dissolved, and The Home was wholly a ladies'
philanthropy. In the late Forties the Magdalen Female Asylum
had begun its interesting history, when the Reverend L. M.
Pease, who conducted a House of Industry under the auspices
of the Ladies' Domestic Missionary Society of New York, rented
and cleaned out a notorious brothel and received a few ex-Mag-
dalens as residents, giving them shirt-making as an employment.
Mindful of the proprieties, the Ladies' Domestic Missionary
Society disapproved of the new activity; and the shirts did not
meet haberdashers' standards. But the minister persisted, got a
trickle of funds from other sources, put the residents of the
Asylum to partially sustaining work at bread-making and straw-
braiding, and by the early Fifties was finding work as domestics
in country places for over a hundred women yearly.

Societies to abolish capital punishment and to improve the
discipline and sanitation of prisons, founded in earlier years,
continued their humanitarian campaigns. The New York
Moral Reform Society, a ladies' organization chartered in 1834,
sent Margaret Prior and other missionaries on prison visitations
and found "an urgent necessity for reform"; the Society pre-
vailed upon the state legislature to order better arrangements
for the segregation of the sexes in the prisons and forced the
appointment of women matrons. In 1839 the Society was
reorganized on a national basis, and thereafter it brought the
crusade into seventeen states.

Dorothea Dix began in 1841 her pioneering work for better
care of the paupers and insane. She wrote a friend four years
later: "Have visited eighteen State penitentiaries, three hundred county jails and houses of correction, besides hospitals
and houses of refuge. I have been so happy as to promote and
secure the establishment of six hospitals for the insane, several
county poorhouses, and several jails on a reformed plan." With
unusual concentration of energy she clung to her chosen task,
and by 1854 she had influenced the legislatures of eleven states
to take the insane out of the jails and almshouses and place
them in asylums under medical care. In the latter year a Congressional bill which Miss Dix had sponsored passed both

Houses, setting aside 12,225,000 acres of the public lands, the proceeds to be used for the maintenance of insane asylums; but President Pierce had particular reasons for declaring the bill unconstitutional and vetoed it. It was in the work of caring for the mentally and physically defective, however, that the generation's reformative program was most successful—in this field simply ameliorative work did not reveal such disparity between hope and result. Samuel Gridley Howe's institution for the blind, in Boston, deservedly won national admiration, and its appeals for funds were widely answered.

The American Peace Society, founded in 1828, continued, under the leadership of William Ladd, the Reverend L. D. Dewey, and Elihu Burritt, to advertise the merits of its cause. The Society maintained close relations with European pacifist bodies and persistently memorialized Congress and the state legislatures to declare an annual concert of prayer in behalf of peace. For every contribution sent in by a church organization New York headquarters refunded half the money in the form of peace-teaching booklets.

Nobility also began at home, and general interest in commemorating the nation's history was manifest. George Bancroft was writing his interminable proof that Providence was on the side of the Americans—the first volume of his *History of the United States* appeared in 1834; the fourth in 1854; the twelfth, and last, in 1882. And Bancroft, promptly in 1834, became by common acclaim the greatest American historian. In monuments of more concrete stuff women did much to make the commemorative gestures possible. When the Massachusetts legislature began an institution, in 1857, by declaring the twenty-second of February a legal holiday, the action was in response to a women's lobby. The Bunker Hill Monument was an idea launched in the Eighteen Twenties; but after Amos Lawrence had pledged ten thousand dollars and Judah Touro of New Orleans had sent a like amount, contributions languished until Mrs. Sarah J. Hale and her lady associates bestirred their sex. Throughout the summer of 1840 women were busied in making jellies and conserves, wax floral pieces, crazy-quilts, embroidery, and other pretties for a great bazaar. The fair was held at Quincy Hall, Boston, in September, and netted the thirty thousand dollars necessary to complete the fund.

Anne Pamela Cunningham founded the Mount Vernon Ladies' Association in 1853, to purchase Washington's plantation home. Edward Everett provided more than a third of the needed two hundred thousand dollars by donating the fees of his lyceum lecture on the moral character of the First President. Mrs. Harrison Gray Otis sponsored the Mount Vernon Ball, at the Boston Theatre in 1859, which realized the final ten thousand dollars; and Mount Vernon was dedicated, in Miss Cunningham's presentation speech, as "the sacred heritage of America's children."

The first upon whom the Industrial Revolution bestowed the boon of leisure were the young ladies—the demoiselles—and married women who had not yet borne the second child. It was the young ladies who set up the feminine arbitrament over fashions, commercial diversions, and drawing-room manners. (The French were notoriously smart at these things, and the feminine tyrannies were promptly imitative.) The mature complement to these gay interests was a sampling of humanitarian work, and the Benevolent Merchant had his proper consort, the Lady Bountiful.

All the pother about *outré* furniture and extra carriages and ballroom invitations—the "ripeness of vanity" for which Donald Grant Mitchell berated the ladies—served to maintain an interesting little world in which a woman could believe her economic inferiority was even a blessing. She had no finger in the business which supported the household. "It appears as if the gentlemen would atone for their all-absorbing passion for business," said Mrs. Pulszky, a Hungarian visitor, "by the privilege

they give to the ladies of idling their time away." When idling
diversions were not enough, the lady had the privilege of patting gentle poultices onto the social ills. It was pleasanter to
be ineffective than to be called unfeminine.

The Sentimental sanctions of particular feminine virtues
and particular spheres of feminine influence were so beguiling
that the number of lady rebels is at first surprising. But when
a writer in the *Home Journal* lists "American excess of family
quarrels" among the "positive evils of society," there yawns
a not unusual gulf between sentiment and practice. If middle-
class society had given women the compensations of pride and
power that Southern "chivalry" bestowed, there would have
been no feminist revolt in the ante-bellum decade. As it was,
the social and political extremes of that revolt enlisted only
a small minority of women in the North; for most of the sex
it was profitable to be effeminate.

"It is impossible to conceive anything more superlatively
beautiful in the organization of the human family, than that
which was designed by the considerate Creator of the Universe,
in the formation of WOMAN for the sole comfort and happiness of man," said Uriah Judah in 1856. "Without some kindred spirit to prevail in HARMONY with ours, of what avail
is life?" The statement was hardly representative, because the
word "sole" expressed an emphasis no longer tasteful; but it
reflected the general shift in appeal, from the old idea of
authority to the new idea of the love-force. There had been
given to each sex the propensity of love toward the other—
"that strong, delightful feeling," as Warren Burton said, "by
which they are drawn together and kept in pairs." And a very
serviceable chain had been made of it.

First link: the innocence of girlhood. "Its honor and
purity, its grace and happiness, constitute the inner sanctuary
of every family, and watchful pride of every brother, the father's
deepest stake in life's chances of good and evil, the mother's
burthen of prayer. And it is not alone," trailed off the eloquent
pen of Nathaniel Parker Willis, "that girlhood is, of all human
phases of existence, the loveliest and most like our imagina-

LADY BOUNTIFUL

Sara Payson Willis ("Fanny Fern"), *Fern Leaves from Fanny's Portfolio*, 1853; drawing by Fred. M. Coffin, illustrating a sketch entitled "The Little Pauper." "There seems to be happiness enough in the world, but it never comes to her. Her little basket is quite empty; and now, faint with hunger, she leans wearily against that shop window. There is a lovely lady who has just passed in. She is buying cakes and bon-bons for her little girl, as if she had the purse of Fortunatus. How nice it must be to be warm, and have enough to eat! Poor Meta! She has tasted nothing since she was sent forth with a curse in the morning to beg or steal; and the tears will come. There is happiness and plenty in the world, but none for Meta!

"Not so fast, little one! Warm hearts beat sometimes under silk and velvet. That lady has caught sight of your little woe-begone face and shivering form. O, what if it were her child! And, obeying a sweet maternal impulse, she passes out the door, takes those little benumbed fingers in her daintily gloved hands, and leads the child,—wondering, shy and bewildered,—into fairy land."

tions of life in heaven—the fairest to look upon and the most
rewarding to fondness and devotion. [Dividends!] There is a
deeper reason . . . the hallowed duties to which it is but the
novitiate, the type which it is to hand down. . . ."

And after the girl, the sweetheart:

> To the fond youth, when manhood's dawn appears,
> A vision mingles with his future years.
> A form, enrobed in soft, yet brilliant dyes,
> Flushes the near horizon of the skies;
> Dipped in the colors of his heart, he sees
> The fairy creature of his destinies.
> At length the sweet ideal of his mind
> To real woman turns, and reigns enshrined.

So conjured Alfred B. Street (*A Poem*, 1852). Next in the gallery comes "A bride, in the morning of her days; standing on
the threshold of a new existence; crowned like a queen with
the virgin coronal, soon to be laid aside, for ever; with the
uncertain future before her; repeating those solemn pledges,
and assuming those solemn responsibilities which belong not
to maidenhood; robed in the vestments of innocence, and giving her young, confiding heart, into the keeping of another;
seems to me a more touching spectacle"—Frederick Cozzens
concluded his tender appreciation—than a funeral.

Then "love makes its strength native and progressive,"
earth's cares fly away, joys double, susceptibilities are quickened; love masters self, and having made the mastery, stretches
"onward and upward toward infinitude." It is the Bachelor of
the *Reveries* who tells this; and an anonymous writer in a gift-
book for newlyweds, *The Marriage Offering*, proceeds, "The
only fountain, in the wilderness of life, where man drinks of
water totally unmixed with bitter ingredients, is that which
gushes for him in the calm and shady recess of domestic life."
Mrs. Stowe speaks to the nymph of that recess: "A woman must
be very insensible, who is not moved to come upon a higher
plane of being, herself, by seeing how undoubtedly she is
insphered in the heart of a good and noble man. A good man's
faith in you, fair lady . . . will make you better and nobler

even before you know it." Miss Fredrika Bremer contributes
the reminder that the married woman is her husband's domestic
faith; to her hands he must be able to entrust "the key of his
heart, as well as the key of his eating-room. His honor and his
home are in her keeping; his well-being is in her hand. Think
of this, O wife!"

And then the mother, guarding the infancy of immortal
souls. "While receiving sustenance from the breast, an attach-
ment is formed for the mother," said Lebbeus Armstrong,
"which uniformly proves to be the first ligament to bind man
to woman in the most tender and indissoluble affection." Put
the links together, and they make a garland and a chain. They
encircle the fifteen virtues appropriate to the sex (Elizabeth
Starling gave that number, in *The Noble Deeds of Woman,*
ranging from benevolence and loyalty to self-control and courage) , and they imply the moral responsibilities: woman's influence in the conjugal relation, "where it often has wrought
almost miracles of reformation, transforming the lion into the
lamb, the proud infidel into the meek and teachable disciple
of the cross" (as the Reverend J. F. Stearns told his congregation at Newburyport) — as mother, as sister, as daughter;
"indeed, few monsters are so hardened that the idea of an
amiable and affectionate daughter, yearning with all her youthful solicitude, over the happiness and reputation of a parent,
will not bring them to at least a momentary pause, and perhaps
lead to repentance and amendment of life."

It was woman's province, then, to be a pure and improving
adornment of social life; to be both a housewife and an Egeria,
and to take her full reward in contemplation of a successful
husband and spotless window-curtains. She needed very little
formal education to produce either result; and she had little.
She read much, but her reading was ephemeral literature which
congratulated her upon her limitations. Theodore Parker complained, "How dull it is to visit most of the ladies of the best

circle even in Boston! Their conversation turns upon subjects of no consequence, and they are discussed in a spirit and manner fully equal to the subject." But if their chief interest seemed to be in suckling small darlings and chronicling small beer, they were following the course of least resistance. The proper retort to Parker's complaint was Lydia Jenkin's article in *The Lily*: "That society thinks women capable only of revolving in a very limited circle, is shown by the general tenor of social conversation, and by writers—especially novel writers. Even men who claim the greatest liberality on the subject of women's rights and abilities, often contradict their avowed sentiments, by their general conversation. This *may* be the result of habit, still the effect is none the less crushing."

Women reached the self-assurance of feminism by intermediate steps—participation in other moral reforms, notably Temperance and antislavery. The church congregation, with its sociable interest in humanitarian causes, was the first training-ground; the next was the reform convention, where women were welcome to listen and where they slowly won the privilege of speaking. The first example was furnished by a British woman, Frances Wright, resident in the United States from 1825 to her death in 1853; she had radical views on theology, political equality, and woman's rights and expressed them in public lectures—this at a time when the first public examination of a girl in geometry, at Emma Willard's seminary in Troy, evoked a storm of ridicule which very nearly persuaded the New York legislature to discontinue its partial endowment of the school. In 1832 Lydia Maria Child published a *History of Woman,* a discreet volume, but offering American women their first manual on the distinctive history of their sex. In 1836 a Polish woman resident in New York, Ernestine L. Rose, circulated a memorial petitioning the New York Legislature to give married women the right to hold property in their own names; she obtained five signatures. But in the same year Angelina Grimké published an *Appeal to the Christian Women of the South* (urging that they exert moral suasion against slavery), and her sister Sarah Moore wrote a pamphlet of simi-

lar message, an *Epistle to the Clergy of the Southern States—*
women in politics!

These were tiny offenses to call down so loud a chorus of
rebuke from editors and clerics. But romantic flowers opened
quickly in the Thirties and Forties; and feminism, like antislavery, gained by the overwrought behavior of its opponents.
Samuel Young, addressing the Young Men's Association for
Mutual Improvement at Albany in 1837, opposed crude satire
—"whether it is expected that fleets and armies will ever be
officered and manned by women?"—with the soft answer:
"Women will never accept of any station which is repugnant to
the native modesty, and delicacy of the sex; and whenever the
ferocity of man shall become softened and humanized by a
proper infusion of female benevolence, wars will be impossible,
and fleets and hostile armies unnecessary." Within another year
hostility to their speaking in public (on antislavery) had made
feminists out of the Grimké sisters, and Sarah published *Letters on the Equality of the Sexes and the Condition of Woman.*
The emotional arguments that had induced the sisters to
manumit the slaves they had inherited at their father's death
were transferred to the new aspect of human equality; "the
page of history teems with woman's wrongs," Sarah wrote,
". . . is wet with woman's tears."

A "National Woman's Antislavery Convention" was held in
New York in 1837. The Grimké sisters in that year spoke
throughout Massachusetts in behalf of antislavery, and in the
next year Angelina addressed the House of Representatives
of that Commonwealth. "This quiet woman arose, utterly for-
getful of self," reported Lucy Stone; "with anointed lips, and
with eloquence rare and wonderful she pleaded. . . . The
curious forgot their curiosity; the mobocrat dropped his brickbat before the solemn earnestness of this woman. . . ." But
Angelina was married a few months later, and Sarah gave most
of her attention to school-teaching. For the next few years (to
quote Mrs. Stone [1] again) "Abby Kelley remained to bear

---

[1] Not "Miss" Stone. Lucy, the wife of Henry B. Blackwell, chose to retain her
maiden name as a mark of individuality, but she took the realistic form of prefix.

THE ORATOR OF THE DAY DENOUNCING THE LORDS OF CREATION

Harper's Weekly, 1859.

alone the opprobrium still heaped upon the woman who so far departed from her sphere as to speak in public. Whatever of tribulation any of us have known in the advocacy of this reform, it has been play compared with the long, unrelieved moral torture endured by Abby Kelley, in the battle which finally secured the right of free speech for every woman."

The relation of the feminist movement to the older crusade was again emphasized in 1840, at the World's Anti-Slavery Convention in London. Several women delegates elected by American societies were refused admittance to the floor. Mrs. Lucretia Mott, one of the rejected delegates, met Elizabeth Cady Stanton, wife of a delegate, at this time; here began that curiously intimate companionship which was a driving force in the American feminist movement for fifty years. "So entirely one are we," said Mrs. Stanton, "that . . . to the world we always seem to agree and uniformly reflect each other. Like husband and wife, each has the feeling that we must have no differences in public." Lucy Stone was arranging to be a lecturer for the Massachusetts Anti-Slavery Society at the time she made her first public speech on woman's rights, in 1847. Susan B. Anthony and Antoinette Louisa Brown entered the feminist movement by way of Temperance; each made her first speech in 1847, for that respectable agitation.

The first Woman's Rights Convention met at Rochester, New York, in 1848. The cause seemed unpromising then; but at the convention at Worcester, Massachusetts, in 1850 nine states were represented, and the leading Transcendentalists and progressive Unitarians publicly identified themselves with the cause. National feminist conventions were held almost annually during the Fifties, and local meetings were frequent. Samuel Young's sympathetic disclaimer in 1837—"That the breath of woman should be put into requisition to blow the flames of political discord, in its existing state of exasperation, is incompatible with the native modesty and dignity of the sex"—was junked by the ladies themselves in their first national convention, and thereafter organized feminism demanded full political equality. The Worcester convention resolved "That women are clearly entitled to the right of suffrage, and to be considered eligible to office; the omission to demand which, on her part, is a palpable recreancy to duty, and a denial of which is a gross usurpation on the part of man, no longer to be endured." Two years later, at the national convention in Syracuse, that tone had mounted to the strident note of Elizabeth Jones' "Men may sooner arrest the progress of the lightning, or the clouds, or stay the waves of the sea, than the onward march of Truth with her hand on the sword and her banner unfurled. I am not in the habit of talking much about rights; I am one of those who take them. . . . The right to vote. That includes all other rights. I want to go to the Legislative Hall, sit on the Judicial Bench, and fill the Executive Chair. Now do you understand me?"

Women had already gained extensions of the right to work —and not by eloquent, untactful avowals of their natural privileges, but by accepting the casual favors of the economic shift. Harriet Martineau, visiting the United States in the mid-Thirties, listed four occupations (the full list) that she found open to women: they could teach, make hats or clothing, work as domestic help or in the factory. The increase in factory production of textiles meant an increase in the number of working women; in 1845 the textile mills were employing 75,710 women (and 55,828 men). A catalogue of that year lists women workers in a great variety of industrial occupations—as makers of gloves, glue, gold and silver leaf, snuff and cigars, trusses, harness; as laundresses, stereotypers, leechers, and soda-room keepers. The census of 1850 places 61,500 women (and 35,061 men) as makers of men's and boy's clothing, and it notices the predominance of women in a new industry, the manufacture of rubber articles.

A stray paragraph in the *Nebraska Palladium* (Bellevue), October 31, 1854, declares that "the number of females at present holding office of Post Master is 128." (One of the by-skirmishes of the feminist movement was the campaign against that word "female," begun by Mrs. Sarah J. Hale in the columns of *Godey's* in 1855.) The *Palladium* reported that "Unmarried females only can hold the office of Post Master"; the interesting circumstance was that they received the same compensation as men. No other occupation showed such equality in the wage-scale.

Godey's began in 1852 to carry paragraphs under the heading, "Employment of Women," recording the latest entrances of the sex into the commercial world. The magazine itself was largely staffed by women, in the editorial chambers and the press-rooms. Type-setting, by the middle Fifties, seemed likely to become exclusively a women's job.

The Philadelphia department stores, in about 1850, were first to employ girls as clerks; and Amelia Bloomer, while traveling in 1853, discovered another innovation that was to cut a wide swath. "Stopping over night at the Delavan House in Albany," she wrote, "we were very agreeably surprised on entering the dining-room for supper to see about a dozen young women in attendance on the tables. This was something new. When we visited the house last winter the waiters were all men, as is usual in such places. Now not a man was to be seen in that capacity; but in place of their heavy tread, and awkward motions, was woman's light footfall and easy, graceful movements. In a conversation with the proprietor we learned that the change was made in May . . . entirely satisfactory . . . the only objectors being a few women . . . preferring black men."

As public schools were opened in the new towns of the West and elementary schools multiplied in the Eastern states to take care of the new demand for common education, women captured most of the jobs. The full-born emergence of the lady poet and the lady novelist from the foam of Romanticism has been noticed; in a lovelier metaphor, as Wendell Phillips put it, "Woman has touched the wand of literature with her enchantment, and it rises to her level, until woman has become author as well as reader. And what is the result? We do not have to expurgate the literature of the nineteenth century before placing it in the hands of our youth."

The rise of the lady journalist was another gain of the generation. Mrs. Ann Stephens, who became literary critic and editorial writer of the *New York Evening Express* in 1837, was the first woman of the nineteenth century to hold either of those positions on a metropolitan newspaper. She was on the *Express* staff for thirty years; and when, in 1857, she turned over the literary criticism to Mrs. Elizabeth F. Ellet (authoress of *The Women of the American Revolution*), lady journalists and lady editors were not novelties. Mrs. Sarah Jane Clarke Lippincott (as "Grace Greenwood") and Lydia Maria Child had become distinguished by their sprightly, capable work as newspaper correspondents and editors. Miss Cornelia Wells Walter was writing solid, readable editorials for the *Boston Transcript,* while Margaret Fuller was doing literary criticism for the *Tribune* of a quality which vied with Greeley's editorials. Mrs. Sarah J. Hale, who had established the first of the ladies' magazines, in Boston in 1827, had moved to Philadelphia to enter an association with Louis Antoine Godey which left the editorial management of the *Lady's Book* practically in her hands.

Jane Grey Swisshelm began the *Pittsburgh Saturday Visiter* in 1848, writing crisp editorials as unique and strong-minded as her spelling; and in the next year Amelia Bloomer published the first numbers of her delightful *Lily,* a journal which began with Temperance, advanced to a sturdy and sometimes dizzy feminism ("Woman," wrote Dinah Taylor in an 1853 issue, "is the great and grand Archimedian lever, whose fulcrum is childhood, whose weight the world, whose length is all time, whose sweep is vast and endless eternity"), and reached its apotheosis with the campaign for dress-reform. Rebecca Sanford's *True Kindred,* begun at Akron in 1848; *The Una,* published by Paulina Wright Davis and Mrs. Caroline H. Dall, which was commenced at Providence in 1853 and dedicated throughout its short and starved life almost entirely to the suffragist cause; and Mrs. Anna McDowell's *The Woman*

Advocate, founded in 1855, fill out the list of feminist journals. These little magazines did not have literary contributions or moral support from the prominent lady novelists and lady poets. Accolades and antislavery, profitable adulation and avowed feminism, did not go together. Thomas Wentworth Higginson, addressing the National Woman's Rights Convention at New York in 1857, hammered the point: "The first obstacle . . . is the feminine. I feel a sense of shame for Ameri-

THE FEMALE GENIUS

"The celebrated Mrs. M. E. Southworth Braddon Cobb, engaged in writing her last new sensation novel, to contain 25 elopements, 43 separations from 'bed and board,' and 742 divorces for neglect, abandonment, etc., etc., etc." *Yankee Notions,* 1866.

can literature, when I think how our literary women shrink, and cringe, and apologize, and dodge, to avoid being taken for 'strong-minded women.'"

The learned professions remained practically a monopoly of the other sex. Yet a story by Mrs. Joseph Hanaford, in the *Family Keepsake* for 1856, contains a portentous hope: "Thank you, Caroline," says the young lady, "for permitting me to continue my studies, undisturbed, so long [Caroline had been reading Mrs. Hemans]. I love mathematics, and I hope to become celebrated some day for my scientific abilities. I wish to have my name inscribed in fadeless characters on the high list of those 'that were not born to die.' I have an ardent ambition to be known among the wise and learned whose works are now regarded by me and others with profound respect." Caroline, pursuing the Muse, was on the better path toward having her name in fadeless characters; her room-mate was riding for a fall. One young lady, Maria Mitchell, discovered a comet in 1847; the recognition she won, augmented by her later researches, was an aspiration of many women, ambition-heartening and a little pathetic.

From the Sixteen Forties, when Mistress Margaret Brent was colonial attorney for Cecilius Calvert, the Lord Proprietor of Maryland, until Arabella Mansfield was admitted to the bar of Iowa in 1869, there were no lady barristers within these shores. The medical fraternity almost unanimously opposed the attempts of women to qualify for general practice. Antoinette Louisa Brown, "beautiful, intellectual, and very religious," entered Oberlin College in 1845 and was graduated from the Ladies' Literary Course; then, to the consternation of the faculty, she elected to remain and take the theological course. All Oberlin's opportunities were open to women—so declared the charter of the College. And Antoinette, with one other of her sex (Lettice Smith, who never preached), studied with the gentlemen; but when the Theological Class of 1850 had its commencement, the two ladies were allowed to be present only as spectators, not to receive degrees. In 1853 Miss Brown was called and ordained by a Congregational church in rural New York; in her generation she was the unique exception. This ordination was the work of a single congregation. The Universalist Church was first to admit women to full fellowship; Olympia Brown, admitted to St. Lawrence University in 1860, was the pioneering lady.

The feminist movement scored a mite of success in the slow work of humanizing the law. A Vermont statute in 1847 secured to the wife the real estate owned by her at the time of marriage or acquired by gift or bequest afterward; but the husband's consent remained necessary for sale or conveyance. New York State in 1848 granted women equal property rights without reservation. No palpable gains were made elsewhere, unless a loosening of the divorce laws in Massachusetts—for which women lobbied earnestly—may be counted. A feminist parallel to Thoreau's campaign of civil disobedience was provided by Miss Harriot K. Hunt of Boston, who annually protested the tax-levy she had to pay. Her protest to the city authorities "and to the citizens generally" in 1853 was typical —a logical, eloquent statement: "No reasonable or satisfactory answer has ever been given to woman on this subject, only that *man* represented her, through fathers, husbands, brothers, and sons. Your remonstrant had no such *representation,* and there are many in like situation, 'State, county, and city tax'; the former the expense of the constitutional convention in which she had no voice (but petition), and how farcical that power of petition, when she can neither express *assent* nor *dissent* to its doings, but be unjustly taxed, and like an idiot, lunatic, or infant, be *compelled* to meet it. . . . Your remonstrant pays her taxes *compulsorily,* instead of *cheerfully,* feeling within *her* that element of patriotism which inspired *her* as well as *your* forefathers, in the utterance of that deep, full and clear sentiment, 'Taxation without *representation* is tyranny.' This is respectfully submitted."

The Bloomer dress, a loose-fitting costume introduced in 1851, had a five years' notoriety. The philosophy of dress-reform was expressed by Gerrit Smith: "Only let woman attire her person fitly for the whole battle of life—that great and often rough battle, which she is as much bound to fight as man is, and all the common sense implied in the change will put to flight all the nonsensical fancies about her inferiority to man." But it didn't work out so. Street gamins had a lively sense of the ludicrous, and most people had devout if erratic regard for propriety in dress. It may be noticed that in Boston the Bloomer dress was emphatically shunned, because a woman of ill repute was first to wear it in that capital. Fear of becoming identified in any manner with the hussies restrained many women from uttering their private sympathy with the feminist movement. The fact that a notorious abortionist of New York, Madame Restell, advertised herself as a "woman's physician" as much as any other factor deterred women from the study of medicine. Says Mr. Ellwide, the Broadway merchant, to his partner Mr. Promptcash, in Mrs. Sidney Bateman's comedy *Self* (1856), "Oh, by the way! that embroidered velvet must be sold at once, or shipped to California. We shall lose by that investment. It's growing vulgar to wear such high-priced goods, since the sporting gentry began buying them for their wives."

There is no orderly progression to the feminine emancipation; all the phases seem coexistent. At almost the same time that Mrs. Elizabeth Wilson, in Cadiz, Ohio, was writing *A Scriptural View of Woman's Rights and Duties* to prove that the Bible really didn't set its seal on woman's inferiority, "James the Barber" in Seneca Falls, New York, was catering to women who wanted their hair bobbed (they called it "shingling"). While ladies anxious to appear palely spiritual were bleaching their complexions by drinking vinegar, Elizabeth Cady Stanton was urging the duty of all young ladies to pay for their own amusements instead of imposing the tax on their young men. And it is possible that a future historian will find the beginnings of the gynecocracy in the early Eighteen Fifties, when an unprecedented volume of clothes-buying and geegaw-buying was evidence that the wives of upper middle-class families were claiming the greater share of the purchasing-power. That the word "lingerie" was introduced in 1852 and quickly supplanted the humbler phrases—"white work," "white sewing," and "the under wardrobe"—is one of those little clues which point to important social changes.

For all the attention to "the Rights and Sphere of Woman," marriage remained her chief business and home her emotional focus. The generation which on the one extreme produced Andrew Jackson Davis' statement, "Divorces are natural until

BLOOMER FASHIONS

Peterson's Magazine, 1851. This was one of the very few fashion-plates with which the popular magazines dignified the new style. The specifications were as follows:

"BLOOMER EVENING DRESS.—Pantelettes of white satin; short, full skirt of pink silk, embroidered at the bottom. Corsage tight, open half way to the waist in front, over a worked chemisette. Loose sleeves, with white under-sleeves. White or pink satin boots.

"BLOOMER WALKING DRESS. — Full Turkish pantelettes of Mazarine blue silk, ruffled. Short, full skirt of blue silk, the same color as the pantelettes. Marseilles vest, open half way to the waist over a plaited linen bosom; small collar turned over. An over-dress of embroidered silk, high at the back, but open all the way in front, so as to show the vest. Loose sleeves, with full white under-sleeves. Hat of gray beaver with a rich plume."

the harmonial plane is reached," as well as John Murray Spear's doctrine of spiritual counterparts, also invented that practical and absurd device, the matrimonial bureau. (The advertisement of the Caroline Fry Marriage Association, "the best and oldest," in the *Tribune* in 1852, offered "CHEAP WIVES for poor and deserving young men . . . particular attention paid to the proper matching of temperaments.")

Instructive books, "convenient subsidia of improved education," were a curiously important element in the domestic life. The generation's abundant supply of guides for the proper conduct of the marital and appetitive affairs represented the quick polishing-up that young wives and benedicts needed; their amazing sales suggest how decorous and misty the premarital education of women must have been.

Birth-control found its way into print. Robert Dale Owen's *Moral Physiology,* first published in December, 1830, the pioneer book on the subject in the United States, went through a number of regular and pirated editions; probably twenty-five thousand copies were sold, despite that all respectable newspapers and journals refused to carry its advertisements. The most noteworthy successor was H. C. Wright's *The Unwelcomed Child; or, the Crime of an Undesigned and Undesired Maternity* (1858). Of similar quasi-frankness were Dr. R. T. Trall's *Marriage and Parenthood* and his *Home Treatment of Sexual Abuses.* A wonderful book translated from the French by Dr. William Jackson of Boston, *Woman: her Health, Beauty, and Intellect, preserved from premature Decline*—demonstrating that solitary vices lead to gangrenes, rickets, cramps, cankers, nervous afflictions, scrofula, insanity, indigestion, and pulmonary consumption, was Americanized into such evasive generalizations that an uninformed person could read all 304 pages without having a glimmer of what the book was about. By the close of the Fifties this interest had strayed into the near-pornographic, and in the late spring of 1859 a New

York house published a translation of Michelet's *Love,* comparable in its ecstatic descriptions to the writings of Ellen Key in our own century. It was the first book of its kind in the United States, and within four months it reached its fourteenth edition. Whither this interest tended was shown in the publication that August of a hastily assembled miscellany, "the whole forming a remarkable Text-Book for all Lovers, as well as a complete guide to Matrimony. By Theocritus, Jr."

Eliza Leslie, Lydia Maria Child, and Catherine Beecher very nearly established a tradition that the first duty of a literary lady was to present her generation with a cook-book. Of the editions of Miss Leslie's *Seventy-Five Receipts, More Receipts,* and *New Receipt Book* there was no end; twenty editions were printed of her *Lady's House-Book,* containing "approved directions" for washing, quilting, making fires, evening parties, straw bonnets, various kitchen duties and parlor diversions.

William Andrus Alcott and Orson Squire Fowler were master producers of household manuals. Alcott, the author of at least eighty-five volumes for home, school, and Sunday School, published *The House I Live in; or, The Human Body,* in 1836; this handbook of physiology was followed early in 1837 by *Ways of Living on Small Means*—which offered advice on housing, the hire of domestics, speed of eating, household medicines, "gadding," and a hundred other details, and the *"Young"* books followed in quick succession. *The Young Woman's Guide to Excellence* appeared late in 1839; in its second edition, dated 1840, the publisher listed Alcott's other works under his imprint, all "standard family books," with copies supplied "in extra style for presents": *The Young Husband,* then in its fifth edition; *The Young Wife,* in its ninth; *The Young Housekeeper,* fourth edition; and *The Young Mother,* ninth. *The Young Husband* had passed its twentieth edition and Alcott's *The Physiology of Marriage* was in its fifteenth when the prolific writer published the volume which became the model "doctor-book" of the American family, *The Home Book of Life and Health* (1856).

Orson Squire Fowler's two volumes, *Love and Parentage, applied to the Improvement of Offspring,* "including Important Directions and Suggestions to Lovers and the Married concerning the Strongest Ties and the Most Momentous Relations of Life," and *Amativeness; or, Evils and Remedies of Excessive and Perverted Sexuality,* "including Warning and Advice to the Married and Single," had both reached a fortieth edition by 1844. (But it was Alcott's *Young Husband* which contained the priceless pearl, this advice on indulging the

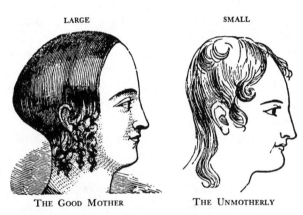

LARGE   SMALL

THE GOOD MOTHER   THE UNMOTHERLY

THE BUMP OF PHILOPROGENITIVENESS

Orson Squire Fowler, *New Self-Instructor in Phrenology and Physiology,* 1859.

whims of a wife: "The intelligent husband, while he will not believe in those singularly terrific consequences, which are supposed by the vulgar to follow from an ungratified appetite, however improper and irrational it may be, will never treat these wayward feelings with unkindness.") In 1846 Fowler published *Matrimony; or, Phrenology and Physiology applied to the Selection of Congenial Companions for Life,* notable both for its excellent sale and the motto on the title-page: "Natural waists or no wives."

Supplementing this abundance of domestic advice were numbers of guide-books on the social graces, introducing the middle class to the art of etiquette. Elias Howe's *Ball-Room*

Hand Book, for one, followed the festive couple from carriage to polka and on to the parting speeches. The matter, for instance, of requesting a lady to dance: "You stand at a proper distance, bend the body gracefully, accompanied by a slight motion of the right hand in front, you look at her with complaisance, and respectfully say, will you do me the honor to dance with me, or shall I have the pleasure of dancing with you, will you be pleased, or will you favor me with your hand for this or the next dance, remaining in the position you have assumed, until the lady signifies her intention by saying, with pleasure, sir, or I regret to say I am engaged, sir, you may then request to see her card, or to be pleased to name the dance for which she is not engaged, and after having made the necessary arrangements you politely bow, and withdraw."

In the late Thirties it was yet necessary to protect the art from the charge that it was undemocratic; and *A Manual of Politeness for Both Sexes* (1837) hastened to state that "Agreeableness of forms is one of the most essential elements of a placid and happy life . . . the habit of delicate sensations tends to give additional refinement to delicacy, while vivacity of imagination and sensibility are improved by it," before it discussed such matters as the stages of the curtsey and the behavior of ladylike knees ("To cross them one over the other, and to embrace them with the hands joined, is deemed vulgar"). *True Politeness; a Handbook of Etiquette for Ladies,* published a decade later, reflected the growing concern with the moral affinities of good manners; it gave warning that *double entendre* was detestable in a woman, "especially when perpetrated in the presence of men"; that a lady should pretend not to understand any indelicate expressions which might be uttered in her presence; that "it is, in general, bad taste for ladies to kiss each other in the presence of gentlemen with whom they are but slightly acquainted"; and topped off the subject with the excellent advice, "Never sing more than one or two songs consecutively."

CHAPTER EIGHT

The Temperance Family

*H*AYDEE is the heroine of a Temperance story; she rests, now, among the brittle pages of Amelia Bloomer's *Lily*. She was wooed and won by a rising young merchant, Charles Dudley. He loved his bride "to mad idolatry," and many happy hours they passed with fond smiles and soft words. (The beautiful bride was named Haydee because the authoress loved her Byron and was shaky in her spelling. *Don Juan* evoked a delectable sensation of mingled pleasure and shock which remained fresh through long familiarity. Literary aspirants kept the third and fourth cantos of Byron's epic close by, as Washington Irving kept his Stilton cheese, to nibble ever and anon.)

Little did Haydee dream of the foe hovering in her path of marital bliss. One night Mr. Dudley, having been in the company of a false friend, returned home intoxicated. But when he saw the tear-stained cheeks of his young wife, he became contrite. "Haydee," he announced, "I have this night revelled too freely in the wine-cup, and am fevered and excited, but no more shall my lips be polluted with the filthy drug." What price a promise, against the adder lurking in the lees! Months passed, and Haydee became aware that his erstwhile fondness had changed to estrangement. "As time divulges all things, so it brought to light the cause of Charles' actions towards his wife. The serpent of the still had charmed him!"

Then to her innocent babe Haydee turned for consolation. But the little one, exposed to the stern necessities of Temperance fiction, sickened and died. The broken-hearted mother drooped away, and in two weeks she rested by the side of her child. Charles Dudley was in a groggery when his wife breathed her last. Too late he awoke to his loss. Then, in the last paragraph, he vowed over the new-made grave that he would forsake the cursed bowl and live to Haydee's memory. "And well did he keep that vow. He now rests beside her in his last sleep."

Read, and weep. Let the tears glow unashamed, like diamonds on the cheek. Let deliquescent melancholy—treasurable emotion—implant in the heart the beauties of Temperance. . . .

The value of "story" was formally recognized by the captains of the anti-rum army in 1836. Setting one of the final seals on the respectability of imaginative prose, they decided to dip their pellets of education into sugar. Temperance annuals and gift-books soon became a stock item in the book-shops. Every one of the generation's "family magazines" used Temperance stories and poems, often by their star writers. Specialized journals appeared in due course, "executed in the finest style of Mechanical Art, and replete with the elevating, the refining, the purifying elements of Temperance."

The publishers of Temperance leaflets curtailed the printing of even such classic exhortations as Lyman Beecher's *Six Sermons,* and narrative homilies of the type written by Theodore Ledyard Cuyler—*Somebody's Son* and *Somebody's Daughter*—became characteristic propaganda. Lucius Manlius Sargent's Temperance stories, the first three of which appeared in 1835, were enormously popular; within the next quarter-century no other items of Temperance literature were reprinted as often or circulated as widely. All twenty-one of Sargent's tales were published in a single volume in 1851, with a worthy preface: "The perusal of some of these narratives is well known to have turned the hearts of many persons of intemperate habits, from drunkenness and sloth, to temperance and industry. Many years have passed since their first publication, in separate numbers. It may not be uninteresting to the children of parents, once intemperate, to cast their eyes upon these pages, whose influence, under the blessing of Heaven, has preserved them from a miserable orphanage."

Even the theater, that old bane of the Puritans, lent its gas-lit charms to the crusade. Timothy Shay Arthur's *Ten Nights in a Bar-Room* was adapted for the stage soon after its appearance as a novel and became a minor classic. *Little Katy; or, The Hot Corn Girl,* a successful play of 1854, was typical of the genre. The curtain rose upon a home of affluence and comfort, glycerined in a felicity of moral apothegms and obtrusive affections. Then, in successive scenes, the husband slipped on the peel of intemperance, gambled, committed forgery, and was nabbed. The wife, toiling at the needle, sought strength for her labor by tippling rum—with disastrous effects to her maternal sensibilities. Little Katy was driven forth, bruised and weeping, to sell "hot corn" on the streets, and caught her death of pneumonia.

The Drunkard; or, The Fallen Saved, was in its day the most beloved of the Temperance plays. Mr. Greeley's *Tribune* was moved to prophesy that Utopia was just around the corner when *The Drunkard* was appearing simultaneously in four New York theaters, accumulating a record of hundreds of performances. It followed the due sequence—"the degradation of himself and vileness of associates, loss of time, etc.," as the program summarized, to the protagonist's delirious despair and the brink of suicide. Thence, however, the play shifted toward a happy ending; and the fifth act offered, according to the program, "his restoration to society and sobriety by the aid of a Temperance philanthropist." *The Drunkard's* first New York showing was in the Lecture Room of Phineas Taylor Barnum's Museum; and it was but proper that the actor portraying the "Temperance philanthropist" bore an unmistakable resemblance to that great and good man, the exhibitor of the Fiji Mermaid.

The reformers' overture to "products of the fancy" was perhaps the least of three circumstances in 1836 that announced a distinctive epoch in the Temperance movement. The second was the devising of a sturdy international organization. Delegates from societies in nineteen states and in Canada organized the American Temperance Union, to be a mother-bird to all the fledgling locals in North America. The convention met, appropriately, at Saratoga Springs, where the salubrious fountains of nature gave point to the lecturers' praises of cold water; and here it was that all distinctions between distilled spirits and other beverages were rabidly sloughed. It was proposed that the phrase "ardent spirits" be scratched from the Pledge and the inclusive prohibition, "intoxicating liquors," be written in. Delegates who saw little evil in the moderate use of unfortified wine or unneedled beer were out-talked and outvoted.

The action of the convention did not settle the issue; the local societies had to be drummed into line. The victory was not easy. Dr. Benjamin Rush, who wore the mantle of leadership in the Temperance cause from Revolutionary times until his death in 1813, had recommended the temperate use of fermented and malt liquors as a corrective of grosser habits; and many disciples of the Doctor held high place in Temperance societies in 1836. They made up in literateness what they lacked in numbers. For a time the salvationist labors of the Temperance men were all but suspended while the brethren wrote pamphlets on the merits or evils of the grape. The Bible was lugged into the argument: whether or no the miraculous wine that graced the wedding-feast at Cana of Galilee was unfermented, and whether the tonic that the Apostle Paul recommended to Timothy for his stomach's coddling possessed an alcoholic content, were matters discussed with such a great show of learning as to leave the conscientious scholar bewildered and saddened. The teetotalers gained a notable victory when President Eliphalet Nott of Union College, whose published lectures expressed the belief that the Scriptures approved the use of "slightly" fermented wine, quailed under the lances of controversy and agreed that the Bible placed all fermented liquors under the ban. The moderate reformers were assaulted from another sector by Edward Cornelius Delavan, a retired merchant of Albany, who was the first philanthropist on record to have rolled out the wine-casks from his own cellar, broken in the bulkheads, and let the aromatic stuff flow into the gutter. Delavan, who had been a connoisseur of wines in his time, now assembled a remarkable *exposé* of shady practices in the business, to demonstrate that there was no such thing as a good, pure wine in the stock of trade.

The choicest items in his pamphlet, *Adulterations of Liquors,* were, for all Delavan's experience, hearsay. A friend had purchased a bottle of "genuine Champaigne" of a New York importer and found the bottle to contain *"one quarter of an ounce of sugar of lead."* Delavan "had been assured" that after whisky was diluted for commercial purposes, arsenic was used to restore the bead. The Reverend Thomas P. Hunt furnished a dreadful account: during a series of lectures in Philadelphia he induced a manufacturer of liquors to abandon the trade. The convert informed the lecturer that the "nutty" flavor of Madeira was produced by the immersion of a bag of cockroaches until the insects were dissolved in the liquor. Mr. Hunt had since been "informed by several" that this was no uncommon practice. "I would give you the name of the person who gave the receipt for using cockroaches, but he gave it in confidence, and is now occupying a much more moral and useful station than that of poisoning his customers."

The outcome of the agitation was that the Temperance movement as a whole became thoroughly committed to the principle of total abstinence. It was a demand upon the individual that he be noble, denying himself the mild comfort of the simple fermented beverages to set a good example for his spirit-tippling contemporaries. It offered the spiritual pleasures of a tiny martyrdom, and it was further attractive in that it incorporated the prevalent fiction of the First False Step.

The axiom was firmly established that great appetites from small drams grow, that the moderate drinker of today is the drunkard of tomorrow. The Reverend Charles Giles stated in November, 1835, that 56,000 people were annually destroyed by drink in the United States alone; "500,000 drunkards are now living in our blessed America, all moving onward to the dreadful verge. What a scene of immolation!" Science, of a sort, reinforced the dismal picture. President Nott assured his students in 1838 that cases of the death of drunkards by internal fires, kindled often spontaneously by fumes of alcohol which escaped through the pores of the skin, were so numerous and incontrovertible "that I presume no person of information will be found to call the reality of their existence into question."

The *New York Times,* on January 9, 1836, reported an experiment made at Berwick, Maine, by a student of medicine, on the blood of a common drunkard. The sot had kept to a rum diet for some five days; the student remarked that the drunkard's blood was so much encumbered with alcohol that it constituted a fire-hazard. The sot asked to be bled, for proof. "A bowl containing this blood was handed to one of the spectators who lighted a match, and on bringing it into contact with the contents of the bowl, a conflagration ensued, burning with a blue flame for a space of twenty-five or thirty minutes."

Mrs. Bloomer exclaimed in her magazine for April, 1850, over the fatal results of a swilling-bout between two yokels at Auburn, New York. "Another murder has been perpetrated! Another added to the countless throng who yearly rush unprepared into the presence of their Maker! Another slain to glut a fiendish thirst for gain!" The contestants had downed, rapidly, three pints of Irish whisky each, when the defending champion had suddenly fallen to the floor and expired. Mrs. Bloomer expressed her sympathy for his mother and sister, "for we know they mourn as those who have no hope."

Fear was one of the busiest weapons in the arsenal of Prohibition, but it was not the only one. And the movement received its share of the diathermic impulses that played through this sunny era. The crusaders had few doubts of the issue and enjoyed many moments of happy confidence in a beverageless millennium. "Many are rejoicing," wrote the Reverend Orin Fowler in 1835, "in the lively hope that the day is nigh, even at the doors, when drunkenness with her burning legion of evils will cease from the earth; and the gospel of the

THE DRAM-DRINKER

The New-York Organ, 1849. "The miserable creature who forms the prominent object is true to the life. Observe the clutch of the hand, and the sucking action of the mouth, as he takes his dram — how he enjoys it, and prolongs the pleasure by taking it slowly, projecting his under jaw and lip to prevent a drop from falling. His apparel betrays the loafer, and the crape on his old hat, probably indicates that his wife is dead, from want perhaps, or it may be from a broken-heart!

"The child stretching its little arm to reach the bar with the empty bottle, is clad in its mother's bonnet and shawl, because it has none of its own. Degraded parents are waiting for the child's return with the maddening fluid, to plunge again into drunkenness. Desolate must be that home, dreadful the examples amid which this poor child is doomed to grow up. How can it escape degradation?

"And who is this officiating as the minister of death? A young woman! By a refinement of diabolical art and wickedness, woman, whom God gave to be a help meet, a refiner and purifier, is stationed here, like sin at the gate of death, to mix the cup of troubling, and hold it to the lips of visitors. How her own heart is hardened. No remorse or shame is on her countenance, even while she doles out to this poor child of her own sex, that which is to destroy its parents and blast all its hopes! O, is not this a scene over which even angels might weep, if there were tears in heaven!"

grace of God will have free course and be glorified, and the whole family of man become temperate, holy, and happy." He expected to see that day.

In this golden age poetry would be irrevocably divorced from its corrupt alliance with alcohol.

The young littérateur met a tradition which blandly permitted him to assume a connection between having a piece printed in the *Knickerbocker* and having a friendly nip with his fellows or his Muse. Thomas Moore could not write until he was warmed with punch; Byron composed with gin and water by his side; Barry Cornwall made no rhymes without his bottle of sherry. . . . So long, perceived the wiser Philistines, as poets decked the amphora and the drinking-horn with metrical laurels, would there be romance and charm about the social glass. The editor of *The Young American's Magazine* was one who set about smashing the tradition; by way of showing the flair which cold water could inspire, he replied in kind:

> It is said that Byron wrote
>   Under GIN exhilaration.
> Grant he did; does that promote,
>   Reptile spirit, thy salvation?
> Does there not remain the proof
>   That the Muse, if he had sought her,
> Would have bid him stand aloof,
>   After quaffing Albion water?
> Did he try the other side?
>   He has not professed it, hath he?
> No one says he ever tried,
>   Ever heard of Hydropathy.

This theme of lyrical regenerativeness in the Temperance movement was strikingly expressed in the Washingtonian crusade. The crusade flared up in 1840 and blazed for five years. The lava of evangelism surged over the solid rock of education; the volcanic orgy spewed a fire of repentance and salvation. Like all literal or vicarious camp-meeting revivals, it burned itself out; but, also like them all, it played high jinks with body and soul while it lasted. A grave concern, rooted in the national Protestantism, over the manners and morals of one's neighbors runs through every phase of the Temperance movement; the presence of this social militance is obvious and inescapable. But it was the distinguishing privilege of the Washingtonian Temperance societies to add another religious element—regeneration through confession.

On an evening in 1840 six convivial friends—artisans by day, tipplers and gamesters by night—sat about a table in Chase's Tavern at Baltimore. A trifling incident, the report of the arguments being advanced by a Temperance lecturer in a near-by hall, served as the spark. The lassitude of gentlemen who had been places and seen things was transmuted into an ardent pledge of personal purity and a zeal for promulgating their just-adopted creed. The name of Washington was chosen for the infant society. Parson Weems, other biographers, and hordes of school-teachers had already calcimined the hearty, human Washington into a paragon of manly, and priggish, virtues. The harried ghost of the First President was, thus innocently, invoked to become the spiritual father of a total-abstinence society. The ghost's pride was broken; and within the next decade the saddened wraith suffered himself to be hailed like an errand-boy by scores of Spiritualist mediums.

The charter society entered upon its bloom when President William K. Mitchell suggested that the meetings be given over to the narration of personal experiences by men whom the Pledge had pulled from the gutter. These "experience meetings," first-person narratives of dreadful degeneracy and joyous redemption, touched off obscure fellows with inspired oratory, caught the interest of thousands who could not be reached by educational addresses or didactic fiction, and carried the torch of Temperance at the head of an ecstatic procession of inebriates. It was a reformation of drunkards by drunkards; grounded in the Sentimental tradition as it was, it became a national epidemic.

A delegation of five Baltimoreans introduced the ways of the tabernacle to New York. On upturned rum-kegs the speakers related their own grapplings with the serpent. After the series of eighteen meetings, eighteen hundred penitents had pledged themselves to total abstinence, and a local Washingtonian Temperance Society was girded to carry on the work. In Boston, later in the season of 1841, John Hawkins, advertised as "more than twenty years a confirmed inebriate," took sure possession of his audiences. Into the rest of the country organizers brought the heated methods of the Washingtonians. Within three years five hundred thousand intemperate drinkers and one hundred thousand habitual drunkards, if the societies' own statistics do not exaggerate unduly, attested on Washingtonian cards that they had been reclaimed and made pure. "The drunkard found himself an object of interest," related a convert, touching the pulse of the movement. "A few leaders in the ranks of intemperance having signed the Pledge, it appeared to be a signal for the mass to follow; and on they came, like a torrent sweeping everything before it. It was for weeks the all-absorbing topic."

A closely knit organization, the Sons of Temperance, was founded by foresighted leaders to consolidate their gains before the Washingtonian spirit waned. The sixteen founders, in convention at Teetotalers' Hall, New York, late in 1842, declared the objects of the order to be protection of its members from intemperance, elevation of their characters, and mutual aid in case of sickness. The Sons of Temperance was financed by an initiation fee and by dues; it offered the sickness and death benefits of a fraternal lodge; and it borrowed a few ceremonies from the Odd Fellows and the Masons to provide the essential trumpery. Until the late Fifties the order flourished. In 1850 it boasted nearly six thousand local units, embracing two hundred and fifty thousand paid-up members. It had the benefit of a sturdily woven hierarchy, the clannishness of the "fraternal spirit"; and, offering the first answer to the objection that without the saloon artisans had no place of informal social assembly, the order made its meeting-halls "pleasant places of resort and social intercourse." In behalf of the American Temperance Union the veteran John Marsh led an opposition to the Sons of Temperance because the newer society had a few secret grips and wouldn't admit outsiders to its meetings. But the anti-Masonic agitation had receded too far into the past to be capitalized a quarter-century after William Morgan's body had been washed ashore.

The Temple of Honor was founded in New York in 1845 —a blend of Temperance society and Protestant fraternity. The Temple, explained Mr. William L. Stacy, who became Most Worthy Templar of the National Temple in 1849 (and was also Most Worthy Associate of the Cadets of Temperance, Grand Worthy Patriarch of the Sons of Temperance for the State of Massachusetts, President of the Boston Parent Washingtonian Society, and high in the councils of various benevolent lodges), embraced "all that is excellent in older associations with additional advantages." It practised "unceasing and universal abstinence"; no person was admitted who did not acknowledge the existence of God; there were passwords and dazzling regalia. The growth of the order was most extensive in the plantation regions of the South.

Another Temperance secret society, the Independent Order of Rechabites, was introduced into the United States from England in 1842 and garnered a hundred thousand American members. There arose also the Independent Order of Good Samaritans and the Daughters of Samaria, the Daughters of Temperance (not to be confused with a later organization named the Original Daughters of Temperance!), the Independent Order of Good Templars, and several other associations of abstemious ladies and gentlemen—however diverse the orders, departments, and banners, all the members belonging to *one great Temperance family.* The italicized phrase is the property of the Reverend Lebbeus Armstrong, author of a devotional history, *The Temperance Reformation* (1852). His impressions were somewhat rose-tinted.

Father Theobald Mathew could have testified that all was not dulcet in the one great Temperance family. He came to the United States in 1849, after enormous success as a total-abstinence crusader in Ireland. He was a Catholic, and therefore, in the Know-Nothing view, a menace. He had, eight years previously, signed an address drafted by Daniel O'Connell urging the Irish in America to support the antislavery movement; this fact, brought to light in 1849, amounted to a gross indiscretion. Jefferson Davis and seventeen of his Southern colleagues voted against a Senate resolution requesting Father Mathew to visit the legislative body. "Dissenters" (as the priest called them in his journal) in considerable numbers attended the services where he followed the celebration of the Mass with a plea for Temperance. He was not squeamish about appearing in public under Protestant auspices; but the "dissenters," not taking seriously his earnest assertions of "single-mindedness in the all-absorbing cause of Temperance," were moved to little enthusiasm. Among the Americans of his own faith, however, he strengthened the reform; and in the wake of his course through twenty-five states "Father Mathew" societies germinated in spontaneous tribute.

Two American orators stood out, in popularity and results, from the herd of amateur and professional workers. John H. W. Hawkins was one of these. There are newspaper rhapsodies of his skimming the keys of pathos, earnestness, informality, humor, vehemence, tremolo, pause, and thunder. "Now," reported a scribe who heard him at the Odeon in Boston, "he assumed the melting mood, and pictured the scenes of a drunkard's home, and that home his own, and fountains of generous feeling, in many hearts, gushed forth in tears." Hawkins had that most effective equipment of the Temperance spellbinder, a past to draw upon. He was a hat-maker in Baltimore when the Washingtonians, in their first months of activity, converted him. At once he assumed the rank of a leader and, abandoning his trade, became a professional lecturer. Probably no one since Peter Cartwright discovered such zest and holy satisfaction in swinging 'round the circle. In his first ten years of the itinerant life he traveled more than one hundred thousand miles and took the stump at least twenty-five hundred times, in his idle stretches supervising the labors of numerous subordinate zealots. It was he, incidentally, who revived the Congressional Temperance Society, founded in 1833 to discourage "the use of ardent spirit and the traffic in it, by example and by kind moral influence." The Nation's legislators had backslid until, in 1842, Hawkins jerked them up.

An even brighter aureole played upon John Bartholomew Gough. Gough, too, was converted by the Washingtonians. The conversion occurred at Worcester, Massachusetts, in 1842. He attended the "experience meetings" regularly and, as the Monday nights went on, developed the narrative of his besotted past. He felt the first flush of oratorical success and decided to become a professional Temperance man. His reputation soon became more than local, and in 1843 a deacon of Boston, president of the Boston Temperance Society, sponsored Gough's first appearance in that adytum of culture. Gough, an ex-resident of Boston, was met there by a Lady with a Muckrake who flaunted an ancient bill for board and lodging. Extricated from this ooze by the good deacon, he was escorted to Tremont Chapel for his first metropolitan appearance. The one-night stand was immediately extended, so successful was the orator, to a split week. In this apprentice year other New England dates followed, from which Gough received an average gross of two dollars and seventy-seven cents. By 1845 his average income from a single engagement was fourteen dollars and forty-two cents. His brother lecturers in the cause seldom received over four dollars for an evening.

He was of nervous temperament and began a lecture haltingly. But soon he warmed to the task, as he got into the sure ground of his own moist history. Of the D. T.'s that enlivened his waking hours. Millions of monstrous spiders, surrounding him and crawling over his body. Sensations of falling, falling, into some terrible abyss, where fiend-like forms perched on crags mocked and gibed him. The finger of scorn pointed by public opinion. "What had I done to make me so shunned and execrated by my kind? Conscience gave me back an answer—I drank!" Then followed several anecdotes, alternately humorous and pathetic, to slacken the pace before the direct exhortation to all tipplers in the audience to come forth and sign the Pledge. In the days when he was making his reputation, his appeal was tempestuous and terrifying: "Ye mouldering victims, wipe the crumbling grave-dust from your brow; stalk forth in your tattered shrouds and bony whiteness to testify against the drink! Come, come from the gallows, you spirit-maddened man-slayer, grip your bloody knife, and stalk forth to testify against it! Crawl forth from the slimy ooze, ye drowned drunkards, and with suffocation's blue and vivid lips speak out against the drink! Snap your burning chains, ye denizens of the pit, and come up, sheeted in fire, dripping with the flames of hell, and with your trumpet tongues testifying against the deep damnation of the drink!"

Hurling that sonorous flood against his audience, he invoked the sinners toward the platform. As they came, and members of the local Temperance society put them to the Pledge, and congratulations were being showered upon the newly saved, Gough's panting energies sought surcease in a hymn. Before the gladiator could sleep that night, he required a tubbing, and food, and hours of attention—this last supplied by his wife, a schoolma'am of New England stock, "morally sweet and pure, and a devoted Christian." In 1844 she brought him into the fold: he confessed his faith and became a member of the Mount Vernon Congregational Church of Boston. Then, with his feet firmly set upon the Rock of Ages, with Mary Gough by his side, and with the accumulated sins of his past transformed into javelins for the battle, he was triply fortified to lead in the Temperance war.

But early in September, 1845, Gough had occasion to visit New York and make final arrangements for his appearances there in the coming winter. At Springfield, Massachusetts, he despatched a letter to his wife, which concluded, "I hope to spend a pleasant and profitable Sabbath in Brooklyn. I shall think of you." Arrived in New York, he walked to the Croton Hotel, registered, took tea, went to his room and performed his ablutions; returning to the lobby, he informed the clerk that he was going to visit some friends in Brooklyn and might not be back that night. Nor was he; not for several nights.

A certain sporting gentleman was informed of Gough's whereabouts within two days of his vanishing. And while Gough's frantic wife harried the police to cast their drag-net, and the good folk of Montreal—where Gough was scheduled to lecture—went lectureless, this gentleman attended to his editorial labors and in his leisure moments debated the ethical thing to do. By Saturday he had decided that the inalienable right of an American citizen to enjoy himself in his own way had a certain time-limit, and that his journal could use an exclusive news-story. So Mr. Camp, of the *Police Gazette,* taking a policeman with him for a witness, went to the bawdy house and confronted the unhappy lecturer.

The best defense that Gough could muster had to do with a stranger, described very vaguely, who must have put a drug into that raspberry soda the lecturer remembered drinking. A pamphleteer gave sentence: "What can we answer, but bid him die for shame, or spend the remainder of his days in tears and penitence, happy if by doing so he may obtain remission of his sins at the latest hour."

But the clear fact is that Gough did not die of shame or languish in obscurity—that in the next year his engagements multiplied and his fees doubled. The ladies and gentlemen of his day knew what they wanted: they wanted to become perfect and to be quite comfortable in the becoming. He offered something of an answer, a creed of self-perfectibility by perfecting the conduct of other people; and, lapse from grace or no lapse from grace, he was too good to lose.

While Gough was—at last—in the home of his Brooklyn friend, recuperating from the raspberry soda and its train of evils, he received innumerable letters "full of Christian tenderness and loving sympathy," which—after the manner of lady murderesses—he pasted into a scrap-book, to gladden his later years. The congregation of his church appointed a committee which visited New York and consulted with all parties concerned, from the night clerk at the Croton Hotel to the flossies in Walker Street. The committee reported that "in judging the character of another, our decision must be regulated by what we know of his physical propensities and natural temperament of his peculiar constitution. With such allowance, then, as Christian charity requires us to make on this score to all, we are brought to the conclusion that there has been nothing in this unhappy affair which ought to affect the standing of Brother Gough. . . ." And they commended to the continued confidence and sympathy of his brethren one whom "God has hitherto honored as an instrument of doing so much to withstand the progress of sin, and who has now been permitted to fall into the fiery trials which, we trust, may fit him more perfectly to serve in the cause."

And the fiery trials did just that. When Gough returned to the platform in December, he had perfected the transition whereby Temperance became Prohibition. He described a trinity—total abstinence, religious injunction, prohibitory legislation. He appealed to the moderate drinker "on a higher ground than mere self-preservation. I ask him to abstain for the sake of others, in view of the terrible nature of this evil, and of the fact that *drunkards are all drawn from the ranks of moderation*; that, when death makes gaps in their ranks, they are filled by recruits from the army of moderate drinkers." And if the moderate drinkers did not listen to his appeal, Gough would be delighted to have them clapped into jail. As early as 1846 he began an "educational campaign" for a prohibitory amendment to the Constitution.

Hawkins, Gough, and other proselytes who had been inspired by the Washingtonian societies were laymen; but the greater part of the active workers for total abstinence had some connection, past or present, with the Protestant ministry. More than three hundred thousand ministers were enrolled under the pledge of Total Abstinence a year before that pledge was made an official policy in 1836. The national organization formed in that year spurred these ministers to work for the cause; and in most pulpits, following the suggestion of the American Temperance Union, at least one sermon a year was dedicated to Total Abstinence.

The missionary spirit, directed towards the dregs of the cities, welded Temperance and religion; a zealot laboring in the vineyard of one perforce was laboring for the other. The alliance produced such fruit as the Five Points Mission in New York, supported by the National Temperance Society. In its building, at the corner of Cross and Little Water Streets, an ordained minister held religious services on Sunday mornings and supervised Temperance meetings on Friday and Sunday nights; a Christian merchant led prayer-meetings on Thursday evenings; members of the Ladies' Domestic Missionary Society conducted school for the neighborhood children on week-day mornings and gave the pitch at singing-classes on Wednesday nights. Under the same auspices the two adjoining buildings were open, as the sign announced, as a "Retreat for the Inebriate, the Friendless, and the Outcast."

It was this religious tinge to the reform that admitted women to whole-hearted participation in the movement. Their presence rather annoyed the more venerable leaders, who had ordered these things better in the early years of the century. But the issue had been threshed out in the middle Twenties, and the reward for the reputation of their sex for abstemiousness was that women could work publicly for Temperance without being called immodest.

Certain idealists bespoke that the refining influence of woman over the rougher sex provided the means of victory for Temperance. "It is for the unmarried females to say how long this scourge shall remain," declared Roswell Rice; and the plea was frequently reiterated that young ladies shun the company of every man who had not signed the teetotal Pledge—and let him know why.

One of James Russell Lowell's most treasured images of his beloved Maria White was of her presentation, in the name of the women of Watertown, of an elaborate banner to the Watertown Washington Total Abstinence Society. The ceremony took place on a wooded hill, in the presence of a thousand or so of the villagers. The beautiful lady was dressed in snowy white; she had a wreath of water-lilies and oak-leaves about her brow and a water-lily at her bosom. At such festive affairs as the Washingtonians' annual celebration on April 5th (upon which date, in 1840, the six friends in the Baltimore tavern had smashed their winecups) the lady abstainers played a happy part.

But their work was much more than ornamental. Societies were formed to alleviate the sufferings of drunkards' families. Temperance women came into the shabby habitations of the poor, soothed fevered brows, and left baskets of food. The Martha Washington Societies, Ladies' Benevolent Societies, and chapters of the Daughters of Temperance took as their province the work of uplifting, by gifts and Christian advice, the home life of the drunkards whom their brothers in Temperance reclaimed.

And in this earnest generation the lady saloon-smasher romps her way into history. Mrs. Caroline M. Sweet of Portland, Maine, had a bibulous husband who spent the hours in a rum-shop; she invaded the place with an ax and demolished glasses, bottles, and bar before she was subdued. The fine was ten dollars and costs; friends of Temperance instantly paid it. In Cambridge City, Indiana, a young benedict (whose name the editor of the local gazette regrettably withheld) "became intoxicated, and continued so for three days, to the great mortification of his young wife and acquaintances." The mortified lady found him in one of the ratty dives called, in a forgotten vernacular, "sink-holes." She seized a club and set to work. With the first lick she smashed a large crock of whisky. The proprietor seemed about to remonstrate, and the club attended to him. Then, barkeep and customers having fled, methodically she broke jugs, bottles, and flasks and knocked out faucets and bungs. The doggery-keeper feared publicity and forbore to make a formal complaint. Occasionally in New York State, in the months immediately following the repeal of the licensing law of 1845, the tinkle of broken glass and the glad cry of the lady saloon-smasher rang out upon the air.

If wives and mothers were gracefully marching in the Temperance army, why not the little ones? There was an old restraint, the idea that a young child was incapable of understanding the solemn obligation of the Pledge; and youngsters under fourteen, or at the least twelve, had not been admitted to "the little band" which "with our hand the Pledge now sign to drink no wine." But by 1836, when the emotional appeals of Temperance had become the dominant chords, the children were conceived fair game. In that year the Reverend Thomas P. Hunt began to interest boys and girls in Cold Water societies. The Sunday School was his medium of approach; through his exhortations there he organized hundreds of children's societies. And, although there was no central organization, the work was maintained with great success.

King Arthur and his noble knights have been endeared to children, not because they were pugnacious roustabouts, but because the legend has to do with pageantry and purity. So it was with Temperance: the healthy aspirations of the boys to be Sir Galahads or Sir Lancelots, with girls the cleanly adoration of white as a color and a symbol, and with both the glamour of parades. In Temperance celebrations they paraded, in their white and blue uniforms, perhaps vested with a band of satin worn like a baldric; fluttering their inscribed banners, singing their cold-water songs, doing good for the cause of Temperance and, unwittingly, for the Cult of the Child.

Children were furnished with pledge-cards by their elders, given the scent of the unregenerate, and set loose.

One little wonder-worker became nationally celebrated. The inspired doings of this child were first set in print by the

Temperance Recorder in June, 1839; the detailed story was reprinted by scores of periodicals and familiarized by platform anecdote and parlor conversation. The narrative begins with a country school-house wherein a Temperance lecturer was addressing an audience made up in principal part of the school-children. (The meeting was after school hours, to be sure; otherwise an unconverted selectman would have been heard from, and there might have been a change of teachers.) Nearing the close of his address, the lecturer exhibited a large sheet of paper on the upper part of which was printed the Pledge; he besought some child to take that sheet and enroll upon it as many people of the neighborhood as would fill the sheet with their signatures. Little Mary volunteered—amid titters from her school-fellows, for Little Mary's father was a notorious drunkard.

That evening Papa came home intoxicated, as usual. Little Mary allowed time for him to sober up, and in the morning she exhibited the Pledge. "He looked at her maliciously and indignantly," the original account has it, as he whammed her one. But not even a bleary-headed drunkard could strike prostrate an eight-year-old girl without being horrified at his deed. Little Mary's father resolved instanter to reform. But pride kept that resolution a secret. And Little Mary, after partaking of the furtive consolation of her frail mother, betook herself—and the Pledge—to school. That day she obtained the signatures of the teacher and of nearly all the attending children. For a fortnight the little darling canvassed the neighborhood, winning with her innocent sweetness the signatures of young and old. Meanwhile, his conscience fermenting, Little Mary's father kept aloof. He interposed no command against her proselyting, nor offered any encouragement.

But the morning arrived when he inquired of her how many signatures she had garnered. She brought the list and, standing diffidently by, ready to dodge fist or boot, waited while he counted the names. "Mary, you have got one hundred and fifty names signed on your paper!"—and he was evidently pleased. Little Mary bounded upon his lap, implanted a kiss upon his grizzled jowl, and spoke these earnest words: "Father, now you sign it, and that will make it one hundred and fifty-one!" The signature was inscribed forthwith, and the sheet was filled. Papa then set about the social regeneration of his

COLD WATER ARMY PLEDGE.

We, Cold Water Girls and Boys,[a]   Wine, Beer, and Cider we detest,[d]
Freely renounce the treacherous joys[b]   And thus we'll make our parents blest;[e]
Of Brandy, Whiskey, Rum, and Gin;   "So here we pledge[f] perpetual hate[g]
The Serpent's lure to death and sin:[c]   To all that can Intoxicate."[h]

a Prov. viii. 4: Zech. viii. 5.   b Isa. lvi. 12: v. 11, 12: xxviii. 7: Prov. xx. 1.   c Prov. xxiii. 32: I. Peter v. 8.   d Eph. v. 18: Prov. xxiii.
31: Deut. vii. 26.   e Prov. x. 1: xxiii. 15: III. John 4.   f Jer. xxxv. 6.   g Ps. xcvii. 10: Rom. xii. 9: Ps. cxix. 128.   h Rom. xiv. 21.

CERTIFICATE OF MEMBERSHIP.

This Certifies, That *Isabella F. Hamilton* having taken the above Pledge, is a Member of the CONNECTICUT COLD WATER ARMY.

Countersigned,   *Th. S. Williams* President Conn.
                                     Temp. Society.

Olcott Allen   *Chas J. Warren* Secretary.
Leader of the   Division.

COLD WATER ARMY PLEDGE

From the original in possession of the New York Historical Society.

family. To remove himself from his former associates of the bar-room he took a farm "on shares," and began a new life of industry, frugality, abstemiousness, and Christian devotion. The narrative leaves Little Mary's father as a member of an evangelical church and superintendent of its Sunday School, and Little Mary herself, beautiful in her teens, a teacher in that School.

Perhaps, comes the ungentlemanly thought, there never was any Little Mary. The narrative depends for its veracity upon the lecturer who gave the little girl the Pledge-sheet and who professed to have visited the family in its after-years of non-alcoholic contentment. No editor bothered to verify the story, of course; it was simply clipped and printed. Then it was in black and white, and it was true!

The success of the Little Marys, the Martha Washington ladies, the Stacys, the Marshes, the Hawkinses and the rest is not to be measured by statistics. Certainly there were many "repeaters" among the signers of the Pledge, who were converted periodically or were complaisant in signing cards whenever their signature would please someone. And certainly Temperance in some degree, or total abstinence, was practised or admired by a majority of the middle class. A correspondent of an Albany newspaper in 1849, not in the least abashed by the absence of trustworthy figures, stated that there were then more than 1,500,000 people in the United States who abstained from the use of ardent spirits or from furnishing them to others; that over 5,000 Temperance societies were active, including more than 600,000 members; that more than 2,000 distilleries had closed for lack of business, and over 5,000 merchants had abandoned the traffic. The first two statements are probable; the fourth, unlikely; and the third is simple evidence that the process of consolidation and expansion operated in the distilling and malting businesses as it operated in other industries. The correspondent added the gratuitous estimate that at least

20,000 families were then in ease and comfort who would have been in poverty and disgraced by drunken members were it not for the Temperance agitation. But Parke Godwin, auditing the spiritual accounts of the reform, found that the gains were being constantly diminished by reactionary forces in American society. He gave a perspicacious list: the great inducements to accumulate wealth by trafficking in liquor; the frequent profligacy of the rich; the despair of the poor, the defeated ones in an exploitative society; and "the merely animal education that is the lot of the mass."

The shortest way to check these forces, it seemed to reformers who wanted immediate triumphs, was by legislative fiat. In 1836 the editor of the *Pennsylvania Temperance Recorder* summed up the growing conviction that moral suasion was insufficient to enforce Temperance: "If the legislation of bygone days, days of darkness, sustains a false public sentiment, it is important that the legislation be changed." The American Temperance Union from its inception denounced the licensing system as governmental participation in an immoral traffic. And, overcoming but not silencing the large majority of the Temperance forces not agile enough to leap from the principle of voluntary total abstinence to that of coercion by police and judiciary, Temperance associations armed themselves with petitions and memorials and drove down upon the state legislatures.

In Georgia the intermeddling of the reformers with the old-line politicians resulted in an antic confusion almost disastrous to the cause of Temperance in that state. Elsewhere the lobbies were more adept. In 1838 the sale of spirituous liquors in taverns and stores became a misdemeanor in Tennessee, and the fines collected from violators were laudably devoted to improvement of the public schools. Mississippi in 1839 prohibited the sale of vinous or spirituous beverages in quantities less than a gallon. Massachusetts in 1838 acquired a law forbidding the sale of spirituous liquors (except for purposes "medicinal or mechanical") in quantities smaller than fifteen gallons. The statute provoked a political thunder-storm, beclouding the legitimate differences between Democrat and Whig. At the next state election Marcus Morton won the governorship from the Whig incumbent, Edward Everett, who had affixed his signature to the troublesome statute. Morton (a Temperance man, incidentally) denounced the statute, and the legislature willingly repealed it in 1840.

Local option had its charms for legislators afraid to ignore Temperance petitions; it seemed a workable compromise to stave off the bitter pill of prohibition. Rhode Island, Illinois, and Connecticut, within five months of each other in 1839, conferred upon the towns or counties the right of deciding by majority vote whether or no liquor licenses should be issued in the locality. The legislatures of several other states, in the Eighteen Forties, authorized local option. In New York—the leading state in the number of Temperance societies, in total membership, in financial contributions, and in the distribution of Temperance literature—a powerful lobby floated a local-option bill into the legislature upon a sea of petitions. After the representatives of the metropolis were made tractable by the specific exemption of New York County from the provisions of the bill, the measure was passed and received the Governor's signature in May, 1845. Nearly five-sixths of the incorporated municipalities in the state prohibited the sale of intoxicants in 1846. In the following year the electorate changed its mind. The law's failure to banish intemperance or to secure a noticeable degree of enforcement in the no-license towns split the forces of reform into groups of divergent opinions; and in June the legislature repealed the statute.

The victories of local option evidently were highly perishable. The general experience was that the electorate couldn't make up its mind with any finality, that the no-license town of yesteryear had wide-open groggeries tomorrow. The difficulties of local enforcement chagrined the Temperance leaders. They turned to another device—state prohibition.

The two Southern states that had dabbled with prohibition repented and repealed—Mississippi in 1842, Tennessee in 1846. But in the ten years from 1846 through 1855 the device was put on trial in many states. A prohibitory law was enacted in Delaware in 1847, but the courts intervened with a lethal decision. In 1849 Wisconsin promulgated a remarkable law forbidding anyone to engage in the liquor traffic until he had posted bonds to pay all damages that the community or individuals might sustain from his business. The retailing of liquor to be consumed on the premises was forbidden in Iowa in 1851, and Maine, Vermont, and Ohio inhibited the liquor traffic. In 1852 three more states joined the ranks of the purified-by-statute; in the next two years, another two; and in the gala year of 1855, no less than six.

One of the six was Iowa, going the whole route after the partial measure of 1851; and another was New York. In 1854 Myron H. Clark became Governor at Albany. Clark was the author of a prohibitory law which his predecessor had vetoed. His candidacy brought the reformers rallying; Delavan with his money-bags, Greeley with his newspaper, and Marsh with his experience were in the vanguard, and in the second rank stood William E. Dodge, Henry Ward Beecher, Chancellor Reuben Walworth, and other famed publicists, ministers, and philanthropists. A prohibitory law passed the legislature and became effective on July 4, 1855. Mass-meetings throughout the state hailed that day as marking the emancipation of the people from a second tyranny; and a gathering in the Broadway Tabernacle of New York City called upon the Honorable Fernando Wood to stand forth as the protector of the law and exhibit "a manly front and a bold determination to carry out the will of the legislature."

The Mayor personally deplored the law, but he took a stand four-square for enforcement. The sustaining of the laws, His Honor declared, was a principle upon which rested the corner-stone of all the national prosperity and greatness. And then he issued instructions to the police for their guidance in this enforcement—instructions which have not ceased to be a source of awe and admiration: "Whether liquors exhibited in your presence . . . are intoxicating liquors . . . you must judge with great circumspection, and be careful to avoid seizing any thus exempt. An error in this regard may lay you liable to severe personal responsibility." And further, "Keeping liquor with intent to sell or give away, is not an offense fully within the scope of the eye. . . . You can not see the violation . . . for an intent can not be seen. . . . These violations . . . do not . . . compel you to arrest or seize without complaints."

The judiciary performed its part, relieving the policemen of the city from the hazardous obligations of enforcing an uncongenial law. The state statute was declared unconstitutional in March, 1856.

And elsewhere, even where there were no Fernando Woods, the result was dust and ashes. Prohibition was one of the most promising fruits in the generation's orchard of social progress. It had been sprayed with Sentimental theory and watered by high aspirations. Ripened and opened, underneath the delicate beauty of its surface was an industrious little army of cankerworms. Legal coercion didn't work. In Indiana the courts relieved the electorate of the task of expunging the prohibitory statute. The legislature of Illinois rescinded in 1853, of Nebraska in 1856, of Delaware in 1857. In other states the work of sweeping out the residue was left to the legislators of the next generation, to be performed by direct repeal or by vicarious undermining of the essential provisions. The prohibitory law of New Hampshire was so imperfect and ineffective that it had value as a piece of practical politics, and it was left unrepealed. Vermont retained its statute. And only Maine is left.

Maine is another story. Here, and nowhere else but in the neighboring states of uppermost New England, were the economic aspects of the liquor problem emphasized. With the rural citizens, who recognized their own limitations, and the employing class, who were instructed to appreciate the relation of intemperance to labor inefficiency, to support them, the Temperance leaders had power and organization. Neal Dow, the chief of the reformers, was of unusual political astuteness. He trained himself for the state-wide task by making Portland into a no-license town in 1842. The next nine years were a bitter struggle of alternate gains and defeats; but in 1851 the manufacture and sale of intoxicating liquors in Maine became a crime. Enforcement was encouraged by the granting of all fines to the prosecuting officers, and the customary safeguards against arbitrary search and seizure were removed for this particular statute. "The jackdaw Mayor of Portland, this man with the fancy vest," an unfriendly state senator labeled him; but the National Temperance Society, holding its first annual banquet in February, 1852, naturally lionized Dow. At the conclusion of a banquet strewn with complimentary toasts (drunk in cold water) General Sam Houston had the honor of presenting to "the Honorable Neal Dow, for his service to fellow-men, as the author of the Maine Law," a gold medal which the General declared "a magnificent specimen of art, having cost about two hundred and fifty dollars."

But the work in Maine was not done. Problems of enforcement remained; party tenets shifted, and in 1856 the Maine Law was repealed. It was replaced after a two years' struggle by a similar law with stronger teeth; this second Maine Law was not dislodged. And for the next three generations legislatures and Temperance reformers tinkered with it, piling up amendments designed to make it quite enforceable. In 1933 the people of the state added the perfecting touch.

CHAPTER NINE

The Pure Sciences and Some Others

"*T*ELL ME," sang the young lady (in *The Birthday Gift* for 1853),

> Tell me I HATE the bowl—
> *Hate* is a feeble word,
> I loathe—ABHOR—*my very soul*
> *With strong disgust is stirred*
> When I see, or hear, or tell,
> Of the dark BEVERAGE OF HELL.

This erotic type of venom, screeching its hate-song to make the world nobler, was not the property solely of the young lady, nor was alcoholic tipple the sole object of this passion. The hellish brew came in for most of the odium; but there were other drinkables and esculents which various good persons disliked thoroughly, with italics and capitals. Dietetic reform was a popular evangelism in the Sentimental Years. And, like other reforms, it used up a great deal of emphatic hating.

Let every man with a shred of ethics, besought Larkin B. Coles, M. D., put away "this nerve-prostrating, mind-benumbing, soul-paralyzing drug, this fleshly, ungodly lust!" It happened to be tobacco of which he spoke. Orin Fowler brought clerical sanction to the physician's plea: it was the duty of "every friend of humanity—of every lover of his country—of every Christian—and of every minister of Christ, to *abstain,* himself, *immediately,* and *forever,* from all use of tobacco, whether by *smoking, chewing,* or *snuffing,* except it be *medicinally.*" The "except" clause was necessary because tobacco cured the toothache.

Tobacco was not fashionable, common though it was. Young dandies lounged in doorways with their cigars, as a symbol of independence. Business men smoked at home, in their "dens" if they had kindly wives, or in the back yard if the clothes had been taken off the line; but not in their offices, where they might set a bad example to the clerks. Many sturdy

CITY NUISANCES
Godey's Lady's Book, 1855.

women smoked pipes as they did the kitchen-work or labored at the wash-tub, but most of them would have perished rather than leave a smoke-trail on their way to the grocery. The dining-rooms and parlors of private homes were sacrosanct unless the ladies gave permission. One of Harriet Beecher Stowe's fictive ministers had in his youth acquired a taste for "the almost universal clerical pipe," but, upon his observing a delicate woman in distress at its vapors, he reflected that whatever could offend a woman must surely be uncomely and unworthy a Christian man—and put the pipe away. George Winfred Hervey, author of an egregious little book, *Principles of Courtesy,* set rules for the social behavior of smokers: never go into the street with a cigar or pipe in your mouth; never smoke in a city unless standing in the company of chimneys, on a fireproof roof.

The argument was simply transferred, with inconsequential changes, from the cold-water school's tiltings against liquor. Tobacco dulled the capacity to sniff the fragrances of nature. The Divine Author had furnished abundant resources of beauty, to be apprehended through the optic, auditory, and olfactory avenues; tobacco dammed all three. It subverted the taste for natural, unseasoned food. It drained the nation of untold intellectual power, making potential geniuses into mediocrities and potentially useful citizens into obscure dullards. "The eye of angels is upon us, the eye of God is upon us," shouted one of the anti-tobacco crusaders, "and shall we fetter, and palsy, and ruin our intellectual capabilities, in the paltry pleasure of using one of the most poisonous, loathsome, and destructive weeds?"

Down the corridors of time steals the pathos of the abstemious Amos Lawrence, successful merchant. In one of the psychic upheavals of adolescence he had resolved to quit rum-drinking; and although, working at the store in Groton, he purveyed gallons of it daily, he clung to his resolve. He decided, too, not to use tobacco in any form. But he loved the aroma of it; and throughout his days he kept fresh Havana cigars in his desk, not to smoke, but only to smell. One of the sweet compensations of life in his generation was that Lawrence, in answer to an earnest college student who requested the formula for success, could relate these two abnegations, and conclude, "To this simple fact of starting just right I am indebted, with God's blessing on my labors, for my present position."

Farther toward the fringe of crusading Philistinism were those (most of them, sadly, Doctors of Medicine) who feared one or both of the homely beverages, coffee and tea. Coffee, which in the fifteen years between 1821 and 1836 had taken favor and come into general use, was labeled an amorous excitant. Not only that, but it forced the maturity of the sexual capacities by several years—to the great distress of public morals. Tea-drinking was little better than toddy-guzzling. Indeed, if you worked yourself to the right pitch, as did William Andrus Alcott, you perceived that tea-drinking was just as bad, and you had the distorted pleasure of harrying thousands of good women with pangs of shame. Declared Alcott, "The female who restores her strength by tea, the laborer who regains strength by spirituous liquors, and the Turk who recruits his energies by his pill of opium, are in precisely the same condition."

These ferreters of new evil gathered, from heaven knows where, verisimilar instances of intoxication from tea-drinking; and from their case-books one gleans that with many tea-bibbers the tongue was unloosed, the countenance flushed, the eye preternaturally animated, and even the gait unnatural. Those symptoms which Mrs. Lydia Pinkham and other venders of patented remedies were to ascribe to an entirely different cause —cold feet and hands, loss of appetite, and "particular difficulties, especially the weakening ones"—were traced to the ladies' fondness for tea. One learns of drinkers of green tea (the deadliest kind) who used the beverage to uphold them through difficult auctorial tasks or other brain-labor, and were in consequence occasionally found upon the floor, in a state of insensibility. One reads of the "tea disease," characterized by hunger-like gnawings in the stomach, to which a fluttering in the left side was gradually added. Many ulcerated ladies, undoubtedly, paid good money for the prescription, "Put away the teapot."

The eating of fruit, especially after dinner, was "abominably bad," advised Edward Johnson, M.D.; and although the doctor was an Englishman, his dietary theories must be noticed here, for Johnson was an internationally known Hydropathist whose writings were amply circulated in the United States. The doctor's full scheme need not be followed (certain indelicate and absurd theories of activity in the digestive tract have much to do with it); but its culminant truth—supported by "many years of investigation and medical practice"—was that bread, meat, and potatoes were the alpha, beta, and omega of diet, and that if an invalid couldn't gain strength on these foods, he was simply ripe for dying. Eggs for invalids? Nonsense. Eggs required (ah, those years of investigation!) a special, stronger variety of gastric juice and so debilitated the constitution.

But Lewis Hough, a domestic deep-thinker, asserted that fruit was man's natural food; primitive man ate fruit from the bough, the correct manner. The perfect man, Hough announced, did not drink water; there was ample moisture in fruit, and—in perfect fruit—ample sustenance. But since the fruits, under artificial cultivation, had been removed nearly as far from their perfect natures as man had removed himself from his, Hough conceded that his contemporaries required some additional nourishment in the form of coarse, whole-grain wheat bread. "The purpose of nutrition"—he steered toward a familiar reef in the Transcendental sea—"is merely to replenish the waste, which takes place in the organs from the action of the soul through them, in its maturing for a future state."

Not so near the periphery were the exponents of vege-tarianism and farina-ism, cults which have survived. The best known of the "physiological reformers" is Sylvester Graham, whose surname now distinguishes a grit-like breadstuff in common use. A mediocre writer, he was most successful as a lecturer. He began his active years in propaganda as general agent of the Pennsylvania Temperance Society, in 1830; within another year his lectures were advocating, besides total absti-nence, these principles of diet and conduct: "Graham" bread, allowed to age for twelve hours or more before being eaten; hard mattresses; light clothing; daily exercises; a bath at least three times a week; "roughage" fruits and vegetables; and cheerfulness at meals. In 1832 he added chastity to the list. A religious cast was omnipresent in Graham's teachings; and Cornelius Mathews was not very unfair in scoffing, "The fiend

Infidelity is to be put out of the way by nothing less than spare diet and a course of vegetables."

Several Eastern cities boasted "Graham boarding-houses," at which only the whole-grain bread was served, vegetables generally were substituted for beefsteak, and the lodgers were encouraged to tub frequently. A special table for Grahamites was laid at the Transcendental colony, Brook Farm. There was a Grahamite bookstore in Boston, an "American Physiological Society" for the distribution of Grahamite tracts, and for three years (1837–39) a *Graham Journal of Health and Longevity*.

To the lasting credit of these physiological reformers, most of them spoke kindly of sunlight. That the light of the moon was "prejudicial" to sleepers was a prevalent folk-notion; the physiologists pooh-pooh'd it and recommended that the windows of a bedroom be opened now and then. And they were death on corsets. "Enormous deformities of every or any part, may be produced by gentle pressure, which may easily be endured by us," as the *Syracuse Health Journal* sounded the warning, "and after we have become accustomed to such pressure, by lacing or otherwise, it becomes a second nature, and we feel unnatural without it, even when it is undermining our constitution; the same as the drunkard without his potations." This folly was often denounced; and the new fashion for men of a leather belt around the middle occasionally came in for its deserts: "Why should man, who was created for strength and endurance, cripple and enfeeble himself by wearing a band tight around the abdomen, where nature has not allowed a bone, or anything but the most free expression and motion?" Farther in dress reform, farther than Amelia Bloomer and the other feminists who popularized the loose-fitting "Turkish costume" in the early Fifties, went Lewis Hough, who insisted that "the external surface of the body," all of it, was designed to be "continually in contact with the atmosphere." (Incidentally, his natural, nude, fruit-eating man was to be interested in coition once a twelvemonth, no less and no oftener.)

The identity of social and political liberalism with "physiological" liberalism is too significant to escape comment. The humanitarians, social revisionists, and innovationists were the same ones who descried new ways toward physical perfection and were most hospitable to new recipes for mental hygiene.

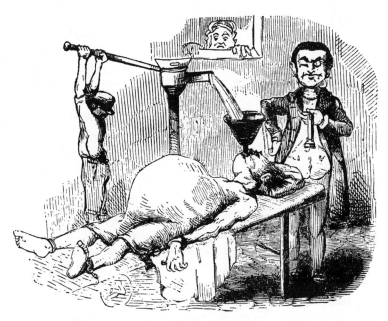

THE WATER CURE
Yankee Notions, 1852.

As ardently and uncritically as progressive ladies and gentlemen embraced the gospel of total abstinence, they embraced Hydropathy. The therapy outlined by Vincenz Priessnitz, the Silesian founder of the "water-cure," filtered into the United States at the beginning of the Forties; by the middle Fifties no less than twenty-seven Hydropathic sanatoriums, most of them in rural spots where the water was alleged to be remarkably good, were receiving paying guests. Some of these establishments, notably the one at Saratoga, became focal points of the wanderings of society people. Six to ten dollars a week—

it seems incredible now—purchased treatment, room, and board at, for instance, the Jamestown Water Cure, beside "the lucid lake of Chautauqua," offering "an abundance of water of dewey softness and crystal transparency, to cleanse, renovate, and rejuvenate the disease-worn and dilapidated system."

Orthodox medicine was too torpid to trip as gaily as the younger therapies. The national zest for formal education meant that many new colleges of medicine would be founded within the span from 1835 to 1860. Yet the one conspicuous advance in medical technique during these years, the use of anæsthetics, was in no sense a primary triumph of the Æsculapians, but was borrowed—in the first instance, from itinerant lecturers on the kerosene circuit, and in the second instance, from an experimental dentist.

Vagrant showmen who billed themselves as "professors of chemistry" included as a regular part of their entertainment a request that some of the gentlemen in the audience step to the platform and inhale nitrous oxide ("laughing gas"). The spectators were amused by the antics of the volunteers, and young subjects enjoyed the experiment as a piece of bravado. So, after the showman had departed from the hamlet of Jefferson, Georgia, Dr. Crawford W. Long, a resident physician, obliged the young men by giving them ether as a substitute for the Professor's nitrous oxide; and the inhalation of ether became a popular vice in Jackson County. The insensate behavior of the ether-drunk lads gave Dr. Long another idea; and on March 30, 1842, he performed a surgical operation upon a patient under the influence of ether—as the patient, "James M. Venables, of the County of Cobb and State of Georgia," did "on oath depose and say" before a justice of the peace.

William Thomas Green Morton, after graduating from the Baltimore College of Dental Surgery (the first chartered college of dentistry in the United States), began the practice of his craft in Boston. He experimented with opium as a painkiller, but found it violently unacceptable to ladies with tender stomachs. On September 30, 1846, he first used ether, and the event was promptly chronicled in the public press. Whether Morton was in any manner indebted to the prior experiments of the Georgia physician was not demonstrable; the way was clear for the two gentlemen concerned, and their partisans, to argue the question as acrimoniously as they pleased—and so they did. A physician of the Massachusetts General Hospital made use of the anæsthetic, with Morton in attendance, in a surgical operation on October 16, 1846. Morton was granted a patent, in the following month, on "Letheon, or Sulphuric Ether." The name "anæsthesia" was suggested to the patent-holder by Oliver Wendell Holmes, as more "appropriate and agreeable." Doctor Holmes, incidentally, was for a time all but outlawed by the medical fraternity for his unprofessional suggestion that septic poisoning of women in childbirth was generally due to the uncleanly hands of the attending physician.

For three years a hard-minded opposition refused to concede the important place of anæsthetics in medical practice. Publicity given the mistakes of certain bungling doctors was a cause, but the stubborn objections were echoes of the old repressive morality. Pain, it appeared, had great ethical value. Ether and chloroform could be used as intoxicants. Their use in childbirth contravened the statement in Genesis, "In sorrow shalt thou bring forth children"; and the interesting view was urged that the pangs of childbirth were endurable without the use of an anæsthetic. Dr. Walter Channing, Professor of Midwifery and Medical Jurisprudence at Harvard, in 1849 published a summary of over five hundred instances of the successful use of sulphuric or chloric ether, and most of the doubters within the profession were satisfied.

The circulation of such volumes as Mrs. Hester Pendleton's *The Parents' Guide for the Transmission of Derived Qualities to Offspring and Children,* uncontroverted by the learned profession, indicates the status of genetic knowledge. In the particular subject on which, in view of the high birth-rate and the high percentage of infant mortality, the humanitarian spirit should have urged the physicians to better their knowledge and improve their technique, considerations of moral delicacy intervened. Dr. Charles D. Meigs, Professor of the Diseases of Women and Children in the Jefferson Medical College, Philadelphia, declared, "So great, indeed, is the embarrassment arising from fastidiousness on the part either of the female herself, or of the practitioner, or both, that I am satisfied that much of the ill success of treatment may be justly traced thereto." It was perhaps for the best, was his remarkable thought, "that this great degree of modesty should exist even to the extent of putting a bar to researches, without which no very clear and understandable notions can be obtained of the sexual disorders. I confess I am proud to say that in this country generally, certainly in many parts of it, there are women who prefer to suffer the extremity of danger and pain rather than waive those scruples which prevent their maladies from being carefully explored."

Dr. Samuel Gregory, of the New England Female Medical College, wrote two volumes with a single thought: *Letters to Ladies, in favor of Female Physicians for their own Sex,* and *Man-Midwifery Exposed and Dissected.* The male obstetrician was an intruder in the private affairs of the opposite sex; "the Romans would not have been more startled to see Lucina, the patron goddess of childbearing women, haranguing the assembled gods or launching the thunderbolts of Jove than they would have been to see his majesty presiding in the puerperal chamber." Doctor Gregory asserted that "a fearful calamity which sometimes happens to parturient women, termed *puerperal convulsions,*" of which there was no generally accepted explanation [three plain words tell the story: doctors' dirty hands], was in truth caused by *"female delicacy,* grievously shocked by the presence and personal attentions of gentlemen," and cited, among a number of proofs, a case in Weymouth: the physician, "having expended much time with a patient, pronounced the birth impossible without the aid of art, and started home for his forceps; but, before he returned, Nature, relieved from her embarrassment, had anticipated his services, and dispensed with his skill."

Faddist therapists who shouted their wares through newspapers or pamphlets battened on their fees. In the welter of diverse enthusiasts it is difficult to discover the sound practitioners; for physicians and professors of medicine were, in the absence of influential fraternities within the profession, unchecked by common restraints. Germs of sentimental humanitarianism and germs of specimen-cabinet science wove ephemeral patterns on the pages of the professional manuals. Many honest physicians recognized the inadequacies of their knowledge and in their frequent perplexities were content to prescribe calomel or a placebo. Bleeding passed very reluctantly out of fashion. In jars on the counters of apothecaries' shops leeches still crawled their rounds and dreamed of human blood. Many a college-trained physician was stimulated by the inadequacy of his manuals to seek his own arcanum and purvey it to all and sundry. And so they swarm: Regulars, Irregulars, Broussarians, Sangradoarians, Morrisonians, Brandethians, Beechitarians, Botanics, Regular Botanics, Homeopathians, Hydropathists, Rootists, Herbalists, Florists, Eclectics, Electricals, Magnetics, Experimentals, Thomsonians, Reformed Thomsonians, assorted proselytes, pill-rollers, and unlabeled quacks.

"TO THE AFFLICTED OF BOTH SEXES," begins an advertisement in the *New York Times* for January 20, 1836, which may be taken as typical of a large and swarming family. "HUNTER'S RED DROP. This remedy is the only absolute specific that has ever been discovered for the cure of Venereal Disease—it removes every vestige of Poison from the system in a very few days, and may always be used with the very greatest safety under any circumstances whatsoever. Now to be obtained from S. Drewer, Boot and Shoe Store, exclusive agent." From backstairs laboratory to shoe-store, that was the route of one remedy. From hack manual to doctor's prescription to ignorant apothecary, that was the route of another. Druggists, asserted a writer in the *Moral Reformer,* generally did not know enough Latin to carry on their trade, allowed drugs to lose their strength by faulty storage, and filled prescriptions with dangerous carelessness; but even this critic recognized the rights of individual liberty: "Nor will I presume to say, that the apothecary should be *licensed* before he be permitted to sell."

Whether the rights of the individual included the liberty of women to inform themselves about their bodies and their bodies' diseases was, as we have noticed, a delicate moral issue. Elizabeth Blackwell settled the question for herself (with the assistance of a college faculty in an unguarded, tractable moment) by gaining admission to the Geneva Medical School of Western New York in October, 1847; in May, 1849, she received the first degree of Doctor of Medicine bestowed upon a woman in America.

Paulina Wright as early as 1844 audaciously had given public lectures to women on physiology, employing a mannikin —a *"femme modèle"* imported from Paris, the first to be exhibited in this country. Its trail of blushes and swoons is reminiscent of Louis Agassiz' note upon his forlorn experiment, in 1847, before a Teachers' Institute in Massachusetts. His subject was the grasshopper; he passed a jar of the insects about, asking each teacher to take one and examine it in consonance with the lecture. The ladies and gentlemen giggled and squirmed; "it was at the time a great innovation," wrote Agassiz, "and excited much laughter and derision."

Paulina Wright became actively identified with political feminism; but Elizabeth Blackwell, although heartily in sympathy with the political movement, was foremost a physician and shrewdly minimized the distinction of sex. "Much is said of the oppression woman suffers; man is reproached with being unjust, tyrannical, jealous. I do not so read human life," she declared. "The exclusion woman suffers . . . has risen naturally . . . simply because woman has desired nothing more, has not felt the soul too large for the body. But when woman, with matured strength, with steady purpose, presents her lofty claim, all barriers will give way, and man will welcome, with a thrill of joy, the new birth of his sister spirit, the advent of his partner, his co-worker, in the great universe of being."

But there was no welcoming thrill of joy among the students of the Medical Department of Harvard College when they learned, at the opening of the fall term of 1850, that the faculty had decided to admit a "female pupil." She was Harriot K. Hunt, forty-five years old, who had been practicing medicine, without benefit of class-room, for fifteen years. The students formally resolved (and in consequence Miss Hunt withdrew her application) "That no woman of true delicacy would be willing, in the presence of men, to listen to the discussion of the subjects that must necessarily come under the consideration of students of medicine. *Resolved,* that we are not opposed to allowing woman her rights, but do protest against her appearing in places where her presence is calculated to destroy our respect for the modesty and delicacy of her sex."

Some part of the delicacy of the sex could be preserved, however, in classes for women only. This facility was first offered by Samuel Gregory's School of Medicine, in Boston, which opened its first term in November, 1848. The course occupied six months. Gregory pointed out that women could afford to charge about a third of the ordinary fees. This threat of ruinous competition, with the scant system of education at Gregory's school (at the better medical colleges a man had to attend lectures for at least ten months before he could get his degree), naturally aroused professional resentment; and despite a Female Medical Education Society in Boston whose chief interest was in assisting young ladies through the course, the Gregory Medical School and its successor, the New England Female Medical College, maintained only a precarious existence.

The Female Medical College of Pennsylvania, opened at Philadelphia in 1850, also had its philanthropic helpmeet, the Ladies' Medical Missionary Society, which asserted in its constitution that "the BIBLE recognizes and approves *only woman* in the sacred office of *midwife*" and singled out for particular "aid and sympathy" the lady medical students who desired to become missionaries. The sympathy was timely. Devotional and medical qualifications were insignificant beside the temptations to immorality which presumably would beset a spinster missionary; and no denominational body would appoint a woman, save as adjunct to her missionary husband.

The Philadelphia college had to train its own women lecturers, to supplant the diffident and poorly fitted men who made up its first faculty, and for its first twelve years was unable to give its students an opportunity to visit hospital wards. The first hospital to offer clinical training to women was the New York Infirmary, chartered in 1854, at first simply a dispensary but after 1857 including a lying-in ward. Dr. Marion Sims, whose experiments upon slave women in Alabama have been called the foundation of gynecology in America, in 1850 founded the first Woman's Hospital in the world. This hospital, in New York, was made possible by the generosity of several women of the city; but Dr. Sims refused to appoint a woman to its medical staff.

The Eclectic School at Rochester and other irregular colleges admitted women more readily than the orthodox schools; but within the Fifties five established colleges of medicine opened special classes for "female pupils." Elizabeth Blackwell estimated in 1859 that about three hundred women had graduated somewhere from some semblance of a medical course. "It is not until they leave college, and attempt their work alone and unaided," she commented, "that they realize how utterly insufficient their education is. . . . A few gain a little practical knowledge, and struggle into a second-rate position."

"Nature is responsible for my unqualified opposition to educating females for the medical profession," declared Dr. Nathan Williams before the New York Medical Society in 1850; and nature, indeed, had moral ramifications through the whole field of science. The editor of *The School Master* remarked in 1836 that young people who collected and exchanged natural objects "have neither time nor disposition to devote to vicious pleasures. Their kind and generous propensities are called into exercise."

Boy and man, students of science collected specimens. They collected them, and they named them—often with pleasing originality. They possessed specimen-cabinets and specimen-boxes; they put their rocks and butterflies and fossils away, and collected more. The Pennsylvania Lyceum, founded in 1835, announced the common object of the naturalists' societies that sprang up thickly in the Thirties and Forties—to further "the knowledge of minerals, plants, and other departments of nature"; and it well represented the enthusiasm of this quest. Within the first six months of the Lyceum the members had collected sets of "elementary specimens in geology and mineralogy" sufficient to furnish county lyceums in each of the eleven hundred counties of the Republic. So greatly had the zeal for picking up rocks and carrying them home outrun the actual study of science that the Pennsylvania Lyceum then had little to do but wait for eleven hundred county lyceums to be formed. Each set, incidentally, consisted of forty-one lithic fragments of moral improvement and differed no whit from any of the other sets.

To the zest of filling specimen-cabinets (ultimately to be willed, in many cases, to institutions of learning) adults added the higher delight of describing new species. Gentlemen rushed their initial findings into print, for the only sound defense of one's claims was priority of publication. In the absence of systems of descriptive science adapted to America a confusing duplication of nomenclature had sprung up. Ornithology, and that thanks to Alexander Wilson, was indeed the only branch of natural science in the United States that had been adequately organized by 1836. Standard textbooks of American authorship were sorely needed, and in the course of the generation they appeared.

Constantine Samuel Rafinesque, the quaint and admirable "botanist - naturalist - geologist - geographer - historian - poet - philosopher - economist - philanthropist" (so he labeled himself), was still alive in 1836. Four years later, in miserable and undeserved obscurity, he died, secure from the knowledge that he had described twice as many fishes, plants, and shells as existed in the wide regions he had traversed. Timothy Abbot Conrad, the paleontologist, outlived Rafinesque by thirty-seven years. The eminence Conrad had enjoyed before the Civil War was sadly impaired when a new generation of scholars decided that to cite other authors from memory (Conrad's wasn't very good) and frequently to redescribe and relabel one's own discoveries of new species were grave faults.

In 1836 Benjamin Silliman, Yale's Professor of Chemistry and Natural History, was making an investigative tour of the gold-mines of Virginia. Gerard Troost was in the eastern mountains of Tennessee, casually obeying the legislature's mandate to look for gold-deposits and intensively searching for fossils. Alexander Bache left for Europe that year, to increase his knowledge of marine surveying; George Catlin was swirling down the St. Peter's and the Mississippi in a canoe. Henry Rowe Schoolcraft hearkened to the request of the Massachusetts Historical Society that he complete his work on the Ojibway language and award its publication to the Society; and James Pollard Espy received the American Philosophical Society's prize medal for his monograph on the origin of storms.

John James Audubon was in the midst of the stupendous *Birds of America* and the *Ornithological Biographies*. Amos Eaton's perennial *Manual of Botany* turned up in a new, enlarged edition. Isaac Lee published his *Synopsis of the Family Naiades,* a delight and an inspiration to the conchologists of the time. James Dwight Dana, just appointed Silliman's assistant at Yale, found he had leisure to write his *System of Mineralogy*. Lardner Vanuxem and his colleagues were beginning the survey of the geological history of New York State, and John Torrey was entering his duties as State Botanist. The history of science in America for the next quarter-century did not belie the zest and the productiveness of the year 1836.

Other states followed the example of New York in financing surveys of the regional natural history and in publishing catalogues of the plant and animal life. James Dwight Dana, with the Wilkes Expedition in the Polynesian archipelago, returned to Cambridge in 1842 and in the next year began publication of the series of reports—on mineralogy, geology, crustacea, and corals—which brought him high professional reputation. Bache launched the definitive labors of the United States Coastal Survey in 1843. The eighth edition of Eaton's botanical manual appeared in 1840, describing 5,267 species of American plants; but meanwhile, and through the Fifties, explorations of the West were accumulating new data faster even than the voracious cataloguers could absorb it. John Torrey and Asa Gray commenced publication of their *Flora of North America* in 1843; five years later they had to suspend the series and set about elaborating their old reports.

Yale College signalized the year 1836 by establishing a separate chair of Mathematics; and Denison Olmsted, his department pared down to Natural Philosophy only, had time to write his textbooks. Olmsted's manual of astronomy, first published in 1839, went through forty or fifty editions, so great was the popularity of star-gazing. Yet as late as 1860 there were but six observatories in the United States. Astronomy was predominantly an amateur's sport—the educational pastime of boys with pieces of smoked glass, the coy diversion of young ladies whose responsive sensibilities fluttered at the scintillant beauty of August nights. Professors and students alike learned their astronomy from textbooks. William Cranch Bond's intelligent interest in celestial phenomena was so notable that President Josiah Quincy of Harvard College paid his respects to him, requesting that he transfer his apparatus to Cambridge and pursue his observations there, under the auspices of the university.

Although no salary attached to the offer, Bond agreed. Dana House was fitted up for him by popular subscription, and a cupola was built upon it to accommodate one of his telescopes. Four years later the brilliant comet of 1843, which zoomed across the heavens as a portent of William Miller's millennium, served incidentally so to whet the popular curiosity about astronomy that a subscription could be raised for the procuring of the best telescope that Europe could manufacture. In 1850 (by which time, thanks to a bequest endowment, he had come into a salary) Bond took several daguerrotypes of the star Vega, the first successful experiment in solar photography.

Five years earlier Joseph Henry and Stephen Alexander had made their first experiments in comparison of the temperature of the solar spots with that of other parts of the sun's disk—practically beginning a branch of modern solar physics. Henry's knack of inventing laboratory gadgets and his exposition of the fascinating mysteries of electromagnetism developed a popular reputation comparable only with the esteem that Agassiz and Silliman enjoyed. When Congress got around to the founding of the Smithsonian Institution, in 1846, the legislators expressed their conception of the English donor's intent ("an establishment for the increase and diffusion of knowledge among men," was the phrase in Smithson's will, with no explanatory details) by ordering a building "for the reception of objects of natural history, a chemical laboratory and gallery of art, and the necessary lecture-rooms"—in other words, a museum of natural wonders, a Chamber of Mysteries, and a picture-gallery and lyceum-hall for the benefit of the inhabitants of Washington. Henry was appointed Secretary of the Institution. Congress provided the architecture, Henry provided the interest in pure science; the juncture proved rather incongruous. Henry could not prevent the trustees from establishing a "Scientific Reading Room," but he did succeed in turning most of the resources of the Institution upon the encouragement of original research by prizes, subsidies, and publication.

The college professors had little opportunity and less desire to retire into their laboratories, write up their findings in terms of the recondite algebras, and cultivate the snobbishness of "pure science." Their knowledge was for the practical and spiritual use of students and readers; these scientists belonged to their times and were not reluctant to admit the relationship. Denison Olmsted wrote *Letters on Astronomy*, recasting his formal textbook into epistolary form for the enlightenment of young ladies. Amos Eaton wrote frankly of his *Index to the Geology of the Northern States,* "I have adapted the style to the capacity of ladies, plough-joggers, and mechanics." Espy trouped about the country to enlist popular interest in his curious theories about storms. Agassiz and Silliman performed as earnestly on the lyceum-platform as in class-room or laboratory.

One of the most active minds of an ebullient generation was Matthew Fontaine Maury's—Maury, whose primary studies and bread-and-butter work had to do with current charts and sailing directions. The by-projects that he suggested and outlined in detail concerned, among other matters, great-circle sailing; the study of the causes and effects of the Gulf Stream; a ship canal from the Illinois River to Lake Michigan; redemption of the swamp lands of the lower Mississippi; a canal and railroad across the Isthmus; the "lane route" for transatlantic steamships; and the colonization of the surplus "black and other population of the South" in the valley of the Amazon. Lardner Vanuxem divided his affections among geology, Mormonism, Millerism, Phrenology, feminism, and Egyptian antiquities.

Within the lecture-rooms and laboratories one finds the same benign optimism that tinged the outer world. The great Silliman, whose lectures at Yale College were so popular that ladies were allowed to attend them, had no difficulty in reconciling everything into one benevolent whole. Darwin's great book fazed him only temporarily; and in 1862, nine years after he had become a Professor Emeritus, he announced: "In Nature, in God's creation, we discover only laws—laws of undeviating strictness, and sure penalties affixed for their violation. There is associated with natural laws no system of mercy; that dispensation is not revealed in Nature, and is contained in the Scriptures. . . . I feel that Science and Religion may walk hand in hand."

Louis Agassiz, stamped with European distinction, arrived in Boston in 1846 and began a series of lectures on the "Plan of Creation." He was thirty-nine, enjoyably famous; enthusiasm beamed in his glance, he was found fascinating. He weighed, deliberately, two choices—to return to Europe and pursue the esoteric delights of science, or to remain in America and adapt his pulse to the popular rhythm. The *American Journal of Science* recorded, late in 1847, Agassiz' acceptance of a professorship at Harvard, and added, "Every scientific man in America will rejoice to hear so unexpected a piece of good news." Agassiz married into one of the most eligible of New England families. He set about being one of the most American of Americans and succeeded admirably, even to the extent of becoming an apologist of slavery for ethnological reasons. He made available to students in America the learning and methods of European zoölogists, published a textbook on the *Principles of Zoölogy,* shared with his wife the direction of a school for young ladies in Boston, wrote for the best magazines, and gave a great number of peptonized lectures before mixed audiences. Agassiz had a theory of the manifold origin of the human race which he described often. He who reads (in the *Christian Examiner* for July, 1850, or in many another place) may run.

Agassiz' first concern was to demonstrate the harmony of his theory with the Biblical account in Genesis—a history which, he pointed out, alluded only to the branches of the white race and nowhere referred to the colored peoples. In defense of the dignity of science he asserted that the investigator was privileged to inquire "into the origin of that first human pair, who have been considered as the acknowledged source whence all mankind have sprung. Such an investigation into the ways of nature, into the ways of the Creator, and into the circumstances under which organized beings were created, is a question wholly disconnected with religion, belonging entirely to the department of natural history." And then, getting into the department of the *non sequitur:* "But at the same time, we deny that, in the view we take of these questions, there is any thing contradicting the records in Genesis."

To the most esteemed scientist in the United States there was ample evidence that "time does not alter organized beings."

Cuvier's researches upon fossils; seeds of ancient Egypt that, discovered in modern times, germinated and produced plants differing in no whit from nineteenth-century plants; skeletons found in ancient sarcophagi which exactly correspond to those of modern animals—the proof was too extensive to be worth considering at length.

Agassiz cited the several beasts of prey, with common characteristics in teeth and claws, metabolism, and demeanor which clearly showed that they constituted a natural unity in the Creation. "But because they agree so closely in all these prominent features, has anyone ever thought that the wolf, tiger, and bear originated from a common stock, and that their resemblance was owing to this common origin? Have we not here, on the contrary, the plainest evidence, that, with the most distinct origin, without even the possibility of a mixture among such races, they exhibit a closer resemblance, and dispositions more alike, than the races of men?" And, pursuing that remarkable thought to its human analogy, Agassiz stated that it was not in oversight that the Scriptural account omitted any reference to the inhabitants "of the arctic zones, of Japan, of China, of New Holland, or of America"; but because the several races of men were of diverse origin, and none but the Hebraic and Caucasian had any biotic reminiscence of Adam and Eve.

In November, 1859, Charles Darwin sent to Asa Gray a copy of *The Origin of Species*, with an humble little petition that the author be given "credit for at least an honest search after the truth," and hoping that after the first horripilation the reviewer would "keep the subject under my point of view for some little time" before he wrote his criticism. Gray's long review, in the *American Journal of Science* for March, 1860, fittingly closes an epoch. The summary was detailed and very respectful, carefully withholding approval but containing no word of derogation. Agassiz, an American only by adaptation, was immune to those neural shocks and untouched by the economic shifts which brought wide changes of thought and feeling in the years after 1861; a relic of the Sentimental Years stranded on a strange beach, Agassiz continued to shout against

Darwin. The new generation of students listened to him with proper deference, went out into the world, and taught the Darwinian thesis.

The reader who skims through the Phrenological literature of the quarter-century from 1835 to 1860 will find, in the back pages of volumes entitled *The Truths of Phrenology Vindicated* and the like, pages of testimonials crowded into small print—words of approval from college professors, divines, and Congressmen. Bump-fingering was a science, glib and triumphant. And the science had vibrant moral overtones which were a part of the national music.

The basic topographical labors—the division of the brain into forty-three "organs," the naming thereof, and the drafting of the primary charts—had been performed by European masters. Dr. Joseph Francis Gall, of Swabia and Vienna, after his scalpel had delaminated hundreds of cerebrums and cerebellums and his fingers had sifted over some thousands of scalps, introduced the science in 1796. John Gasper Spurzheim played Brill to his Freud; and George Combe felt extensively of British skulls, to give the science validity to English-speaking peoples. Spurzheim came to Boston in 1832 as missionary of the new knowledge; Combe's textbooks came into American circulation at the same time. And college students, mimicking their anthropoid relatives in this respect as in divers others, felt of one another's heads. Henry Ward Beecher kept a Phrenological bust in his study-room at Amherst; Orson Squire Fowler, a class-mate, there began his career as dean of the science by charging each applicant two cents for a "reading."

John Quincy Adams and other weather-beaten survivors of a more rational age hooted at the science, but the scoffers were few. Webster was at first dubious, but he weakened as Phrenologists garlanded his massive skull with bay upon bay of flattery. (That, after the Farmer of Marshfield had gone to his eternal home, Jeffries Wyman dissected his skull and found Webster's brain to be rather small, incommensurate with its great cranium, was one of those untoward circumstances which cultists are adept at discounting.) The popular attitude toward Phrenology was decidedly favorable, if it hedged somewhat short of complete endorsement. Elisha Barrett, "Professor of the Theory and Practice of Physic in the Medical Department of Transylvania University," expressed the prevailing attitude in his letter to Andrew Boardman: "I am not a practical Phrenologist; that is, I have not made the study and observation of the special organology a matter of practice sufficiently to speak with confidence. I can only say, from study and observation, that I am well satisfied of the truth of the general principles and doctrine of the Phrenological physiology of the brain." Indeed, a frequent disparagement of the science was that, while probably true, it was unnecessary, because a person revealed his character, without possibility of concealment, in his glance and his conversation.

Orson Fowler, immediately after his graduation from Amherst in 1834, adopted the title of Professor, issued handbills, and began lecturing on Phrenology. Fowler cleared forty dollars in his first stand. Good showman that he was, he appealed to ladies with cut-rate prices and other inducements. The first of the American professors of the science, he built Phrenology into a remunerative and dignified activity. What an American could not do to make Phrenology fashionable was performed by George Combe; the great English exponent came to this country in 1838 and lectured for two years.

Fowlers and Wells, at 135 Nassau Street, New York, became a thriving publishing house. Here was issued the *American Phrenological Journal*; the volume *Phrenology Proved, Illustrated, and Applied,* which ran through some thirty editions; numerous writings by Orson Fowler on an incredible variety of subjects; and many works on Hydropathy and kindred uplifts. When, by 1845, the field was overcrowded with showmen, Fowler published directions in the art of reading one's own bumps and making one's own Phrenological chart. His earnest enthusiasm for the science he had helped to popularize was undiminished even when, in his old age, alien races had

EXAMINING ROOM IN THE PHRENOLOGICAL MUSEUM OF FOWLERS AND WELLS

New-York Illustrated News, 1860.

taken over his charts as a variant to fortune-telling and Phrenological lecturers were no longer *à la mode*.

Phrenology in the United States unloosed its pinions and soared into universality. It became a key to life "throughout all its multifarious aspects and interrelations," in the definition of one of its Professors; its comprehensive analysis succeeded where "all past and present fractional attempts to expound and improve humanity have signally failed."

Every mental factor had its corresponding "organ" in each hemisphere of the brain. The mass of each organ varied according to the vigor of its influence, and the hillocks and vales of the cranial shell served as indices to the diverse importance of the mental faculties. These faculties were commonly grouped into nine major classifications ("Animal, Domestic, Moral, Self-Perfecting, Sensory, Perceptive, Literary, Reflective, and Aspiring") and comprised forty-three items in all, governing the sum total of human activity. The science has been mutable in minor detail; charts have varied with the education of the "Professor" and the demands of the trade (currently, to allow for our lustful propensities, the organ of Amativeness is represented as very large indeed). The chart here reproduced is that published by Fowlers and Wells, the standard of its time.

With all the mental traits engrossed under forty-three rubrics some of the organs had a great deal to attend to. Among the "animal appetites" is Bibation, which relates to "the drinker; love of liquids; fondness for water, washing, bathing, swimming, sailing, stimulants, water scenery, etc."; and Destruction includes "the exterminator; executiveness; severity; sternness; harshness; love of tearing down, destroying; hardihood; teasing, etc.; revenge." Orson Fowler's definition of Love runs, "sexuality; gender; desire to love, be loved, and fondled; passion; sexual admiration, courtesy, and blending."

The infinite diversity of human character and feeling was accounted for by the action of the organs working in combination. The sum total of human activity was, then, the number of possible combinations to be made from the labeled items—

multiplied by factors of the fourth dimension. For Phrenologists recognized the time-element and were certain that the skull changed its contours as specific mental faculties were consistently exercised or neglected. Lorenzo Fowler, upon concluding an eighteen months' lecturing tour, felt of his own bumps and found that Observation, Form, Size, Eventuality, Language, and Comparison had become enlarged. Another "Professor" examined the head of "Mr. S. of R." in 1836 and found a marked depression between Firmness and Kindness—a cavity which should have been occupied by the bump of Devotion. The lecturer exhorted his subject to cultivate religion. In 1842 the Professor examined the gentleman again; lo, the depression had become a protuberance. The gentleman acknowledged that, having taken the Phrenologist's homily to heart, he had become a "praying man" and had been continually devout.

Abnormalities in human behavior were explained by the inflammation or other vagary of particular organs. Case-histories were marshaled into plausible books, wherein one learns, for instance, of the Irish laborer—a Mr. Hunter of Wilmington—who was injured by a powder-explosion, the charge plowing a furrow in his skull, taking its course along the borders of Time and terminating near Mirthfulness. Mr. Hunter, mortally injured, began at once to sing and continued to sing until his death nine days later. An intimate reported, "His principal song was 'Erin go bragh,' and he sung it with a better tune than I ever heard it sung before or since. It beats all how musical his voice was. He sung very loud, and seemed to take a great deal of pleasure in it." So much for violent stimulation of the organ of Music. One may learn, too, of "Mr. C.," appropriately of Boston, who was subject to violent pains in the forehead (the seat of the intellectual organs), during which spells he was observed to think, study, and write; and of that citizen of Hatfield, Massachusetts, a man of talent but "deranged in the matter of love, while he is sane in other respects." This person complained often of a sensation of compression and of a buzzing sound exactly in that portion of the head where the organ of Friendship is located.

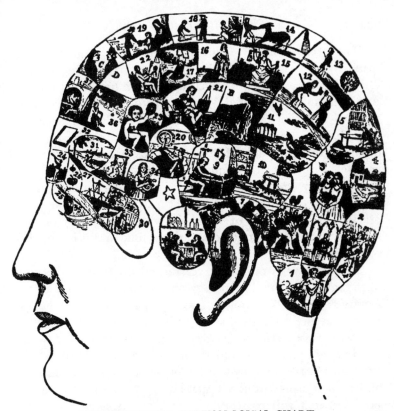

THE SYMBOLICAL PHRENOLOGICAL CHART

American Phrenological Journal, 1852, published by Fowlers and Wells. Below is the key to the "definition of the faculties, according to their numbers":

Domestic Propensities
1. Amativeness
2. Philoprogenitiveness
3. Adhesiveness
4. Inhabitiveness
A. Union for life
5. Continuity

Selfish Propensities
E. Vitativeness
6. Combativeness
7. Destructiveness
8. Alimentiveness
9. Aquisitiveness
10. Secretiveness
11. Cautiousness
12. Approbativeness
13. Self-esteem
14. Firmness

Moral Sentiments
15. Conscientiousness
16. Hope
17. Spirituality
18. Veneration
19. Benevolence

Semi-intellectual Sentiments
20. Constructiveness
21. Ideality
B. Sublimity
22. Imitation
23. Mirthfulness

Intellectual Organs
24. Individuality
25. Form
26. Size
27. Weight
28. Color
29. Order
30. Calculation
31. Locality
32. Eventuality
33. Time
34. Tune
35. Language

Reasoning Intellect
36. Causality
37. Comparison
C. Human Nature
D. Agreeableness

The great Horace Mann said that a young man should spend his last dollar, if he had but one, in learning from a Phrenological examination what occupation he should pursue. And Phrenology, declared Warren Burton, "would teach the voter to look first to Conscience, next to Intellect, but closely to both. It would inform him, moreover in regard to party opinions, that the political oracle who possesses the largest Perceptives, surmounted by equal Reflectives, and above all, and indispensably, crowned with the loftiest Conscientiousness, is most likely to belong to the right party, and be the safest oracle. Let the genius of Freedom, with Christianity on one side and Phrenology on the other, sit sublime in this her mighty continental home."

Orson Fowler would have rearranged the seats at the head of the table and put Phrenology on the right-hand side of the genius Freedom. Phrenology was a thing of practical utility, which was the ultimate goal of universal nature. "In connection with a sister science [Hydropathy, apparently] it is sweeping into oblivion those old theories, unnatural customs, and erroneous institutions, by which past ages have been enthralled, and even the present is yet spellbound. So great is its moral power, that it will prostrate and ride over *whatever* religious doctrines, forms, or practices conflict with it. If even the Bible could be found to clash with it, then would the Bible *go by the board. Nothing could save it*; for it would war with truth, and must suffer defeat." Contrariwise, if the Bible were found to harmonize with Phrenology, then the Bible could claim the support of Nature's immutable laws, and infidelity and atheism were overthrown.

The violet-like Fowler made just such a comparison, in a volume published in 1844 entitled *Religion Natural and Revealed; or, the Natural Theology and Moral Bearings of Phrenology . . . compared with those Enjoined in the Scriptures.* Book-jackets not having been invented, Fowler incorporated a model review of his volume in its preface. "Requiring some minor qualifications, but tenable in every material position, as well as unanswerable in every leading argument. It asks no favor, but investigation—it yields nothing to the religions that be. Its pathway is *philosophy*. Its goal is eternal right. Strewed behind it in all its course, are the nauseating carcasses of hydro-headed error in all its forms. It stands high on the hill of *Science*. Its roots run deep into the nature of man. Its branches yield all manner of delicious fruits, for the healing of the nations, and the renovation of mankind. Its moral truths are food to the hungry, a cooling beverage to the thirsty soul, a foundation to those whom the tides of error are sweeping onward to destruction, and a feast of reason, with a flow of soul—sight to the blind, feet to the lame, health to the invalid, vitality to the dying, and life to the dead." In short, quite a useful book. And Fowler sent it forth "upon the angry sea of sectarian contention, to calm its troubled waters; to harmonize conflicting sentiments, and to disseminate truth, and love, and moral purity among mankind." If the book failed somewhat, the fault was not obscurity; *Religion Natural and Revealed* ran through ten editions in four years.

The Bible came out of it pretty well. Man's large organ of Veneration demonstrated that religious sentiments were natural to him. Both Phrenology and the Bible recognized a spiritual essence, the soul. Both enjoined sentiments of justice, penitence, and forgiveness; inculcated hopes of immortality; demanded filial piety, moral purity, connubial love, patience, hospitality, and the rest of the moral virtues. Both interdicted profanity, murder, and kindred vices. The Biblical emphasis on Charity corresponded to the large domain given Benevolence in the Phrenological chart. But wherever the newer humanitarianism was in conflict with the Old Testament, Phrenology belabored the Old Testament. The toughest knot of sectarian controversy, the doctrine of original sin, was solved by "the Phrenological doctrine of hereditary descent"; a little of original vice, that is, had survived along with a little of original goodness, original Inhabitiveness, Vivativeness, and the other pristine organs.

That Phrenology was a moral science in its own right anyone could surmise from the location of the moral organs—at the very top of the head. ("The feet," explained Fowler, "are the menials of the body, and accordingly, are placed at the bottom of all, because they are the servant of all, and because they can describe their appropriate function there better than anywhere else.") The moral organs were large—further proof of their importance in the science. But, possessing neither cosmology nor mysticism of its own, Phrenology was stretched too far when its Professors tried to make a cult of it.

This truth, however, was generally half-accepted, so to speak —that cranial bumps showed the human character; and that gestures, intonations, postures, all reveal the innate man. "In nine cases out of ten it will be found," wrote one of *Godey's* contributors, "that the most inveterate liars, after long practice and experience, still retain the winking, blinking, skulking look, and the shuffling, faltering tongue." To the Sentimental generation, life was imitating literature: the magnate strutted, the villain slunk, the hero strode, the heroine minced. And while life was conscientiously a window-dressing of the soul, the naïve analyst was likely to be right. So: intellectual men always carried their heads forward (the intellectual lobe was located just behind the brow), pompous gentlemen threw their heads back (in the direction of Dignity), firm persons inclined not a hair's breadth backward or forward (the organ of Firmness was aligned with the body's center of gravity). Light, easy sneezers were easy-going and amiable, but inefficient, persons; people whose sneezes were loud and explosive were resolute and forceful in character. "Coarse-grained and powerful organizations have a coarse, harsh, grating voice; while in exact proportion as persons become refined and elevated mentally, will their tones of voice become correspondingly refined and perfected." The demarcation between folklore and "science" wears thin. In Comparative Physiognomy the border is almost transparent.

This last system would seem to be a gallimaufry of Gall, Leibnitz, and St. Francis of Assisi—three writers with whom

Mr. James Redfield, sponsor of the science and author of *Comparative Physiognomy*, was probably unacquainted. It is likely that he was enabled to write his masterwork simply by virtue of being a good American of keen sensibilities. Several books on Physiognomy ("How to Read Character at a Glance") were in circulation among the enlightened of the middle class when Mr. Redfield's volume appeared, in 1852. Other systems of Physiognomy were to Redfield's, however, what gold-bricking is to alchemy.

COMPARATIVE PHYSIOGNOMY

James W. Redfield, *Comparative Physiognomy, or, Resemblances between Men and Animals*, 1852. "The next example which we present of a resemblance to the lion is John Jacob Astor. The history of this individual, in connection with his face, is a confirmation of the principle stated at the outset. A sordid look, we see, is compatible with the lion, otherwise there would be no pertinence in the allusion to "the lion's share." But there is no littleness in anything that he thinks or does. It is not emulation that makes the lion-like individual do things on a larger scale than others. He has the desire of doing great things, but they are little in his estimation when he has done them. He therefore takes no pride in what he does; and to show that what others stare at, is nothing in his eyes, he may give it away."

First, the St. Francis: "We are hard-hearted indeed if, having studied our relationship to the inferior animals, we are not disposed to treat them more kindly. We sympathize with them, for we perceive the same faculties which warm our breasts animate theirs." Add the Leibnitz: what a delightful world of moral affinities this is! "It must have been an agreement in the first place between the Laplander and the reindeer that brought them together. The former must have seen the adaptation of the latter to his own necessities and pursuits; and the latter, when brought into the service of the superior, acknowledged, by his submission and acceptance of favors in return, that no violence was done to his nature, but that there was afforded a wider field for the exercise of his predominant faculties." Add Phrenology to these two strains, and the melody is Comparative Physiognomy.

Mr. Redfield's volume had many illustrations. Beside the head of an eminent person was, for purposes of comparison, the head of a bird or beast—starling, crow, wolfhound, okapi, whichever completed the best resemblance. The visual likeness confirmed a spiritual similarity. One example may suffice— Jenny Lind, who was *not,* in the light of Comparative Physiognomy, the Swedish Nightingale: "The truth is, Jenny Lind represents a lioness. There is something in the unimposing dignity and active strength of the lioness. . . . It is no objection to this resemblance that her voice is powerful, resonant, and of great compass—for it is the counterpart of the most splendid bass that was ever heard." The ethical message of it all was that man possessed within himself a menagerie of beasts and birds, clean, unclean, wild and tame; "to name them and govern them by morality and religion, is his highest duty and his highest delight."

CHAPTER TEN

The Children's Hour

*A*DAM never played marbles, nor drove a tandem of boys with a string; he never skated on a pond, nor played "hooky" from school. All the gay, irresponsible things young Adam—were reviewed by a philosopher in New York State whose sympathy bridged the ages. And Eve: she never made a playhouse, nor took tea with another little girl, nor pieced a baby quilt and cuddled a doll. "They never played 'blind man's buff,' or 'pussy wants a corner,' or 'hurly burly.' " How blank must have been their declining years, mused Mr. Samuel H. Hammond, "wherein no memories of early youth came welling up in their hearts, no visions of childhood floating up from the long past, no mother's voice chanting a lullaby to the ear of fancy in the still hours of the night, no father's words of kindness speaking from the grave in the churchyard where he sleeps! ADAM and EVE, and they alone of all the countless millions . . . had no childhood."

This bit of Sentimental furfur, from a volume entitled *Country Margins* (1855), bespeaks an important social development—the new attitude toward the child. The fashion-plates in the ladies' magazines are eloquent of the change; for the children are very often there, in preposterous clothes imitating mama's and papa's but with their hoops, ropes, and dolls. The little ones are at play, and the grown-up ladies, stiff though they be in the latest frounces from Paris, are beaming at them. Childhood had been discovered. The first fifteen or eighteen years of life were no longer primarily a rigorous apprenticeship in the business of being an adult; little ones were being seen and heard.

When the history of the Cult of the Child is written (and some of the later chapters will be ruefully amusing), the narrative will take its impetus from another humanitarian force, the expansion of the emotional and social life of the average woman. And it will give much attention to other aftermaths of the Industrial Revolution: the fantasy-life of the harassed adult, the dream of regression into childhood—to have one's cake, that is, without having to work for it; the philosophy of natural virtue and virtuous simplicity, with its facile deduction that the child is more natural, simple, and virtuous than the adult; the "love-force"; and the remarkable discovery that every male person had a chance of becoming President.

"All our social misdirections and disorders run straight back into the lessons of childhood," declared the Reverend F. D. Huntington, one of the Sentimental generation's favorite ministers. "Into the lessons"—the hurtful impressions of disagreeable facts as they forced themselves into the child's world. The statement now sounds like a platitude; but as late as the Eighteen Twenties it would have been phrased, most social misdirections and disorders run straight back to the lack of lessons in childhood. A positive expression of the new attitude was Paul Siogvolk's "A child is not a mere finite sequence of matrimonial union, sometimes welcome and sometimes obtrusive, but is the germ of an existence at least as important as our own." "Love is the sanctioner and fulfiller of law," declared Huntington, urging that, in the training of a child, authority be preceded and accompanied by sympathy. Siogvolk, using the pages of the *Knickerbocker* in 1852 to appeal for greater liberty for children, asked, "What matters it if childhood do go somewhat astray? May not its very error be its destined pathway to rectitude? May it not be that we are sacrilegiously interfering with the ways of PROVIDENCE in thus arbitrarily mapping out the travels of an immortal soul?"

That heterodox query introduces a subject of much concern to the generation, the place of the child in the Church. The Sunday School movement was in full bloom. Its steady increase was not left to chance but was being promoted by an interdenominational body, the American Sunday School Union. This body was also interested in the circulation of good books among the Sunday scholars. The shift in the religious education of children away from catechismal dogma, toward "applied Christianity," was encouraged by the Union's publications, of which *Useful Lads; or, Friendly Advice to Boys in Business* may be taken as a typical description of practical morality. The chapter-titles are "Temper and Behavior," "Obedience," "Punctuality and Exactness," "Personal Habits and Appearance," "Industry," "Improvement," "Truthfulness," "Care of Property." Founded in 1824, the Union was distributing over $125,000 worth of books annually by 1848. In the latter year about two hundred thousand men and women in the United States were teachers of Sunday Schools.

The regeneration of a child's nature by baptism seemed a beautiful, vital symbol. The thought was caressed in many fugitive essays, and the Reverend Nehemiah Adams wrote a novel to show the moral beauties of immersion of the very young. Its protagonist says of infant-baptism, "It makes you love God the Father in such a way as the Lord's Supper makes you love the Savior. I think, sometimes, that the baptism of children is our heavenly Father's sacrament." Few thoughts, perhaps, could be so beautiful (or so fuddled). But other friends of the little ones resented the suggestion that a child stood in need of any regeneration, symbolical or otherwise.

Worth far more than baptismal fonts, stated the Reverend J. B. Waterbury, were the faith and example of Christian parents. Parents must recognize in their offspring the gift of God; and in the human race "at that very period, where the lower animals abandon their young, begins to operate that high moral care which, having instinctive love as its base, rises and reaches to the very termination of the child's earthy existence."

So, in the good family, there developed a moral likeness between parent and child. Such was the popular belief, and the reading-books for young children mirrored the principle. Mrs. Sigourney wrote a book of *Letters to Mothers* to direct the moral blossoming, urging that mothers use poetry as an aide ("Its melody is like a harp to the infant ear, like a trumpet stirring up the new-born intellect"). Emerson would have had the mother receive instruction from the infant. He would not permit his children to be baptized, because, as he told Fredrika Bremer, the nature of a child was purer than that of an adult.

"Almost all children are as pure as Eve was," declared Dr. Samuel G. Howe; "but the tempting apples are left hanging so thickly around, that it would be a marvel if they did not eat." Vested orthodoxy was becoming touchy at the inroads of humanitarian innovation; and that sentence (which appeared in a report by the doctor of his success in training the blind, deaf, and dumb Laura Bridgman to appreciate and love the world about her) was snapped up. It was heresy. If children shared Eve's purity, then they were born with a moral character; they shared Eve's holiness until they tumbled from their original righteousness, as she did. And what becomes of Original Sin? The battle mounted to a roar when Horace Bushnell published his *Discourses on Christian Nurture*.

That booklet, by the pastor of the North Church ("Orthodox") of Hartford, appeared in 1847 under the innocent label of the Massachusetts Sabbath School Society. Its message was that the child should be so trained as never to know the time when he became regenerated in Christ. The technical experience of "repentance of sin" was to be practically a prenatal occurrence. "The child is bathed by love as it enters upon its present being, and the kiss of maternal tenderness is the first quickening influence which greets its undeveloped nature." Reared in this same lavabo, under an incessant sprinkle of mother's kisses, the child would seem to have loved virtue from his earliest moment; his spiritual regeneration would have occurred without a struggle. The variance of *Christian Nurture* from their Bible soon was hotly indicated by protesting conservatives. Bushnell was engaged in a combat of pamphlets and counter-pamphlets which went through several volleys. The Sabbath School Society suppressed the tract; its author republished it. And the students of the Harvard Divinity School, planning the college anniversary program, elected Bushnell to deliver three sermons.

There was as merry a war over the attitude of the schools toward the child. The Keates and the Busbys had to be dealt with. Outside the school-room a clamor of discussion, pro and con, over corporal punishment, was counterpoint to the school-room whimperings of swinged and feruled pupils. Such discipline was an old fashion, and schoolmasters were a generally conservative class. Children were whipped for truancy, tardiness, "for unkempt hair, or task unconn'd"; summoned out of the spelling-match line and told, "Put out your hand," if they forgot to pronounce the word before they spelled it; and perhaps feruled if they read from books laid flat on the desk instead of being held slantwise at the approved angle. A master in the Eighteen Forties boasted of having welted a dozen boys consecutively for not having learned the difference between "immorality" and immortality." In one of the public schools of Boston, no more harsh in its discipline than many others, a tabulation in 1844 listed floggings to the respectable total, on an average, of one hundred and thirty a day. The school's enrollment was about two hundred and fifty students; it was a coeducational institution.

The *Southern Literary Messenger,* leading belletristic ornament of the South, printed in 1841 a little essay entitled "Corporal Punishment as a Moral Discipline." It was written by a schoolmaster of Petersburg, Virginia, and was published not as a pathological document, but in common with the other items in the magazine as a deserving piece of literature. It had humor, and eloquent persuasion. "Flagellation," wrote the essayist, "is compendious and economical of time. It is refreshing—composes the wandering thoughts, brightens the wits, quickens the animal spirits and braces the nerves. It is a sort of Animal Magnetism, a galvanic battery—a thunderstorm to purify the moral atmosphere." And as to those persons who argued against corporal punishment, the essayist pointed out that they owed their very skill in argument to having had, in their boyhood, scholarship flogged into them.

The perverse joys of the paddle and the rod were an old privilege of the teaching craft; and the masters defended it valiantly, even—when an opponent of Horace Mann's ability pressed them hard—hysterically. The brief for the defendants Birch and Ferule was ably set forth by a schoolmaster of Baltimore in the *Evangelical Review* in 1849: (1) swishing had "the highest authority," from which Christians should not dissent—the twenty-odd allusions to the rod in the Scriptures; (2) "the divine moral government of the world" embraced corporal punishment, for, as the fate of libertine and drunkard demonstrated, people were "physiologically so constituted that we cannot habitually violate the laws of nature without incurring corporal pain"; (3) well-regulated governments used force when moral persuasion was inadequate; (4) "Experience is the best teacher," and young buttocks had been pinked since time immemorial; (5) the rising generation, not shent as thoroughly and often as the preceding generations of youth, furnished an awful example of the results of leniency: "defaced and broken milestones, bespattered handboards, mutilated works of art, etc." The schoolmaster spoke as one with experience, for the Board of Commissioners of the public schools of Baltimore had made, in the summer of 1848, a concession to the humanitarians. Corporal punishment was abolished in the "male High School" (not in the grammar-schools). After eight months the concession was revoked.

The crusade against the birch was stimulated by newspaper stories in 1836, when a "female seminary" in Massachusetts received uninvited publicity about its teachers' custom of stripping the girls before disciplining them. The unpleasant fact, effortlessly calling up a mental image, led directly to a humanitarian conviction. The birching of girls didn't jibe at all with that deference to women which was the generation's boast. "How, then," demanded Lyman Cobb, "can we expect young gentlemen and boys to treat girls with kindness, and regard them as the gentler, nobler, and lovelier sex," if they saw girls being flogged? "Let the person and character of the female be held sacred."

This worthy precept Cobb stated in a volume named *The Evil Tendencies of Corporal Punishment as a Means of Moral Discipline in Families and Schools,* published in 1847. The author, a school-teacher and writer of many textbooks, enumerated some sixty "objections," each with its complement of "points" and "remarks." To this closely packed ammunition he added a section on ways and means of disciplining without the rod and printed a great many letters from school superintendents and eminent politicians in approval of his thesis. The many "objections" cover all matters from the physical damage to the victim to the moral welfare of the flagellator. Parents or teachers who trounced their children, he stated, were apt, immediately after a vigorous session, to speak in an unkind or irritable manner to other members of the family or school. Cobb remarked that the tendency of drunkards to beat their wives "proves that the system is actuated by a bad spirit," and Horace Mann declared that the exhilaration felt by the teacher just after administering summary punishment was no virtuous sensation, but decidedly was from the Devil—both reformers coming within an ell of recognizing the erotic roots of the folkway.

One particular anomaly of Female Virtue disturbed Lyman Cobb—the fact that some mothers favored whippings for their children and urged husband or teacher to whack soundly. The good Mr. Cobb resolved the difficulty thus: "It may be asked, *can* a MOTHER do this? I answer; it is ONLY the case where all the *finer* and *nobler* feelings of a MOTHER have become blunted by an EXCESSIVE use of VERY STRONG *tea* or *coffee,* or of *wine* or *brandy,* etc.; or, by the use of *snuff;* or, when the LOVE of PLEASURE and GAYETY has taken full possession of the mind, instead of the LOVE OF DOMESTIC HAPPINESS!"

The war between the disciplinarians and the anti-spankers may best be followed in its Boston sector. Horace Mann, Secretary of the Massachusetts Board of Education, reluctantly believed that corporal punishment, "in the present state of society, and with the available corps of teachers," was an occasional necessity. One of his objects in sponsoring normal schools was to train teachers to rely on moral suasion—in his phrase, "the all but omnipotent power of generosity and affection." His *Seventh Annual Report* assailed the teachers of Boston for two malfeasances—their methods of discipline and their slovenly results in the teaching of reading. (In 1837 the Primary School Committee of Boston had recommended the adoption of a certain textbook, Gallaudet's *The Mother's Primer,* and its use became general. From *The Mother's Primer* children learned words first and the letters of the alphabet afterwards; the school-teachers, however, had not been taught in that manner, and they adapted their instruction most indifferently.) Mann's *Report* was almost polemical, and the schoolmasters rallied to defend the old ways.

Thirty-one schoolmasters signed the *Remarks on the Seventh Annual Report,* which included the patriarchal lament, "It is quite offensive now-a-days to ears polite, to talk of authority, and command, and injunction," and the homily, "How careful should men of influence be to guard against encouraging that excessive love of freedom which can brook no restraint." Mann answered in a pamphlet which was a masterpiece of political art. He pleaded that his name had been attached to ideas he had never approved, spoke of "mutilated and garbled quotations" and "the forced transposition of paragraphs" to distort his actual statements, and added that the schoolmasters' pamphlet was very badly written. He published a letter from George Combe wherein the great Phrenologist said to Mann, "You love what is good, and by elective affinity are attracted towards it, and draw it towards you, be it French, German, or American." He intimated that the Boston masters were overpaid, getting fifteen hundred dollars a year in contrast with the seven hundred dollars or nine hundred dollars paid better schoolmasters in smaller towns of the state. And in the matter of corporal punishment Mann played his sentimental trump. The schoolmasters, in defending their right to flog, had made no distinction of sex. "Would you whip the sensitive, trembling girl, who comes to school effusive of sweet affections, and as inoffensive as the flowers which she brings as an offering to her teacher?"

Probably they would not; but they demanded the right to do so if they felt like it. And the exchange of pamphlets went on to Mann's final blast, *Answer to the 'Rejoinder' of Twenty-Nine Boston Schoolmasters, Part of the Thirty-one who published 'Remarks'.* . . .

The regulation adopted by the Boston school system that teachers keep a written record of corporal punishments, enforced from the year of the pamphlet war, coöperated with the popular humanitarianism toward the physical comfort of the school-children. By 1860 the daily average of floggings in the public schools of Boston, taken in the aggregate, was only seventy-four—an amazing reduction of educational violence within one generation.

Greater amenity in the school-room was in part an effect of the refining influence of the gentler sex. Teaching in the public schools was becoming a woman s occupation; the trend gathered momentum in the late Forties, and in 1852, out of eight thousand teachers in the public schools of Massachusetts, six thousand were women. Of the 120 teachers in the Brooklyn public schools that year, 103 were women; in Philadelphia, 699 of a teaching staff of 781.

Even in schools where "mildnesse, and gentle entreatie" was the mode, the scholars were under physical strain. The school-day was inordinately long, and there were six school-days in the week. Humanitarians became aware of the evil, but one difficulty in the way of practical reform was the extreme

Rousseauism of the proposed remedies. Horace Mann made inquiries of leading physiologists in 1840 and put their answers

DECIDING UPON THE PEOPLE'S EDUCATION
Common School Assistant, 1839.

in his next *Report.* Children over eight years of age, ran the replies, should have no more than four hours of schooling on a winter day, nor more than five in summer; no homework;

and should have intervals of rest or play after each hour. Younger children should not study for more than a half-hour at a time. One physiologist added that if a child showed "alarming symptoms of precocity," he should be removed from school altogether.

The city physician of Boston in 1854 protested against over-work in schools, as repulsive to "fact, feeling, and physiology." A Committee of Inquiry found the teachers amazed at the suggestion that the scholars' tasks were excessive; ill health among their pupils arose, they suggested, from indulgence in confectionery, late hours and excitement at parties, "chewing pitch," and other indiscretions which it was the province of the parents to correct. The Committee was responsible for a statute added to the school regulations, limiting homework assignments to the maximum a boy of ability could perform in an hour and providing that no out-of-school lessons at all should be required of girls.

No such solicitude for the tender sex affected the course of study at the fashionable seminaries for young ladies, where the proprietors strove with the complex task of imparting nicety in manners, acquaintance with the French language, and some measure of English literacy to the little buds of the new aristocracy. Thomas Wentworth Higginson, in a fervent article, "The Murder of the Innocents," in the *Atlantic* for September, 1859, quoted the daily schedule at a seminary noted for the gloss of its finished product. The girls rose at five and studied until the breakfast hour (seven to eight), then were in the class-room for six consecutive hours, until two. After dinner, from three to five, they had opportunity to attend to their sewing, letter-writing, school politics, and all the small miscellanies of existence. From five to six was a study-hour; six to seven was "tea"; and two hours were left for study until bedtime. At another seminary, one with rather more swank, the girls rose at six-thirty; after a study-period and breakfast, from nine until twelve-thirty they attended recitations. A half hour for "recreation and lunch" intervened before a two-hour period of "studies exclusively in the French language." And the remainder of the day was crowded with recitation and study, until half-past nine, when "lights in the sleeping apartments must be extinguished."

EXERCISES WITH INDIAN SCEPTERS
Godey's Lady's Book, 1849.

Yet at the time Higginson was protesting in the *Atlantic,* already the tendency of private schoolmasters was to advertise "Especial attention given to physical education." The endeavors of Mrs. Sarah J. Hale and other social workers to obtain playgrounds for city children were bearing fruit; and the cult of physical education, then meek and apparently harmless, was claiming a part in the educational process. In the decade following the Sentimental Years it infected the colleges. The Jutes had come to the aid of the Britons.

The generation believed fervidly in education; "cultivated conscience and intellect" triumphing over "mere animalism" was an analogy to free America triumphing over the sordid monarchisms of Europe. Universal education was recognized as an essential bulwark to the republican idea; the task of educating the young passed from sectarian and other private interests to the State. This transition opened the way to other changes, in curriculum and in teacher-training. On the frontier this development was comparatively unhindered, for there was no propertied conservative class to object to the cost of State-supported education. Michigan in 1837 added a state university to complete a full program from primary school to college. In the East private interests retained control of the colleges. And before the principle of free common-school education could prevail in the older states, strong prejudices had to be overcome—the belief that education was not one of the "civil things" that were the proper concern of government, and that to compel a citizen to contribute to the support of the schools against his will was an infringement of individual liberty. Henry Barnard and Horace Mann were leaders in the struggle.

Mann was the most effective of the educational reformers of his time, and he has left the deepest impress upon American education. A "manipulator" in the office of the Messrs. Fowler, in New York, after feeling Mann's cranial bumps, reported, "We seldom find so large a brain in the tophead, in the region of the organs of reason, imagination, sympathy, dignity, perseverance, wit, and moral sentiment, joined with so little basilar brain in the animal and selfish organs." His busy ten years as Secretary of the State Board of Education in Massachusetts amply confirmed this complimentary description. The existence of the Board itself, the first transplanting of Prussian educational organization into this country, was largely due to Mann's efforts; and that the American structure of "grades" so closely mimics the Prussian departments is evidence of the permanence of Mann's work. Henry Barnard founded the *American Journal of Education* in 1855, in effect the first national journal of the teaching profession. He had established, in the Forties, a state system of public schools in Rhode Island and had done similar pioneering service in Connecticut.

Between the establishment of a public school system in Pennsylvania in 1834 and the introduction of a state-wide structure of elementary education in New York in 1849, property owners were generally convinced that the dangers of an illiterate but enfranchised democracy outweighed the taxation necessary to support free schools. In acknowledgment of their utilitarian origin the schools shunted Latin out of the elementary grades. The entrance requirements of the colleges protected the liberal studies in the high schools from being displaced by the bookkeeping arts; but most college students were trained in the private academies.

A Massachusetts philanthropist, Edmund Dwight, in 1837 offered to contribute ten thousand dollars toward a school for the professional education of teachers if the legislature would duplicate the sum. The result was the opening of the first public normal school in the United States, at Lexington in 1839. New York State was next to follow. David P. Page wrote the standard text on principles and methods of school-teaching, quoting liberally from Horace Mann. Page's text, Mann's twelve *Reports,* and the volumes of Barnard's *Journal* were the literary seeds of the modern profession.

One of the Graces was admitted into the school-room, and there was talk of inviting a sister Grace or two. Since music was put to admirable use in setting tonal mood in churches, argued D. H. Barlow in *Godey's,* the legislative halls of the nation should be equipped with orchestras. Music was not adopted, his suggestion to the contrary, to soothe the savage Congressman; but it did find a place in the elementary schools. A petition drawn in the office of Lowell Mason's private Academy of Music in Boston was endorsed by prominent citizens and forwarded to the School Board in 1836. A committee of that Board, in discussing the memorial, offered strong persuasions that music was sufficiently a disciplinary study to warrant its admission into the schools. Music was vindicated by intellectual standards ("Memory, comparison, attention, intellectual faculties—all are quickened by a study of its principles"), moral criteria ("Happiness, contentment, cheerfulness, tranquillity—these are the natural effects of music"), and physical improvement ("It appears self evident that exercise in vocal music, when not carried to an unreasonable excess, must expand the chest and thereby strengthen the lungs and vital organs"). It was particularly commended as a means of recreation without idleness: "Its office would be thus to restore the jaded energies, and send back the scholars with invigorated powers to other more laborious duties."

After an experimental year under Mason at one grammar-school, the youngsters were led by him in a public exhibition.

WILD WOOD FLOWERS.

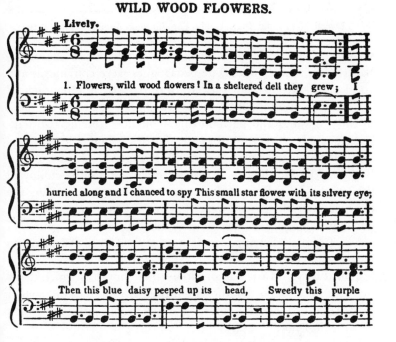

1. Flowers, wild wood flowers ! In a sheltered dell they grew;

hurried along and I chanced to spy This small star flower with its silvery eye;

Then this blue daisy peeped up its head, Sweetly this purple

orchis spread, I gathered them all for you— I

gathered them all for you; All these wild wood flowers, Sweet wild wood

flowers—All these wild wood flowers, Sweet wild wood flowers.

Lowell Mason and G. J. Webb, *The Juvenile Singing School*, 1844.

sang the little ones, and with other lyrics made the South
Baptist Church resound. The pedagogues were convinced; and
vocal music from 1838 onward was part of grammar-school
education in Boston. Professional teachers conducted exercises
in this "refining and harmonizing influence" during two half-
hour periods weekly. Within the Forties other cities in New
England and the most enterprising capitals of the West—
Buffalo, Pittsburgh, Cincinnati, Chicago, Louisville—followed
the example of Boston. In most large towns, by 1860, the
public-school fledglings were singing in unison. And vocal
music was lugging a sister luxury, drawing, into the course of
study. But not dancing. If mothers wished their offspring to
know the schottische and the lanciers, on themselves be the
responsibility. "Music has an intellectual character which dancing has not," reported the committee of the Boston School
Board, "and above all, music has its moral purposes which
dancing has not."

The solid stuff of education was little changed, but it was written in more amiable, sprightly fashion. To these qualities the Peter Parley books owed their wide success in school and home. Samuel Griswold Goodrich, who hid behind the elfin pseudonym, wrote a *Geography for Beginners* which sold two million copies; and his *Universal History upon the Basis of Geography* was also a publisher's darling. The greater part of the *Universal History* was written not by Goodrich, but by a scrivener ghost, Nathaniel Hawthorne, who got a hundred dollars for the job. Hawthorne worked at it with the aid of his sister Elizabeth and turned in the completed volume in 1836. Goodrich wrote his employee, "I like the History pretty well; I shall make it do," signed the manuscript "Peter Parley," and it was published the next year. The book's circulation passed a million copies.

The *Universal History* was hack-work, and therefore close to the ideals and prejudices of its readers. Written for a generation boastful of its moral refinements, intensely nationalistic, and with naïve conceptions of cause and effect, the book accurately mirrors these qualities.

Of Adam and Eve: "The whole number of inhabitants on this globe is about eight hundred million. All these are descended from Adam and Eve, whom the Bible tells us lived in the Garden of Eden. What an immense family to increase from one pair!"

Of the glory that was Rome: "Splendid as the Roman Empire was, it was destitute of real glory. Its splendor was acquired by robbery, and its fame, though it might dazzle a heathen, will be regarded as a false renown by the Christian."

Of the second French Revolution: "They raised large armies, and drove Charles X and his family out of the kingdom. They then asked the good and glorious La Fayette what sort of a government they should have. He would have chosen a republic, like our own; but he knew that this countrymen were not like us. He therefore told them that the government must be a limited monarchy." The primary cause of the

American Revolution was, in Peter Parley's opinion, the Stamp Act, devised "to take money out of the pockets of the Americans for the use of the king and ministry."

The usual practice of elementary textbooks was to foot up each chapter with a set of questions. The only possible way of answering many of these questions was to prattle the text verbatim. Thus, in the *Universal History,* as part of his lesson on Austria the young innocent was asked, "How may Austria be considered at the present day? What is a curious fact?" The requisite answers lay in two sentences of the text: "At the present day, Austria may be considered one of the leading kingdoms of Europe. It is a curious fact that the emperors of Austria have had a great many beautiful daughters." Whenever the text failed to provide it, the answer was surely to be gleaned from the general fund of moral truisms. The Anderson-Davenport *History of the United States,* used in the public schools of New York and Philadelphia, was simply and undisguisedly an aid to parrot-training. Its text was a series of questions and answers "containing all the events necessary to be committed to memory," a Table of Chronology, and the Declaration of Independence and the Constitution in full.

Teachers might be educated, or enjoined, to cease thwacking their pupils without excellent provocation; they might find it rather easy, after some practice, to radiate moral sunshine about the school-room. But, whatever the normal schools might attempt, the teachers were too much the product of their previous training to be capable of divorcing instruction from textbooks. And the venerable technique of book-learning by rote, lingering into a generation when the tradition of exactness was loosened, produced manuals of facile and blurred information. The pupils of the Chicago common schools, who studied Hutchinson's *Class Book on Rhetoric* ("wherein are exhibited the Graces and Styles of English Composition and Public Oratory"), recited such glib definitions as "The difference between a metaphor and an allegory is that the metaphor is short, the allegory prolonged"; "The qualities of a good style are perspicuity and ornament. Perspicuity implies the setting up of a sentence so that it may be easily understood"; "An extravagant hyperbole is called a metaphor." *The Southern Reader,* Book Second, after wisely advising the scholar that to read with a singing tone was a very silly habit, told him to mind the stops: "When you come to a comma, make a pause long enough to count one; semi-colon, two; colon, four; period, six."

Wherever refining precepts could be introduced into the manuals, they appeared. *Jack Halyard the Sailor Boy; or, the Virtuous Family,* was used as a reading-text in the Philadelphia schools because the merits of its characters were "of the imitable kind." McGuffey's First and Second Readers were published in 1836, the next two in 1837, and the Fifth Reader in 1844; these worthy texts, brimming with good examples, became as standard as Webster's spelling-book. In the "new method," no-spanking schools, like those which Jacob Abbott and William A. Alcott had conducted in the early Thirties, discipline was so enswathed with sugary admonition that the scholars might have welcomed a physical trouncing by way of variety. Several textbooks gave lists of the virtues and the vices, for the pupils to memorize.

"Aunt Alice," author of *First Lessons in Gentleness and Truth,* published by the American Tract Society as a pre-school textbook, declared that children often suffered a gradual blight of the moral affections after their fifth or sixth year because the young minds were being crammed with thoughts "of the abstruser sciences." None of the common pursuits of learning except reading and spelling, urged Aunt Alice, should be taught children younger than nine or ten; the time gained should be devoted to the cultivation of their moral affections. The earlier chapters of the *First Lessons* were entitled "Honor to Parents," "Kindness to Brothers and Sisters," "Show Respect to Aged," "On Behavior at the Table," "How to Behave at School," "I Must be Industrious and Useful," "Remember the Poor." In later chapters the tot learned about not walking on wet grass, being careful with ink, "Using Tobacco Very Filthy," and the purposes of the scraper and the doormat.

A reading-text for children of seven or eight years relates of the truant: "Father told Henry a story the other day, about playing truant, which I do not think he will soon forget. It was about a man who was hung for killing another man; and he began his naughty actions when a boy, while running away from school. There was an exhibition of some sort in a town near by, and he wished very much to go. He thought his father would not be there, and therefore would not find him out. But his father was there, and saw him. The boy had to be punished; but I am sorry to say the punishment did not cure him of his fault. I suppose the boy was not really sorry for what he had done. The boy went on from one bad thing to another, and grew up into a very wicked man, and at last committed murder."

Children's literature prior to 1830 had been didactic without guile. It was a molasses-and-sulphur tonic compounded for the most part by ministers or elderly ladies and intended usually for Sunday reading. But in 1827 Nathaniel Parker Willis began the *Youth's Companion,* and in 1833 Goodrich launched *Parley's Magazine,* both journals presenting a copious miscellany of information, tales, games, and puzzles, and abounding in blurry little woodcuts. The Sunday School Union, in accord with the tendency of the generation to obscure sectarian differences, encouraged its writers to leave dogmatic instruction out of their volumes. With the sulphur reduced to a trace, the little dears actually liked the tonic and were known to save their pennies to buy the Union's doses. As part of the growing amenity of home life, parents came to understand an obligation to provide their children with children's books.

Every one of the household manuals, it seems, included a warning to watch carefully what books entered the domestic sanctuary. But however much immoral literature there was in mid-century America (and there was a distressing quantity), none of it was "juvenile." Warnings to the contrary, there was no such thing as a naughty book for children. Expurgated editions of *Tom Jones* and *Moll Flanders* to serve as children's reading had gone out of fashion at the beginning of the century. Jacob Abbott's *The Young Christian*, first published in 1832, became an international success, and American editions were still being reprinted in the Fifties. This book, persuasively virtuous and written in simple language, was the most popular exemplar of the new gentle method of religious instruction. But the dominant type of juvenile literature was fiction, or at least an alluring pretense of fiction. Mrs. Sarah J. Hale wrote children's stories; so did Mrs. Sigourney. Lydia

SYMPATHY FOR THE LAMBKIN

Aunt Alice's First Lessons in Gentleness and Truth, 1854. The innocent animal is being driven to the butcher's block. The children do not think this right and are mingling generous tears with their unavailing pleas. Mother will have to explain that the lamb's destiny, while apparently cruel, is all for the best.

Maria Child's *Flowers for Children*, all three volumes (1844, 1846, 1855), were thornless flora, beloved by girls but burgeoning with too feminine ecstasy to please both sexes. Miss Eliza Leslie, having written the generation's standard cookery-books, presented the young ladies with the several annual numbers of *The Gift;* her own volumes of short stories for girls were pleasant tales brightly related, which met cordial welcome. Miss Catherine Sedgwick, for many years principal of a famous school for girls, published several volumes of children's stories which reviewers declared made Miss Sedgwick the leading prose-writer of her sex.

Most important in this professional field were two diligent and inexhaustible gentlemen, Jacob Abbott and Samuel G. Goodrich, whose books were primarily designed to satisfy the male child's thirst for knowledge. Goodrich began his labors in emulation of Miss Hannah More, whose *Moral Repository* had been a delightful discovery of his youth; he made a pilgrimage to Britain and received the old lady's blessing before he published his first work. The thesis upon which Goodrich and Miss More agreed was that geography, history, and nature-lore were more seemly elements of juvenile literature than were fairies and giants. The first *Peter Parley* book appeared in 1827; new ones came along until not even Goodrich knew exactly how many there were. The original scheme concerned a kindly old gentleman, marvelously well-informed, talking to an inquisitive set of little prigs. In time Goodrich abandoned the tenuous thread of fiction, and the *Peter Parley* books became practically textbooks; but the geniality and simplicity of style remained. Goodrich calculated, twenty-nine years after his first volume, that he had written or edited about one hundred seventy books. About seven million copies of the *Peter Parleys* had been sold, he reckoned, and they were still selling in 1856 at three hundred thousand copies a year.

Jacob Abbott was the literary father of that prodigy, Little Rollo. The first of the *Rollo* books appeared in 1834. The very young Rollo was induced (he was never *made* to do anything, but was persuaded, in the best manner of the experimental schools then being introduced into the United States) to learn to talk, to see objects for himself, think about them, and ask questions. In the next volume he was taught to read and found how that art, undertaken in earnest, quickly became a very pleasant one. In four succeeding volumes Rollo was exhibited at work, at play, at school, and during vacation—the morals appropriate to each situation being elicited by one or another of the benevolent adults from whom Rollo never escaped. Thereafter Rollo became as ageless as the Katzenjammer Kids and survived in that suspended boyhood for twenty-four volumes in all. His counterparts, of both sexes, lived in other

THE IDLE BOY

The Youth's Casket, 1857, illustrating the following poem:

Thomas was an idle lad,
And lounged about all day;
And though he many a lesson had,
He minded nought but play.

He only cared for top or ball,
Or marbles, hoops, or kite;
But as for learning, that was all
Neglected by him quite.

In vain his mother's kind advice,
In vain his master's care,
He followed every idle vice,
And learned to curse and swear.

Think ye when he became a man,
He prospered in his ways?
No; wicked courses never can
Bring good and happy days.

Without a shilling in his purse,
Or cot to call his own,
Poor Thomas went from bad to worse,
And hardened as a stone.

And oh! it grieves me much to write
His melancholy end;
Then let us leave the dreadful sight,
And thoughts of pity lend.

But may we this important truth
Observe and ever hold:
*"That all who're idle in their youth
Will suffer when they're old."*

series by Abbott—the *Lucy, Jonas, Franconia,* and *Gay Family* books. Abbott also wrote informational volumes for children, among them the long-cherished series of illustrated books innocently named (because of their uniform covers) the *Red Histories.*

There is no measuring-rod to gage the tenaciousness of this moral instruction; but there happens to be an indication of the quantity of factual matter that the public-school pupils could retain awhile, at least until the final examinations. The annual test of pupils in the primary schools of Boston in 1845 was, contrary to custom, uniform for all the schools. The questions, 154 in all, embraced History, Geography, Arithmetic, Grammar, Definitions, Natural Philosophy, and Astronomy (the first five were the required stuff of the curriculum; the latter two were elective subjects). The proportion of correct answers in the tabulated papers is not impressive; with a possible score of 100, the median was 37.5. It was somewhat discouraging to Horace Mann that even among the "medal" scholars there should be some to define *bifurcation* as "washing," *esplanade* as "a body of people," *convocation* as "something that is not heavanly," *connoisseur* as "one that is not acquainted with any art," *evanescence* as "smell," and *Hades* as, bafflingly, "Hell from beneath is moved because of thee." The young mind crammed with historical facts had a way of compressing them: to the question, *In what century was the great French Revolution, and who were some of the characters who figured in it?* there were several insistences upon the seventeenth century and the untoward information that "Napoleon Wellington Blutcher" or "Generals Washington, Wolfe and Montcalm" were participants.

Nearly all the medal scholars knew something about the Norman Conquest, Oliver Cromwell, the Pilgrims, and the American Revolution. The definition of *embargo* as "a prohibitation to pass a stoppage of trade" was not a bad answer. In arithmetic the scholars were really good. For *a short sentence containing an active transitive verb and an objective case,* one pupil's "Wm struck me" was certainly adequate. In supplying *a sentence containing a relative pronoun and an adjective in the comparative degree,* there could be small quarrel with "The days are longer now than what they used to be," or "He who is Sick if not careful will be Sicker"; and the young Penrod who wrote "She was the prettiest girl, that I ever saw," in answer to the same question, at least deserved a mark for his gallantry.

But, mulling over the not very happy results, Horace Mann deplored the excess of book-teaching and the superficial psittacism it produced—the helplessness of the children when, their books put aside, they were called to the blackboard and requested to answer questions not in the texts. More students knew the date of Jefferson's Embargo than could define an embargo; and while the pupils of the Boston schools were comparatively adept in "the mere osteology of language," it seemed regrettable to Mann that a child who could parse correctly the words of a stanza of "Childe Harold" had no glimmer of the sense of the verse. His chief recommendations were simplification of the school organization to provide a single principal; [1] the abolishing of prizes and medals; changes in methods of instruction; less flagellation; and the selection of teachers on a merit basis by competitive examination.

Four of these recommendations had become fact, and the fifth partially adopted, when in 1919 two Professors of Education made an interesting experiment. Thirty questions, equally representing six subjects, were selected from the Boston examinations of 1845; this abbreviated test was given to eighth-grade students in more than two hundred cities. The median score in 1919 was 45.5—eight points nearer perfection than the median of 1845.

Among the comparatively underprivileged scholars in 1845, 61 per cent knew that Lake Erie flows into Lake Ontario; among the fortunate eighth-graders in 1919, 47 per cent asserted that Lake Ontario flows into Lake Erie. In the 1845 examination 92 per cent of the pupils computed the problem, "What part of 100 acres is 63 acres, 2 roods, and 7 square rods?" correctly. By 1919 roods were out of style; so the question was supplemented by the note, "A rood is a measure of land no longer in use. There were 40 sq. rods in a rood, and

---

[1] The Boston system began with the primary school, receiving children at five years. In their seventh year children went to grammar-school and writing-school—in the same building, but with different principals. Classes shifted from one room in the morning to another in the afternoon. In the fourteenth year pupils chose between the Latin High School, leading to college, and the English High School, preparing for the counting-room; each was a two-year course.

4 roods in an acre." With this help 16 per cent of the students in 1919 succeeded in answering the problem correctly. On fifteen of the thirty questions the Boston group excelled the pupils of 1919. They were eighth-grade pupils of the Teachers' College era who variously defined *connoisseur* as "a business man," "a French word meaning 'come again,'" "a motor truck," "to fight for something else," "to think"; *misnomer* as "ill treatment," "a man who studies about certain things," "liking"; *infatuated* as "soaked with," "to get angry"; *monotony* as "harmonization," "about plants," "to get a divorce"; and *dormant* as "a bedroom." It is instructive to remember that the expense (salaries, building, maintenance) of the Boston public school system amounted in 1845 to fourteen dollars for each of the 17,306 pupils; whereas the corresponding expense to the citizens of Detroit for their city's public school system in 1921 amounted to two hundred and seventeen dollars for each of the 143,677 school-children.

Would the very young child who died too soon to attend Sunday School or hear Aunt Alice's lessons abide in heaven? Michael Wigglesworth's *Day of Doom,* a lugubrious chant which the children of colonial New England had memorized along with their catechisms, set forth a tableau in which the Presiding Magistrate addressed the swarm of infants risen from their tiny graves:

> You sinners are, and such a share
>   As sinners may expect.
> Such you shall have, for I do save
>   None but my own elect. . . .
>
> A crime it is, therefore in bliss
>   You may not hope to dwell;
> But unto you I shall allow
>   The easiest room in hell.

The Judge's leniency was the utmost that the penal code (Calvin's *Institutes*) permitted. The acetic Calvin himself

admitted that infant damnation was "a dreadful decree, I confess." But it was one of those matters which he had heard the
Trinity, in ecumenical conference, decide upon: babies were
doomed to eternal torment, in consequence of the fall of Adam.
The Lutheran Church had disowned the Anabaptists because
those heretics affirmed that children were saved without baptism. Wigglesworth's doggerel and Jonathan Edwards' lurid
envisioning of a hell paved with the skulls of babes remained
sound Presbyterian and Congregational doctrine until, in the
second decade of the nineteenth century, the revolt against
creed gained momentum.

The newly flourishing middle class had no taste for such
strong medicine as infant-damnation. Women could not endure
it; and however little was their direct influence in ecclesiastical
conferences, women dominated the social activity of the parish.
Little babies, whose only crime was in dying, consigned to
flaming, roaring torment! Infinite wrath and total depravity
were disagreeable enough, but because they could not be vis-
ualized, they were not so awful as this other. Theodore Parker
linked the three malignant attributes: "Why you could not get
a woman that had sense enough to open her mouth, to preach
these things anywhere. Women think they believe them; but
they do not. Celibate priests, who never knew marriage, or
what paternity was, who thought woman was a 'pollution'—
they invented these ghastly doctrines."

Mothers' need of abiding assurance that their departed children were not wailing under the Divine wrath was answered
by bevies of lady poets and by all manner of literary consolation for bereavements present and potential. One B. F. Barrett
wrote a book, *Beauty for Ashes*, to demonstrate the afterworld
happiness of children. They all went to heaven and lived in
an outdoor palace of beautiful objects—not real gardens, fountains, and arbors, but illusions created by guardian angels.
"Now let the mother believe all this, and will she not derive
support and comfort from it? Will it not give her *beauty for
ashes*, the oil of joy for mourning? Will she not dry her tears,
suppress her sighs, chide her murmurs?" It was a happy fancy,

if it was considerably more fairyland than anything else; for, with the appallingly high mortality of infants and children, mothers were entitled to whatever compensations of the spirit they could persuade themselves to accept.

CHAPTER ELEVEN

The Chariot of Fire

A HARVARD student, in 1837, wore a dark-brown coat on Sunday; he was haled before the faculty committee on discipline for having been garbed in an illegal color. On a Sunday in 1845, shortly after President Polk and his family had returned from church, a servant brought in the card of the Honorable Mr. Jennifer, late Envoy Extraordinary and Minister Plenipotentiary to Austria; the servant was instructed to deliver the message that the President declined seeing company on the Sabbath.

Sunday-observance was so widely practised that it seemed likely to be written into the Federal statutes. Sabbath laws were as strict in Alabama as in Connecticut. The National Lord's-Day Society was an influential body; John Quincy Adams, presiding officer at its annual meeting in 1844, wrote an account of the "snarling debate" over the difference between the terms "Lord's-Day" and "Sabbath" and of the issuing of many addresses—to innkeepers, to close their bars on Sundays; to army officers, not to exact military services from the soldiers on the Lord's Day; to canal commissioners, railroad directors, and Post-Office authorities. In several states the operation of trains, except to transport the mails, was prohibited on Sundays; and by 1850 forty railroad companies had been persuaded to discontinue Sunday trains voluntarily.

"Our Constitution borrows from the Bible its elements and its proportions and its power," averred Lyman Beecher, "and this is the secret of its success." It was a safe thing to say, in 1838. The framers of the Constitution were dead, and Deism itself was outmoded and forgotten. Atheism offered only feeble evidences of its existence—a journal called *The Age of Reason* and a few pamphlets. Thanks to the Irish and Continental immigrants, the Roman Catholic Church was gaining adherents in the United States at a rate more rapid than that of any Protestant denomination; but its relations to the civic authorities were often a story of conflict. When Beecher spoke of the Bible, he meant the King James Version; and so did the judges

THE NEW YORK GERMAN STADT THEATRE ON SUNDAY EVENING

Harper's Weekly, 1859; drawing by A. Fredericks illustrating one of a series of "Sketches of the People Who Oppose Our Sunday Laws."

and mayors who had a vague but decided impression that Christianity of the Protestant brand was part of the common law in America.

"Home missions" and public charities were sometimes practically identical. Particles of Christian instruction were scattered through the public-school materials, and daily readings of the Bible were the routine in most schools and colleges. Free pamphlets and cheaply priced books were religious agencies which penetrated every cranny of the settled country. Literature was never assessed at a higher educational value, and tracts never distributed more liberally, than in the United States of the three decades preceding the Civil War. The American Baptist Publishing and Sunday School Society was annually distributing, in the Forties, twelve thousand bound volumes and a hundred thousand tracts. Every Wesleyan in the "traveling connection" was a colporteur for the Methodist Book Concern and got twenty per cent commission on his sales. The Concern's catalogue for 1843 lists about three hundred and fifty volumes for general circulation, a like number of pamphlets and tracts, and almost five hundred titles of juvenile books. The American Bible Society in the same year issued 216,000 copies of Bibles and Testaments. But the greatest distributive agency was the American Tract Society, founded in 1825 by a merger of several denominational publishing houses. In its first eighteen years the Society issued a total of 68,418,138 copies of books and tracts; and in the following years, through its force of twenty-five or more colporteurs, it put into circulation more than four million copies of its leaflets and other publications annually.

In this versatile era, with its flood of informal literature and its casual assumption that a substratum of plain Christianity underlay its works, the pastor who best fitted the scene was the one who said, "Much harm has been done by the idea that a certain gloom, and a restriction of the lively emotions, bear some relation to piety. They bear the same relation to it that rust does to the sword-blade—*they eat into it.*"

For a stranger in Brooklyn on a Sunday morning who asked the way from Fulton Ferry to the Plymouth Church—Mr. Beecher's church—"Just follow the crowd" was a sufficient direction. In the clear light that streamed through plain-glass windows, the congregation was informal and unhushed, until the seats were taken, the doorway was clogged with standees, and Henry Ward Beecher entered the pulpit. The organ struck a chord, and a hymn was sung, while Beecher strummed with his fingers on the arm of the ministerial chair and smiled benignly. Then Beecher prayed, in a voice soft, liquid, persuasive; every listener felt that the words came spontaneously. In the sermon his voice had full range, from a tender bit of pictorializing to the thundering measure of righteous wrath. Beecher was the paragon type of ministers who were being *heard,* in the Sentimental generation, outside their local congregations or the theological reviews. Tremendously popular, he accepted the social obligations that went with such eminence; "When I married him," said Mrs. Beecher, "I merely had to share him with the congregation, but since then he has married the Platform and the Press and the Goddess of Liberty, and I miss him a good deal."

Friendly, colloquial, fond of humor and the simple virtues, Beecher preached a simple, everyday religious faith, accepting a denominational creed (first Presbyterian and then Congregational) as a blithe matter of routine—because it was feeling, not reason, that mattered. "We are a singing church," he declared, "and when we are dead, and men come and scrape the moss from our grave, they will say: 'These were Christians who sang much.'" His sententious discourses reappeared on the printed page with all the loose ends of thought still untied, for Beecher cherished his informality. It bespoke his sincerity, his fresh communion with truth; "when a man holds back feeling until it chokes in the sand, that he may present a correct and refined discourse, *he betrays Christ to rhetoric.*"

This straining for spontaneity in feeling and even in utterance and the emphasis upon the note of joy in religion, characteristic of Beecher and other widely liked ministers, were escapes from an old restraint. Most of the clergy who occupied pulpits in 1836 had undergone in their student days a period of doubtings and spiritual turbulence—when some fresh Platonic current, released by the opening of a book, wafted into the study-room. The fear of death; the unexplained puzzle of the nature of the "unpardonable sin"; the fear that some boyish obscenity would invoke a lethal bolt of lightning in punishment—these almost common memories of childhood were barriers against the philosophical idealism that had been shaped in Romantic Europe, of which a divinity student was certain to encounter literary evidences. Sometimes the barriers held, and the generation had an ample number of sectarians to carry on doctrinal battles. But often the censorial authority of the subconscious was broken through. Orville Dewey related the experience in his own case—how, at Andover, he found "many a solid text of the Old Testament evaporating in the crucible of exegesis, leaving no residuum of proof." He encountered differences between words and ideas, between the abstract thesis and the living sense. The more he attempted to believe in the doctrine of literally eternal punishments, the more he doubted; and the terms "Unity" and "Trinity" did not seem as interchangeable as he was expected to believe. Dewey skirted the commitment of ordination; preached for several months as an agent of the American Educational Society, still cautiously feeling his way toward wider horizons of faith; and, accepting a call from a Gloucester congregation, in the quiet of that village resolved the problem. His answer was liberal Unitarianism.

Romantic thought entered the United States in three main ways, and possibly by a fourth; for it may be that general endoglandular changes are effected (as great climatic changes occur) by forces which biochemists have not yet charted. Each of the three ways—theological, literary, and the economic shift —was both a borrowing from European precedent and a rebirth. If this book were a comparative history, a long list of published sermons and metaphysical books by English and German authors would have to be cited in partial explanation of the "new thought" in America, the religious revolution which is most strongly marked in New England. Not that the influences that produced the Unitarian organization were merely regional; but that in New England the reconstructive tendency becomes overt, in the votes of the church congregations, and becomes lucid in a body of sermons of a quality that only New England clergymen could produce.

A protest against intellectual belief as the key of entrance to the Church, against a pietistic rigor in private life, against interminable prayers and ministerial cant; a religious justification for the social conscience—"good works," humanitarianism, benevolence; a view of life as a period of healthful development in Christian experience, with personal conviction rather than dogmatic authority as its inspiration: that was the "new thought" at its best. The sermons of Dr. William Ellery Channing, the kindly heresiarch who fathered Unitarianism, are noteworthy in its literature. Channing in 1819 delivered a carefully prepared address on the infinite beneficence of God; the sermon in pamphlet form was circulated by the thousands in New England, and its author became the leader of the break from Calvinist orthodoxy. "Man is God's child, made in his image and object of his love; his reason and conscience are divine witnesses to truth and light, and when governed by them he walks in the ways of God"—this credo swept aside the concept of a God of arbitrary will and discriminatory grace. Channing's sermons asserted the dignity of human nature, the divinity of the soul, man's moral kinship with Christ, the power of moral intuition. Progressively widening his social sympathies, Channing by 1840 had advanced so far from a dogmatic attitude as to declare, "The adoration of goodness—this is religion," and so far toward perfectionism as to say, "The soul itself, in its powers and affections, in its unquenchable thirst and aspiration for unattained good, gives signs of a Nature made for an interminable progress, such as cannot now be conceived."

By 1836 the majority of the Congregational churches in the New England cities had voted Calvinism out and Unitarianism in. The Trinitarian Congregationalists defended themselves ably in the smaller towns, although they lost most of their church-buildings in eastern Massachusetts. (The law of the Commonwealth was that the church-edifice and all the religious property belonged to the town and that the local voters had the ultimate right of choosing the town minister. In 1853, by constitutional amendment, Church and State were completely separated.) In towns where they lost the religious property, usually the Trinitarians organized new churches. Their theologians attempted to make some doctrinal concessions to the rising spirit of romantic liberalism; but the best they could produce was the ingenious contredanse arranged in 1828 by Professor Nathaniel Walker of the Yale Divinity School—that "man's acts are not necessitated by a rigid law of cause and effect, but that his choices are so connected with antecedent conditions of soul and environment, that to God's perception it is certain what they will be, although he possesses full power of contrary choice."

For what they lacked in liberalism, the orthodox Congregationalists attempted to atone in zeal. They were separated from the Calvinist national organization, the Presbyterian Church, because they valued their congregational independence and because of a few differences in doctrinal interpretation; for Jonathan Edwards had left his impress upon Calvinism in New England, and the flinty Scotch-Irish brand that the Presbyterian organization represented was Calvinism as restated by John Knox. Yet the Congregationalists and the Presbyterians in 1801 had agreed to combine their forces for the missionary work of carrying religion into the new settlements of the West. They had, then, some common interest in hundreds of Western churches at the time the Congregationalists showed flashes of evangelical fervor. The Presbyterian theologians then regretted this alliance with the Congregationalists; and their fears seemed confirmed when the chief Presbyterian seat of learning, Princeton Seminary, became fitfully aglow with the new ardor. From 1830 onward the Presbyterian hierarchy pressed frequent prosecutions for heresy against the younger members and was unflinchingly orthodox in the face of a growing liberalism within the Presbyterian communion. Vindictive in their mistrust of the popular spirit, the rigid theologians in 1837 abrogated the union with the Congregationalists and disowned all the presbyteries and synods formed under it. The

Presbyterian organization thereby exscinded five hundred and thirty-three churches, with over one hundred thousand communicants. Thereafter the "Old School" Presbyterians had their greatest strength in the South; and the "New School" party, creating a new organization, gathered four-ninths of the Presbyterian communicants. This was the only schism in a major denomination during the generation in which the slavery issue was not the point of cleavage.

The Unitarians had not greatly desired an organization, or even a label; but they had acquired both and had the regular machinery of a theological party—officers and missionaries, money and tracts. This machinery exercised an automatic conservatism; and Dr. Channing himself paused while the currents of liberalism swept past him. Channing in 1835 borrowed a copy of *Sartor Resartus* from Emerson, and the Sage of Concord mentioned the incident in a letter to Carlyle. "His genius," he wrote, "cannot engage your attention much . . . but please love his catholicism, that at his age can relish the *Sartor,* born and inveterated as he is in old books." Channing, five years later, commented sadly that he deplored the new movement among the younger Unitarian ministers, the speculation which, "anxious to defend the soul's immediate connection with God," was "in danger of substituting private inspiration for Christianity." He was fifty-seven years old in 1836; his years of creative emotion belonged to the past generation. He was aging rapidly and illness kept him indoors. Visitors called, said little, and listened long, while Channing talked steadily—occasionally taking a note on his own conversation and tossing it into a pigeonhole, for future literary use.

The Unitarian machinery received a severe shock in 1841, when Theodore Parker, in the South Boston pulpit, disowned faith in the supernatural and scouted the assumption of a special Divine ingredient in the miracles of the Bible. Channing did not agree at all, but he expressed his attitude, "Let the full heart pour itself forth!" Orthodox Unitarians lamented that Parker reduced the miracles of Jesus to the level of the feats of Cagliostro and John Dee; but their orthodoxy was to be battered again and again. Unitarians had ceased to fear "the great and dreadful God" of the Old Testament; but, Parker made his repeated protest, they had not learned to love "the beautiful and altogether lovely" God of the universe. His valiant battle in behalf of the love-force did not capture the citadel or break the sectarian boundaries; but it soared above them and outside them, stimulated the nonsectarian movement of Transcendentalism, and had popular influence which was directly reflected in antislavery votes.

Emerson called Parker one of the four great men of the age. This prodigally energetic minister expressed most of the dynamic idealisms of his time, enforcing them with a wealth of book-learning and with a clear and uncompromising passion for righteousness which bespoke the academic life in its best form. He was acquainted with nineteen or twenty languages, and his reading extended, as he remarked, from dream-books and demonologies to "the Pseudipigraphy of the Old Testament, and the Apocrypha of the New." Mrs. Seba Smith and Antoinette Louisa Brown were given the privileges of his pulpit, and in his own sermons he insisted on the right of women to equal education and equal opportunity. He replenished his stock of sentiment and inspiration in the company of women; [1] there is a delicious note, "The other day I met a woman in the street, and our *eyes met*. I felt a sensation of unspeakable delight which lasted all the morning. I cannot tell why it was, but so it was. It was involuntary delight."

In public prayer Parker addressed God as "Father and Mother of us all." This Creator was immanent in both matter and spirit; Divine love was shaping society to the Divine pur-

[1] Disappointed at not finding a certain lady at home, Parker composed the poem:

> Unheeded grow the precious flowers,
> No eye woos now their beauty;
> I only came for plaintive hours,
> To strengthen for sore duty;
>
> But the new sadness of the place
> Upon my heart is stealing;
> Nature without that July face
> Will paralyze my feeling.

pose, by an evolution which antedated even the appearance of man on the globe. "I see daily sights in Boston of awful sin and misery," runs a note of Parker's, "not the product of lust alone, but of intemperance, ignorance, poverty, and manifold crime, which make me shudder. All that I can do seems like putting a straw into the ocean to stop the tide. But I do not despair of mankind. No, never! It is better than ever before."

The Spirit of the Age appeared in 1849, an ebullient little magazine numbering William Henry Channing (nephew of "the" Dr. Channing, who died in 1842) and Henry James *père* among its editors. "True Christianity is Social; true Socialism is Christian. Religion and politics are as indispensable as Spirit and Body," announced the prospectus. "The New Church is Divine Love flowing in as holiness; the New State is Human Love rising up to brotherhood. The piety of this church will be charitable, and the charity of this state will be pious." This rhythmic elegance is certainly from the pen of Henry James, who was then compounding his own theology, Christian Socialism. Geographically and intellectually roving, he had picked up Robert Sandeman, Swedenborg, Fourier, and various Gnostic interpreters of the Scriptures; ingesting the lot, he was, in his own phrase, "filled to the brim with the sentiment of indestructible life." Although he did not put his system into a book until 1857 (*Christianity the Logic of Creation*), he began to bid for converts in 1849. Fredrika Bremer attended a lecture by James ("a wealthy, and, it is said, a good man") in New York that November. "His doctrine was that which recognizes no right but that of involuntary attraction, no law of duty but that of the artist's worship of beauty, no God but that of the pantheist, everywhere and yet nowhere." The lecture called out a rejoinder by his coeditor Channing, a discourse "like a clear, gushing river," opposing the idea of a personal God to the idea of pantheism, "developing from that divine personality the thence derived doctrine of duty, of social law, of beauty, of immortality, as applicable to every man, to every human society." His rebuttal was sound Unitarianism, as became a nephew of the late Dr. Channing. But it may be observed that the Transcendentalists desired both the Divine personality and the Divine abstraction, and had both.

Near the core of Unitarianism—the misleading label of the denomination to the contrary—was the glorification of Christ. Jesus, separated from the Godhead so that he became human as well as divine, was all the more endearing. The insistence upon Christ as teacher held the Unitarians away from the individualism of the Quaker doctrine. Without the teaching of the Infinite Spirit in the human soul—the inward light, as the Friendly phrase is—the New Testament certainly could not be understood; but Christ's words and the drama of his life and death were a powerful stimulus and indispensable guidance to the inward religion of the soul. And this importance of Christ as teacher, conservative Unitarians held, was commended to the world by miraculous evidences. Samuel Lothrop exhorted his congregation in Boston not to rely too much upon the Old Testament or the Pauline epistles, but to make Christianity the doctrine of Christ—to draw one's inspiration from the Gospel, an ample foundation for religion if the rest of the Bible were blotted out.

From the glorification of Christ to the glorification of man was such an easy step. Edward Everett Hale handled the transition very dexterously, preaching at Brookline in 1842: "When I see that no man has ever been able to show where Christ's divinity ended and where the powers and qualities which he showed in common with a perfect man began, I cannot but believe that the nature of man, when carried to this perfection, is more beautiful, more spiritual, more divine, than, without this exhibition, there were reason to suppose. . . . When I find that man's nature is assumed by a being who is entitled to style himself the Son of God, I find strong proof of the dignity of man's nature." Henry Ward Beecher frequently emphasized the dignity that one possessed simply by being a featherless biped. "There is no religion in the Bible, any more than there is a road upon the guide-board," he told his congregation; "the Bible is the rule, the direction. Religion is *in*

A METHODIST PRAYER-MEETING

in a camp-meeting tent at Millennial Grove, Eastham, Massachusetts. *Ballou's Pictorial Drawing-Room Companion*, 1858.

the man, or it is not anywhere." Again, more strikingly, "The great truth which God is driving through our times, as with a chariot of fire, is the *importance of man."*

The Universalist Church gained in social favor by the revolution in the Congregational ranks. The Universalist thesis that God's nature, "his whole essence, is Love" had become respectable. The denomination's old doctrine of no future accountability for one's sins and "immediate entrance into glory" did not jibe with the social conscience and was discarded. The heartening idea was stressed that "God will, in his own good time, gather together, into his immortal kingdom, all rational intelligences, where they will be inexpressibly happy, world without end"; the other Universalist doctrines were few and simple, and especially in the smaller towns of New England the denomination enjoyed a steady growth. Universalists, like Unitarians, consistently pried into social problems; and the two churches were side by side when, in the Fifties, the "New England conscience" became a major force in practical politics.

The radical movement within the Congregational churches was indicative of change in every Protestant denomination. The typical expression of Protestant Christianity was becoming an unselective, complacent humanitarianism. Many professional churchmen, even, were outgrowing the old squeamishness over points of doctrine. Moncure Conway, the Virginian, had left the Methodist Church to become a Unitarian, and Father Taylor, famous for his gusty sermons in the Seamen's Bethel of Boston, upbraided him for the transfer. "I answered that if I could, like himself, be a Methodist and ignore the Trinitarian dogma, I would have done so; but Methodism in Boston and that in the Baltimore Conference differed. The old man relented. 'Well,' he said, 'our Southern brethren *are* very strict about matters of which they know nothing.'"

The Methodists were at last making efforts to secure an educated ministry. A "call" issued in 1839 forecast the change in policy: "We firmly believe that none are competent to take upon themselves the holy office of ministers of Christ, but they who are called of God and anointed with the Holy Ghost; nevertheless, we see no reason why the Divine Call should exempt them from the necessity of making preparation for an enlightened and successful discharge of their duties." In April, 1847, the first Methodist seminary in the United States, the Methodist General Biblical Institute at Concord, New Hampshire, introduced its twelve students to its three professors and began the educative process. The Garrett Biblical Institute, in Evanston, Illinois, was next, opening in 1854.

Denominations which had been steadfast to formal preaching were now cordial to the new tendency of extempore sermonizing, and even were inviting laymen occasionally into their pulpits. Low-church Episcopalians were forcing discussion of the propriety of relaxing the liturgy. Many presbyters, including several High-churchmen, subscribed to a memorial presented to the Right Reverend Bishops in Council Assembled in 1853, which besought a liberalizing modification of the liturgy and a widening of the doors of ordination. The Reverend Edward A. Washburn of St. John's Church, Hartford, expanded the appeal: "Our system does not reach the mass of the American middle class. We do not mean, of course, that it excludes them altogether, but that a comparatively small portion of them enter its communion. Methodist and Baptist take hold of such classes; we do not. . . . The Church asks today reality, not theory; it wants men to come out of these old one-sided positions and unite in its principles; to hold, to teach, to toil for the Church . . . the Church in its living meaning, in its broad catholic activities."

Meanwhile, as Episcopalians were asking for gates, leaders in other denominations were crying out for fences. Dr. Richard F. Storrs, Jr., pastor of the Church of the Pilgrims, Beecher's chief competitor for the souls of Brooklynites, became an ardent advocate of a fixed mode of Congregational worship. The *Christian Enquirer* and other Unitarian periodicals in the mid-Fifties published articles by staunch Unitarians in behalf of liturgical forms. Similarly anxious for a set ritual in the Dutch Reformed Church was Dr. George W. Bethune, that interesting homilist who edited the first American edition of *The Compleat Angler*. In the *Princeton Review* for 1855 appeared an article urging the preparation of a Book of Common Prayer for the optional use of Presbyterian divines. An anonymous volume published that same year, *Eutaxia; or, the Presbyterian Liturgies,* excited discussion among the brethren; it professed to demonstrate, by historical proofs, that the principles of Presbyterianism in no wise conflicted with the discretionary use of written forms, and it urged their adoption.

Gerrit Smith in 1840 tendered the Presbyterian church in Peterboro, New York, a series of resolutions to the effect that sectarianism was "unscriptural and wicked," and calling for "a common Christianity to take the place of the Methodist and Presbyterian and Baptist and other sects which now divide and afflict and corrupt Zion." The church did not oblige its communicant; but later Smith held an antisectarian meeting at Oswego, in which Presbyterian, Baptist, Universalist, and Unitarian laity were represented, and his resolutions carried.

Several articles in the popular magazines bespoke a "national religion." If the Reverend George B. Cheever was correct in thinking, "He [God] is beginning to prepare the American church, by a vast access to her numbers, elevation of her purity, and increase of her light, for the magnificent scale on which her enterprises are hereafter to be conducted," then a united, national, Protestant establishment would be most desirable. William M. Evarts, in his "Moral Destiny of the United States," calculated that in one hundred and seventy years from 1840 "the descendants of the present inhabitants of the United States" would number one billion. Cheever was not disposed to postpone the great work until then: "Let the bare existence of a truly Christian nation, with a population of five hundred millions be supposed, and the world's evangelization follows almost inevitably." Nor was the world's evangelization being neglected in Cheever's generation; the missionary activity which got under way in the Eighteen Twenties was being continued and expanded.

Sustaining the natural inertia of organizations and the vested interests of church-officers against any grand coalition was the widely held sentiment that good people did not differ about essential things; they were divided over forms, and ordinances, and such other doctrinal matters as did not involve the abiding principles of Christianity. "They should tolerate each other's views, meet and act together where they may," wrote Nehemiah Adams; "but I do like to see a man heartily attached to his own denomination, without bigotry." Beecher spoke from his pulpit that he could see in the New Testament authority for Episcopacy, for Presbyterianism, and for Congregationalism. "To me it seems, therefore, that the Apostle's idea was that the Churches should be governed according to their necessities, taking one form or the other, as was best suited to them. The only ground on which all Christians can have perfect union is the ground of *love*." It was a beautiful thought; but after the slavery issue was threshed over in the national assemblies of the three largest Protestant denominations, there was not enough intrasectarian love in any of them to hold the denomination intact.

The ethical aspects of slavery were much too prominent to allow a nation-wide church to pretend indifference; and, in the absence of any possible concord on an important moral issue, a religious body, unlike a commercial enterprise, could not retain its variant elements on the mere plea of expedience. The ecclesiastical conferences or assemblies passed resolutions condemning "all diverse and schismatical measures tending to destroy the peace of our churches" as long as postponement was feasible; and when it was not, they proceeded to arrange a division, with as much good feeling as the circumstances permitted. The Southern Baptists withdrew from their national associations in 1844; the Methodist Church split at about the same time. When the General Assembly of the New School Presbyterians in 1857 exhorted all its people to eschew such tenets as that "slavery is an ordinance of God . . . scriptural and right," the twenty-one Southern presbyteries withdrew to form their own denomination. The Episcopal Church alone of the major Protestant churches avoided the slavery rift—probably because its controversial energies had been engaged since 1835 in a truceless discussion between High- and Low-churchmen.

The American Tract Society, too, perished of the slavery dispute. In 1856 the directors' policy of avoiding the question was under raking fire; antislavery churchmen demanded that, at the least, the Society publish tracts against such generally acknowledged sins of slavery as the separation of families and the withholding of the Bible from the Negro. The Society made a weak effort to please, and fell apart in 1859.

The epileptic chapter in the religious history of the generation has to do with Millenarianism, an invocation of the prophetic books of the Bible to give the Perfectionist impulse an immediate reality. The leader of the movement was William Miller, who had the stuff of inheritance and experience that the great evangelists of the backwoods have been made of —rural isolation (northern New York); God-fearing, hard-working parents who added to their progeny every year (William was the oldest of a brood of sixteen); a Protestantism with hell-fire and salvation (in this instance, the Baptist sect); and a Bible and Concordance for the youngster to pore over. William's appetite for reading made him at first seem "queer" to his parents and neighbors, then gained the youth deference as a probable genius. After he was married and had become a farmer near Poultney, Vermont, his talent in producing occasional literature—Fourth of July hymns and the like—made him a notable figure in the community. He took larger doses of philosophy than his Baptist-conditioned system could stand; was for a time a Deist, treating sacred subjects with the usual levity of the village freethinker; in due time had an emotional reversion, purged himself of the cynicism, and was thereafter a

Bible man. After his second conversion the Good Book was his chief study; and, as became his superior attainments, he fastened upon the prophecies of Daniel and the wonders of Nebuchadnezzar's dream. By 1823 Miller had calculated, in five different methods, the time of the chaining of the Beast and the end of the world; each calculation ended with the same date, 1843. Miller had to wait a bit longer than most prophets for the requisite command from the Lord, but in 1831 he received it. The Voice said, "Go tell it to the World!" Ultimately, after some quibbling with the Voice, Miller agreed: " 'Why,' I said, 'if I should have an invitation to speak publicly in any place, I will go tell them what I find in the Bible about the Lord's coming.' " Instantly the constraint was lifted from his soul; and within half an hour a young man called, emissary from a neighboring village, asking him to lecture to the church-folk.

For the next several years Miller moved among the rural communities of New England and New York, proclaiming the nearness of the Second Advent. The Baptist Church made him a "Reverend" in 1834, but he was welcomed in the pulpits of other denominations. Natural, honest, sometimes a Yankee farmer cajoling his peers with homely truths, and again a scholar with the whole of Scripture at his tongue's command, Prophet Miller ignited the religious spirit wherever he went and left communities aflame with revival zeal. Pastors who had their own doubts about Miller's thesis nevertheless invited him to address their flocks, because he did awaken enthusiasm for the Power of the Word in sleepy congregations and persuaded his listeners to try to become perfect.

Miller faced his first critical audience when the Reverend Joshua V. Himes, pastor of the Chardon Street Baptist Church, Boston, invited the Prophet to lecture to the city folk in 1840. Himes discerned in Miller's preachments the yeast of a national fermentation, a revival of such enthusiasm and extent as this country had not seen since the frontier upheaval of 1800. He attached himself to the Prophet as manager, arranged for invitations to city pulpits, and warmed the old gentleman into redoubled fervor. Time was slipping by; anxious Christians had to "get right with God" in a hurry, for Miller's calculations might be true!

A sprouting of minor lecturers to carry the Millenarian message was coincident with the appearance of five periodicals crammed with excited letters from brethren and sisters who had seen the Light. Millerism became a cult; and, much though it grieved the Prophet himself, its tendency was to take its followers out of their old denominational ranks. Once Miller became no longer a guest revivalist but the head of an all-devouring enthusiasm which made sectarian differences insignificant and normal churchly activities unimportant, pastors regretted their earlier tolerance and defended the ramparts of denominational Christianity. The ablest defense was a pamphlet written by the Reverend John Dowling, a Baptist clergyman of Providence. Dowling rallied his brothers of the cloth: "An intelligent and pious member of my church lately remarked to me, 'Sir, if this doctrine is true, we certainly ought to know it; and to whom are the Christian communities to look for instruction on this subject, but to those who are appointed as watchmen on the walls of Zion, to sound the note of alarm when the day of evil approaches, and to blow the blast of triumph when the glorious Jubilee dawns.'" Miller was too learned a scholar, however, for ministers to squelch with text and sermon. He could outquote and outexpound the best of them. And among ministers who were staunch to the literal Word, who believed that "days" in the prophetic passages always meant "thousand years," and who accepted the conventional dates for the "first captivity in Babylon," the commandment to rebuild Jerusalem, and like key-points of Miller's computations, Millerism enlisted some of its most active converts.

Beset occasionally by city hoodlums and at the center of a storm of criticism and controversy ("I find as I grow old I grow more peevish and cannot bear so much contradiction," he wrote), the venerable Prophet warded off fatigue by the whole-hearted fervor of his convictions, writing books for Himes to publish and lecturing with intense vigor as the millennial dawn brightened the horizon. Miller possessed a homely nobleness. He was sixty-one in 1843; his face was massive and round, his hair was still auburn and his eyes an unfaded blue. "He is of about medium stature," a Phrenologist described, "a little corpulent, and in temperament a mixture of sanguine and nervous. His intellectual developments are unusually full, and we see in his head, great benevolence and firmness, united with a lack of self-esteem. He is also wanting in marvelousness and is *naturally* skeptical." But it was Himes who was master of the show, who prepared the charts and published the tracts and hallooed the devotees into frenzy. For Himes esteemed enthusiasm for enthusiasm's sake and apparently believed that unreined ecstasy was the best expression of Christian faith. Miller was forced to realize, in the crucial year of 1843, that the movement had outgrown its prophet, and he wrote letters of warning that Satan was attempting to get the advantage by scattering coals of wild-fire among the Millenarian workers. "Keep cool," he wrote; "let patience have its perfect work."

"Keep cool," indeed! Even the heavens turned fanatical. The resplendent comet of 1843, one of the greatest ever to approach this sphere, streaked across the noonday, blazing its rival light against the sun. This wonder was a portent of that immediate time when the planets should wander from their orbs and dash against each other, the beginning of that upheaval celebrated in the hymn-book of the Millerites, *The Millenial Harp:*

> We, while the stars of heaven shall fall,
> And mountains are on mountains hurled,
> Shall stand unmoved amidst them all,
> And smile to see a burning world.
>
> The earth and all the works therein
> Dissolve, by raging flames destroyed;
> While we survey the awful scene
> And mount above the fiery void.

But, pending their ascension, the Millerites displayed no such serenity. Lurid accounts of the Second Coming, in print and from pulpit, excited followers already frantic lest they be not prepared for the Day or fearful that some of their loved ones would remain scoffers and be doomed. "All will be wild and mad confusion" at the hour of Gabriel's trump; "The earth *rocks; she reels to and fro*; and from her *very bowels, heaves* up on every side her *burning flames*; she throws her fires of melted lava up to the cloud-top height, and pours them forth, in furious madness, on cities, villages, and the affrighted *People,* too, who flee in *frantic wildness."* Prepare. . . .

The paranoiac diversions appeared; cases of derangement and suicide increased as the days of the year 1843 followed a bewilderingly normal progression. A hundred and twenty inmates listed as "religiously insane" in the report of the Worcester Asylum for 1842; thirteen of the twenty-seven persons committed to the Maine State Insane Asylum in the same year listed as victims of religious excitement—these were part of the early toll. The tension and the casualties increased as the wait for the ascension was prolonged through 1843 into 1844. The latest possible date for the Second Advent, according to Miller's calculations, was March 21, 1844.

Millerite congregations overflowed the restricted space of church auditoriums and lecture-halls; Tabernacle Tents were pitched for camp-meetings, and in Boston and New York huge wooden assemblies were built. (The rumor that the Boston Tabernacle was insured for seven years was an invention of scoundrels.) How many converts were there? Millerite editors, doubtless wooed by the euphonious sound of the word, claimed a million. A third or fourth of that number would be a more reasonable estimate, but any figure must be simply a guess.

The converts had rue and wormwood for their breakfast portion on March 22, 1844. A twenty-four hours' vigil; not one celestial wonder, not one clarion blast from Gabriel. The enfeebled, harried old Prophet remained in seclusion for several days. On May 2 he issued a statement of some pathos and dignity: "Were I to live my life over again, with the same evidence I then had, to be honest with God and man, I should have to do as I have done. . . . *I confess my error, and acknowledge my disappointment*; yet I still believe that the day of the Lord is near, even at the door; and I exhort you, my brethren, to be watchful, and not let the day come upon you unawares." When he appeared in public again, at the Boston Tabernacle late in May, he was eloquent and serene.

The Prophet was steadfast, and the followers took heart. For most of them the ridicule of unbelievers ("What! not gone up yet?"—"We thought you'd gone up. Aren't you going up soon?"—"Wife didn't go up and leave you behind to burn, did she?") made a graceful rescension from Millerism impossible. There was some error in the calculations. . . . Presently it appeared. The final date, by the revised estimate, was "the tenth day of the seventh month" of the Jewish year—in late October, certainly no later than the 22d. Himes launched a new periodical; Miller and Himes went to Ohio to lecture during the summer; and in the East leadership shifted to a frenetic group of self-elected interpreters. Miller's simple Perfectionism became obscured by morbid excesses or by symbolic balderdash. Disciples greeted each other with kisses, washed each other's feet, and prepared white robes so as to be clothed in outward purity for the time of the Advent.

A worldly-minded person who visited a Millerite campmeeting at Bridgeport came away with a handful of rings and jewelry thrown away by the believers; they would have no need for the stuff after the ascension. A dressmaker in Philadelphia placed above her door the sign, "Behold the Bridegroom cometh"; and a shopkeeper in the same city posted the notice, "This shop is closed in honor of the King of Kings, who will appear about the 20th of October. Get ready, friends, to crown him Lord of all." These two tradespeople illustrated the sudden rush for poverty. As one believer wrote in an Adventist journal, "How, my dear brethren and sisters, do you expect to gain admittance to the marriage supper of the Lamb, if the Lord comes and finds you dealing in the articles which the daughters of Zion lust after? See that you stand not among those merchants spoken of in *Rev.* xviii, 15." There was considerable excitement over the election of a President of the United States that autumn; but canvassers for Clay or Polk had no luck with Millerites, who answered that mundane politics would have come to an end by November.

The time of the prophecy arrived. *The Midnight Cry,* Himes' organ, published a farewell number, carrying an unflattering woodcut of Gabriel and bearing the capitalized message: "At 3 o'clock in the morning, 22nd October, he will surely come. Child, believe it." And the faithful were ready—gazing heavenward, holding vigil on the housetops. The terror-stricken, the dazed, the hallelujah-shouters, and the ones whose fault was in loving too much and thinking too little. Gerrit Smith wrote to "beloved Nancy" at half-past eight on the evening of the 21st, "We have just had family worship—perhaps for the last time. . . . I know not, my dear Nancy, that we shall meet in the air. You will be there—for you have long loved and served your Savior. I seek salvation, though it is in the last hour. And how my eyes have flowed at the welcome thought that we shall meet our dear Fitzhugh and Nanny!"

After the undistinguished morning of the 22d, Himes attempted to stave off ridicule by denying, boldly and absurdly, that he had had any part in the October hysteria. Too heart-broken and ill to write, Miller dictated an "Apology and Defence." George Storrs, one of the fanatics who had driven the chariot of Millerism pell-mell, announced that the whole business was a delusion caused by Mesmerism. The greater number of the night-watchers, whose allegiance to Millerism rested primarily in their fear of damnation if the trump *did* sound, managed well enough to survive the disappointment. But at least fifty thousand Millerites were genuine disciples of the faith; these underwent days of chastenment and spiritual travail. Some, of course, emerged as infidels, denouncing all things of faith. Many humbly awaited an explanation of the undoubted mistake; many others offered their own explanations. The theory that gained most credence was that the end had indeed come, but in heaven, not upon earth; that Jesus had left the seat of mercy and entered into his Kingdom, and those who had not been attentive to the Millerite prophecy had had their names blotted from the Book of Life. This was the "shut-door" theory; its adherents in time changed their ideas as to Miller's relation to the millennium but retained their lively interest in that promised occurrence. They organized as the Seventh-Day Adventists. Another group took shape as the Advent Christian Church, which holds to the general imminence of Christ's return but respects the statement that "no man knoweth the day nor the hour wherein the Son of Man cometh."

Miller's thesis had been that the coming of Christ was to be immediate, not to await a thousand years of peace, as *Revelations* xx: 2, 3, seemed to indicate. Other Millennialists held different views. Harriet Livermore had a theory of her own, which she expounded before the House of Representatives. She declared (and what she meant only Harriet knew), "Only by His death, can the serpent's sting be extracted from our souls; but our bodies—I mean true believers in Christ—are already dead with Him; and their restoration is a concern of His resurrection from the dead."

The second coming of the Lord should be interpreted as an allegory, thought Sylvester Judd, a Unitarian minister; and his book *Philo; an Evangelical* (1850) related how Christ would come into the world again—in the person of his followers; how in their virtues and moral beauty His own qualities would be reproduced; how they would bear the cross and die His death.

A number of clerical savants dabbled in eschatology. John Dowling regarded the angel's cry in *Revelations* xiv: 8, "Babylon is fallen, that great city, because she made all nations drink of the wine of the wrath of her fornication," an explicit and beautiful prediction of the spread of evangelical truth throughout the world; this extension of the faith, together with the downfall of Babylon, was to usher in the millennium. Popery's throne was already tottering; Mohammedanism was on the wane, pagan darkness beginning to disappear; and soon "the brazen rampart around the millions of China and Japan shall be melted before the rising rays of the Sun of Righteousness." Dowling thought it probable that the angel had already begun his flight, the take-off being marked by the rise of the missionary spirit in the early decades of the century.

A pervasive complacence held that the millennium was being actively promoted in America, where various benevolent societies were doing good deeds in many fields, where the Sabbath School had become a common institution, bethels were established for seamen and books donated for their sea-chests. Bibles from American presses were being distributed among families destitute of the Word; missionaries were sent to the heathen; young men of piety and talent were given scholarships at Divinity Schools; the Temperance reform was marching irresistibly forward. One didn't have to be a scholar to understand that the United States was doing the needful to promote the Second Kingdom.

Dr. Joseph F. Berg, pastor of the Second Reformed Protestant Dutch Church of Philadelphia, was a very learned scholar, however, and he bore American nationalism to a dizzy peak. His *Prophecy and the Times; or, England and Armageddon,* discoursed upon the predictions "included under the sixth and seventh vials of the Apocalypse of St. John, the last sub-division of the closing period in the pre-Millennial history of the Church of God"—*id est,* Dr. Berg's own times. He twisted the Lion's tail with a Biblical wrench. Among the various resemblances between England and Babylon Dr. Berg cited the little known fact that Albert, the Prince Consort, was a Papist.

The Doctor suspended his researches into the millennium long enough to deliver a counterblast to Spiritualism, *Abaddon and Mahanaim; or, Demons and Guardian Angels.* Error confounded in that sector, he returned to his specialty. *The Stone and the Image; or, the American Republic the Bane and Ruin of Despotism,* appeared in 1856. The stone cut out of the mountain without hands in Nebuchadnezzar's vision the pastor-scholar insisted was a symbol of the United States—"a government that shall be free from antichristian oppression." "The hostility of Satan and all the powers of despotism to this country is symbolized by the great red dragon" of *Revelations;*

but the Republic had been wonderfully sustained against "the Roman persecuting power" and was destined to conquer the new Antichristian force which, as the nineteenth chapter of *Revelations* promised, was to succeed "the Papal dynasty." (Dr. Berg admitted, "I may be reminded of the negro race held in involuntary servitude, and this system of bondage may be adduced as testimony against the glory of our land. I answer, the glory of the firmament is in the sun, and yet even that is not without its dark spots.") The Reverend Ethan Smith, in the thirty-six lectures of his *Key to the Revelations,* set forth similarly flattering auguries of the Republic's destiny, pronouncing the Protestant church in the United States "a seat for the commencement of the special showers of the Spirit of Grace in the last days . . . clearly destined to give a new and correct model to the whole militant church of Christ."

And the Shakers—a communistic sect which repudiated the lusts of the flesh and worshipped with a hand-clapping, dancing syncopation—received word of heavenly doings, from the best possible sources. To the United Society at Lebanon, New York, four angels collaborated in sending a lengthy discourse "from the Lord God of Heaven to the Inhabitants of Earth"; several Prophets and Apostles contributed testimonials of its accuracy and divine origin, which were printed in the book (1843). Six years later Paulina Bates, in a New Hampshire colony, compiled *The Divine Book of Holy and Eternal Wisdom,* "revealing the word of God, out of whose mouth goeth a Sharp Sword." Sharp indeed for slaveholders and other sinners, who were warned of the wrath to come. The volume was a symposium of the revelations Paulina Bates had received at intervals, and it contained the testimony of Adam, Eve, Noah, and all the patriarchs. The Latter-Day Saints, meanwhile, building a creed about revelations of like celestial authority, were showing that courage and high fortitude sometimes arose from a clannish, primitive religiosity. In 1836 Joseph Smith built the first temple of the New Zion, in Kirtland, Ohio. In 1860 New Zion had been moved to a valley in the Western desert, and Salt Lake City, thirteen years old, was flourishing like the green bay tree.

CHAPTER TWELVE

Toward the Seventh Circle

*W*HEN seekers came "down in front" and knelt while friends prayed for them, when believers' meetings, for prayer and heart-searching, preceded the evangelical sermon in the big tent, the revivals seemed to generate a parching heat, inviting for immediate relief the special showers of the Spirit. "Sanctification by grace" was a Wesleyan phrase, and in rural communities it sometimes meant that the agitated heart vibrated with a consciousness of superlative piety. The problem of evangelical ministers was to make Christians *stay* converted, to throb at a sustained tempo of holiness. Charles G. Finney, a Presbyterian by leniency of his synod but in faith allied with the simpler Methodism of the frontier, devised the formula. In 1843, after having labored as a revivalist for almost twenty years, he underwent a fresh "baptism of the Spirit." Then he explained: the exercise of faith (on the human side) and the agency of the Spirit (on the divine side), together, made the perfect life. The privilege of Christians was to live without sin; when man's will consecrates his "constitutional powers of body and soul" to God, perfection is his. Finney's doctrine, which captured Oberlin College and radiated from that point, was the ultimate denial of the Calvinist tenet, the unworthiness of man.

Christian Perfectionism was not, of course, the discovery of any person or group in the nineteenth century. It was a very old idea. And a certain almost inevitable twist to that doctrine was also very old. Since the martyrs emerged from the catacombs, there had been exponents of Christian simplicity who were really simple Christians—who succeeded, by an antinomian trick of justification, in indulging freely in various phallic pastimes without damaging their credit in heaven.

An American gentleman of the Eighteen Thirties, or later, who wished his fun unrestrained and his virtue unimpaired had three choices of conduct. The commonest was marriage, with the assurance that the marital ceremony bestowed upon the gentleman complete rights to the woman's body—an assumption so general that very few wives dared, or cared, to question it. Another choice, not necessarily excluded by the marriage-vow, was to accept professional services. Patrons of the shuttered houses could assuage their moral sensibilities, if they wished, by thoughts of the physiological dangers that beset the denial of virile appetites. Commercial prostitution increased noticeably in the Eighteen Thirties, as urban society began to overshadow the agrarian. The trade came under quasi-legal protection.

In the generation prior to the Civil War a surprisingly large number of people muddled their spiritual values so dexterously that the third choice, "free love," acquired almost a religious sanction. Tertius Strong at Brimfield, Connecticut, Dr. Thomas Nichols at Modern Times, New York, Simon Lovett at New Haven, and C. E. Dutton at Albany were local leaders of a movement which stretched far enough westward to establish lively colonies in Ohio. The scandal-monger Lenderman has described the Sunday-afternoon meetings in Cincinnati (at the Mechanics' Institute!), "a delectable intellectuo-sensuo-spiritual repast" served up for a "highly appreciative audience, judging from the frequent applause manifested in stampings, and clappings, and hissings." Among the speakers when Lenderman was visitor towered "an unshaven bison from the backwoods, who prided himself on being a perfectly illiterate but natural philosopher—a hairy, skinny, wrinkled, and bold champion of Free Love. If the ladies wanted something natural, unsophisticated, here they had it."

Unsophisticated in a different sense was the fantasy of Erasmus Strong, leader of the Perfectionist group in Syracuse, New York. Strong envisioned men and women flying in all directions, across each other's courses, apparently in earnest search. Certainly the meaning was that couples were wrongly mated and should find their true affinities. If they failed, it seems not to have been from lack of trying.

It was John Humphrey Noyes, strangely enough, who labeled the restiveness of certain communities in 1835 "an epidemic of lasciviousness."

Noyes' early life is a record of successive "conversions" that didn't take, backslidings, interminable meditations on the manner of becoming perfect (never a doubt of the possibility), and bland irregularities of conduct. He didn't like Andover, where the students of divinity were more concerned with orthodoxy than with spirituality. Noyes left that seminary after a year and gave the Theological School of Yale a try; here, devoting himself to prayer, contemplation, and study, he attained knowledge of the way to perfection. The Bible and Wesley's *Christian Perfection* were the books he studied. The philosophy that Noyes evolved was largely Wesleyan, but distinctive in two features. One of these was the hoary antinomian idea of "security"—that after becoming perfect a person never went amiss again—which Wesley had discarded. The other was the cheerful concession Noyes made to his own prurience.

"I have been wishing today," Noyes wrote in his diary at Andover, "I could devise some new way of sanctification—some patent, some specific for sin, whereby the curse should be exterminated once for all." Less than two years later he had evolved just such a grand program and preached at the Free Church of New Haven upon the text, "He that committeth sin is of the devil." Noyes was rebuked for his radicalism by a fellow-student the next day, and to the point-blank question, "Don't you commit sin?" he made the simple reply, "No." Nor did he. He went to New York City and painted the town red—because he felt impelled by spiritual instinct to assert his freedom from any system of external restraints. "I drank ardent spirits," he explained, "that I might reprove the spirit of legality which still hovered about me, and that I might practically transfer the keeping of my soul from the temperance pledge to the Spirit of God."

Noyes spent several months among a group of Perfectionists at New Haven and helped edit their magazine; he corresponded with the leaders of "Perfection" colonies in New York and New England and entertained the notion of disseminating his goodly doctrines far and wide. But, principally because he was incapable of working harmoniously with other preachers of sanctification, he concluded that the quality of proselytes was more important than their quantity, and he returned to his home town (Putney, Vermont) to begin the work modestly. There, in the winter of 1836, he commenced a Bible school and gathered about him "a few simple-minded, unpretending believers, chiefly belonging to my father's family." From this circle developed the Putney Community; from that developed the Oneida Community, established in Madison County, New York, in 1848. This colony of holiness retained its communal features until the year in which Noyes' first cousin, Rutherford B. Hayes, was elected President of the United States.

Allan Estlake, a member, described the Oneida Community as an object lesson in the possibility of realizing heaven on earth. Noyes did believe that the second coming of Christ was imminent, and he fancied his own colony as a preparatory experience in perfect holiness. He made an intricate distinction between being free from sin and being past all improvement. As a book might be true and perfect in sentiment, yet deficient in typographical accuracy and stylistic grace, so Noyes thought of himself—not pretending to perfection in externals, only claiming purity of heart "and the answer of a good conscience toward God."

When Charles Nordhoff visited the Oneida Community, he asked for a definition of "salvation from sin" and was told that it was a special phase of religious experience, based upon spiritual contact with God. God was to be approached by prayer, and instinctively; "All religionists of the positive sort," Nordhoff learned, "believe in a personal God, and assume that he is a sociable being." From this assumption it followed that ills of the physical body might be removed through prayer. The Community anticipated Mrs. Eddy and her immediate creditors in the practice of "faith-healing" and kept written testimonials to prove it. Mrs. M. A. Hall, thus, was ill of consumption and given up as a hopeless case by doctors; in June, 1847, Noyes and a Mrs. Cragin came to the sufferer's bedside and supplied the power of faith. "From a helpless, bedridden state, in which I was unable to move, or even to be moved without excruciating pain," avowed Mrs. Hall, "I was instantly raised to a consciousness of perfect health. My eyes, which before could not bear the light, were opened to the blaze of day, and became strong. My appetite was restored, and all pain removed."

The members of certain other Perfectionist groups professed, in their ecstasy at being perfect, the power of working miracles, the gift of tongues, and complete wisdom. The Oneida communists discovered many Spiritualist mediums among themselves, and Noyes' authority was threatened by the conflicting importance of messages from the other world. He met the difficulty by demonstrating that spirit communication compared, in truth and beauty, most unfavorably with inspirational thought—communication with the will of Christ. His own thought was without question inspirational in nature; and lacking a standard to differentiate between true and unreliable spiritual communication, the members of Oneida were constrained to allow first rank to the thoughts of Mr. Noyes. In following his persuasions, indeed, the members had little to lose. The farming operations of the Oneida Community were successful; the multiple enterprises were well managed by a single mind. Vegetarianism was not unpleasant to people of their temper; the prohibition of tobacco and liquid stimulants accorded with their own ideas of the good life. And if the members were prohibited the blessings of monogamy, there were compensations.

THE PROPHET NOYES AND HIS FAMILY
William Hepworth Dixon, *New America*, 1867.

Noyes developed the idea of "complex marriage" (he didn't like the phrase "free love") in 1835, during a visit to New York in company with an expert libertine and apologist, Simon Lovett. During this excursion Noyes' freedom from sin proved again a very convenient attribute; "I did nothing of which I had occasion to be ashamed," he wrote, "but I lost reputation with those who saw only external attributes." He had his fun and still remained virtuous, which was the spring whence his philosophy flowed; and at Putney and Oneida Noyes and his fellow-communists had fun, all on a plane of impeccable unselfishness. Their test of perfection was, indeed, an altruistic promiscuity. The curse of selfishness asserted itself most generally, Noyes knew, in a man's proprietary attitude toward his wife; hence the test of a man's sanctification was his willingness to share his marriage-bed. Estlake expressed it fervidly: "No matter what his other qualifications may be, if a man cannot love a woman and be happy in seeing her loved by others, he is a selfish man, and his place is with the potsherds of the earth. There is no place for such in the 'Kingdom of Heaven.'"

The result was, in practice, a gynecocracy, modified by Noyes' own guidance in the distribution of favors. He had little patriarchal authority, but he possessed a Buchmanesque genius in making people talk to him of their most intimate problems and in persuading them of his own superior wisdom. "Special love," a fondness for one particular woman so great as to make one think favorably of monogamy, was an offense against the Community; for one could not love a single person much without loving everyone less. Nordhoff was present at a "criticism meeting" when it was related of the young benedict being criticized that he had fallen into the error of selfish love; had been summoned to the head of the Community for counsel; and had been persuaded, for chastenment, to allow another man in the Community to satisfy his wife's philoprogenitive desire.

"Against all precedent in nature," stated a member of the Oneida Community, "man has by brute force usurped the prerogative of the physically weaker sex"; that error was corrected in the Community, where the lady did the choosing. If a gentleman desired special attention, he could put his request only through the mediation of a third party, preferably a woman; so that the young lady was free to decline or accept without embarrassment. But the patriarchs of the tribe claimed the virgins, by a happy theory of "ascending fellowship," that edification and improvement came from associating with one's superiors. It was of the greatest importance, in the Noyesian credo, that girls' first impressions of sexual experience should be received from older gentlemen "who would be more likely to elevate them with the consciousness of having innocently exercised a pure and natural function on the spiritual plane, than would men to whom self-gratification would be a greater temptation"; Noyes apparently had complete supervision over these matters of ascending fellowship.

In as neat an inversion of logic as the generation achieved, the sinless life was the promiscuous one. Sexual affairs were all-absorbing to the Community; so that a disciple could write, blithely and innocently, "Life became a state of continuous courtship, both seeking to attract each other by commending themselves to the highest ideal of either by loyalty to truth and to community principles." Beyond "affectional happiness" was selective parentage, a science which Noyes fostered under the not attractive title "stirpiculture." He hoped that the Community would produce a race spiritually perfect by inheritance.

This sanctified intermixing was regulated by confession, occasional "fasts" (periods of continence, declared sometimes when the Community was undergoing affliction of some sort), and mutual criticism. The confession of Christ was found helpful whenever Perfectionists did not feel at peace within the community. In Noyes' colonies the expression, "I confess Christ a good spirit," apparently had mystic virtues; by repeating the charm the unhappy Perfectionist conquered his insubordinate feelings. "Criticism meetings," whose efficacy Noyes had learned at Andover, were rigorous ordeals for the subjects—who were penned in the center of a gathering and dissected with brutal candor. These meetings, salutary exercises in humility for the victims and strengthening the communal associations of the group, were in good part responsible for the solidarity of the Oneida society during more than thirty years.

Hopedale, founded by the Reverend Adin Ballou, a Universalist, likewise had extraordinary vitality. The colony, founded in 1841, occupied five hundred acres in western New York and by 1851 had one hundred and seventy-five adherents. The members professed cordial and complete faith in the religion of Christ according to the New Testament and acknowledged all the moral obligations of that faith. The "Preceptive and Parentive Circles" of the organization tolerated no unchastity and served as "the confidential counselors of all members and dependents who may desire their mediation in cases of matrimonial negotiation, contract, or controversy." There were no economic restrictions "other than those which Christian morality everywhere rightfully imposes." The community was supercharged with religious enthusiasm and considered itself a model of social regeneration, presage of a new Christendom. It dissolved in 1858, when the religious inspiration had abated.

"Not a reading man but has a draft of a new Community in his waistcoat pocket," Emerson wrote to Carlyle in 1840. "George Ripley is talking up a colony of agriculturists and scholars." A company of New England's brightest and most hopeful met at Dr. Channing's house that autumn to discuss the project; some of these, a twelvemonth later, became the stockholders of Brook Farm. They were Transcendentalists, a name suggested by favorite passages in Kant's *Critique of Pure Reason* and by Wordsworth's expression,

> transcendental truths
> Of the pure intellect, that stand as laws.

Brook Farm was designed as a philosophical and moral experiment, with competition and the ordinary rules of trade excluded but the right of private property retained. Agriculture was to be the basis of its life, "it being the most simple and direct in its relation to nature"; but the hours of labor were to be brief, so that the members should have "leisure to live in all the faculties of the soul." The members found the agricultural work more exacting than they had supposed it would be; but, stimulated by Transcendental visitors from Boston and Cambridge on the week-ends, the community was sustained with equivocal success. In 1844 Brook Farm took on new characteristics as a Fourierist colony, and during its remaining three years it was an earnest propagandist of that system.

Another Transcendental endeavor to found a "New Eden" was the small cluster of Fruitlands, begun by William Lane and Amos Bronson Alcott in 1843. "The pure soul, by the law of its own nature, adopts a pure diet and cleanly customs," said Alcott; and the group followed a strictly vegetarian regimen. "We rise with early dawn," Lane and Alcott described the life to a prospective member, "begin the day with cold bathing, succeeded by a music lesson, then a chaste repast. Each one finds occupation till the meridian meal, when usually some interesting and deep-searching conversation gives rest to the body and development to the mind. Occupation . . . engages us out of doors or within, until the evening meal—when we again assemble in social communion, prolonged generally until sunset, when we resort to sweet repose for the next day's activity."

Unitarianism had rejected the binding force of every dogma of traditional Christianity save supernatural revelation. Transcendentalism rejected that. The revelation came from within, in a burst of glory, bringing an intuitive knowledge of God and a positive assurance of the spiritual nature of man; and with that bright optimism each Transcendentalist reconstructed the meaning of God, society, and self. So many egocentric universes had a basis of association only as long as idealism looked upward, toward vagueness, for its nourishment, and not straight ahead, toward clarity.

The initial impulse in the making of a Transcendentalist was a wordless emotion, one that may be within the experience of any of us—a moment of exaltation, the sudden and delightful discovery of absolute harmony between oneself and the outside world. Emerson's vigor was sustained by the frequent recurrence of these expansive feelings. In most people this exhilaration, after roaming the cerulean spaces, takes a mundane, amative direction. Emerson's journals—thoroughly honest, if he did intend them for publication—make clear that he was never seriously troubled by impulses of the flesh; and the Transcendental group as a whole was characterized by an attractive pure-mindedness. "Continence, or chastity in personal indulgences," Bronson Alcott listed as one of the five "sacraments of inspiration and thought."

Lowell was speaking to a group of friends when the exaltation came. "The whole system rose up before me like a vague Destiny looming up from an abyss," he confided to George Loring. "The air seemed to waver to and fro with the presence of Something I knew not what. . . . I cannot tell you yet what this revelation was. I have not studied it through. But I shall perfect it one day, and then you shall hear it and acknowledge its grandeur. It embraces all other systems." Lowell's dissective bent ruined it all. These pseudo-mystic feelings were too evanescent to be "studied through"; Lowell became a good Brahmin and a poor Transcendentalist.

Three factors brought the Transcendental philosophers into a fairly coherent unit—the communal experiment at Brook Farm, the magazine *The Dial* (1840–44), and Emerson. The author of *Nature* was a focal point, a benign center of conversation and hospitality. He was innately the patron. Emerson wrote to Carlyle in 1836, "O my friend, if you would come here and let me nurse you and pasture you in my nook of this long continent, I will . . . doubt not give you . . . sound eyes, round cheeks, and joyful spirits." He actually did as much for certain native geniuses; he was the host of the Transcendental company, as Elizabeth Peabody in Boston was its hostess. "His range includes us all," said Lowell; and at another time he said, with that certain condescension which spared none of his eminent acquaintances, "Waldo Emerson is an amusing instance of a . . . man who is keenly alive to the incongruousness of *things,* but has no perception of the ludicrousness of *ideas."*

Most active in diffusing the ideas of the "Spiritual Philosophy" was Amos Bronson Alcott; he, and not Emerson, was by general repute the leading Transcendentalist. Alcott's favorite mode of radiating his phrases was through gatherings he called "Conversations." Fredrika Bremer described one of these meetings: "There were present from forty to fifty people, all seated on benches. Alcott sits in a pulpit, with his face toward the people, and begins the conversation by reading something aloud. On this occasion it was from the writings of Pythagoras." The discourse did not captivate Miss Bremer. "Alcott drank water, and we drank—fog. The good Alcott hears an objection as if he heard it not, and his conversations consist in his talking and teaching himself."

These sentences of Alcott's contain the central ideas of Transcendentalism: "Love is the genius of spirit." "Man is man, in virtue of being a Person, a self-determining will, held accountable to a spiritual ideal." "What is the bad but lapse from good." "Nature and spirit are inseparable, and are best studied as a unit." "The Person is One in all the manifold phases of the Many, through which we transmigrate." "Ideas are solvents of all mysteries, whether in matter or in mind." To these should be added Emerson's general definition of the reformative impulse. "There is an infinite worthiness in man, which will appear at the call of worth."

The leading Transcendentalists possessed, what was as uncommon then as now, an acquaintance with contemporary philosophical literature—Kant, Herder, Cousin, Fichte, Jacobi, Schelling. In 1838 George Ripley launched one of the movement's most important services, the fourteen volumes of *Specimens of Foreign Standard Literature,* making available in translation much German and a little French Romantic belles-lettres. The unusual width and depth of their reading provided the Transcendentalists with an elaborate logomachy, making the stuff of perfectibility, the nature-cult, pantheism, and the love-force into a phraseology so distinctive that the intimate connection of Transcendentalism with the broad Romantic movement in America has been obscured. This logomachy also served to let Emerson, who in truth never released his grip on reality, write with the disjointed brilliance of a neophyte yogi who has not yet learned to concentrate; to let Margaret Fuller conceal her critical gifts beneath convolutions of tortuous phrases wherein a sentence's worth of idea becomes a paragraph of print; and to allow Bronson Alcott, the Orpheus of the movement, unwittingly to convince most of his contemporaries that Transcendentalism was an eccentric fantasy.

After the discovery that Fourier had constructed a social scheme which assigned definite place and task to brotherhood, manual energy, and the other social tools, many "apostles of the Newness" felt the want of a Fourier to make blue-prints for the spiritual world. "Everything seems to come from the Infinite, to be filled with the Infinite, to be tending toward the Infinite," wrote Lydia Maria Child in 1843; but after a few years of strolling the uncharted Infinite the traveler wanted a cosmography.

The scientific works of Emmanuel Swedenborg were published in London in 1845, done into English by J. J. Garth Wilkinson, who enriched the volumes with prefaces which Emerson said "throw all the contemporary philosophy of England into shade." The New Church itself had been quietly sustained in the United States since the beginning of the century, but the Swedenborgian revival of the late Forties was impelled by Fourierists and free-lance thinkers as Wilkinson's volumes came into circulation. Swedenborg's elaborate mysticism was welcomed by the Brook Farm group. A critic in the *Arcturus* (April, 1841) had complained of Transcendentalism that "the sect has a narrowing influence, from the reiteration of its favorite topics. These are of progress, of insight, of the individual soul. Most true and weighty are they; yet, by being

eternally harped on and insulated, they lose their effect."
Thanks to Swedenborg and his translators, it was now possible
to soar into the cosmos with a new phraseology—the doctrines
of Forms, Orders and Degrees, Series and Society, Influx, Correspondence, Representation, and Modification.

Andrew Jackson Davis met Swedenborg's ghost in a graveyard near Poughkeepsie in 1844, and the two had a mutually
instructive conversation. The ghost commissioned Davis to bol-
ster the "inefficient" efforts of Christ to regulate mankind, and
Davis promised to do his best. Emerson did his part, in a lecture on "Swedenborg, the Mystic." *The Harbinger,* journal of
Fourierism, adopted Swedenborg and in the thirty months of
its existence printed almost forty articles and reviews on
Swedenborgianism. John Sullivan Dwight exclaimed, "In
religion we have Swedenborg; in social economy Fourier; in
music Beethoven." Charles A. Dana wrote, "The chief characteristic of this epoch is its tendency, everywhere apparent, to
unity in universality; and the three men in whom this tendency
is most fully expressed are Swedenborg, Fourier, and Goethe."

And another field of knowledge adopted the mystic Teuton.
George Bush, professor of the occult therapy, wrote a book,
Mesmer and Swedenborg, demonstrating how snugly the doc-
trines of the two illuminati interlocked.

Franz Antoine Mesmer regarded the publication of his
thesis *L'influence des planettes sur le corps humain* (following
the taking of his Doctorate at the University of Vienna in
1766) as the formal inauguration of Animal Magnetism. The
science was in fact a compounding of the "Etheriall Sperm"
of Fludd, the "magnet" of Paracelsus, and the "strong persuasion" of that remarkable faith-healer of the seventeenth century, Valentine Greatrakes. Mesmer baited the medical
fraternity to prove that Animal Magnetism was not curative;
they tried and failed. He devoted himself to the remunerative
practice of the science while disciples developed the theory
of a "universal magnetic fluid." Mesmer's treatment of his first

case, an epileptic woman, to whose limbs he applied magnetic plates, was one of the curative procedures. More common was the use of the *baguette,* a magnetic rod which the Mesmerist pointed at the ailing organ and from the tip of which the subtle fluid flowed from the superior vitality of the Mesmerist to the passive frame of the patient. An elaborate form of group-cure involved the *baquet,* a circular tub filled with water, bottles, and patients, with iron rods to magnetize the water and a pianoforte to play airs during the performance. All the phenomena of the hypnotic trance were soon associated with Mesmerism.

For Continental learning the United States was largely dependent upon prior British publication and British interest. Despite scattered conversions among the first two generations of the nineteenth century, Mesmerism aroused no consistent following in England until the early Forties. The rise of the science in the United States followed immediately. By 1848 this country was a laboratory for "biological" experiments. The exhibitions of the Professors began with a call for volunteers from the audience. The subject was given a small metallic battery to hold and gaze upon; the Professor, meanwhile, made gestures to encourage the flow of the magnetic fluid. "After fifteen minutes," described an observer, "the battery was removed, and the operator would seize the right hand of the subject with his left, and press the thumb firmly between the middle and ring-finger . . . then, looking the subject firm in the eye, would press the thumb of his right hand with great force, in the region of intuition and clairvoyance—between the eyebrows, at the root of the nose." In simple, he would hypnotize the subject. After the Professor had moved on to his next stand, teachers and parents frequently had to interfere to stop their charges from mesmerizing one another.

Blendings of Phrenology and Mesmerism produced several systems which are distinctive by little else than variance in phraseology and the intense jealousy among the several founders. Dr. Joseph R. Buchanan began lecturing on "Neurology" in 1841 and published *The Phrenological Portion of Neurology* two years later. In 1854 he published a more complete description of his science, which had taken in so much territory that the volume was named *The Neurological System of Anthropology*. The usual distribution of the Phrenological organs he discarded for a system of his own, which located organs on the face and neck, as well as in the skull; and he had much to say of an impalpable fluid, "Nervaura." Nervaura was a subtle emanation from the nervous system, differing not only for each individual but for each organ; it was the mediating link between consciousness and electricity. Being mundane, nervaura could be transmitted from one organism to another through an iron bar; but being also spiritual, it could radiate out from the cerebral centers and so transmit the will of one strong mind into the minds of the multitude. Thus had Napoleon and other great ones swayed the sentiments of a people.

Buchanan preferred (unnecessarily, it would seem) to supplement the cerebral radiations of his own nervaura by making use of the printed word, and he published a *Journal of Man* devoted to his science. In public lectures he placed his finger upon the cranium of the "subject"; along Buchanan's arm and out his finger flowed the nervaura, and, if all went well, the subject responded according to the Phrenological organ the "fluid" entered. If Bibation were excited, he wanted a drink; if Inhabitiveness, presumably he wanted to go home. A more occult variation, requiring a person of greater sensitivity than the Doctor himself, was the placing of a letter against the forehead; the sensitive person could then describe the personality of the writer. Buchanan called this technique "psychometry." Mrs. Theresa Pulszky, one of Kossuth's retinue, met the Doctor in his own bailiwick, Cincinnati; Buchanan had with him a sensitive young man, and Mrs. Pulszky tested his powers with a specimen of her husband's handwriting. She was quite awed by the accuracy of the characterization.

Etherium, the substance upon which J. Stanley Grimes founded his system of "Etherology," performed all the duties once commonly ascribed to the astral ether, and many besides; it connected the planets and communicated "light, heat, electricity, gravitation and mental emotion, from one body to another, and from one mind to another." It supplied the motive power for the human body in this wise: entering the body through the "external senses," etherium passed to the "phreno-organs" of the brain; here it was modified and transmitted to the organ of Consciousness, and thence, through the motor nerves, to the muscles. "And, as the motor nerves make some resistance, motion is the consequence." Released by this motion, the etherium passed to the external world and mingled with the general mass of the universal fluid.

The diversion of etherium from its usual channels, explained Grimes, was the real cause of all Mesmeristic phenomena. It accounted, too, for the influence of immoral associates upon susceptible persons. He had seen persons whose Phrenological organizations indicated sobriety, honesty, and virtue but who had devilish reputations. The untoward circumstance was their extreme susceptibility to "etheropathic" influence; they had fallen into vicious society and conformed to the will of evil associates—even though those associates were quite unaware that they were radiating malevolent etherium.

Dr. R. H. Collyer, of English birth, became one of the most zealous exponents of Mesmerism in this country. For his own elaboration of the hybrid science he chose the name "Psychography"; his pamphlet under this title, with the subtitle "The Embodiment of Thought," was published in 1843. The title-page bears this illustration: two persons are gazing into a bowl of molasses; dotted lines (representing the magnetic stream) are radiating from their foreheads to a point on the surface of the dish. The text explains that one of these persons is the Doctor, the other, a young lady, the "subject." "When the angle of incidence from my brain to the surface of the molasses was equal to the angle of reflection from her brain, she distinctly saw the *image* of my thought at the point of coincidence."

The Reverend Laroy Sunderland had already been an evangelical preacher, good enough to give his customers the jerks, then an ardent crusader for Abolition, when he became a "Phrenopathist"; he added no less than one hundred and fifty organs to those mapped out by orthodox Phrenologists.

This enthusiasm exhausted, after five years, he followed his independent interest in Mesmerism and formulated a system he called "Pathetism," publicly introduced in 1847. He was the first American to explain the phenomena of the trance without resorting to magnetic fluid or psychic effluence of any kind. Sunderland apparently discovered the principle of autosuggestion independently of Continental influence. John A. Wroe and John Reid invented "Electro-Biology, or the Science of Impressions," an ornately mystic system whose most lucid suggestion was that "Man, himself, is a real, living, self-acting Galvanic battery." And stemming primarily from Mesmerism was Roswell Park's "Pantology," "an exhaustive analysis of human knowledge, in which all the fragments, even of minor importance, find a distinct and proper place." So much for the small fry; the catalogue reaches a genius.

Andrew Jackson Davis was one of an all but numberless flock of children born to an humble couple in rural New York. He had only one month of district schooling and no other recorded education. In his seventeenth year his home town, Poughkeepsie, was excited by the lectures on Mesmerism delivered by Professor J. Stanley Grimes. A local tailor tried his hand at magnetizing young Davis, with such success that the two turned professional—the tailor as monitor and Davis as clairvoyant. Davis discovered in 1844 that he had an "inward" monitor and needed no assistant. In the following year he published *Lectures on Clairmativeness,* a word he invented to describe his psychic power. He asserted his ability to project his vision through all space, seeing "things past, present, and to come. I have now arrived at the highest degree of knowledge which the human mind is capable of acquiring." Using two admirers as magnetizer and scribe, he dictated during periods of trance *The Principles of Nature, Her Divine Revelations, and a Voice to Mankind*—eight hundred octavo pages of closely packed inspiration, published in 1847. Produced in the same occult mode, several volumes followed under the general title of *The Great Harmonia;* and thereafter Davis wrote a number of books without the aid of the trance. He began by discussing the Primal Germ and ended on the outermost circle of the illimitable universe.

There have been few revelations of such magnitude. The core of Divinity he explained: "There are in the Godhead and Godbody (that is to say, in the imperishable mansions of Father-God and Mother-Nature) all the persons that were ever developed on any star in the firmament or the earth beneath; all men, all spirits, all angels, all archangels and seraphs which people the immeasurable spheres of life and animation; for we live and move and have our being in the Divine Existence, 'whose body Nature is, and God the soul.'" Man's primary duty was faithfulness to the dictates of his "highest attractions" —those impulses generated in the organs of Veneration, Sublimity, Ideality, and Marvelousness. Davis announced a "divinely-originated and supernally-authenticated" set of twelve commandments, the first being, "Obey the normal requirements of self-love." The second was, "Obey the law of Conjugal Love with all thy heart and with all thy mind"; the sixth, "Obey the law of Universal Love with the total ingenuousness of thy inmost nature"; and the tenth, "Obey the whisperings of the spirit of true beauty."

In the intervals between the auctorial trances Davis supported himself and his two assistants by giving clairvoyant readings. The fame of his seances and news of his uncommon manner of composition helped his first "inspired" volume to reach thirty-four editions. His enthusiasm for the moral regeneration of mankind was the quintessence of Sentimental hope; he rewrote the prevailing philosophy of the love-force on a cosmic page. It was Andrew Jackson Davis who gave modern Spiritualism its vocabulary and suggested its theology; without him and the group clustered about his periodical, *The Univercoelum,* the rappings of the Fox Sisters might have been but a nine days' wonder in western New York, little more important than any village ghost.

The first number of *The Univercoelum and Spiritual Philosopher* appeared in December, 1847, announcing its devotion to "philosophico-theology, and an exposition and inculcation of the principles of Nature, in their application to the individual and social life." Its editor-in-chief and his two most active associates in the writing and editing were Universalist ministers. *"What is sin?"* inquired Davis. "Sin is a name for excess; a mark missed by man in his development; a ditch, into which, when with ignorance or passion blind, we stumble for a season"—an echo of the doctrine which the Universalist Church formerly stressed, the denial of eternal punishment, and a parallelism of the Transcendentalist statement, "What is the bad but lapse from good." From faith in Davis' clairvoyant revelations (which the *Univercoelum* regularly published) to faith in spirit-knockings and like manifestations from the other world was but a slight transition.

The leading article in the first number was by the Reverend William M. Fernald, "On the Necessity for new and higher Revelations, Inspirations, and forms of Truth, for the benefit of Mankind at the present day." All the men and women who contributed to the early volumes of *The Univercoelum* shared an electric expectancy; something most portentous, some new communion of man with the Godhead, was about to occur. A lady contributor in 1848 stated that the spirits of the departed "may be all around us without our discovering them, because our spiritual vision is not strong or clear enough," and that ultimately every disciple of truth might be aware of the union of the two worlds, the quick and the dead. Even the Reverend George Bush, who wrote a pamphlet solemnly warning the public against the errors and falsities in Davis' *Principles of Nature,* declared in his tract that Davis had been used as a mouthpiece by uninstructed and deceiving spirits, and that "if we mistake not, the indications are rife of a general demonstration about to be made, or now being made, of the most pernicious delirium breaking forth from the world of spirits upon that of men."

Two girls in their teens, Margaretta and Katherine Fox, on the evening of March 31, 1848, enjoyed themselves hugely. They pressed their toes against the baseboard of the bedstead and produced the raps that are generally accounted the first phenomena of modern Spiritualism. The girls had experimented with the ghostly racket on previous nights; this time they fairly excelled themselves. Mamma, prescient that the night was an extraordinary one, ran to call in the neighbors for witnesses. Was it a spirit? Three loud raps. Had it been murdered for money? Three loud raps. The spirit was one "C. R.," foully done to death in that very house long before Mr. John D. Fox and family had become the tenants. Though the spirit did not care to give its full name, it was quite willing to give the age of everyone present and to rap the correct replies to other parochial questions. The good people of Hydesville Village, New York, were credulous and agape at the marvel. The Fox family soon abandoned their overtenanted house, and fifteen-year-old Margaretta went to Rochester to stay with a married sister, Mrs. Leah Fish. Leah seems to have been the first to recognize the commercial possibilities of the (shall we say?) racket; and shortly the spirits bade Margaretta to charge a fee for her exhibitions.

Thereafter the spiritualistic epidemic spread—increasing numbers of mediums and an increasing variety of occult phenomena. From Rochester to Auburn, to New York City, to Bridgeport; to Philadelphia, Charleston, Cincinnati; the movement extended, not sporadically, but in waves of spatial sequence, like the widening ripples of water in which a stone has been thrown. Or like the unrecorded whisperings of a grape-vine telegraph.

The one positive tenet of Spiritualism, the possibility of communion with the spirits of the dead, was not unattractive to most Christians, even though the Spiritualist conception (as became obvious on reflection) carried with it the denial of basic Christian doctrines. For, as one disciple expressed it, it was not "an incredible thing, nor one unworthy of Heaven, that the Key-stone in the arch of evidence should be furnished by angels, whose joy over penitent sinners would leap at the permission thus to awaken the dormant energies of men to the high theme of glorious salvation." Those hard-shell sectarians who saw portent of great evil in the rise of Spiritualism were disposed to accept most of the phenomena, but to ascribe them to devils. One encounters awful warnings against these occult forms of infidelity and the "multitudes of *nothingarianism*"; a polemic volume went so far as to charge the Spiritualists with planning a new political party to carry out the scheme of de-Christianizing American institutions, in particular to eradicate the Blue Sunday Laws.

Clairvoyance itself was not new in the United States, even though it had not assumed the language of a cult until Andrew Jackson Davis began his writings. In August, 1843, to take one of the isolated instances, crowds of Philadelphians descended upon Brandywine Hundred to see an entranced girl prophesying strange things and holding conversations (in Latin) with God. By 1848 there were several professional clairvoyants who issued prescriptions and medical advice while in a state of trance; they were not slow to add spirit-rapping to their accomplishments. Many Fourierists and Swedenborgians early were converted to Spiritualism. Liberal ministers became its ablest propagandists. Within two years after the demise of *The Univercoelum* in June, 1849, six or seven Spiritualist organs were being published, in most of which the coterie of Harmonial Philosophers were associates. The longest-lived of these journals was *The Spiritual Telegraph* (1853–61), edited by Charles Partridge, a wealthy merchant, and the Reverend S. B. Brittan, a Universalist minister.

Benjamin Franklin—whose *Autobiography* was readily accessible—became the most ubiquitous of all the spirits, a more industrious seance-attendant than even George Washington. Through Leah Fish at Rochester in 1849 Franklin described the most favorable conditions for the production of spiritual manifestations. Darkness was requisite, the blacker the better; the spirits were uncomfortable and taciturn when the audience gave too close attention to the medium; they relished a musical overture, or cheerful conversation, at the beginning of a "sitting." A spirit which penetrated the veil in Darien, Wisconsin, was more particular as to the musical overture, insisting on "Jim Crow" rendered on the violin, while (chronicled the *Spiritual Telegraph*) "he beat time with great violence, precision, and apparent pleasure."

The *Poltergeist* was loose in 1850 and was never recaptured. In March of that year a series of violent disturbances broke out in the house of the Reverend Austin Phelps, a Presbyterian minister of Stratford, Connecticut. Windows were miraculously smashed, turnips covered with hieroglyphs grew out of the carpet, scraps of mysterious writing materialized in quantity; the minister's little boy was transported to the high branches of a tree and there was found with his pants off; a brass candlestick rose and dashed against the floor until it succeeded in breaking itself; a large potato dropped from the empyrean onto the Doctor's breakfast-table. For about eighteen months the phenomena, marvelous if somewhat annoying, were frequent in that household. Skeptical visitors present during certain of the manifestations noticed an incidence between the erratic behavior of the Doctor's son and daughter and the violent occurrences. The mysterious writings were in a school-boy scrawl. When the little fellow was despatched to a school in Philadelphia, the spirits destroyed his books, tore his clothes, and so disrupted the school routine that the boy was remanded to Stratford.

This, the first instance of "possession" in modern Spiritualism, was followed by other instances of spirit playfulness. As late as 1858, when the Spiritualist movement was in its decline, strange things were reported from Duquoin, Illinois; there, in the house of "Mr. L.," reported a witness, "near the fireplace was the youngest daughter, a very pretty girl, moving around in a kind of waltzlike dance, her arms in a horizontal position, seeming paralyzed, and humming a singular air. Strangest of all, every piece of furniture in the house was keeping perfect time with the movements of the girl, and a clock on the mantel piece had ceased running, but a continuous stream of sounds rung from its bell. A square table cut the queerest antics of anything in the room. First it would tip forward on the two front legs, then on the two hinder ones, and lastly spin around on one leg like a top, and again tip forward and backwards. A fire-shovel was dancing a jig on the hearth. . . . A green light, interspersed with orange colored rays, seemed to envelop the upper portion of the girl's body, giving her a supernatural appearance, and the most melodious sounds followed."

The demoniac visitation at Stratford is particularly noteworthy because in reporting upon it Andrew Jackson Davis laid down the doctrine of "spirit control." He remarked that the minister's boy "frequently failed to discriminate, during certain moments of mental agitation, between the sounds which he himself made and those sounds which were made by a spiritual presence"; surmised that a benevolent spirit, to restrain the boy from being impelled to some foolhardy deed by "the electrical state of his system," made the young fellow unconsciously instrumental in tying himself to the tree (and removing his pants); and concluded that the spirits possibly had employed some impressionable member of the family to write some of the messages and arrange some of the "expressive tableaux." Thereafter, whenever a medium was discovered *in flagrante delicto,* the excuse—entirely acceptable to Spiritualists—was that the medium, highly susceptible to the magnetic power of the spirits, occasionally endeavored to perform the very action that the spirit was planning to do. In such circumstances the task of exposing trickery was a thankless one—nor did any person apparently possess enough of the spirit of scientific inquiry to make a conclusive demonstration. Horace Greeley vouchsafed, in 1850, that whatever might be the cause of the rappings and other wonders manifested through Mrs. Fox and her three daughters, it was unquestionably shown that the ladies themselves were not the source; and, comparatively, Katherine Fox's confession, made public by Mrs. Norman Culver in 1851, that she produced the raps by cracking her smaller joints, was of trifling moment.

Mr. Hiram Pack, 488 Pearl Street, New York, and other cabinet-makers, added to their savings by making "medium" tables, with the rap-producing machinery concealed in the bed of the table and operated by wires carried down the legs. James Russell Lowell commented, in January, 1853, that "the

A PRACTICAL USE FOR TABLE-TIPPERS

"Mrs. Jenkins, being about to remove on the first of May, has engaged the celebrated medium, Mr. Turner, to move her furniture, thinking it will be cheaper than to employ a carman." *Harper's New Monthly Magazine,* 1854.

Rappers are considered quite *slow* nowadays"; everybody was talking about the Tippers, and washstands, tables, and bedsteads were "behaving as if inspired." Lowell added, base scoffer that he was, "Judge Wells . . . is such a powerful medium that he has to drive back the furniture from following him when he goes out, as one might a pack of too affectionate dogs."

The most striking manifestation of spirit-power, the levitation of the human body, was introduced by Henry Gordon, a medium of New York, in 1851. On one occasion Gordon was apparently transported sixty feet, from one house to another. While Dr. R. T. Hallock, Secretary of the New York Conference of Spiritualists, was addressing that organization on June 28, 1852, Mr. Gordon, one of the audience, began to float upward and was swaying above his chair when (so Dr. Hallock affirmed) the attention of the audience was riveted by the spectacle and the gentleman returned to his seat. It was afterwards declared that the intention of the spirits had been to convey Mr. Gordon over the heads of the audience to the rostrum, but that they had been embarrassed by so much attention. A few other mediums were sometimes successful at levitation, but the phenomenon was an extraordinary act of grace on the part of the spirits. Trumpet-blowing, performances on the tamborine, slate-writing, the materialization of spirit-hands, luminous apparitions, and the sudden appearance of birds and other material objects ("apporting," a phenomenon especially favored by lady mediums, whose skirts were ample and opaque) were the common manifestations.

The phenomenon called "speaking with tongues" was not infrequent. Less often, mediums wrote spirit-messages in languages of which the medium professed no knowledge. Some of these messages defied the best linguists in the United States. An accumulating mass of inspired literature, dictated by great literati and orators from the hither world, and paintings produced by mediums who were but the supine agents of great artist-spirits, attested that the creative afflatus survived after death. A personal letter "from a gentleman formerly Senator" to a lady of Providence was printed in an 1853 number of the *Spiritual Telegraph*: "Since I wrote you last, I have had some of the most extraordinary manifestations from my old friend Calhoun. . . . I have also had communications from Webster, through a writing medium, of the most extraordinary character. A gentleman of the highest intellect present at the time, said he had read all the old philosophers from Plato down to Bacon, and he had seen nothing to equal these communications from Webster." John Murray Spear transcribed utterances from Seneca, Jefferson, Plato, and Aristotle, among others of the great departed; Andrew Jackson Davis received communications from Franklin, Solon, St. Paul, and St. John.

A medium of Rochester, the Reverend Charles Hammond, came under the influence of Thomas Paine in December, 1851. His lot was simply to take pen in hand and place himself "in the attitude of writing"; gradually all care and thought would vanish from his mind, and as his thoughts disappeared, his hand began to move. He expressly disclaimed any personal credit; often he could not tell what word he was writing until the word was completed. Paine had said his bookful by the first of February; and in March, 1852, the manuscript was published, under the title, *The Pilgrimage of Thomas Paine and others to the Seventh Circle in the Spirit World*. The medium explained in his foreword, evidently not untruthfully, that he knew nothing of the history of Thomas Paine. "Having been connected with the ministry for over twenty-two years, I was not inclined to read his productions"; and the poor fellow added, "Since I have become a writing Medium, I have found no leisure to read any book." But, as his own words show, he knew that Paine was an infidel, and therefore one whose first-hand confession of the glories of heaven would be most impressive.

The volume is Paine's recital of the discarding of his earthly, false wisdom as he passes through various experiences in the afterworld, and of his ultimate conversion, after some hours of argument with William Penn. Paine journeys past various arches and temples incrusted with symbolism, returns to earth for a little social-service work after the manner of Marley's ghost, and at last is transported to the Seventh Circle, or Court of Beauty. Paine's literary style had changed greatly since his death, for this utterance is typical of the *Pilgrimage*:

"Onward did not stop. Onward never stops. It works, labors, acts, and moves for the good of the mind. Dulness waits, cringes, fears, doubts, moves not. It waits to see, to know, and to understand the mysteries of nature. It will wait, and wait in vain. It will wait, and wait without improvement. It will wait, and improvement will wait also."

All these physical manifestations of a spirit-world were but the spectacular aspect of a new religion. Spiritualist doctrines were never definitively formulated; the movement was too individualistic properly to be labeled a cult. But the great mass who became Spiritualists enlisted to slake their religious doubtings. Spiritualism offered such a comfortable answer to the old problem of heaven and hell. In the religious ebullition of the thirty years up to 1850 material heaven and hell had vanished for most people; and there was no great cheer in the prospect of meeting one's beloved relatives and friends, in after-life, as disembodied spirits in a nebulous Godhead. The family was the unit of the social structure and of everyday Christian living; Spiritualism completed the swing of the pendulum from Calvinism and arrived, in this particular, at the same point—the assurance of meeting, recognizing, delighting in, one's departed friends in the after-world. Spiritualism was the better in that this promise was not limited to a selected few, the "saved." The unity of the family triumphed over bereavement. Nor, thanks to the communication of the spirits through "mediums," did one have to wait for death to renew the bond of affectionate companionship with the dead. Participating to the full in the love-force of the times, Spiritualism minimized the after-effects of sin; one did not have to be good, in a doctrinaire sense, or sanctified by grace, to be assured of life after death.

The behavior of spirits who appeared at seances attested that, at least for a while after entering the other world, departed persons were in about the same condition as to morals, tastes, and prejudices that had characterized them in earthly life. A colloquy in 1855 between William R. Gordon and the spirit (speaking through a medium) of an Irishman killed in a railroad accident has its significance: "What becomes of the wicked?" asked Gordon, and Pat replied, "Och! dthey go into the lowest shpere, fwhere dthey will progriss, afther a while." The spirit later vouchsafed, in Gordon's painful transcription of the brogue: "If one man murdhers anodher, whin he comes to quit dth' form, he must look for dth' speret of dth' mur-

SPIRITUALISM TESTED AND PROVED

Robert Hare, *Experimental Investigation of the Spirit Manifestations*, 1855. This apparatus, devised by Professor Hare for a rigorous scientific test, he described as "the instrument by which spirits were enabled to move a table under the influence of mediumship, yet in no wise under the control of the medium employed, even clairvoyance being nullified." The medium's hands rested on a metallic plate supported by brass balls, through which no motion could be imparted to the table. Nevertheless the table moved, and the various movements, transmitted by pulley and band to the "ouija" disk, spelled many interesting spirit communications.

dher'd man, an' ask his pardon; for he will be onaisy in his conscience. All dth' hell dthere is, is in conscience. An' dth' sowl is not responshible for deeds committed by dth' passionate animal speret."

A widespread belief, which has been glimpsed in Tom Paine's "pilgrimage," concerned a sequence of concentric zones arranged in groups of seven, a symbolism taken over from

Swedenborgianism and older mystical systems. Robert Hare, sometime Professor of Chemistry in the University of Pennsylvania, was told by the spirits that the satellites of Jupiter were the spiritual spheres of that inhabited planet. Josiah Gridley (who declared that he found in Spiritualism, after half a lifetime of searching, the answer to "the unutterable desires of my thirsty soul") gave the exact dimensions of the various spiritual spheres for earth-folk, the first being five thousand miles from the equatorial surface.

The common idea of the progress of the spirit was expressed, as clearly as anywhere, in Gordon's *Three-Fold Test of Modern Spiritualism*. Summarizing the doctrines of the movement, he named "a pantheistic theology, the identification of God with matter, or a Soul of the World, or vital principle of the Universe; hence, man's responsibility is only to the laws of nature. . . . The physical demonstration of the immortality of the soul is perfectly obvious from the 'inherent and immutable laws of progression,' that every particle of matter in the universe, ascending through multifarious forms, from the angular to the circular, 'will ultimately pass to the perfection of a spiritual essence.' "

Not a complete cosmology, all this; and not overly lucid as far as it went. Problems of good and evil, sentience and knowledge, Spiritualism elided. Ignoring the critical intelligence and little concerned with the ethical imagination, Spiritualism was distinctively an emotional faith; and it captured the allegiance of probably one million people in a population of twenty-five million. It was fittingly the last wave in the religious flux of the generation. At no time in its later history has Spiritualism, the world over, numbered more than three-fifths as many adherents as it counted in the United States in the middle Fifties.

In partial counterpoise to this leftward search for spiritual moorings—Swedenborgianism, Spiritualism, and other ports of call—was the shift of many wearied liberals to the ritualistic faiths. Timothy Dwight, sobering after his potations of strong metaphysics, spoke in ardent loyalty of "The Church"; he meant the Episcopal Church, suddenly and for the first time become almost fashionable in New England. And the Roman Catholic faith gained many distinguished converts—among the sometime Transcendentalists, Orestes A. Brownson, the voluble writer, and Isaac Hecker, founder of the Paulist Order.

Immigration had brought about a tremendous increase in the number of Catholics in the United States, and the Church had its American hierarchy, holy orders, seminaries. But this organization stemmed from the Congregation *de Propaganda Fide* of the Church of Rome, and American bishops held commissions as *in partibus infidelium*. There was reason.

CHAPTER THIRTEEN

The Ostrich in the Sand

MARIA MONK was a bad girl, and her mamma put her in the Magdalen Asylum of Montreal. A short while after her dismissal, a little book, *Awful Disclosures of Maria Monk,* was published in New York (January, 1836). It purported to be Maria's story of the wrongs she saw and experienced during seven years as novice and Black Nun in the Hôtel Dieu nunnery, which was also a Montreal institution. The lady may have substituted the fictitious address for the real one, to gain respectability and sympathy; or she may have been persuaded to the fabrication by the enterprising gentleman who actually wrote the book. The *Awful Disclosures* was a garishly sadistic account of the cloistral life, replete with flagellations and other juicy horrors. Miss Monk, it appeared, had fled to New York and there given birth to "the fruit of her connexion with a Catholic priest."

The first reviews were chary. The Protestant *New York Observer* confessed doubts as to the truth of the narrative, but remarked that none the less "our opinion of convents and of the confessional will remain the same. They undoubtedly afford great facilities for the perpetration of the crimes here alleged." By mid-February enlightened persons were convinced that the thing was nonsense, and the *New York Times,* having cagily forborne to notice the book as long as doubt existed, in the brief space of a two-inch review called the *Disclosures* a tissue of palpable lies, a detestable publication, a tissue of abominable lies, a vile fabrication from beginning to end, a subject too loathsome to be touched, and a vile appliance to the lowest tastes, the most gross ignorance, and the most blind superstitions of the day.

But meanwhile the book was selling—forty thousand copies; and it was reprinted day by day in the columns of a newspaper. Editorial denunciations and other rebukes hardly affected the credibility of the *Disclosures* for those prepared to believe it. In the previous year, 1835, the inventor Morse had exposed the designs of the Vatican and the Order of Jesuits in fostering treasonable and monarchical intrigues in America; that was the alarmist story of his book, *Foreign Conspiracy against the Liberties of the United States.* Maria Monk supplemented Morse's account of political villainy by adding a dreadful exhibit of moral pollution. The *Disclosures* became a stock item of "shocker" literature, and it may readily be found today (on the rack beside *Napoleon's Dream Book* and *The Devil's Ball-Room*). The Native American spirit which it represented has also enjoyed long life.

Irish immigration was the largest factor in the increase of Catholic communicants in the United States from about 550,000 in 1830 to more than three million in 1860. "Whatever respect we may have for the peasantry of Ireland or Germany," wrote Orestes A. Brownson, a New Englander converted to Catholicism, "much soever we may honor them for the firmness with which, under the severest trials and temptations, they have held fast to the orthodox faith, we can by no means take them in respect to civilization as the advance guard of humanity." There was no doubt among "native Americans" who the advance guards of humanity were. And a few of these chosen ones, in the early Thirties, hastened the golden age by setting fire to some Catholic buildings and claiming the rights of pillage.

The clustering of Irish and other poor in the cities offered valuable blocs of voters for whichever faction of the democracy could capture them. Politicians had three sturdy devices for the manipulation of the tenement-area dwellers—the legend of equality, the show of benevolence, and hard cash. The natural tendency of unprosperous citizens was opposition to the political party of the merchants and bankers, the Whig party; the usually successful politicians in the slum districts were those who headed a personal faction within the Democratic ranks. These factions were reliable and sometimes decisive elements at the polls. The sporadic outbreaks of anti-Catholic violence in the Atlantic cities were secondarily moral bludgeonings of

THE SPIRIT OF OUR ELECTIONS
Yankee Notions, 1861.

the dreadful Vatican; but primarily the riots were protests of other factions against the Irish fingers in the political pie.

In New York City the Irish invasion of Tammany Hall was well under way by 1836. The civic program for the Fourth of July showed a Donnybrook tinge. The Federal troops, after being reviewed by their major-general at Battery Park, were to march to the City Hall, where the Mayor and Council were to be saluted, "after which the troops will fire a feu de joie and be dismissed." Then the municipal parade was to form, with the Hibernian Universal Benevolent Society and the Hibernian Provident Society among the five units trooping after the Grand Marshal and the Civic Band. The procession was to follow a roundabout course, starting at East Broadway and Pike Street and ending at the Methodist Church on Duane Street—"Here music, Address to the Throne of Grace, Oration, and Collection." City Hall Park, obviously, would be thronged with spectators—a good place for the refreshment business.

Irishmen were awarded the concessions. Their tents and stocks of beverages were in place on Sunday, the 3d. That evening "several young persons," as the family newspapers referred to the hoodlums, belabored the Irish proprietors and ripped up the tents. On the morning of the Fourth the *Times* had its appropriate editorial on the only national holiday of Americans: "Its rejoicings are the hosannahs of a free people on the altar of their country's liberty, and the aspirations of gratitude sent up by them for past blessings, are mingled with pledges, that the past is but a solemn earnest of the future, that what has been well won, shall be well maintained." That evening the hue and cry was raised on the East Side, and a bloody riot between Irish and anti-Irish produced an imposing total of casualties. On the 5th belated celebrants kept missiles flying. "Alderman Brady," reported the *Times,* "was struck by a brickbat and knocked down." The outcome of the rioting was the addition of more policemen to the municipal force— Irish policemen.

When the large cities adopted systems of tax-supported public education, the Irish groups demanded a division of school funds to give parochial schools a share—or, failing that, a modification of the system of Bible-readings in the public schools. The Bishop of Philadelphia explained, in March, 1844: "Catholics have not asked that the Bible be excluded from the public schools. They have merely desired for their children the liberty of using the Catholic version, in case the reading of the Bible be prescribed by the controllers or directors of the schools. They only desire to enjoy the benefit of the Constitution of the State of Pennsylvania, which guarantees the

IGNORANCE IS BLISS

The Lantern, 1853. An anti-Catholic cartoon inspired by the controversy over Bible-reading in schools. The prelate is Bishop John Hughes.

rights of conscience, and precludes any preference of sectarian modes of worship." But there was no pouring oil on such turbulent waters. As election time approached, the Philadelphia mob made several experiments, not wholly successful; three Catholic edifices and a row of houses occupied by Irish residents were burned, but several of the rioters got themselves killed. In New York similar affairs were scheduled, to occur a few days before the city was to change mayors. But Bishop John Hughes, aggressive leader of that diocese, promised an armed resistance, and placards calling the mob to assemble were replaced by others announcing cancellation of the exercises.

The large number of virulent pamphlets on the "Bible question" evoked headstrong pamphlets in reply. In this emotional fever was rekindled the old suspicion that the Catholic European nations were determined to bring this free and enlightened Republic under the dominion of the Papal See. So grand a conspiracy could not, in the mere fitness of things, be grappled with openly and directly. It required masks, capes, and poignards—or something like the paddles and passwords of a high-school fraternity.

In Philadelphia, a city lacking the bustling commercialism of New York or the Unitarian and Harvardian distractions of Boston, the Native Americans meditated longest on the imaginary conspiracy—and founded the first Know-Nothing bodies. The Order of United Americans was established in 1845, a secret social organization with principles "in unison with the innate feelings of every deserving American." That was to say, it aimed to create a renewed commonalty of sentiment among true-born Americans, to check the progress of the political demagogue, and to avert from the Union "the jealous influence of all foreign Powers, Princes, potentates, or prejudices." It offered fraternal benefits in return for its fees; "by means of this we are enabled to minister to the comforts of a brother—to smooth the pillow of sickness—to bury the dead—to comfort the widow, and to protect and cherish the orphan." In 1848 the Order became aggressive, expanded beyond Philadelphia, and at the close of 1852 claimed thirty thousand members. Similar organizations had blossomed in those five active years —the United American Mechanics, the United Sons of America (with a ladies' auxiliary, the United Daughters), the Sons of Liberty, the Order of the Star-Spangled Banner, and several less important sodalities.

Place the thumb of your left hand between the fore and middle finger, bending the third finger. Then casually lift the hand to your face, and, as if rubbing your bristles, draw the little finger two or three times across the cheek. Do all this with artful carelessness; if the stranger you are addressing is not a fellow-member, probably he won't notice anything curious in your behavior. But if he is, he will close the thumb and forefinger of his left hand and make as if to put them in his vest pocket. Just to make certain you say to him, "What news do you carry?" He will answer, "Your news first." A brother Know-Nothing!

"We come together under circumstances that are calculated to develop all our better feelings; pledges that will dissipate our selfishness; obligations that will make us continually stand by and love each other; and objects in view that will ever keep our sympathies in full flow and our social delights in ever-fresh existence." Touching, if familiar in other connotations. What mattered was not the abracadabra of the conclaves, but the impact of Know-Nothingism upon society. Its voice was heard, claimed *The Republic,* from the snowy mountains of Vermont to the green plains of Texas; and with the help of that great power which stood beside the patriots of '76, the Native American movement would not rest until the American people were "reunited, re-nationalized." Thomas R. Whitney, editor of that journal, expected that seven-tenths of all the native-born Americans ultimately would come into the societies.

Four Know-Nothing journals voiced intense, dramatic propaganda. *The Republic* was begun in January, 1851, its prospectus advising those who "shrink from the touch and contagion of everything and anything homespun, or (*sic*) 'to the manor born' of this Nation," to avoid both the journal and its editor. "The interests of mechanics and working men and women, who have been sorely pressed by the unfair competition and combinations of pauper Europeans, will receive attention at our hands," promised *The Republic,* "and while we aim to supply them with a large share of good and wholesome reading, in the Literary Department, we shall ever strive to warm into full life the latent fires of patriotism that dwell in our hearts." That was warm enough for 1851; but three years later the good and wholesome fiction had been crowded out, and the pages were taut with expletives and exhortations. Equally vigorous was *The Know-Nothing and American Crusader,* with its motto, "God and our country! Deeds not words!" surmounted by a youth extending his right hand to a star and trampling the Papal tiara under foot; and *The Wide-Awake and the Spirit of Washington,* with the slogan, "God forbid that we, their posterity, should be recreant to our trust." More cryptic was the *Mystery,* whose banner announced it to be "published nowhere, sold everywhere, edited by Nobody and Know-Nothing."

The militantly Protestant movement aimed toward the eradication of parochial schools and the education of youth in the public schools or none; the general use of the Bible as a textbook in the public schools; a Sabbatarian revival to drive "bands of infidel foreigners" and "shameless freethinkers" out of the sight of church-goers; the election of native Americans of Protestant stock exclusively to all public offices; and an unremitting counter-attack against "the aggressive policy and corrupt tendencies of the Roman Catholic Church." The literature of Know-Nothingism exhibited ominous facts on Popery: the information, for instance, that Washington had Roman Catholics in mind when he issued his famous warning against foreign entanglements, and that "the valley of the Mississippi has been mapped as well as surveyed by the Jesuits of the Vatican"—as indeed it had been, in the Sixteen Seventies! A volume entitled *Young Sam; or, the Native American's Own Book* (1856) included chapters on "Abominations of Jesuitism," "Catholics Owe No Allegiance to the United States," "Licentiousness the Fruit of Celibacy," "Pope Equal with God," "Nunneries"—captions which adequately reveal the typical literature.

Know-Nothing candidates overwhelmingly carried the Massachusetts state elections in 1854 and were partially successful in New York, Delaware, and Maryland. Politically, Native Americanism proved a haven for remnants of the Whig party, a last refuge for voters who didn't want to commit themselves on slavery or slave-state expansion. The Roman Catholic immigrant was a convenient whipping-boy. For all the talk about the suffrage-power of the foreigner and of special factions stealing into American ballot-boxes and voting away American liberties, no definite program emerged other than the simple negative of voting for non-Catholics. No concerted attempt was made toward building a legislative dam to stop the flood of immigration—the idea that America was traditionally an asylum for the oppressed of all nationalities was as generally endorsed as the idea of "America for native Americans," and people did not bother to reconcile the two contradictory platitudes. The vagueness of the party was one of its beauties. Southern Whigs, far removed from any "immigrant problem," came into the American party, as the group of Nativist organizations, merged for political strength, named itself, and seized control. To the Know-Nothing platform they added two hush-clauses: "The suppression of all tendencies to political divisions, founded on geographical discriminations, or the belief that there is a real difference of interest and views between the various sections of the Union," and a pledge of "tender and sacred regard" for the legislation of 1850 designed to keep anti-slavery sentiment out of politics.

To the national convention of the American party in 1856 the name of Millard Fillmore was presented, "free from solicitation, unblemished by cunning, or wrinkled by selfishness." The party made an ardent campaign, and the candidate hoped for the best. Horace Greeley commented, on the morning of the election, that a few Fillmourners would waste their votes that day: like a squad of men, Greeley said, who take their stand on the outskirts of Waterloo and keep firing at a mark—"be the mark what it may, the scarlet woman, fancied disunion, foreign influence or what not"—while the battle rages. Only Maryland's electoral votes went to the Native American candidate.

Another of the Sentimental ebullitions had, for the time being, played out. They were subsiding rapidly in the late Fifties. The emotional lava that had fed them all was gathering under the Krakatao, slavery.

Manifest Destiny, too, had lost its vigor as a national crusade. The wane began when emphasis was transferred from the first great imperial task to the second. To reclaim the wilderness and bring the vast area of North America under one flag was the first; the acquisitive diplomacy of the Mexican War cleared the way toward its fulfillment. The second task was implied in James Buchanan's avowal in 1850: our Union was the Star of the West, whose genial and steadily increasing influence would dispel the gloom of despotism from the ancient nations of the world. But, unhappily, this task required a greater altruism and promised a smaller profit.

At the close of the Mexican War, Congress and Executive paused to watch, with pardonable pride, the triumph of democratic principles in France. President Polk declared that the world had seldom witnessed "a more interesting or sublime spectacle," and Congress formally congratulated the French people upon their exemplary revolution. Then came a genuine opportunity to dispel the gloom of despotism from an ancient nation.

Shortly after the crushing of the Hungarian rebellion of 1848, Americans began to hear of the banished patriot Louis Kossuth, who had taken refuge in Constantinople. Congress empowered the President to permit a vessel of the United States Navy to convey Kossuth to these shores. Several of the

Hungarian exiles found their way to the United States without such assistance—notably "the stout little curmudgeon," Governor Ujhazy, and "the valiant little Demoiselle Jagello," who were stuffed with dinners and paraded at dances throughout the social season of 1850.

KOSSUTH

"attended by the spirits of freedom and history, and the Guardian Genius of Hungary, with his own good angel calmly bearing him through space to America." *Gleason's Pictorial Drawing-Room Companion*, 1851.

The well-heralded Kossuth reached New York in December, 1851. Twelve days after his arrival Senator Isaac Walker announced that the United States must interpose "both her moral and physical power" against the interference of one nationality (which was to say, Austria) in the affairs of another. Senator Lewis Cass in the following month sponsored a resolution that the United States could not view "without deep concern" the intervention of European powers to crush a nationality's independence. In March Senator William H. Seward drew attention to the commercial advantages accruing to the United States as soon as the republican idea should triumph in Hungary.

Meanwhile Kossuth had become a fad, and oppressed Hungary an inspiration—his portrait in a thousand shop-windows; the allegorical statuette of the patriot warrior trampling the crowned eagle of Austria; the Kossuth soft hat, the Kossuth flare-sleeved overcoat, the Kossuth mode of exuberant moustache; civic banquets and private receptions, at which the hero's fine person, honest eye, and fluent eloquence roused loud appreciation. "We hear of respectable young men and women who have actually taken to study of the Magyar dialect," remarked a *Lorgnette* essay; "in all the *bals costumés* the Hungarian costume is just now carrying the day, even against a Buena Vista hussar coat, or the lace trimmings of a *Debardeur*. Street mountebanks are wearing Hungarian caps; the Hungarian balsam is in new demand; and Miss Lawson, who divides with the *Home Journal* the honors of being Pythoness of modes, is about to offer to the enchanted town a Jagello hat!"

Pro-Hungarian enthusiasm had been too long in the boiling, however, to be sustained at high heat after the novelty of Kossuth's presence had subsided. Kossuth's own impetuousness did much to ensure that the pugnacious aspect of the Monroe Doctrine was to remain confined to problems of the Western Hemisphere. He wanted funds, public or private, to sustain a second Hungarian revolt, and he pushed his request late and soon. "Have you seen the 'great Hungarian'?" wrote Orville Dewey to a friend. "Behold, we have on our hands a world-disturbing propagandist, a loud pleader for justice and freedom, who does not want to settle but to fight; who will not rest on his country's wrongs, nor let anybody else if he can help it." Theresa Pulzsky, one of Kossuth's company, stated that the party had been warmly greeted in every part of the States they had visited—at the firesides of the rich, amidst crowds of street-folk, in the shops of the working classes. Yet, for all the "tearful sympathy" and "delightful sensibility" that Mrs. Pulzsky noted, whenever Kossuth turned the conversation toward money the hosts tried to be reminded of something else.

The next few years saw a number of experiments in jingoism; but all these were sectional, identified with the "peculiar institution." In 1858 President Buchanan, as a last hope to minimize the slavery issue, attempted to promote an imperialist diversion which should be of national interest: the United States should acquire Cuba, by force if necessary, and assume a protectorate over the northern provinces of the Republic of Mexico; for a third immediate project, our military and naval forces ought to open a route over the Isthmus of Nicaragua. But nobody seemed interested then. Southern jingoists who might have welcomed the proposal were already involved with William Walker's filibuster in Nicaragua; or were busy with plans to renew the maritime slave trade; or thought, why make acquisitions for the Federal Government that shortly may be made for a Southern Confederacy? Northern friends of Manifest Destiny were not interested, because at this time any expansionist project inevitably took its dominant tone from the aggressive friends of slavery.

In the Northern states in 1835 rowdies broke up several antislavery meetings. The National Administration endorsed the refusal of Southern postmasters to deliver antislavery literature to the addressees; and early in 1836 the House of Representatives voted to table, without reading or debate, all petitions for legislation adverse to slavery. The majority of Northern Congressmen were reflecting the wishes of their constituents when they voted to hush up the disquieting subject. But a group of Abolitionists, who had framed a national organization in 1833 and possessed a vigorous, eloquent journal, *The Liberator,* insisted on proclaiming with pen and speech their utter detestation of slavery, slaveholders, every Federal statute or custom that in any way supported slavery; and this group could not be squelched.

Slavery was a cancerous sin—that was the blunt argument. No soft answer could turn away such righteous wrath, and after the middle Thirties there was no softness in the replies. Slavery sympathizers in the North were put on the defensive, whether they hated "naygurs" in manifestation of the snobbery of the mob or hated them because free Negro labor seemed a threat to their own unskilled jobs; or whether they belonged to the better-situated ranks who believed that the primary function of government was to protect property rights—all kinds of property. The South, at a moral disadvantage, put on the garments of a melodramatic purity. Southern ministers, many of them genuinely desirous of ending slavery by some peaceful and gradual process, produced a great bulk of sermons and essays in defense of slavery as a Christian institution, while Southern statesmen exclaimed over the political and cultural beauties of a civilization erected on the backs of a servile class.

The murder of Elijah P. Lovejoy, an antislavery editor, in Illinois in 1837 was the culmination of a phase of violence which quickly passed. The humanitarian impulse was at work in the North, and in the next decade the tide of middle-class sentiment flowed away from the pro-slavery attitude. But the flow was not toward the opposite shore; it was toward a stagnant center.

The attitude that became characteristic was voiced by Nathaniel Hawthorne, in a campaign biography of his friend Franklin Pierce published in 1852. It was odd that a literary genius should express the middle-class philosophy so capably; but Hawthorne's defense against the environment of lading-bills and crying babies to which he was bound was a partial surrender: he accepted the institutional ideals that he found generally accepted, as his way of least resistance, and retreated into the haunted world of his moral introspections. Hawthorne described slavery as one of the evils which Divine Providence does not leave to be remedied by human contrivance, but which, in its own good time, by some means impossible to be anticipated, Providence "causes to vanish like a dream."

The reformative impulse could not ignore slavery, but spokesmen for the middle class insisted that only the most gentle means should be used in combating it. The Reverend A. C. Dickinson, with many another, held that Christianity indicated the proper method. "As the Gospel has gained foothold," he wrote, "the people have become at once enlightened and purified, and gradually advanced to higher degrees of civil liberty. The Constitution of the State has felt its soft and plastic touch. All changes in advance of the proper preparation, would be real evils instead of blessings." So he deprecated the zeal of antislavery agitators for immediate results, bidding them "recognize the master's civil rights; urge the slave to a quiet acquiescence of the necessities of his lot, and a diligent use of his faculties for improvement—*then* your way to the heart of each is opened." These were admirable sentiments in the library; but the slaveholder resented (only a little less fiercely than he resented the Abolitionist attacks) both the suggestion that he himself was in need of any enlightenment or purification and the proposal that his Negroes should be educated.

When Daniel Webster sought outside his New England affiliations for a platform which would make him a truly national leader, he adopted an attitude on slavery practically identical with the Reverend Dickinson's. Dr. William H. Furness of Philadelphia wrote to Webster on January 9, 1850, urging that he "throw that great nature which God has given him into the divine cause of human freedom." Apparently Webster was not ready to reply; he delayed answering for thirty-seven days, then stated the attitude which was to take the Senate by surprise on the 7th of March. "But now, my dear sir, what can be done by me, who act only a part in private life," was his modest beginning. "In my opinion it is the mild influence of Christianity, the softening and melting power of the Sun of Righteousness, and not the storms and tempests of heated controversy, that are, in the course of these events,

NO COMMUNION WITH SLAVEHOLDERS

"Stand aside, you Old Sinner! WE are HOLIER than thou." *Harper's Weekly*, 1861. This Northern satire on the Abolitionist attitude, depicting the repudiation of Washington by John Brown, Beecher, Seward, Lincoln, and Greeley, appeared in the issue of March 2, scarcely six weeks before the attack on Sumter.

which an all-wise Providence rules, to dissolve the iron fetters by which man is made the slave of man."

There was comfort in remarking how greatly the Negro's moral and physical condition had improved in the comparatively short while that the African had been transplanted to America. President Buchanan, in one of his annual messages, called the attention of Congress to this happy effect. Slavery, "however deformed by evil," asserted the *New York Review* in 1838, "has been and is working out *good*"—and proceeded to rebuke a Southern writer for defending slavery as the permanent state of a certain class of humanity rather than a temporary condition.

Obviously the commercial relations of Northern merchants, manufacturers, and mill-owners with Southern planters and merchants would be neither intimate nor profitable if a wide moral gulf yawned between them. Governor William L. Marcy of New York, addressing the state legislature in 1836, descried a particular irritant: "In our commercial metropolis the Abolitionists have established one of their principal magazines, from which they have sent their missiles of annoyance into the slave-holding States. The impression produced in these States, that this proceeding was encouraged by a portion of the business men of the city of New-York, or at least not sufficiently discounted by them, threatened injurious consequences to our commerce. A proposition was made for an extensive voluntary association in the South, to suspend business intercourse with our citizens. A regard for the character of our States, for the public interest, for the preservation of peace among our citizens, as well as a due respect for the obligations created by our political institutions and relations, calls upon us. . . ."

Calls upon us, indeed; for so convenient a whip as the threat of economic boycott did not lie idle when there was occasion to use it. A publishing firm refused to print two volumes by Theodore Parker because they contained discourses unfavorable to slavery—not because the volumes were unsalable in the South, but because it was requisite that the firm's entire list be "pure" if it were to keep the patronage of Southern booksellers. Publishers of family magazines found it advisable to exclude any criticism of the "peculiar institution." Godey evaded the subject with an elegant gesture: "I allow no man's religion to be attacked or sneered at, or the subject of politics to be mentioned in my magazine. The first is obnoxious to myself and to the latter the ladies object." Charles J. Peterson did not escape so easily; his refusal to accept manuscripts from Grace Greenwood after that steady contributor to *Peterson's Magazine* had spoken for antislavery prompted Whittier to hit him off:

> A moony breadth of virgin face,
>   By thought unviolated;
> A patient mouth, to take from scorn
>   The hook with bank-notes baited!

The nasty use of the boycott was that of Northern merchants who wrote to the Southern correspondents of competitive firms that the merchants with whom they had been trading were fanatical bigots whom their fellows in commerce disowned. This dodge was certainly worked in Boston, and probably elsewhere.

There was another aspect, of course—one illustrated in a little volume entitled *Five Years' Progress of the Slave Power* (1852). A shoe-dealer, for instance, "full of chivalry and peculiar-institutionalism," sets out from Charleston or Savannah to lay in his annual stock. His neighbors have heard that Lynn is a hotbed of Abolitionist abomination, and they serve notice that no wife, child, or bondman of theirs shall wear a scrap of Lynn's tainted leather. The shoe-dealer, calling upon a wholesaler in Boston or New York, announces his disinclination to buy anything made in Lynn. As it happens, the wholesaler has just the article he wants—leather well tanned and cut, well stitched and sewed, not in Lynn but in Hopkinton. To be sure, if the buyer were willing to take Lynn shoes, he could have them at a better price, since they were much less in demand in the Southern market. But he prefers those from Hopkinton? Very well.

What had the merchants to gain if Virtue were allowed to pass judgment on the slavery system? Nothing that their common myopia perceived. When Webster made his final bid for the Presidency, in 1852, the commercial interests were friendly to the statesman who, besides being sound on money matters, insisted that slavery was politically a dead issue. The bellwether merchants of New York arranged a gigantic mass-meeting at Tripler Hall to further the Senator's prospects; they spent twelve thousand dollars on advertising, an amazing quantity at the prevailing rates. George Griswold, director of many corporations, was the chairman, and the one allowed to write the biggest check toward paying off the expenses of the futile campaign.

The American Colonization Society, founded in 1817, was protracting its unimportant existence. The colonization idea was to slough the whole annoyance by transplanting the Negroes back to Africa—a facile solution which would have intrigued the Sentimental generation had not the first twenty years of the Society demonstrated how inadequate were the resources of private philanthropy in competition with the fecund production of young Negroes in the slave-breeding states. David Christy conceived another use for Africa: speed the redemption of that continent by Christianity and civilization; the moral effect of several million educated and devout Africans in their native habitations would be irresistible to the sensibilities of the Southern planters, and "every Christian master, as his slaves attained sufficient moral elevation, would say to them, 'Brothers, go free!' "

Throughout the thirty years preceding the Civil War an aggressive propaganda, in books, orations, and sermons, presented slavery as a positive excellence. Ethnical and social reasons were mustered to reinforce Noah's curse on Ham, and the textbook most commonly used in philosophy courses at Southern colleges, Jasper Adams' *Elements of Moral Philosophy,* taught the young men that a slave class was an indispensable element of the best society. But these arguments were the product of a cultural organization in which there was only a very insignificant middle class. They penetrated the North no more successfully than Garrison's arguments pierced Southern consciences.

With the founding of the *Liberator,* in 1831, William Lloyd Garrison placed himself in the van of a strident, irrepressible reform. The crusade employed the printed word, the lecture, and the convention as its educational forces; if it was not repaid in converts, it had the moral satisfactions of having obeyed conscience, of alarming one entire section of the nation, and of irritating most of another. The movement brought together in its frequent conventions a group of earnest, sunny people, wholly convinced of the dynamic perfectibility of man, effusive with sentimentalism, and happily indifferent to the economic and political currents affecting the masses of middle-class society. Abolition of slavery was the common hope that brought into one hall a remarkable company of intellectual free-lances—Garrison, distinguishable by his prematurely bald, "fine intellectual head," at the center of the group, flanked by two or three Quaker vice-presidents; the alert Thomas Shipley, whose avocation was smuggling slaves out of Maryland; Thomas Whitson, the Hicksite; George Mellen, who wouldn't stop talking and whom some subtle person would have to coax off the floor; the Hutchinson family; Abby Folsom (Emerson called her "that flea of conventions") with her shrill and frequent interruption, "It's the capitalists;" Wendell Phillips, Mrs. Maria Chapman, and Edmund Quincy, high-bred delegates from Boston; the Reverend Samuel J. May, the most courteous and disarming of the antislavery lecturers; a smattering of Transcendental philosophers and literary men and women; Abby Kelley, whom Elizabeth Cady Stanton called "the most untiring and most persecuted" of the antislavery women lecturers; and Sojourner Truth, an effective speaker who had been a slave and had cicatrices on her back to prove it—Harriet Beecher Stowe's "Lydian Sibyl." There might be present Father Lamson, with a completely white outfit to match his beard and to signify his philosophy of purity; Henry Wright, a Congregational minister without parish, whose wont was to harry the chairman about parliamentary procedure; or, yet worse for the presiding officer, Nathaniel Peabody Rogers, who objected to any semblance of organization or any restriction on debate.

No contemporary reform stayed on its own track; even Abolitionism, with a goal unusually direct, had its difficulties with a crew of contrary minds. Samuel Sewall and John Greenleaf Whittier led a defection which insisted on adding the ballot to the weapons of the crusade; Garrison was a non-voter and held the American Antislavery Society to his principle. Garrison was also vehement that the institution of the Sabbath had been overruled by the coming of Christ; he had his own ideas about the Bible, about labor, and was an ardent pacifist. "Garrison is so used to standing alone," James Russell Lowell remarked, "that, like Daniel Boone, he moves away as the world creeps up to him. . . . He considers every step a step forward, though it be over the edge of a precipice." This radical zealotry did nothing toward making Abolitionism respectable.

Slaveholders visiting in the North were pleased to discover in the industrial system evidences of a servitude more burdensome than slavery. A North Carolinian wrote to Theodore Parker of a personal experience: the traveler, in a Boston hotel on a Sunday, discovered housemaids scouring the privies. He learned that the women were all Irish Catholics and that regularly on Sunday mornings, at the hour they would have chosen to go to Mass, they performed this special labor. He told them that he was a stranger, a slaveholder from the South—who "would certainly not allow my servants to be thus employed on a day which demanded general rest, especially for servants." The unhappy and embittered spouse of a Northern Abolitionist informed the *Southern Literary Messenger* of the servile routine of wives like herself: the mistress of a family, "although surrounded by several small children, and in circumstances which *gentlemen* deem delicate," was obliged to rise unseasonably and prepare breakfast; if not sufficiently expeditious, she received a tongue-lashing; if she replied in kind, she was a termagant; "and if she weep, her tears are as oil upon the passions of her lord and master, making them blaze the more fiercely." The editor, not above making a *tu quoque* when the opportunity offered, pointed out that "the wretched drudges, even while clanking their chains, dream that they are free; and the black domestics of the South, though their fetters are of flowers, are *called* slaves."

This unpleasant form of counter-attack, frequently used, gave the middle class further reason to believe that antislavery sentiments, not objectionable as a private virtue, were a confounded nuisance as the basis of a national crusade. There was ample scope at home for humanitarianism and uplift—Christianizing the poor, redeeming the inebriate, soothing the rough life of the mariner, promoting education. But the inflammable issue was not to be avoided. The Sentimental philosophy, which in its plausible and oversimplifying way encompassed nearly all social problems, could not absorb the slavery question. The attenuated fabric of middle-class idealism could not stretch quite far enough to conceal the ugly protuberance— although it tried hard enough. When, in the Eighteen Sixties, the national body got rid of the tumor by cutting it out, the fabric was cut too.

President Jackson in his farewell address (March, 1837) had a great deal to say about slavery; but he did not call it by name, for that was unmannerly. The citizens of every state should avoid anything calculated to wound the sensibilities of the people of other states; all measures calculated to disturb the rights of property or jeopardize peace anywhere must be voted down; and so on. Van Buren's inaugural speech, bright and amiable, included an avowal to resist any interference with the "peculiar institution" in the states where it existed. The two spoke for the great majority, who believed in Jackson and had been willing to accept Jackson's own choice for his successor. General Harrison in the campaign of 1840 declared that the Constitution did not sanction the discussion of slavery in slave states by citizens of free states—and shut up on that topic, as indeed on every other political issue. Then came the question of the annexation of Texas; and with it slavery was intimately connected.

Most of the settlers in Texas had come from slaveholding states. Slavery was protected in the new Republic, and the soil was favorable to

> The wondrous staple of the Southern clime,
> Material ruler of our race and time.

Cotton prices were rising in the early Forties, and the textile fiber had become the economic determinant of Southern philosophy. Planters were fearful that Great Britain would make a deal with Texas, exchanging trade and military favors for the abolition of slavery, to obtain cotton untainted by the "peculiar institution." The time was ripe for the absorption of Texas into the Union, and in 1843, when President Tyler got a friendly Secretary of State, the administrative way was clear. There remained the task of interesting a sufficient number of the Northern middle class. The lure of territorial expansion—as Tyler said in 1841, "Could anything throw so bright a lustre around us?"—and the prospect of repatriating the brother Anglo-Saxons who had moved into Texas were worth a great deal. The quantity of Texas debt-certificates held in the North, which the Republic probably would never redeem if annexation were not accomplished, was also a valuable persuasion; and Texas came into the Union in 1845. But none of these persuasions affected the New England conscience, and the ethical objections to the acquisition of Texas were stated in exalted fury. There were no blackguards among the Abolitionists, and very few creditors.

When the presidential campaign of 1844 was under way, Congress had not yet voted for the annexation, and the Texas question was a leading political issue. Henry Clay, the Whig candidate, attempted to make himself over into a second Harrison, hedging on his convictions until it might appear that he had no views at all but a sublime faith in the popular will. He had committed himself against the annexation of Texas before he was nominated, but in the heat of the campaign he took pen in hand again—and wrote his own damnation. It now appeared from Clay's letters that slavery really had nothing to do with the merits of the Texas question, and that if annexation could be accomplished without war with Mexico and with the common consent of the Union, he "would be glad to see it." In his anxiety to become like the average man, Clay had become too average. He had no prospect of attracting the extremist Southern vote; in South Carolina Robert B. Rhett and his like were threatening "immediate resort to state interposition" if "Texas and Southern rights" were not gratified post-haste. At the other extreme, the Garrisonian Abolitionists resolved, in convention that year, that the Constitution was "a covenant with death and an agreement with hell." Garrisonians didn't vote, but of the Abolitionists who did, enough in New York State voted for their own candidate, James G. Birney, to give the pro-slavery Democratic candidate a plurality. And the outcome of the national election balanced on the returns from New York. A closely linked chain of great events followed upon that election: the admission of Texas, the Mexican War, the acquisition of the domain west of Texas to the Pacific coast— the tyrannical importance of territorial expansion and slavery expansion in national politics.

The two kinds of expansion, often confused, were clearly separated by the Wilmot Proviso, introduced as an amendment to a money bill in 1846. The Mexican War was then scarcely begun; President Polk hoped to buy territory and peace and requested two million dollars toward that purpose. The Proviso specified that slavery should be forever forbidden in any territory purchased with the money. It offered a common ground for the Whigs and the "conscience Democrats," and at that time, before a succession of military victories had lent glamour to the war, it was passed by the House and very narrowly failed in the Senate. Within the next few years, in one form and another but with the unvarying purpose of consecrating the acquired territory to free institutions, it was presented again and again.

The hero of the war, General Taylor, was irresistibly the man to be made President in 1848. He was a Southern Whig who had never taken any marked interest in politics. "Old Zach" owned a sugar-plantation—worked by slave labor, of course; but no one knew his views on the "peculiar institution," and during the campaign he did not vouchsafe them. In New York, Willis Hall addressed an opposition meeting: "We know not what are General Taylor's principles. His friends frequently compare him, in this respect, to George Washington. Fellow-citizens, is this a popular government, and have people a right to control it? [Cries of yes! yes!] Tell me, then, how can you control it, if you don't know the principles of the men you vote for? [Cheers.]" But outside that meeting hall, instead of "cheers," was the ready answer: by knowing that the men we vote for have honest, noble characters. The moderates of the antislavery element hoped that General Taylor might be, as Horace Greeley suggested, "an instrument put into our hands by Providence to put down the civil demagogues, that for selfish purposes created the war"; and, indeed, after taking office Taylor gave promise of embodying the social conscience of the North.

When the granting of statehood to California, with the constitution of the region's own choosing—which prohibited slavery—became a subject of Congressional debate, Senator Clay offered a comprehensive recipe to kill all the political eruptions of the slavery infection. His program called upon the South to concede California as a free state; banished the slave-trading business from the District of Columbia; and granted a large sum of money to Texas, ostensibly in return for the state's consent to a reduction of its boundary claims. On the other hand, Congress was to pledge itself never to abolish slavery in the District of Columbia unless the State of Maryland assented, and was to revise the Fugitive Slave Act to provide for stringent enforcement. Clay appealed to the South to make a sacrifice of interest, and to the North to make a concession of sentiment.

The majority of the Northern middle class was willing to make the concession. Was it not for the good of another sentiment, Nationalism? Perhaps there was a masochistic tinge in this voluntary submission; Orville Dewey carried that emotion into a perverse ecstasy, declaring from his pulpit that "I would consent that my own brother, my son, should go into slavery— ten times rather would I go myself, than that this Union should perish for me or mine; and I believe you will feel, that if I *could* have saved this Union from being rent in pieces by becoming a slave, no bosom in all this continent, or the world, would be filled with such joy as mine." Webster, who had sulked in 1847 because he regarded the Wilmot Proviso as thunder stolen by minor politicians from his own arsenal, waited several weeks before committing himself, and on March 7, 1850, pronounced a momentous speech in favor of the Compromise program. Northern Whigs, he was convinced, were ready to yield antislavery convictions for the sake of harmony. In taking the lead in expressing this willingness Webster hoped to bring nearer the crown of his ambition, the Presidency. He had correctly gaged the temper of the middle class in the states between New England and the South, and he could not conceive that the New England Whigs would ever desert Webster. It remained for the young Senator William H. Seward to be mouthpiece for the irreconcilable minority in the North.

And another intransigent opinion was expressed by a political majority in South Carolina and a minority in every other Southern state. Slavery expansion in the Mexican Cession was apparently frustrated, by the hostility of nature in the Arizona country and by the popular vote in California. From this disconcerting fact the "Young South" turned to con the prospects of Disunion.

President Taylor ate too heartily at a Fourth of July celebration that year and died of the cholera morbus; and so tense was the slavery issue that radicals in both camps whispered a poisoner might have been at work. Fillmore, the new President, was in temperament a prudent civilian; he represented, as nearly as anyone could, the golden average of the voters who

THE REFUGEE MOTHER

The Star of Emancipation, 1841. This refined portraiture of a fugitive slave-woman and child celebrates that moment when the pair have reached Canada and safety. With gestures, the mother addresses a pæan in four quatrains to the Queen of the Empire: in part,

> "And here we are, Victoria!
> As free as thought can be;
> May we be thy peculiar care —
> And every refugee."

had elected the Taylor and Fillmore ticket in 1848. He had an honest and unabashed love of the Union. Privately he was antislavery; socially and politically he was amenable to all the temporizing influences. He believed that the plan of establishing colonies in Africa was the only wise one "for ameliorating the condition of our colored race"; and, leaving that to philanthropy and to time, he approved Clay's recipe for immediate ills.

In the South, Disunion sentiment ebbed; the majority of that section chose to trust that the Northern people would see to it that antislavery had been ejected forever as a political issue. In the general rise of prices both cotton-planting and slave-trading were profitable businesses; the economic gains of the next few years provided a poor soil for the germs of secession, and South Carolina alone remained fond of the idea. In the North the idea of comfort was taking on a new materialistic meaning. "The terrible glitter of the mines" was discernible in nearly every fashion of life; and, over the objections of a writer in *Harper's* for 1852, "Tables glitter with galvanized plate; hotels glitter with vanity-teaching mirrors; boats glitter with chandeliers and stained glass; churches glitter with gilt crosses; wives glitter with showy diamonds and daughters." There was no incentive among the majority of either section to press the slavery issue further. Now that a new Fugitive Slave Act had been enacted, with its biased and stringent provisions which gave the slave-hunter every advantage, the Northern middle class did not want to be reminded of the Compromise; so in 1852 it gave its votes to the party most likely to waive the whole uncomfortable subject. General Franklin Pierce, Democrat, insignificant in political and military record, was overwhelmingly elected, and the Whig party began to fall apart.

The old group of forensic statesmen was taking its leave. John C. Calhoun, in his dying whispers to Robert Toombs, resigned the work of Disunion to younger dragoons. Webster had his own way of dying. He privately advised his friends to vote for Franklin Pierce, for it seemed fitting to Webster that the Whig party should commit suttee on the pyre of its great leader. Then he returned to "Marshfield," and within the old mansion, away from all noises of the world except the resounding surf, spoke cordial adieus to each relative and family retainer, listened to a reading of Gray's "Elegy," and breathed his last. Four months earlier in that year, 1852, an escort had brought the remains of Henry Clay from Washington to "Ashland." Young America gained a clear channel for publicizing its desires when George N. Sanders, Congressman from Kentucky, became editor of the _Democratic Review_ in 1852. Stephen A. Douglas of Illinois became most conspicuous in the new group of Congressmen, attaching to himself all the projects of expansion that then hovered in the political brume. The Senator defied the crowned heads of Europe; demanded that the United States protect oppressed nationalities in the exercise of self-determination; denounced any amiable gesture of the Department of State toward Great Britain as "truckling"; favored the subsidizing of internal improvements, a more generous homestead law, and measures to increase trade with the Orient; hoped to see Cuba a part of the United States; and was invaluable in the service of the Pacific Railway project.

Early in 1854 Commodore Matthew Perry, on his second trip as good-will emissary to Japan, was at Yokohama. He set up an exhibit of American products and manufactures, including the telegraph and a working model of a railway train. When he sailed the Commodore possessed the treaty which was to inaugurate diplomatic and commercial relations between the United States and the Rising Sun. Young America was much pleased, and thought about that railway train.

The Kansas-Nebraska Act of 1854, which forced the North to reconsider its attitude on slavery and reopened the channels of controversy which were not closed until the election of 1864, was not of Southern inspiration and was not primarily concerned with the slavery issue. There was need for better communication between the Mississippi Valley and the mines, farms, and ports of the Pacific region; there was an active demand for a trans-Western railroad, and capital ready to support the demand. Prior to the active advancement of the railway project it was needful that the intervening unsettled stretch be given some form of governmental organization. For this wilderness of prairie and mountain Senator Douglas proposed a territorial status; he suggested the name, Nebraska. Apparently to satisfy the claims of Missourians to an equal chance with the citizens of Iowa and Illinois in the westward extension of farm-land and capital, he revised his proposal to call for the creation of two territories, Kansas and Nebraska. The slavery question interested Douglas very little, and for political convenience he inserted in his bill a statement of its intent "not to legislate slavery into any Territory or State, nor to exclude it therefrom, but to leave the people thereof perfectly free to form and regulate their domestic institutions in their own way, subject only to the Constitution" and to the Missouri Compromise of 1820, which had excluded slavery from any portion of the Louisiana Purchase north of Arkansas Territory.

Pro-slavery Congressmen demanded, as the price of their support, an explicit statement that the Missouri Compromise was no longer binding. Douglas was acquiescent and announced the doctrine that the Compromise measures of 1850 had in effect repealed the Missouri Compromise, so that the sole determinant of slavery in Kansas should be the will of the majority of the settlers—in short, "popular sovereignty." Senator John Bell of Tennessee warned his Southern colleagues that slavery could not take root in Kansas or Nebraska in any event, and that the "repeal" paragraph, of no benefit to the South, would rouse "the cauldron of Northern agitation and fanaticism" to boiling. They did not believe him; Kansas, at least, might be brought into the slavery area. So an acrimonious, intemperate debate began, stressing and widening the difference of sectional interests. The enactment of the bill did not quell the debate. An immediate political effect was the defeat of Democratic office-holders in the New England states. In Massachusetts a sweeping change of the elective personnel brought in a legislature which (besides appointing a committee to snoop into the bedrooms of nunneries, to gather anti-Catholic "evidence") forbade state officials to aid in the enforcement of the Fugitive Slave Act, provided free counsel for Negroes arrested under that Act, and directed prosecution, on charges of kidnapping, of any claimant of a fugitive slave who should fail to prove his

MISSIONARIES TO JAPAN

The Lantern, 1852. A cartoon inspired by Commodore Matthew Perry's first amicable embassy.

claim. Other New England states followed this lead in the enactment of similar "personal-liberty" statutes.

Just after the annexation of Texas, Edward Everett Hale had written a pamphlet, *How to Conquer Texas before Texas Conquers Us,* urging the rapid settlement of Texas by Northern men. The idea recurred in 1854 to both interested groups, the planters and the antislavery campaigners. But prudence dictated that slaveholders delay the expensive business of transporting their families and chattels into Kansas until the security of slavery in the territory was assured. That security was to be attained by "border ruffians" who sallied across the Missouri boundary to vote in Kansas elections and rode back again when the polling was over. Kansas was actually settled by people from the states of the Ohio Valley and the Middle East; New England, Missouri, and the Old South furnished only small proportions. These settlers from free states wanted a free Kansas; but the dominant pro-slavery element in the Democratic party staved off its admission of defeat until 1859. Meanwhile, in a guerilla warfare, homes were put to the sack and over two hundred men were killed; "Bleeding Kansas" became a provocative element in the trend of the middle class toward full acceptance of antislavery doctrine; and Southern children became galvanized midgets of hate when their mammas told them about the horse-thief, Abolitionist, and murderer, John Brown.

The Supreme Court, in 1857, ruled upon the most troublesome aspect of the controversy, attempting to smother it under the judicial ermine. A Negro slave of Missouri had been taken by his master to Fort Snelling, Minnesota, and back into the slave state. That cantonment, on the west bank of the Mississippi, was in a part of the Louisiana Purchase from which slavery had been expressly banished by the Missouri Compromise of 1820—therefore, conceivably, the Negro had become a free man when he entered the territory. Interested parties

pressed a suit which reached the Supreme Court. Chief Justice
Roger B. Taney, in a fifty-five page opinion, invaded all the
philosophical aspects of the Negro's status to prove the irrev-
ocable inferiority of the black race, and decided that Congress, in excluding slavery from a territorial domain, had
exceeded its constitutional powers. At last the highest court in
the land had affirmed, though by a divided decision, the contention that the South had expressed for the past decade—that
the Constitution protected slavery in the territories. It had also
endorsed the Southern view of the legal status of the Negro;
and the South regarded the Dred Scott decision as a finality.
But the storm of protest in the North, swelling in newspaper
comment, private letters and conversation, and in resolutions
by state legislatures, battered against the respectability of the
Court. Abraham Lincoln, a lawyer in Springfield, Illinois,
remarked that the Supreme Court had sometimes overruled its
own decisions and "we shall do what we can to have it overrule
this."

And the representatives of the planters' South were unwittingly doing their best to provoke a counter dominance
response from the North. The voice of the Young South had
become a rasping stridor. The human disposition was to conceal a too palpable compromise with expediency; and the best
concealment, from oneself as well as the rest of the world, was
aggression.

When a Southern-born Congressman shot down an Irish
waiter, apparently because the breakfast rolls were cold, Southern newspapers commented temporizingly; the *Charleston
Standard* observed, "If white men accept the office of menials,
it should be expected that they will do so with an apprehension
of their relation to society." Senator Charles Sumner, last of
the forensic Puritans, discussed "the harlot Slavery" and her
advocates in odorous personalities. Two Representatives from
South Carolina, carrying thick gutta-percha canes, stalked into
the Senate Chamber, and while one brandished his cane to
prevent interference, the other rained blows upon the aged
Sumner. Senator Toombs of Georgia, an exhilarated witness,

THE BEGINNING AND THE END OF JAMES BUCHANAN'S ADMINISTRATION

Lithograph, 1861, in the possession of the New York Historical Society.

wrote to a friend a few days later, "Sumner takes a beating badly. He is said to be ill tho' I don't believe it." Forty-two months elapsed before Sumner had recovered sufficiently to be at his post again. Free Soil Congressmen charged that Southern hotheads deliberately sought to provoke duels, in the expectation of using their skilled marksmanship to cripple the opposition to slavery interests; and it may have been so. A more likely assumption is that when a gentleman declared his honor offended by some remote umbrage, his particular honor was in fact offended. But in 1858 John Lyde Wilson of South Carolina published a book of inescapable significance, *The Code of Honor; or, Rules for the Government of Principals and Seconds in Duelling,* a thoroughgoing avowal of the dignity of private fights, with detailed instructions for the chivalric exercise. Christian forbearance, "highly recommended and enjoined by many good men," was no favorite of Mr. Wilson's; it was "utterly repugnant to those feelings which nature and education have implanted in the human character." His preference was all for pistols.

At the opposite end of the tension, a conference of Abolitionists held at Worcester, Massachusetts, in 1857, discussed hopefully and at length the "practicability, probability, and expediency of a Separation between the Free and Slave States." The smoke of so many emotional cross-firings—from the Sumners, Phillipses, Garrisons, and the Hunters, Barnwells, Rhetts —obscured the sound economic reasons that made civil war a poor choice for either section. However much a war may appear in perspective as an event rooted in trade-balances and problems of bread and butter, at the moment of its occurrence either participant is most likely to view it as the rod of last resort to punish an intolerable exhibition of bad manners.

During the early Fifties James Buchanan was the American minister in London—where Lady Palmerston snubbed him and the good democrat fretted at the gelid, barren society of the British capital. But his friend John Slidell wrote from Washington, "The political atmosphere is malarious, and those who are not compelled to inhale it had better keep away."

Buchanan remained abroad until just two months before the Democratic national convention of 1856; he returned with the great political advantage of being unidentified with the disputes of the last several years. "I like the noise of a democracy!" he told his welcomers; "there is no country under God's heaven where a man feels to his fellow man, except in the United States." He was nominated, and elected handily enough. But the Governor of South Carolina called the election simply a postponement of events, and urged that the South "employ the interval of repose thus secured in earnest preparation for the inevitable conflict."

Cotton, taught orthodox economists, was the center pin in the American set-up. "Slavery takes the products of the North," said David Christy, "and metamorphoses them into cotton, that they may bear export." Whatever political eminence the antislavery group might seize, Southern leaders expected the middle class of the North to be mindful of their precarious lot if the center pin should fall. In 1860 Northern votes elected a President whose party demanded that Congress use its sovereign power over the territories to prevent the extension of slavery. And, assuming that a mass of hitherto reluctant allies above the Potomac and the Ohio would defeat any Administration program of reprisal, the South took that election as the signal to secede.

But if the Northern middle class had no clear and common idea on the subject of slavery in the South, it was practically a unit in its fidelity to the idea of nationalism; and that, with which the promoters of an independent Confederacy had not reckoned, emerged as the dominant emotional issue. And within a year after the proclaiming of a "state of insurrection" the North found that even the loss of a major staple was not important enough in dollars and cents to offset the profits of war. For twenty-five years the gain in urban population—accruing to the North and West—had steadily outdistanced the increase in rural population. Almost three-fourths of the country's railway mileage in 1860 was outside the South, as was over ninety per cent of the capital invested in the nation's manufactures. The economic structure of free-state capitalism, embracing so many diverse units and so well equipped with communicating arteries, not only survived the test of war but made that war the instrument of its development, the occasion for a gala barbecue of the little tradesmen, the small farmers, and the major decencies.

A beguiling statement in Laurens Hickok's *System of Moral Science,* one of the preferred text-books for philosophy courses during the Sentimental Years, is that "The rectilineal as opposed to curvature is an analogon of worthiness as opposed to happiness." It was happily possible, the Sentimental generation found, to combine the two geometrical unlikes and, by analogy, to unite their moral apposites. The result of the marriage of straight line and curve was the dollar-mark.

The central experiment of the generation had been toward the reconciliation of unlikes—the humanitarian philosophy of enlightenment, perfectibility, democracy, beside the philosophy of acquisition, laissez-faire, gratuitous benevolence. Under this ægis people had played, very earnestly, many variants of a game which may be called Effects without Consequences. Religion without humility. Sensuality without smut. Laissez-faire without oppression. Benevolence without sacrifice. Little Latin and less tears. Salvation without pangs. Administration without statesmanship. Femininity without feminism. Food, and a cupboard undepleted. Bricks without straw. . . .

The prematurely mature shoots of Romanticism did not survive the blight of the Civil War. Donald McKay's clipper ships passed from the seas. Emerson's "Nature" became the emasculated inspiration of the pretty local colorists, and his American Scholar went to Germany to learn to accrete footnotes and write badly. Walt Whitman alone was the strong man capable of absorbing and overriding the war; and in the post-war generation his upright figure is buffeted by loneliness. Yet much of the human impulses reshaped by the Sentimental generation has survived with only tiny changes; and every day, in perhaps our happier moments, we slosh through that epoch's cultural lag.

INDEX

Abbott, Jacob, 309; writings, 311-313.
Abbott, John, 145.
Abolition movement, 180, 209, 395-6, 399, 402, 417.
Adams, Charles Francis, 49.
Adams, Jasper, 401-2.
Adams, John Quincy, and Lord's Day, 321; and phrenology, 278.
Adams, John S., 149.
Adams, Zelotes, 133.
Advertising, newspapers, 53-4; agencies, 55-6.
Aeronautics, 64-5.
Agassiz, Louis, 268, 274, 275-8.
Agriculture, 14-5.
Alcott, Amos B., and Fruitlands, 358; and Transcendentalism, 359-61.
Alcott, Anna, 143-4.
Alcott, William A., and education, 309; manuals by, 221-2; on natural science, 270-1; on perfection, 193; on tea, 260.
Alexander, Stephen, 274.
Allen, Charlotte, 135.
Allen, Elizabeth, 153.
Allen, Stephen, 356.
Allston, Washington, 166.
American Academy of the Fine Arts, 161.
American Art Union, 162.
American Bible Society, 323.
American Colonization Society, 401.
American Female Guardian Society, 199.
American and Foreign Christian Union, 198.
American House, Boston, 57.
American Institute of Education, 119.
American Journal of Science, 276.
American Lyceum Association, 119.
American Monthly Magazine, on Bulwer, 104; on Hemans, 107.
American Monthly Review, 55.
American Moral Reform Society, 191-2.
American Party, 391-2.

American Peace Society, 202.
American Phrenological Journal, 279.
American Physiological Society, 262.
American Seamen's Society, 198.
American Sunday School Union, 42, 293, 310.
American Temperance Union, 42, 230, 237, 243.
American Tract Society, 309, 323, 337.
American Union of Associationists, 192.
Anæsthetics, 264-5.
Andrews, Stephen, 61.
Antarctica, 20.
Anthon, Charles, 109-110.
Anthony, Susan B., 241.
Anti-Catholic agitation. *See* Native Americanism.
Anti-Monopoly Party, 50.
Antislavery movement, 395-417 *passim.*
Apporting, 374.
Architecture, 159-160.
Arcturus, on American literature, 111; on Braham, 181; on Dickens, 105; on scenery, 147; on Transcendentalism, 361-2.
Armstrong, Lebbeus, on Lind, 186; on mother love, 207; on Temperance, 237.
Arnold, Harriot, 191.
Art unions, galleries, 162.
Arthur, T. S., fiction, 130; play, 229.
Aspinwall, William H., 162.
Astor, John Jacob, 43, 44, 45.
Astor, William B., 43, 45.
Astor House, New York, 57-9.
Astor Library, 43.
Astor Place Riots, 123.
Astronomy, 273-4.
Atheism, 321-2.
Atlantic Monthly, 113-4.
Audubon, John James, 272.
Avery, Mrs. R. J., 144-5.
Awful Disclosures of Maria Monk, 383-4.

(1)